Complete Lyrics and Shorter Poems

Volume 4

Complete Lyrics
and
Shorter Poems

Volume 4

The Caucasus and Courtship
1829–30

Married Life and Final Years
1831–37

Alexander Pushkin

Edited and annotated by Roger Clarke

With translations by
Roger Clarke, Walter Arndt, Maurice Baring, Carleton Copeland,
John Coutts, Babette Deutsch, John Dewey, James Falen,
Irina Henderson, Jill Higgs, Mary Hobson, Walter Morison,
R.H. Morrison, Adrian Room, Eugene Raitch,
Avril Solokov and Irina Zheleznova

ALMA CLASSICS

ALMA CLASSICS
an imprint of

ALMA BOOKS LTD
Thornton House
Thornton Road
Wimbledon Village
London SW19 4NG
United Kingdom
www.almaclassics.com

This collection first published by Alma Classics in 2022

Translation © Roger Clarke, Carleton Copeland, John Coutts, James
Falen and Avril Sokolov for their respective translations

Foreword, Introduction Index of Proper Names, Notes, Extra Material
© Roger Clarke, 2022

Printed in Great Britain by CPI Group (UK) Ltd, Croydon CR0 4YY

ISBN: 978-1-84749-734-5

Contents

Alexander Pushkin (1799–1837) in 1836,
by Pyótr Fyódorovich Sokolóv (1791–1848)

Abrám Petróvich Gannibál
(c.1693–1781), Pushkin's African-born
great-grandfather

Natálya Nikoláyevna Pushkina (1812–6?
Pushkin's wife, 1832 portrait by
Alexándr P. Bryullóv (1798–1877)

Tsar Nicholas I (r. 1825–55),
engraving by Stein after an 1835
portrait by Franz Krüger

Tsar Alexander I (r. 1801–25),
bust (1826) by Bertel Thorvaldsen
(1770–1844). See No. 580

Fountain at Tsárskoye Seló (1816) by Pavel Petróvich
Sokolóv (1764–1835). See No. 627

Two illustrations by Alexándr Notbek for *Eugene Onégin* printed in the *Nevsky
Almanákh* for 1829: (left) Pushkin and Onégin standing on the Nevsky
Embankment in St Petersburg (*EO* ɪ, 48; see No. 576 a); (right) Tatyána at
dawn, holding her letter to Onégin (*EO* ɪɪɪ, 32; See No. 576 b)

General Prince Barclay de Tolly
(1761–1818), portrait by George
Dawe (1781–1829). See No. 723

Alexander Column in Palace
Square, St Petersburg, by L.-J.
Arnoux, 1840s. See No. 761

Statues of young men throwing a *svayka* (right, by Alexándr Loganóvsky)
and *babki* (left, by Nikolái Pímenov), now outside the Alexander Palace at
Tsárskoye Seló. See Nos. 758 and 759

Foreword

This is the last of four volumes, published successively by Alma Classics since 2018, that present for the first time a complete annotated edition of Alexander Pushkin's lyrics and shorter poems with Russian texts and English translations on facing pages.

Pushkin's poetic output was immense. The four volumes together contain more than 750 separate pieces of varying length, subject matter and metre, all displaying something of the sensitivity, passion, intelligence, erudition, wit and technical accomplishment for which Pushkin is famous. Publication of the complete set marks a major step towards Alma's long-term aim of giving readers of English access to all Pushkin's writings in readable modern versions, faithful to Pushkin's meaning and spirit.

Volume 4 contains well over two hundred poems from the period between Pushkin's second Caucasian journey in 1829 to his untimely death in 1837; it encompasses the years of his engagement and marriage, when frustrations with the sterility of metropolitan life were occasionally relieved by productive sojourns elsewhere. The Russian texts reflect the latest Russian scholarship. Of the English translations, some are reprints or revisions of earlier versions; most are new. They are the work of seventeen translators, whose names and contributions are enumerated on p. 413. The volume also includes an introduction to Pushkin's life and work, an index of people and places referred to in the poems, explanatory Notes on each poem, and some extra material on the translations.

These four volumes replace volumes 1–3 of the fifteen-volume *Complete Works of Alexander Pushkin* published by Milner and Company between 1999 and 2003, the rights to which now rest with Alma Classics. In publishing this latest volume Alma Classics wish again to pay a warm tribute to the initiative and drive of the late Iain Sproat, who, as managing director and owner of Milner and Company and chairman of the original project's editorial board, achieved the publication of Pushkin's complete works in English for the first time. Scholars, lovers of Pushkin and general readers wishing to gain knowledge of one of Europe's finest writers owe him the heartiest admiration and gratitude.

– Alessandro Gallenzi, Publisher; Roger Clarke, Editor

Editor's Acknowledgements

I am indebted to Carleton Copeland for providing twenty-eight excellent new translations for inclusion in this volume; I am also most grateful to John Coutts and Professor James Falen for their cheerful cooperation over the reprinting for this book, with or without revision, of the admirable translations they prepared originally for Milner. I am grateful to Derek Davis for sharing with me his annotated edition of Pushkin's travelogue *A Journey to Arzrum*, the commentary to which sheds light on the poems bearing on Pushkin's trans-Caucasian journey of 1829. My thanks are also due once more to Simon Blundell, Librarian of the Reform Club, who has given me his willing assistance in my research. Above all I am grateful to Alessandro Gallenzi for entrusting me with the preparation of these volumes of Pushkin's shorter poetry and for his strong editorial support: it has been an enormous privilege and pleasure for me to direct this ground-breaking project that makes such a uniquely important contribution to the study and appreciation of Pushkin's poetry among English speakers.

I am also deeply grateful to my wife Elizabeth and my daughter Rebecca for their help in proofreading and for their indispensable support in many other ways.

– Roger Clarke

Transliteration of Names

Proper names from antiquity are spelt in the traditional English way. Modern names are generally given their national spelling. For transliterating Russian names I have used the simplified British Standard system, except where it is customary to use anglicized forms – e.g. "Alexander" Pushkin, "Moscow". Because of the unpredictability of stress in Russian and its importance in correct pronunciation and scansion, I have marked the stressed syllable of Russian names with an acute accent over the relevant vowel; the only exceptions are names of one syllable, and those of two syllables where the stress falls on the first (e.g. Pushkin). Russian (and Polish) women are referred to by the female form of their surnames.

– Roger Clarke

Introduction

ALEXANDER PUSHKIN'S LIFE AND WORKS

Family, Birth and Childhood

Alexander Sergéyevich Pushkin was born in Moscow in 1799. His father came of an ancient but largely undistinguished aristocratic line, as Pushkin records in 'My Pedigree' (IV, 635). Perhaps his most famous ancestor – and the one of whom he was most proud – was his mother's grandfather, Abrám Petróvich Gannibál (*c*.1693–1781), who was an African, most probably from Ethiopia or Cameroon. According to family tradition, he was abducted from home at the age of seven by slave traders and taken to Istanbul. There in 1704 he was purchased by order of the Russian foreign minister and sent to Moscow, where the minister made a gift of him to Tsar Peter the Great. Peter took a liking to the boy, and in 1707 stood godfather to him at his christening (hence his patronymic Petróvich, "son of Peter"). Later Abrám adopted the surname "Gannibál", a Russian transliteration of Hannibal, the famous African general of Roman times. Peter sent him abroad as a young man to study fortification and military mining. After seven years in France, he was recalled to Russia, where he followed a career as a military engineer. After the deaths of Peter and his widow Catherine I, Abrám fell into disfavour, but in 1741 Peter's daughter, the Empress Elizabeth, made him a general, and the following year granted him large estates in the province of Pskov, including Mikháylovskoye (where Pushkin was to spend much time); Abrám eventually died in retirement well into his eighties.

Pushkin had an older sister, Olga, and a younger brother, Lev. His parents did not show him much affection as a child, and he was left to the care of his maternal grandmother and servants, including a nurse, Arína Yákovleva, of whom he became very fond. As was usual in those days, his early schooling was received at home, mostly from French tutors and in the French language, and, like many of his contemporaries, he was as fluent in French as in Russian. Some of his earliest poems were written in French.

One result of parental unconcern was that the young Pushkin was given free run of his father's library of French literature, including the works of freethinkers such as Voltaire, plays by Racine and Molière, pastoral, erotic and satirical poetry by writers such as Parny, Grécourt and Boileau, and French translations of the Greco-Roman classics: these became strong influences on Pushkin's early literary output. Even before he began his formal education, Pushkin was a remarkably well-read boy.

School 1811–17

In 1811, at the age of twelve, at the suggestion of a family friend, Alexándr Turgénev, Pushkin was sent by his parents from Moscow to St Petersburg to be educated at the new Lycée (high school), a boarding school that the Emperor Alexander I had just established to prepare the sons of noblemen for careers in government service. The Lycée was housed in a wing of the Tsar's summer palace at Tsárskoye Seló (Russian for "Tsar's Village"), about twenty kilometres south of St Petersburg. From the Lycée the boys had access to the park, with its paths, gardens, canals, lakes, woods, fountains, statuary and monuments to Russian military victories. Nearby were summer residences for those close to the imperial court (or aspiring to be so) and a guards-regiment barracks, with whose junior officers the students, when older, sometimes mixed.

Pushkin's years at the Lycée encompassed a time of momentous events in European history. The year 1812 saw Napoleon's invasion of Russia (the school was instructed to prepare plans for evacuation to Finland), the burning of Moscow and the calamitous French retreat. During the next two years, Russian troops under Alexander I, with their allies, drove the French back across Europe, occupying Paris, dethroning Napoleon and exiling him to Elba; in 1815 Napoleon escaped, briefly returned to Paris and was finally defeated at Waterloo, leaving Alexander the triumphant leader of a transformed continental Europe. These events made a deep impression on the students and are reflected here and there in Pushkin's poems (for example, Vols. I, 25, 35, 44 and 63; II, 289; IV, 595, 661, 723 and 760).

The school's regime was strict. The boys were not allowed to go out of the school building alone, nor could they leave Tsárskoye Seló for any home leave for the whole of the six-year course (though in the final year they were allowed to spend Christmas and Easter with their families in St Petersburg or nearby). Pushkin compared the enforced seclusion to that of a monastery (see the closing lines of I, 4, and I, 12). Nonetheless, visits by families were permitted (though Pushkin scarcely saw his own family till they took up residence in St Petersburg in 1814). The pupils were also encouraged latterly to take part in social events outside the Lycée, and Lycée balls were sometimes arranged. Student accommodation was comfortable by the standards of similar establishments elsewhere, and the curriculum was wide and enlightened: it included Russian, French, Latin, German, state economy and finance, scripture, logic, moral philosophy, law, history, geography, statistics and mathematics.

Though Pushkin did tolerably well at his studies, his behaviour and general demeanour did not always speak in his favour. His marked "African" physiognomy (often seen by himself and others as ugly), his moodiness, his sexual preoccupations and frustrations and his irrepressible wit (often mischievous, risqué or politically incorrect) sometimes alienated his more conservative fellow students, members of staff and others he met. He enjoyed the attention and company of adults with a similar outlook to his own, but was quick to take offence, reacting fiercely to condescension, pomposity or hypocrisy. Nevertheless, he spent six relatively happy years at the school, and felt a deeper affection for that community than for his parents, to whom he was never close. To the end of his life he remained deeply attached to his memories and friends from the Lycée years, often writing verses for the annual reunions of his class (see III, 446, 501 and 540 and IV, 668 and 760).

Poetry in the Lycée Years

Although Pushkin had played with writing poetry and dramas at home (see I, 1 and 2), it was at the Lycée that he took up literary activity in earnest. In this he was encouraged by his uncle Vasíly Pushkin, himself a minor poet and a leading member of Arzamás, a group of progressive writers and intellectuals in St Petersburg. Through his uncle, Pushkin met some of the leading Russian literary figures of the time when they visited Tsárskoye Seló, and his verses won their admiration.

Pushkin's output even at this early period is astonishing for its technical accomplishment, its maturity and its variety of both form and content. His Lycée verse includes, especially early on, some translations, adaptations and imitations of foreign poetry – mostly French, but also Latin and (via Russian or French translations) Greek and English. Some pieces would have been composed as school exercises or for competitions, formal or informal, between students. Even into this derivative or bespoke material Pushkin injects his spontaneous eloquence and wit. His own prolific work includes drinking songs, narrative ballads, a few ceremonial or historical odes, light pieces of conventional philosophy, critiques of other Russian writers, verse epistles to real or imagined acquaintances, album verses, schoolboy banter and humorous epigrams – wry, satirical, bawdy and caustic. A group of poems from the final month reflects the fears and aspirations of Pushkin and his schoolmates for life in the outside world beyond the Lycée (see I, 115, 117, 118, 120 and 121). The predominant subject of these early verses, however, is love: many of the love poems are imitations of French classical and pastoral verse, fictional love tales, or other expressions of a schoolboy's amatory imagination; but some are addressed to living women that he met around the school and the palace grounds – for example classmates' sisters (I, 13), teachers' guests (I, 107) or other visitors (I, 65).

St Petersburg 1817–20

In 1817 Pushkin, having graduated, was attached to the Ministry of Foreign Affairs in a junior rank, with duties that he was allowed to interpret as minimal. He spent the next three years in St Petersburg living a life of pleasure and dissipation. He loved the company of friends, drinking parties, cards, the theatre, and particularly women. He took an interest in radical politics. Like many young Russians of his day, he hoped that the destruction of Napoleon's empire would usher in a period not only of lasting peace and stability internationally, but also of freedom and constitutional government at home, as Alexander I had seemed to promise. Pushkin's hopes on this score and their subsequent disappointment are reflected in his poetry of the time (II, 145, 164, 167 and 186). He also continued to write lyrics, verse letters and epigrams on personal, literary and amatory subjects – often light and ribald, but always crisply, lucidly and euphoniously expressed. His poetry gained admiration for its grace, independence and wit, but very little of it was published at the time. Rather, it would have been copied, memorized and recited among Pushkin's literary friends. The more outrageously radical or scurrilous pieces were in any case unpublishable because of the censorship, but they often achieved a *succès de scandale*, inevitably before long reaching the eyes and ears of government and court and gaining the unfavourable attention of the Emperor himself.

Pushkin's major work of this period was *Ruslan and Lyudmila*, a mock epic in six cantos, published in 1820 and enthusiastically received by the public. Before its publication, however, the Emperor finally lost patience with the subversiveness of some of Pushkin's shorter verses and determined to remove him from the capital. He first considered exiling Pushkin to Siberia or the White Sea; but at the intercession of high-placed friends of Pushkin's the proposed sentence was commuted to an official posting to the south of Russia. Even so, some supposed friends hurt and infuriated Pushkin by spreading exaggerated rumours about his disgrace, and the wound continued to smart for some years (see II, 224, 225, 264 and 265 ; III, 397).

Travels in the South

Pushkin was detailed to report to Lieutenant-General Iván Inzov, who was at the time Chairman of the Board of Trustees for the Interests of Foreign Colonists in Southern Russia based at Yekaterinosláv (now Dnipro) on the lower Dnieper. Inzov gave him a friendly welcome, but little work to do, and before long Pushkin caught a fever from bathing in the river and was confined to bed in his poor lodgings. He was rescued by General Nikolái Rayévsky, a soldier who had distinguished himself in the war of 1812 against Napoleon. Rayévsky, who from 1817 to 1824 commanded the Fourth Infantry Corps in Kiev, was travelling through Yekaterinosláv with his younger son (also called Nikolái), his two youngest daughters, a personal physician and other attendants; they were on their way to join the elder son Alexándr, who was taking a cure at the mineral springs in the Caucasus. General Rayévsky generously invited Pushkin to join them; and Inzov gave his leave.

The party arrived in Pyatigórsk, in the northern foothills of the Caucasus, in June. Pushkin, along with his hosts, benefited from the waters and was soon well again. He accompanied the Rayévskys on long trips into the surrounding country, where he enjoyed the mountain scenery and observed the way of life of the local Circassian and Chechen tribes. In early August they set off westwards to join the rest of the Rayévsky family (the General's wife and two older daughters) in the Crimea. On the way they passed through the Cossack-patrolled lands on the northern bank of the Kubán river and learnt more about the warlike Circassians of the mountains to the south. (Pushkin's impressions from this visit to the Caucasus are reflected in II, 224–227.)

General Rayévsky and his party including Pushkin met up with the rest of the family at Gurzúf on the Crimean coast, where they had the use of a villa near the shore. Pushkin enjoyed his time in the Crimea, particularly the majestic coastal scenery, the southern climate and the new experience of living in the midst of a harmonious, hospitable and intelligent family. He also fell in love with Yekaterína, the General's eldest daughter, a love that was not reciprocated. The impression made on Pushkin by the Crimean coastal scenery and by his acquaintance with Yekaterína are recorded in several poems (II, 229, 237, 238, 239, 241 and 308).

Before leaving the Crimea, Pushkin travelled with the Rayévskys through the coastal mountains and inland to Bakhchisaráy (see II, 241; III, 382 and 542), an oriental town which had till forty years before been the capital of the Tatar khans of the Crimea, and where the khans' palace still stood (and stands).

Bessarabia 1820–23

After a month in the Crimea, it was time for the party to return to the mainland. During the summer General Inzov had been transferred from Yekaterinosláv to be governor of Bessarabia (the northern slice of Moldavia, which Russia had annexed from Turkey only eight years previously). His new headquarters was in Kishinyóv (modern-day Chişinău), the chief town of Bessarabia. So it was to Kishinyóv that Pushkin went back to duty in September 1820. Pushkin remained there (with spells of local leave) till mid-1823.

Kishinyóv was still, apart from recently-arrived Russian officials and soldiers, a raw Near Eastern town, with few buildings of stone or brick, populated by Moldavians, Greeks, other Balkan nationalities and Jews. Pushkin missed the cultivated ambience of St Petersburg and his friends there, and longed to return, chafing at the restrictions of exile and comparing himself to the Roman poet Ovid, who for similar offences had 1,800 years previously been exiled by his own emperor to a nearby part of the Black Sea coast (II, 263, 292, 298; III, 360). Pushkin paints an unattractive picture of Kishinyóv, its squalid streets and raffish inhabitants (II, 277, 306, 309, 313, 317 and 330). But, despite the contrast with St Petersburg, Pushkin still passed a lot of his time in a similar lifestyle of camaraderie, drinking, gambling, womanizing and quarrelling, with little official work. He wrote too – and, as in the Caucasus and Crimea, he took a close interest in the indigenous cultures, visiting local fairs and living for a few days with a band of Moldavian gypsies, an experience on which he later drew in his verses (III, 362, 363; IV, 649).

In the winter of 1820–21, Pushkin finished the first of his "southern" narrative poems, A Prisoner in the Caucasus, which he had already begun in the Crimea (the epilogue, II, 273, he added in May 1821). The poem recalls at length the impressions of his Caucasus visit. The work was published in August 1822. It had considerable public success, not so much for the plot and characterization, which were criticized even by Pushkin himself, but rather, as Pushkin acknowledged, for its "truthful, though only lightly sketched, descriptions of the Caucasus and the customs of its mountain peoples".

Having completed A Prisoner in the Caucasus, Pushkin went on to write a narrative poem reflecting his impressions of the Crimea, The Fountain of Bakhchisaráy (extract at II, 241). This was started in 1821, finished in 1823 and published in March 1824. It was also a great popular success, though again Pushkin dismissed it as "rubbish". Both poems, as Pushkin admitted, show the influence of Lord Byron, a poet whom, particularly at this period, Pushkin admired.

During these years several events of historical importance took place abroad. In 1821 Napoleon died in exile in St Helena. Pushkin continued to write about him, and it is interesting to compare his re-evaluation of Napoleon now and later (II, 289, 341 and 349; III, 357; IV, 643) with his earlier views of the man (I, 25, 35, 44, 63; II, 145). Also in 1821, the Greeks in the Danubian Provinces, expecting Russian support, rose up against their Turkish overlords (see II, 272 and 315). In the event, Alexander refused support, and the uprising was quickly crushed (though it lit the touchpaper of the wider and ultimately successful struggle for Greek independence – IV, 594). The early 1820s saw, too, the crushing of liberal democratic movements in Spain, Portugal, Piedmont and Naples by reactionary forces supported by the Holy Alliance of Russia, Austria and Prussia; these developments, which followed the Russian-instigated suppression of radical groups in Germany, dealt a further blow to Pushkin's post-Napoleonic hopes for an enlightened Russian policy in Europe and for freedom and constitutional government within Russia itself (II, 254, 323, 326 and 332). Alexander's increasingly reactionary foreign policy and his denial of promised reforms at home alienated many other young intellectuals and army officers and fomented the growth of clandestine groups that discussed and plotted the overthrow of autocracy – a process that would culminate in the Decembrist uprising of 1825.

In the winter of 1820–21 Pushkin spent several months' leave visiting friends in the Ukraine. While staying with the Davýdov brothers at their estate at Kámenka, he had a brief affair with the promiscuous wife of Alexándr Davýdov, which exploded in a row that provoked some of Pushkin's bitterest invective (II, 249, 257, 258).

Just before his departure from Kishinyóv in 1823, Pushkin composed the first few stanzas of Chapter One of his greatest work, the novel in verse *Eugene Onégin*. It took him eight years to complete. Each chapter was published separately (except Chapters Four and Five, which came out together) between the years 1825 and 1832.

Odessa 1823–24

In the summer of 1823, through the influence of his friends in St Petersburg, Pushkin was posted to work for Count Mikhaíl Vorontsóv, who had just been appointed Governor General of the newly Russianized region south of the Ukraine. Vorontsóv's headquarters were to be in Odessa, the port city on the Black Sea founded by Catherine the Great thirty years previously. Despite its newness, Odessa was a far more lively, cosmopolitan and cultured place than Kishinyóv, and Pushkin was pleased with the change (III, 354 gives a lively picture of Odessa at this time). He only remained in Odessa for a year, but during this time he experienced two of the most intense love affairs of his life, which left a deep mark on his poetic imagination.

The first of these affairs was with Amalia Riznić, young wife of a much older expatriate businessman. Pushkin's stormy relationship with Amalia is probably reflected in several poems from this time as well as later (II, 327, 328, 337 and 339; III, 458; IV, 637, 652). Amalia left Odessa in the spring of 1824. The second affair was with the wife of the Governor General.

Pushkin did not get on well with Count Vorontsóv, his chief in Odessa (II, 345; III, 396 and 400). This was partly because of temperamental differences and partly because Pushkin objected to the work Vorontsóv expected him to do; but an additional factor was that Pushkin, still smarting from his disappointment over Amalia Riznić, fell passionately in love with the Countess Yelizavéta ("Elise") Vorontsóva, an attractive woman of Polish descent. Elise failed to discourage Pushkin's advances – her husband had mistresses of his own – and they used to meet at a seaside villa with a bathing place beneath the cliffs. Several poems written before and after Pushkin left Odessa seem to relate to her (II, 350 and 351; III, 355, 358, 359, 383, 390 and 395; IV, 629).

Vorontsóv tried hard to get Pushkin transferred elsewhere; and Pushkin for his part became so unhappy with his position on the Count's staff that he tried to resign and even contemplated escaping overseas (III, 357). But before matters came to a head, the police intercepted a letter from

Pushkin to a friend in which he spoke approvingly of the atheistic views
of an Englishman he had met in the city. The authorities in St Petersburg
now finally lost patience with Pushkin: he was dismissed from the ser-
vice and sent to indefinite banishment on his mother's country estate
of Mikháylovskoye. He left Odessa on 1st August 1824; he had by now
written two and a half chapters of *Eugene Onégin* and had begun a new
narrative poem *Gypsies*.

Exile at Mikháylovskoye 1824–26

Pushkin spent more than two years under police surveillance at
Mikháylovskoye, a time he recollected ten years later in IV, 732. The
enforced leisure gave him a lot of time for writing. Within a couple of
months he had completed *Gypsies*, which was first published in full in
1827. *Gypsies*, reflecting Pushkin's experiences of life in the Moldavian
steppelands, is a terser, starker, more thoughtful and more dramatic work
than *A Prisoner in the Caucasus* or *The Fountain of Bakhchisaráy*; along
with *Eugene Onégin* it marks a transition from the discursive romanticism
of Pushkin's earliest years to the compressed realism of his mature style. At
Mikháylovskoye Pushkin progressively completed Chapters Three to Six
of *Eugene Onégin*, many passages of which reflect Pushkin's love of the
countryside and observation of rural life. He also wrote his historical drama
Boris Godunov at this period and his entertaining verse tale *Count Nulin*.

Pushkin was stunned by the sudden loss of Odessan society, and of
Elise Vorontsóva in particular. Despite his love of the countryside, as a
lively and gregarious individual he was also frustrated by the restrictions
under which he was condemned to live – so much so that he again contem-
plated absconding abroad (III, 379 and 437). The disgrace of his second
exile had further alienated him from his parents, who after a fractious
three months left him alone at Mikháylovskoye; they also encouraged his
sister and brother to do the same, though Pushkin tried to keep in touch
with them and other friends by correspondence, sometimes in verse (for
example, III, 377, 378, 388, 405, 427, 431, 447, 454 and 455). One of his
few consolations was the companionship of his faithful old nurse and
housekeeper, whom he genuinely loved and who regaled him with Russian
folklore (III, 393, 409, 466; IV, 732). He was, too, touched and delighted
when, on separate occasions, two of his old schoolfriends travelled out
to pay him brief visits (Nos. 446 and 473). For the rest, he had to content
himself for company with the occupants of the neighbouring estate of
Trigórskoye – the middle-aged widow Praskóvya Ósipova and her son,
daughters, stepdaughter, nieces and other occasional visitors, with whom
he had relationships of varying intensity (III, 365, 385, 392, 402, 403, 434,
436, 437, 439, 445, 456 and 460).

The Decembrist Revolt 1825

In November 1825 Alexander I died suddenly. He left no legitimate children, and there was initially confusion over the succession. In December some liberally minded members of the army and the intelligentsia (subsequently known as the Decembrists) seized the opportunity to attempt a coup d'état. This was put down by the new emperor, Nicholas I, a younger brother of Alexander's. Among the conspirators were several old friends of Pushkin, and he might well have joined them had he been at liberty. As it was, the five leading conspirators were executed, and many of the rest were sent to Siberia for long spells of hard labour and exile. Some of the younger Pushkin's more politically inflammatory verses (e.g. II, 145 and 254) were found among their papers. Pushkin feared that he too might be punished and, in the summer of 1826, appealed to the new emperor for release, with promises of loyalty.

Rehabilitation 1826–31

In September Pushkin was abruptly summoned to Moscow to see the new emperor. Nicholas surprised Pushkin by offering him his freedom, commenting publicly, "Today I conversed with the most intelligent man in Russia"; and Pushkin assured Nicholas of his future good conduct.

Pushkin was enormously relieved to have regained his liberty and to have escaped the fate of his Decembrist friends (III, 488 and 491), and he remained deeply grateful to Nicholas. Initially he foresaw for himself a role of informal counsellor to the Emperor, advocating policies of cautious liberalization and clemency (III, 463, 474 and 506); but in this he was disappointed: the Emperor took little notice of Pushkin's political aspirations, remaining strongly conservative in domestic policy and implacable towards the surviving Decembrists; and Pushkin's more independent friends read his veiled admonitions to the Emperor as pointless ingratiation (III, 506 and 544). Pushkin had to content himself with private expressions of sympathy and encouragement to the exiles (III, 473, 476, 543a and 557). Despite all this, Pushkin continued to respect Nicholas for his personal qualities and for his determination to defend and enlarge the Russian Empire (III, 474, 506; IV, 643, 663, 760); and the Emperor for his part evidently valued Pushkin as a writer and afforded him intermittent support and patronage.

At his interview with Nicholas Pushkin had complained of the difficulty of making money from his writings because of the censorship – about which he had more than once protested, fruitlessly, during the previous reign (II, 310; III,371). In response Nicholas undertook to oversee Pushkin's work personally. In practice, however, the Emperor often delegated the task to the Chief of the Secret Police, and, despite occasional interventions from Nicholas, Pushkin continued to have difficulty with the censorship.

From September 1826 Pushkin spent eight months in Moscow. He then returned to St Petersburg, where he lived for most of the next two years, though he continued periodically to visit Moscow, go back to Mikháylovskoye and stay with friends elsewhere in the country. During this period, denied a public role, Pushkin directed his poetic and social activity primarily to fellow-littérateurs (III, 465, 485, 492, 497, 502, 511, 518, 545, 559, 561 and 562), to gambling partners (III, 507, 523 and 560) and to women friends old (III, 508, 509 and 558) and new (III, 484, 525, 529 and 553). He also reflected poetically on the nature of the poet (III, 493, 494 and 516). In these years he seems to have felt an increasing urge to find a lifelong partner and settle down at last to married life. He first thought of choosing a distant cousin (III, 469), then a lively young Moscow acquaintance (III, 483 and 486). Then, during the summer of 1828, he paid suit to a twenty-year-old St Petersburg girl, Anna Olénina (III, 512, 515, 521, 522, 531 and 532); Pushkin's proposal of marriage, however, was rejected by her parents.

At the very end of 1828, at a Moscow ball, Pushkin first glimpsed the attractive sixteen-year-old Natálya Goncharóva. On his return to Moscow in March 1829 he began to court her, initially with little success. At the beginning of May Pushkin left Moscow for his only visit abroad: after revisiting the Caucasus, he followed the Russian army on a campaign into north-eastern Turkey. Several years later he wrote a prose account of this trip in his *Journey to Arzrúm*, but in the meantime he reflected some of his experiences and impressions in his verses (IV, 563–567, 569–572, 592, 615, 616, 619, 620, 644).

Pushkin returned to Moscow in mid-September and resumed his court-ship of Natálya. The courtship did not run smoothly (IV, 596), but in May 1830 they were at last engaged, much to Pushkin's delight (IV, 613), and they were married in early 1831.

It was during the four years between his return from exile and his marriage that he wrote Chapter Seven (1827–28) and most of Chapter Eight (1829–31) of *Eugene Onégin*. In 1828 he also wrote *Poltava* (published in 1829), a kind of historical novella in verse. This seems to have been the first attempt in Russian at a work of this kind based on the study of historical material. In its application of the imagination to real historical events, it prefigured Pushkin's later historical novel in prose, *The Captain's Daughter*, and helped to set a pattern for subsequent historical novels in Russia. It is also notable for the terse realism of its descriptions and for the pace and drama of its narratives and dialogues. It was during this period, too, that Pushkin began to write fiction in prose, though it was not till late in 1830 that he succeeded in bringing any prose stories to completion.

In the autumn of 1830 a cholera epidemic caused Pushkin to be marooned for a couple of months on another family estate, Bóldino, some 600 kilometres east of Moscow. He took advantage of the enforced leisure to write. It was at this time that he composed *Belkin's Stories* and *A History of Goryúkhino Village*. He also completed Chapter Eight of *Onégin*, another verse tale, *The Little House in Kolómna*, many of his best lyrics (IV, 617–620, 627–634, 637–639, 643, 644, 649–652), and his set of four one-act dramas known together as *The Little Tragedies* (extracts at IV, 640, 641, 647, 648).

The Final Years

There was a strongly imperialistic streak in Pushkin's character, as evidenced in *Poltava* and other verses such as II, 273 and IV, 593. During 1830 nationalist sentiments in Russia were inflamed by a Polish uprising against Russian control. The insurrection was quelled by late 1831, but the crisis in that year evoked from Pushkin some fiercely patriotic poetry (IV, 660, 661, 663, 669).

The 1830s were not on the whole happy years for Pushkin. His marriage, it is true, was more successful than might have been expected (IV, 671). Natálya was thirteen years his junior; her remarkable beauty and susceptibility to admiration constantly exposed her to the attentions of other men; she showed more liking for society and its entertainments than for intellectual or artistic pursuits or for household management; her fashionable tastes and social aspirations incurred outlays that the pair could ill afford; and she took little interest in her husband's writing. Nonetheless, despite all this, they seem to have remained a loyal and loving couple; Natálya bore him four children in less than six years of marriage, and she showed real anguish at his untimely death.

But there were other difficulties. Pushkin, though short of money himself, with a weakness for gambling and with a costly family of his own to maintain, was often called upon to help out his parents, his brother and sister and his in-laws, and so fell ever deeper into debt. Both his wife and the Emperor demanded his presence in the capital so that he would be available to attend social and court functions, while he would much have preferred to be in the country, writing (IV, 710). Though Nicholas gave him intermittent support socially and financially, many at court and in the government, wounded by his jibes or shocked by his supposed political and sexual liberalism, disliked or despised him. Literary rivalries continued to generate fierce invectives (IV, 574, 575, 577, 584, 591, 600, 607, 625 and 636). At the same time, a new generation of writers and readers were beginning to look on him as a man of the past (IV, 621, 642, 665).

In these last years Pushkin wrote less poetry. Now he was married, his love poetry was mostly penned, more formally, for society ladies' albums (IV, 673–677, 679, 733). His masterwork *Eugene Onégin*, completed in 1831, was first published as a whole in 1833. Pushkin commemorated its completion in IV, 622 and, though pressed to write a sequel, steadfastly declined to do so (IV, 694, 729). When he did write, he turned increasingly to prose. He did, however, continue to reflect poetically on poetry itself, on poets and their readers (IV, 606, 612, 621, 625, 642, 665, 690, 692, 738, 741).

In 1833 Pushkin spent another productive autumn at the Bóldino estate. He composed his most famous prose novella, *The Queen of Spades*, and again wrote some remarkable poetry – notably *The Bronze Horseman*, finest of his narrative poems (extract at IV, 704), the beautiful 'Autumn' (IV, 697) and two fine ballads (IV, 702 and 703).

In these years Pushkin also developed his interest in history, already evident in *Boris Godunov* and *Poltava*: Nicholas I commissioned him to write a *History of Peter the Great*: although the subject was a favourite one of Pushkin's (III, 474; IV, 635, 701, 704, 739), he did not complete the *History*, only leaving copious notes for it at his death. He did, however, write in 1833 a *History of Pugachóv*, a well-researched account of the eighteenth-century Cossack and peasant uprising under Yemelyán Pugachóv, which Nicholas allowed him to publish in 1834. He built on his research into this episode to write his longest work of prose fiction, the historical novel *The Captain's Daughter* (1836). Over these years too he produced his five metrical fairy stories; these are mostly based on Russian folk tales, but one, *The Golden Cockerel* (1834), is an adaptation of one of Washington Irving's *Tales of the Alhambra*.

Since the turn of the decade Pushkin had begun, intermittently at least, to reflect regretfully on the follies of his previous life (IV, 595, 605). Increasingly during these last years he came to turn for his poetry to more serious social, moral and philosophical matters. He even began to write with earnestness and commitment on Christian subjects, which in early years had served mainly as topics for ironic verse. These developments are especially evident in the remarkable pieces that he composed in the summer of 1836 while on holiday on Kámenny Ostrov ("Stone Island") on the edge of St Petersburg (IV, 750, 752–754, 761).

Death

Early in 1837, Pushkin's career was cut tragically short. Following a series of improper advances to his wife and insults to himself, he felt obliged to fight a duel with a young Frenchman who was serving as an officer in the imperial horse guards in St Petersburg. Pushkin was fatally wounded in the stomach and died at his home in St Petersburg two days later. The authorities denied him a public funeral in the capital for fear of demonstrations, and he was buried privately at the Svyatýe Gory monastery near Mikháylovskoye, where his memorial has remained a place of popular pilgrimage.

Writings

From his school days till his death Pushkin composed well over 700 shorter verses, comprising many lyrics of love and friendship, album verses, verse epistles, jokes, protests, invectives, epigrams, epitaphs, dedications, ballads, folk songs, tales, descriptions of landscapes, seascapes, cities and works of art, and verses of literary, social and (albeit guarded) political criticism. He also wrote narrative poems, dramas, poetic fairy stories, novels in verse and prose, short stories, history, satire and travelogue. He left numerous letters from his adult years that give us an invaluable insight into his thoughts and activities and those of his contemporaries. And, as a man of keen intelligence and interest in literature, he produced throughout his career many articles and shorter notes – some published in his lifetime, others not – containing a wide variety of literary criticism and comment. It is indeed hard to name a literary genre that Pushkin did not explore in his lifetime; or it would be truer to say that he wrote across the genres, ignoring traditional categories with his characteristic independence and originality. He was exceptionally well read not only in Russian but in foreign literatures, and he translated, adapted and imitated works from ancient Greece and Rome, from Arab, Persian and Hebrew sources, and from France, Italy Spain, Portugal, England, Scotland, Poland and other Slavic lands, and from North America and Brazil. Occasionally too he would present original works as translations to deflect the censors' attention. All Pushkin's writing is marked by an extraordinary polish, succinctness and clarity; a keen sense for the beauty of sounds and rhythms; a deep human sympathy and insight; a great sensitivity to what is appropriate to the occasion; and a directness and naturalness of diction that is never pompous, insincere or carelessly obscure – all qualities supremely evident in these poems.

– Roger Clarke, 2022

Lyrics and Shorter Poems

Volume 4

The Caucasus and Courtship
1829–30

1829

(ОТ МАЯ)

563

* * *

На холмах Грузии лежит ночная мгла;
   Шумит Арагва предо мною.
Мне грустно и легко; печаль моя светла;
   Печаль моя полна тобою,
Тобой, одной тобой... Унынья моего
   Ничто не мучит, не тревожит,
И сердце вновь горит и любит — оттого,
   Что не любить оно не может.

564

КАЛМЫЧКЕ

Прощай, любезная калмычка!
Чуть-чуть, на зло моих затей,
Меня похвальная привычка
Не увлекла среди степей
Вслед за кибиткою твоей.
Твои глаза конечно узки,
И плосок нос, и лоб широк,
Ты не лепечешь по-французски,
Ты шелком не сжимаешь ног;
По-английски пред самоваром   10
Узором хлеба не крошишь,
Не восхищаешься Сен-Маром,
Слегка Шекспира не ценишь,
Не погружаешься в мечтанье,
Когда нет мысли в голове,
Не распеваешь *Ma dov'è*,
Галоп не прыгаешь в собранье...

4

1829

563

* * *

The hills of Georgia are veiled in mists of night;
    close by I hear the Arágva flowing.
I'm sad, yet glad at heart; my very sorrow's bright –
    my sorrow that is overflowing
with you, with you alone… There's nothing here to move
    that sorrow into pain, nothing to overpower
my feelings that are now again aflame with love –
    for not to love is beyond their power.   RC

564

FOR A KALMYK GIRL

Goodbye, my lovely Kalmyk friend,
you almost made me ditch my plans –
I, rightly, like to fraternize and
might have dashed across the steppes
after that covered cart of yours.
Your eyes, it's true, are narrow slits –
your nose is flat, your forehead wide;
you don't go simpering on in French,
nor squeeze your calves in silken hose;
you don't cut bread in pretty shapes   10
beside a teapot, English-style,
nor rave about de Vigny's books,
nor damn poor Shakespeare with faint praise;
you don't resort to meditation
to hide an absence of ideas;
you don't drone arias by Rossini,
nor prance a *galop* at a ball…

Что нужды? — Ровно полчаса,
Пока коней мне запрягали,
Мне ум и сердце занимали   20
Твой взор и дикая краса.
Друзья! не всё ль одно и то же:
Забыться праздною душой
В блестящей зале, в модной ложе,
Или в кибитке кочевой?

565

ФАЗИЛЬ-ХАНУ

Благословен твой подвиг новый,
Твой путь на север наш суровый,
Где кратко царствует весна,
Но где Гафиза и Саади
Знакомы ………… имена.

Ты посетишь наш край полночный,
Оставь же след ……………
Цветы фантазии восточной
Рассыпь на северных снегах.

566

ДЕЛИБАШ

Перестрелка за холмами;
Смотрит лагерь их и наш:
На холме пред казаками
Вьется красный делибаш.

Делибаш! не суйся к *лаве*,
Пожалей свое житье;
Вмиг аминь лихой забаве:
Попадешься на копье.

Эй, казак! не рвися к бою:
Делибаш на всем скаку   10
Срежет саблею кривою
С плеч удалую башку.

No matter! For a full half-hour,
as they were harnessing the horses,
your gaze, your beauty from the wilds,   20
held my attention, mind and heart.
My friends, it's surely all the same
to let one's idle feelings roam
in soirées, theatres bright and smart,
or by a nomad's covered cart.   RC

565

FOR FAZIL KHAN

Your exploit, friend, is brave and bold:
our northern lands are bleak and cold,
and lovely spring too quickly flies.
Yet here your Saadi's tale is told…
Hafez is known among the wise.

Across our midnight world we trace
your eastern footsteps as you go:
so scatter on our northern snow
blossoms of fantasy and grace.   JC

566

THE DELIBÁSH

Gunfire on the hilltops warns us;
both encampments, foe and friend,
watch as, towards the Cossack forces,
rides a *delibásh* in red.

Delibásh, don't charge, hot-headed,
into battle! Hold life dear,
lest your derring-do be ended
on the fine point of a spear.

Cossack, don't rush into action,
or the *delibásh* will slice,   10
with his sabre curved and slashing,
head from shoulders in a trice.

Мчатся, сшиблись в общем крике...
Посмотрите! каковы?...
Делибаш уже на пике,
А казак без головы.

567

ИЗ ГАФИЗА

Лагерь при Евфрате

Не пленяйся бранной славой,
О красавец молодой!
Не бросайся в бой кровавый
С карабахскою толпой!
Знаю, смерть тебя не встретит:
Азраил, среди мечей,
Красоту твою заметит —
И пощада будет ей!
Но боюсь: среди сражений
Ты утратишь навсегда   10
Скромность робкую движений,
Прелесть неги и стыда!

568

КРИТОН

Критон, роскошный гражданин
Очаровательных Афин,
Во цвете жизни предавался
Всем упоеньям бытия.
Однажды, — слушайте, друзья, —
Он по Керамику скитался,
И вдруг из рощи вековой,
Красою девственной блистая,
В одежде легкой и простой
Явилась нимфа молодая.   10
Пред банею, между колонн,
Она на миг остановилась
И в дом вошла. Недвижим он
Глядит на дверь, куда, как сон,
Его красавица сокрылась ...

Cries and clashing... Then a viewer
shouts, "Who's won?" By now the dread
delibásh is on a skewer
and the Cossack has no head.   CC

567

FROM HAFEZ

A camp on the Euphrates

Don't be lured to martial glory,
O my young and handsome lord!
Don't rush off to battles gory
with your daring warrior horde!
Yes, I know: you'll hardly perish –
Azrael, among the blades,
will, I'm sure, your beauty cherish,
and protect it from the shades!
Still, I fear that under battle
you will suffer all the same,   10
lose your shy and modest manner,
tender charm and sense of shame!   JF

568

CRITO

Rich Crito lived as he desired
in Athens, city much admired.
Now in life's prime, he would surrender
himself to pleasures unrestrained.
One day he'd chosen – hear me, friends –
around Ceramicus to wander,
when from an ancient wood close by,
her maiden beauty glowing brightly,
a girl (or nymph?) ran, young and spry,
towards the baths, clad simply, lightly.   10
While passing through the columns there,
she for a moment paused unbidden,
then entered. Crito stopped to stare,
unmoving, at the doorway where
the lovely girl had, dreamlike, hidden ...   RC

569

* * *

Зорю бьют... из рук моих
Ветхий Данте выпадает,
На устах начатый стих
Недочитанный затих.
Дух далече улетает.
Звук привычный, звук живой,
Сколь ты часто раздавался
Там, где тихо развивался
Я давнишнею порой!

570

СТАМБУЛ

Стамбул гяуры нынче славят,
А завтра кованой пятой,
Как змия спящего, раздавят
И прочь пойдут и так оставят.
Стамбул заснул перед бедой.

Стамбул отрекся от пророка;
В нем правду древнего Востока
Лукавый Запад омрачил —
Стамбул для сладостей порока
Мольбе и сабле изменил.
Стамбул отвык от поту битвы
И пьет вино в часы молитвы.   10

Там веры чистый жар потух:
Там жены по кладбищам ходят,
На перекрестки шлют старух,
А те мужчин в харемы вводят,
И спит подкупленный евнух.

Но не таков Арзрум нагорный,
Многодорожный наш Арзрум:
Не спим мы в роскоше позорной,   20
Не черплем чашей непокорной
В вине разврат, огонь и шум.

569

* * *

Drum roll... Dante's tome, well-thumbed,
from my startled hands starts falling;
verses that I've just begun
reading hang on lips now dumb.
Sounds from far back I'm recalling.
Rhythmic drums – your beat I know!
Many a time I heard you rolling
close at hand while I was growing
quietly up so long ago.   RC

570

ISTANBUL

The infidels praise Istanbul
today; soon, though, with iron heel
they'll crush her like a torpid snake,
then off they'll go and leave her crushed.
Though menaced, Istanbul lies sleeping.

The city has disowned God's Prophet:
in her the West's mendacity
has clouded age-old Eastern truth.
Worship and warfare Istanbul has
abandoned for indulgent vice: 10
now, weary of the sweat of battle,
she quaffs red wine at hours of prayer.

Islam's pure fire has been extinguished;
wives roam the graveyards as they please;
to street corners they send old housemaids
to summon men to their harems,
while eunuchs take a well-paid sleep.

In Erzurum, though, in the mountains,
this town of many byways – here
we do not lounge in shameful comforts,   20
nor into wrongful winecups do we
pour ourselves clamour, lust and strife.

Постимся мы: струею трезвой
Святые воды нас поят;
Толпой бестрепетной и резвой
Джигиты наши в бой летят.
Харемы наши недоступны,
Евнухи строги, неподкупны,
И смирно жены там сидят.

Алла велик!
       К нам из Стамбула   30
Пришел гонимый янычар.
Тогда нас буря долу гнула,
И пал неслыханный удар.
От Рущука до старой Смирны,
От Трапезунда до Тульчи,
Скликая псов на праздник жирный,
Толпой ходили палачи;
Треща в объятиях пожаров,
Валились домы янычаров;
Окровавленные зубцы   40
Везде торчали; угли тлели;
На кольях скорчась мертвецы
Оцепенелые чернели.

Алла велик. Тогда султан
Был духом гнева обуян.

571

ДОНЦЫ

Был и я среди донцов,
Гнал и я османов шайку;
В память битвы и шатров
Я домой привез нагайку.

На походе, на войне
Сохранил я балалайку —
С нею рядом, на стене
Я повешу и нагайку.

Что таиться от друзей —
Я люблю свою хозяйку,   10
Часто думал я об ней
И берег свою нагайку.

We keep the fasts, and soberly
drink only consecrated water.
When our fierce horsemen fly to battle
in fearless and excited hordes,
to our harems no man can enter –
eunuchs are strict, cannot be bought,
and wives live meekly, as they ought.

Allah is great!
        From Istanbul   30
there fled to us a janizary.
A storm had burst and bent us low,
an unimagined blow had fallen.
From Ruse fort to old Izmir,
from Trabzon all the way to Tulcea,
town streets were full of murderous mobs,
egging on hounds to share a feast.
Engulfed in crackling conflagrations,
the janizaries' houses crumbled;
all round sharp spikes of iron dripped   40
with blood, and heaps of embers smouldered.
Impaled on stakes contorted corpses
were stiffening and turning black.

Allah is great! The Sultan's rage
still burned within him unassuaged.   RC

571

DON COSSACKS

I too with Don Cossacks fought,
Turks I too sent flying presto!
From the battlefield I've brought
home this whip as a memento.

On campaign I through it all
kept my balalaika by me.
That and whip upon the wall
side by side I'll fasten slyly.

Why keep secrets from a friend? –
I do love my missus dearly: 10
I have thought of her no end –
and my whip I'm keeping near me.   RC

572

ДОН

Блеща средь полей широких,
Вон он льется!.. Здравствуй, Дон!
От сынов твоих далеких
Я привез тебе поклон.

Как прославленного брата,
Реки знают тихий Дон;
От Аракса и Евфрата
Я привез тебе поклон.

Отдохнув от злой погони,
Чуя родину свою,
Пьют уже донские кони
Арпачайскую струю.

Приготовь же, Дон заветный,
Для наездников лихих
Сок кипучий, искрометный
Виноградников твоих.

573

САПОЖНИК

Притча

Картину раз высматривал сапожник
И в обуви ошибку указал;
Взяв тотчас кисть, исправился художник.
Вот, подбочась, сапожник продолжал:
«Мне кажется, лицо немного криво...
А эта грудь не слишком ли нага?»...
Тут Апеллес прервал нетерпеливо;
«Суди, дружок, не свыше сапога!»

Есть у меня приятель на примете:
Не ведаю, в каком бы он предмете
Был знатоком, хоть строг он на словах,
Но черт его несет судить о свете:
Попробуй он судить о сапогах!

572

RIVER DON

There he flows! A happy meeting!
Gleaming Don, I spy you now:
sons from far away send greeting:
let me make a Russian bow.

Gentle Don – the rivers know you:
pride of place is yours, they vow.
Aras and Euphrates show you
honour due: I make their bow.

Cossack horses, over-driven,
feel themselves on Russian soil,   10
once the river Arpa's given
cool refreshment after toil.

Honoured river Don, make ready!
Please prepare your sparkling wines.
Grant your gallant riders heady,
seething juice from richest vines.   JC

573

THE COBBLER

A Parable

A cobbler once reviewed a work of art.
"Dear me!" said he. "They've got the footwear wrong!"
The painter took his comments in good part –
one small correction didn't take him long.
The critic then decried a squinting face…
a bosom scarcely decent… "Not so fast!"
Fretful Apelles put him in his place:
"The cobbler, sir, should not forsake his last!"

A friend of mine is happy to display
sincerely held and widely ranging views   10
on any current topic of the day…
but what he really knows is hard to say.
I wish the man would stick to judging shoes!   JC

574

НА НАДЕЖДИНА

Надеясь на мое презренье,
Седой зоил меня ругал,
И, потеряв уже терпенье,
Я эпиграммой отвечал.
Укушенный желаньем славы,
Теперь, надеясь на ответ,
Журнальный шут, холоп лукавый,
Ругать бы также стал. — О, нет!
Пусть он, как бес перед обедней,
Себе покоя не дает:
Лакей, сиди себе в передней,
А будет с барином расчет.

10

575

НА НАДЕЖДИНА

В журнал совсем не европейский,
Где чахнет старый журналист,
С своею прозою лакейской
Взошел болван семинарист.

576

НА КАРТИНКИ К *ЕВГЕНИЮ ОНЕГИНУ* В *НЕВСКОМ АЛЬМАНАХЕ*

а

Вот перешед чрез мост Кокушкин,
Опершись жопой о гранит,
Сам Александр Сергеич Пушкин
С мосьё Онегиным стоит.
Не удостоивая взглядом
Твердыню власти роковой,
Он к крепости стал гордо задом:
Не плюй в колодец, милый мой.

574

ON NADÉZHDIN

Old Zoïlus would aim a curse...
he thought I wouldn't give a damn.
Alas, I'd make the matter worse
by granting him an epigram...
His sidekick now aspires to fame
and dares me to another bout...
You serf, incapable of shame,
you journalistic joke, get out!
As when a fiend is banned and barred
I conjure you – poor scribbling monkey –   10
begone! Your place is in the yard!
Give me the master – not the flunkey!   JC

575

ON NADÉZHDIN

Now – at an unenlightened publication,
on which a hack has wasted useless years –
with wordy prose of grovelling adulation
    a doltish student priest appears.   JC

576

ON SOME DRAWINGS FOR *EUGENE ONÉGIN*
IN THE *NEVSKY ALMANAC*

a

Just having crossed the Bridge Kokúshkin,
his bottom to the wall applied,
stands poet Alexander Pushkin,
Monsieur Onégin at his side.
Not deigning even once to peer
at fateful Power's citadel,
he showed the place his haughty rear:
don't spit, dear fellow, in the well.   JF

6

....
Пупок чернеет сквозь рубашку,
Наружу титька — милый вид!
Татьяна мнет в руке бумажку,
Зане живот у ней болит:
Она затем поутру встала
При бледных месяца лучах
И на подтирку изорвала,
Конечно, «Невский Альманах».

577

НА КАЧЕНОВСКОГО

Как сатирой безымянной
Лик зоила я пятнал,
Признаюсь: на вызов бранный
Возражений я не ждал.
Справедливы ль эти слухи?
Отвечал он? Точно ль так?
В полученье оплеухи
Расписался мой дурак?

578

ОЛЕГОВ ЩИТ

Когда ко граду Константина
С тобой, воинственный варяг,
Пришла славянская дружина
И развила победы стяг,
Тогда во славу Руси ратной,
Строптиву греку в стыд и страх,
Ты пригвоздил свой щит булатный
На цареградских воротах.

Настали дни вражды кровавой;
Твой путь мы снова обрели.   10
Но днесь, когда мы вновь со славой
К Стамбулу грозно притекли,
Твой холм потрясся с бранным гулом,
Твой стон ревнивый нас смутил,

b

....

Her navel shows through her chemise;
one breast's uncovered – lovely sight!
A rumpled page her fingers squeeze...
alas, she's gripped with stomach blight:
Tatyána's risen with the dawn,
and in the moonbeams' fading light
the girl, to wipe herself, has torn...
"The *Nevsky Almanac*?..." – You're right!   RC

577

ON KACHENÓVSKY

Zoïlus' face – yes, I confess –
I bruised, but hid his real name.
I little thought he'd seek redress,
acknowledging that mark of shame.
Has he hit back, then? (So one hears –
what's said, though, I've not verified.)
Although I've boxed him on the ears,
I can't believe the fool's replied.   RC

578

THE SHIELD OF OLÉG

Olég, Norse warrior, when once you
to Constantine's great city came
with Slavic troops, and, raising banners,
your host to victory laid claim,
you won for Rus new martial glory,
but left proud Greeks ashamed, aghast,
and to Constantinople's portal
you nailed your steel-forged buckler fast.

Bloodshed and war are here again now:
we've marched the same route south as you.   10
But this time, though once more with glory
we've menaced Istanbul anew,
your burial mound has quaked and rumbled,
your jealous roar's caused us dismay,

И нашу рать перед Стамбулом
Твой старый щит остановил.

579

* * *

Стрекотунья белобока,
Под калиткою моей
Скачет пестрая сорока
И пророчит мне гостей.

Колокольчик небывалый
У меня звенит в ушах,
На заре .... алой,
Серебрится снежный прах.
....

580

К БЮСТУ ЗАВОЕВАТЕЛЯ

Напрасно видишь тут ошибку:
Рука искусства навела
На мрамор этих уст улыбку,
А гнев на хладный лоск чела.
Недаром лик сей двуязычен.
Таков и был сей властелин:
К противочувствиям привычен,
В лице и в жизни арлекин.

581

ДОРОЖНЫЕ ЖАЛОБЫ

Долго ль мне гулять на свете
То в коляске, то верхом,
То в кибитке, то в карете,
То в телеге, то пешком?

Не в наследственной берлоге,
Не средь отческих могил,

and there, by Istanbul's defences,
your shield has held our troops at bay.   RC

579

* * *

Chattering with song unending,
by the wicket hops and flies
a motley magpie, and impending
guests' arrival prophesies.

Strangely does a bell-like chiming
in my ears forever go...
Red streaks through the skies are climbing...
silvern gleams the dusted snow...

....   RM

580

TO THE BUST OF A CONQUEROR

You're wrong to think his likeness garbled:
the eye of art has truly seen
upon his lips that smile enmarbled
and anger on his brow's cold sheen.
No wonder that the bust's reflected
this potentate's internal strife:
his feelings ever were bisected –
a harlequin in face and life.   WA

581

A TRAVELLER'S GRUMBLES

Must I so long roam the world round,
on a horse, on wheels of wood,
carriage-borne or wagon-whirled, bound
anywhere, on sledge, on foot?

Not in my ancestral lair,
nor amid my forebears' tombs,

На большой мне, знать, дороге
Умереть Господь судил,

На каменьях под копытом,
На горе под колесом,   10
Иль во рву, водой размытом,
Под разобранным мостом.

Иль чума меня подцепит,
Иль мороз окостенит,
Иль мне в лоб шлагбаум влепит
Непроворный инвалид.

Иль в лесу под нож злодею
Попадуся в стороне,
Иль со скуки околею
Где-нибудь в карантине.   20

Долго ль мне в тоске голодной
Пост невольный соблюдать
И телятиной холодной
Трюфли Яра поминать?

То ли дело быть на месте,
По Мясницкой разъезжать,
О деревне, о невесте
На досуге помышлять!

То ли дело рюмка рома,
Ночью сон, поутру чай;   30
То ли дело, братцы, дома!..
Ну, пошел же, погоняй!..

582

ЛЕГЕНДА

Жил на свете рыцарь бедный,
Молчаливый и простой,
С виду сумрачный и бледный,
Духом смелый и прямой.

Он имел одно виденье,
Непостижное уму,

but on some main thoroughfare,
seemingly, to die I'm doomed –

crushed by wheels, or horses stumbling,
on paved road or mountain ridge,   10
or when down a gully tumbling,
gouged by floods that wrecked a bridge.

Or the plague, maybe, will take me,
or a blizzard freeze me hard,
or a clumsy sentry break my
skull as he lets down the bar;

or I'll, lost and isolated,
fall to an assassin's knife,
or in quarantine, frustrated
by sheer boredom, end my life.   20

Must I suffer this ordeal,
still observe reluctant fasts –
chewing truffle-less cold veal,
missing Yard's superb repasts?

Here's my one wish for the present –
down Myasnítskaya to ride,
free to dream of more that's pleasant:
country living and a bride!

Here's my wish – a glass of rum now,
good night's sleep, then tea in bed!   30
Here's my wish – to be at home now!...
So, drive on, full speed ahead!   RC

582

A LEGEND

Once upon a time – good people –
lived a poor and simple knight:
pale and sad in face and feature:
eager to defend the right...

He had caught a glimpse of glory –
sudden, piercing, never sought;

И глубоко впечатленье
В сердце врезалось ему.

Путешествуя в Женеву,
На дороге у креста   10
Видел он Марию деву,
Матерь Господа Христа.

С той поры, сгорев душою,
Он на женщин не смотрел,
И до гроба ни с одною
Молвить слова не хотел.

С той поры стальной решетки
Он с лица не подымал
И себе на шею четки
Вместо шарфа привязал.   20

Несть мольбы Отцу, ни Сыну,
Ни святому Духу ввек
Не случилось паладину,
Странный был он человек.

Проводил он целы ночи
Перед ликом пресвятой,
Устремив к ней скорбны очи,
Тихо слезы лья рекой.

Полон верой и любовью,
Верен набожной мечте,   30
Ave, Mater Dei кровью
Написал он на щите.

Между тем как паладины
В встречу трепетным врагам
По равнинам Палестины
Мчались, именуя дам,

«*Lumen cæli, sancta Rosa!..*»
Восклицал в восторге он,
И гнала его угроза
Мусульман со всех сторон.   40

Возвратясь в свой замок дальный,
Жил он строго заключен,

deep, oh deep, the vision entered,
far beyond the power of thought.

While he journeyed to Geneva,
Mary – mother, queen and maid –   10
showed herself in wonder to him:
soon he joined the new crusade.

From that hour his heart was flaming:
she alone was all his care;
mortal women's words and glances
he for ever did forswear.

Never was the steely visor
raised: his face he chose to hide.
Ladies' favours were discarded;
prayer beads round his neck he tied.   20

Never did our brave crusader
offer prayer, or give the praise
due to Father, Son and Spirit:
strange – how very strange his ways!

Brightly glowed the Virgin's icon;
gravely knelt the knight below,
gazing up in nightly vigil;
tears were flowing – still and slow.

Then at last the faithful dreamer,
still devoted, took the field,   30
writing *Ave, Mater Dei!*
plain in blood upon his shield.

Palestine! Our brave crusaders
swiftly rode in search of fame;
trembling enemies could hear them
speak their dearest lady's name.

"*Lumen cæli, sancta Rosa!*"
louder than them all he cried –
soon the Saracens, dumbfounded,
fled in fear on every side.   40

Next he travelled homeward, closing
tight the gloomy castle's gate,

Всё безмолвный, всё печальный,
Без причастья умер он.

Между тем как он кончался,
Дух лукавый подоспел,
Душу рыцаря сбирался
Бес тащить уж в свой предел:

Он-де Богу не молился,
Он не ведал-де поста,
Не путем-де волочился
Он за матушкой Христа.

Но пречистая, конечно,
Заступилась за него
И впустила в царство вечно
Паладина своего.

50

583

* * *

Счастлив ты в прелестных дурах,
В службе, в картах и в пирах;
Ты Saint-Priest в карикатурах,
Ты Нелединский в стихах;
Ты прострелен на дуеле,
Ты разрублен на войне, —
Хоть герой ты в самом деле,
Но повеса ты вполне.

584

ЭПИГРАММА

Седой Свистов! ты царствовал со славой;
Пора, пора! сложи с себя венец:
Питомец твой младой, цветущий, здравый,
Тебя сменит, великий наш певец!

Се: внемлет мне маститый собеседник,
Свершается судьбины произвол,

living lonely, sad and silent –
dying excommunicate.

At the last, he lay expiring:
then a devil – in the know –
came to seize his soul and drag it
downward to the realms below.

"Has this man not scorned his Maker?
overlooked the Lenten fast?   50
failed to serve Christ's Holy Mother
in a fitting way?" he asked.

But, of course, our Blessed Lady
stooped to plead her champion's case.
Happy paladin! For ever
safe in heaven, he took his place.   JC

583

*   *   *

You're happy with your sweet buffoons,
at dinner, cards or under arms;
you match Saint-Priest with your cartoons,
Nelédinsky with verse that charms;
in duelling you might be shot –
in battle, maybe, blown to hell;
a hero you'd be – doubt it not –
but rascal you'll remain as well.   RC

584

EPIGRAM

"Svistóv! At last thy grey-haired glories wane!
'Tis time to set thy diadem aside:
a happy, healthy foster-child must reign
instead of thee, famed singer, Russia's pride!"

See: the great poet-counsellor complies,
and Providence's will is now made known:

Является младой его наследник:
Свистов II вступает на престол!

585

* * *

За Netty сердцем я летаю
    В Твери, в Москве
И R и O позабываю
    Для N и W.

586

К ЕКАТЕРИНЕ ВЕЬЯШЕВОЙ

Подъезжая под Ижоры,
Я взглянул на небеса
И воспомнил ваши взоры,
Ваши синие глаза.
Хоть я грустно очарован
Вашей девственной красой,
Хоть вампиром именован
Я в губернии Тверской,
Но колен моих пред вами
Преклонить я не посмел   10
И влюбленными мольбами
Вас тревожить не хотел.
Упиваясь неприятно
Хмелем светской суеты,
Позабуду, вероятно,
Ваши милые черты,
Легкий стан, движений стройность,
Осторожный разговор,
Эту скромную спокойность,
Хитрый смех и хитрый взор.   20
Если ж нет... по прежню следу
В ваши мирные края
Через год опять заеду
И влюблюсь до ноября.

the youthful heir apparent greets our eyes –
Svistóv the Second mounts the royal throne!　　　　JC

585

* * *

To Netty in my heart I fly
　　in Tver and in Moscow –
and R and O are now passed by
　　for N and W.　　　　AR

586

TO YEKATERÍNA VELYÁSHEVA

Just as I approached Izhóry,
glancing upwards at the skies
I recalled your gaze before me
and the blueness of your eyes.
Though your girlish fascination
drives me desperate (I own),
though among Tver's population
as a vampire I've been known,
yet to come and kneel before you
I confess I did not dare –　　　　10
nor, for sure, did I desire to
vex you with a lover's prayer.
Drunken with the ugly pleasures
that the social whirl begets,
your delightfully sweet features
I'll most probably forget –
supple waist and lithesome bearing,
modest looks and winning ways,
shyness in the talk you're sharing,
mischief in your smile, your gaze.　　　　20
Should I nonetheless remember...
one year hence I may look in,
fall in love – until November –
then be on my way again.　　　　IH & RC

587

ЗИМА

2 ноября

Зима. Что делать нам в деревне? Я встречаю
Слугу, несущего мне утром чашку чаю,
Вопросами: тепло ль? утихла ли метель?
Пороша есть иль нет? и можно ли постель
Покинуть для седла, иль лучше до обеда
Возиться с старыми журналами соседа?
Пороша. Мы встаем, и тотчас на коня,
И рысью по полю при первом свете дня;
Арапники в руках, собаки вслед за нами;
Глядим на бледный снег прилежными глазами;   10
Кружимся, рыскаем и поздней уж порой,
Двух зайцев протравив, являемся домой.
Куда как весело! Вот вечер: вьюга воет;
Свеча темно горит; стесняясь, сердце ноет;
По капле, медленно глотаю скуки яд.
Читать хочу; глаза над буквами скользят,
А мысли далеко... Я книгу закрываю;
Беру перо, сижу; насильно вырываю
У музы дремлющей несвязные слова.
Ко звуку звук нейдет... Теряю все права   20
Над рифмой, над моей прислужницею странной:
Стих вяло тянется, холодный и туманный.
Усталый, с лирою я прекращаю спор,
Иду в гостиную; там слышу разговор
О близких выборах, о сахарном заводе;
Хозяйка хмурится в подобие погоде,
Стальными спицами проворно шевеля,
Иль про червонного гадает короля.
Тоска! Так день за днем идет в уединенье!
Но если под вечер в печальное селенье,   30
Когда за шашками сижу я в уголке,
Приедет издали в кибитке иль возке
Нежданная семья: старушка, две девицы
(Две белокурые, две стройные сестрицы), —
Как оживляется глухая сторона!
Как жизнь, о боже мой, становится полна!
Сначала косвенно-внимательные взоры,
Потом слов несколько, потом и разговоры,
А там и дружный смех, и песни вечерком,
И вальсы резвые, и шепот за столом,   40

WINTER

2nd November

It's winter. What's for us to do here in the country?
I greet the man who brings my morning tea with sundry
questions: "How warm is it? Has last night's blizzard stopped?
Does snow lie on the ground, or not? And can I opt
for riding out, or is it best if I inspected,
till lunch, old magazines some neighbour has rejected?"
The snow is lying! So we rise and mount. Away
we canter through the fields at early light of day,
long hunting whips in hand; keen foxhounds, yelping, follow;
we scan the pallid snow, we scrutinize each hollow,   10
we trot to left, to right, until, with noon long past,
two hares flushed out and lost, we jog it home at last.
Some fun was that! Night falls; a snowstorm's howling madly;
dimly my candle burns, my heart is aching sadly,
and boredom slowly, drop by poisoned drop, I sip.
I try to read; my eyes along the letters slip,
my thoughts, though, are elsewhere... At last I stop pretending,
take up a pen and sit, intemperately rending
some ill-matched words from my reluctant, weary Muse.
Sound will not fit with sound... At such a time I lose   20
complete control of Rhyme, my whimsical maidservant:
the lines are feeble, flat – no feeling, no discernment.
Exhausted, I break off my struggle with the lyre
and seek the sitting room; there I can hear the squire
discussing sugar mills and imminent elections;
my hostess, storm-like, casts black looks in all directions,
her steely knitting needles clicking; or she starts
to tell us each our fortunes by the king of hearts.
Oh, life's a bore for those who live in isolation! –
I yearn for a surprise. Maybe in resignation   30
I'm sitting playing draughts, and then up the approach
there drives a covered sleigh or roomy sledded coach:
out steps a family, a matron and two girls –
curvaceous sisters both, each one with flaxen curls –
how much they'll animate the place till now so numb!
How full, dear God, our lives will all at once become!
At first there'll only pass alert but sidelong glances;
a word or two ensues; then conversation chances
to raise a friendly laugh; a sing-song later on;
vivacious waltzes next; then whispered words lead on   40

И взоры томные, и ветреные речи,
На узкой лестнице замедленные встречи;
И дева в сумерки выходит на крыльцо:
Открыты шея, грудь, и вьюга ей в лицо!
Но бури севера не вредны русской розе.
Как жарко поцелуй пылает на морозе!
Как дева русская свежа в пыли снегов!

588

ЗИМНЕЕ УТРО

Мороз и солнце; день чудесный!
Еще ты дремлешь, друг прелестный
Пора, красавица, проснись:
Открой сомкнуты негой взоры
Навстречу северной Авроры,
Звездою севера явись!

Вечор, ты помнишь, вьюга злилась,
На мутном небе мгла носилась;
Луна, как бледное пятно,
Сквозь тучи мрачные желтела,   10
И ты печальная сидела —
А нынче... погляди в окно:

Под голубыми небесами
Великолепными коврами,
Блестя на солнце, снег лежит;
Прозрачный лес один чернеет,
И ель сквозь иней зеленеет,
И речка подо льдом блестит.

Вся комната янтарным блеском
Озарена. Веселым треском   20
Трещит затопленная печь.
Приятно думать у лежанки.
Но знаешь: не велеть ли в санки
Кобылку бурую запречь?

Скользя по утреннему снегу,
Друг милый, предадимся бегу
Нетерпеливого коня
И навестим поля пустые,

to exchange of melting looks, and snatched flirtatious speeches,
and long encounters up a stairway's narrow reaches.
In the half-dark one girl, unmuffled neck and busts,
steps out onto the porch, face buffeted by gusts –
but icy northern gales won't harm a Russian rose.
How burningly a kiss will glow amidst the frost!
How fresh a Russian girl will bloom among soft snows!   WA & RC

588

A WINTER'S MORNING

Look! Frost and sun! A gorgeous morning!
Why sleep as though day's not yet dawning?
Sweet friend, wake up, unseal your eyes
to greet our northerly Aurora,
get out of bed, appear before her,
yourself a star of northern skies.

Recall last night the tempest driving
the snow and heavy storm clouds flying;
you sat so tensely at my side.
The moon, a yellow smudge, was glowing   10
behind the clouds, but hardly showing –
Today... just take a look outside:

A clear blue sky above! Extended
like sumptuous carpets deep and splendid,
agleam with sunlight, snow now lies;
nothing's left black but leafless forest;
the firs, dark-green, stand thickly frosted;
our little river glints with ice.

This whole room's lit with amber radiance,
and in the hot stove's cosy ambience   20
you lie stretched out along its ledge,
delighting in the jolly crackle;
but why not have them fetch the tackle
and harness Chestnut to the sledge?

Through morning snow, dear, let's go gliding,
and, headlong after Chestnut flying,
race to the gate and out beyond,
across the fields where there'll be no one,

Леса, недавно столь густые,
И берег, милый для меня.   30

589

ЕЛЕНЕ

Зачем, Елена, так пугливо,
С такой ревнивой быстротой,
Ты всюду следуешь за мной
И надзираешь торопливо
Мой каждый шаг? ..... я твой.

590

* * *

О, сколько нам открытий чудных
Готовят просвещенья дух,
И опыт, сын ошибок трудных,
И гений, парадоксов друг,
И случай, бог изобретатель...

591

НА НАДЕЖДИНА

Мальчишка Фебу гимн поднес.
«Охота есть, да мало мозгу.
А сколько лет ему, вопрос?» —
«Пятнадцать». — «Только-то? Эй, розгу!»
За сим принес семинарист
Тетрадь лакейских диссертаций,
И Фебу в слух прочел Гораций,
Кусая губы, первый лист.
Отяжелев, как от дурмана,
Сердито Феб его прервал   10
И тотчас взрослого болвана
Поставить в палки приказал.

through woods now leafless, past the mill-run –
haunts of which I've so long been fond.   RC

589

FOR HELEN

Why, Helen, do you follow me
so hastily, with jealous fear,
forever shadowing me here,
and scrutinize suspiciously
my every move? I'm yours, my dear.   JH

590

*   *   *

How many erstwhile hidden wonders
are brought to us by Education,
by Experience, child of painful blunders,
by Genius, friend of contradiction,
and Chance, inventive deity!...   JC & RC

591

ON NADÉZHDIN

One day a not-so-likely lad
offers a hymn to bright Apollo.
"How old is he? Fifteen – too bad!"
(So schoolboy caning has to follow.)
A seminary student next
presents his essays – tedious stuff...
As Horace tries to read the text,
the god of light has had enough.
Our dunderhead completes a page...
"An adult, eh? Expecting thanks...   10
How dare the fool provoke my rage?
Let's flog the fellow through the ranks..."   JC

592

ТЕРЕК

Меж горных стен несется Терек,
Волнами точит дикий берег,
Клокочет вкруг огромных скал,
То здесь, то там дорогу роет,
Как зверь живой, ревет и воет —
И вдруг утих и смирен стал.

Всё ниже, ниже опускаясь,
Уж он бежит едва живой.
Так, после бури истощаясь,
Поток струится дождевой.   10
И вот ……… обнажилось
Его кремнистое русло.

593

* * *

Опять увенчаны мы славой,
Опять кичливый враг сражен,
Решен в Арзруме спор кровавый.
В Эдырне мир провозглашен.

И дале двинулась Россия,
И юг державно облегла,
И пол-Эвксина вовлекла
В свои объятия тугие…

594

ГРЕЦИЯ

Восстань, о Греция, восстань.
Недаром напрягала силы,
Недаром потрясала брань
Олимп и Пинд и Фермопилы.

Под сенью ветхой их вершин
Свобода юная возникла,

592

TEREK

Midst mountain walls the Terek dashes,
at rugged banks its torrent gnashes,
and foams round crags abrupt and wild,
now here, now there, its channel boring,
like a ferocious creature roaring –
then suddenly grows hushed and mild.

Down, downward yet, the water's flowing,
now scarce alive, but moving still,
as, wearied when a storm's ceased blowing,
the rain flood dwindles to a rill.
Yet farther, and the .... river
reveals its shallow, stony bed...

RC

593

* * *

Again we wear the victor's crown:
in Erzurum the bloody fray
was won – a haughty foe goes down.
Now in Edirne, far away,

peace is proclaimed: great Russia grows –
far to the south her sway extends.
Half the Black Sea most surely knows
her power in arms – her tight embrace...

JC

594

GREECE

Awake, O land of Greece, awake!
Your sons strove rightly to be winners,
rightly their will to fight did shake
Thermopylae, Olympus, Pindus.

Sheltered beneath their age-old peaks,
a youthful freedom is arising

37

На гробах ……… Перикла,
На ……… мраморных Афин.

При пенье пламенных стихов
Тиртея, Байрона и Риги   10
Страна героев и богов
Расторгла рабские вериги.

595

ВОСПОМИНАНИЯ В ЦАРСКОМ СЕЛЕ

Воспоминаньями смущенный,
    Исполнен сладкою тоской,
Сады прекрасные, под сумрак ваш священный
    Вхожу с поникшею главой.
Так отрок Библии, безумный расточитель,
До капли истощив раскаянья фиал,
Увидев наконец родимую обитель,
    Главой поник и зарыдал.

В пылу восторгов скоротечных,
    В бесплодном вихре суеты,   10
О, много расточил сокровищ я сердечных
    За недоступные мечты,
И долго я блуждал, и часто, утомленный,
Раскаяньем горя, предчувствуя беды,
Я думал о тебе, предел благословенный,
    Воображал сии сады.

Воображаю день счастливый,
    Когда средь вас возник Лицей,
И слышу наших игр я снова шум игривый
    И вижу вновь семью друзей.   20
Вновь нежным отроком, то пылким, то ленивым,
Мечтанья смутные в груди моей тая,
Скитаясь по лугам, по рощам молчаливым,
    Поэтом забываюсь я.

И въявь я вижу пред собою
    Дней прошлых гордые следы.
Еще исполнены Великою Женою,
    Ее любимые сады
Стоят населены чертогами, вратами,

on ground where Pericles lay dying
in marbled Athens, pride of Greeks.

Fired by the incandescent lines
Tyrtaeus sang – and Rigas, Byron –   10
Greece, who great men with gods combines,
has snapped her slavish chains of iron.   RC

595

RECOLLECTIONS IN TSÁRSKOYE SELÓ

Vexed as I am by recollection,
    weighed down with thoughts both sad and sweet,
I come, head bowed, O hallowed gardens of perfection,
    beneath your canopied retreat.
Thus too the wastrel son, in Holy Scripture's telling,
plunged deeply in despair, exhausted by regret,
but now at last in sight of his paternal dwelling,
    hung his head humbly down and wept.

Consumed by transitory pleasures,
    whirled round by winds of worldliness,   10
oh, how I've wasted all my heart's most precious treasures
    on dreams that never met success –
how long I've wandered, lost! Worn out, though (I confess it),
by smouldering remorse and menace of distress,
I've held you in my thoughts, you refuge ever blessed,
    and visualized your paradise.

I stand, in memory surveying
    the Lycée's joyful opening day;
I hear the cheerful sounds of games and young boys playing –
    I see the friends I met each day.   20
Young lad once more, now idle, now with ardour glowing,
I'm storing in my heart dreams random, ill defined,
and, as through meadow grass and silent woods I'm roaming,
    poetic musings fill my mind.

I see too those commemorations
    that celebrate a glorious past.
Still permeated by Great Catherine's emanations,
    stretch her much-loved majestic parks,
decked with the effigies of gods, with gates and portals,

Столпами, башнями, кумирами богов   30
И славой мраморной, и медными хвалами
   Екатерининских орлов.

   Садятся призраки героев
   У посвященных им столпов,
Глядите; вот герой, стеснитель ратных строев,
   Перун кагульских берегов.
Вот, вот могучий вождь полунощного флага,
Пред кем морей пожар и плавал и летал.
Вот верный брат его, герой Архипелага,
   Вот наваринский Ганнибал.   40

   Среди святых воспоминаний
   Я с детских лет здесь возрастал,
А глухо между тем поток народной брани
   Уж бесновался и роптал.
Отчизну обняла кровавая забота,
Россия двинулась и мимо нас летят
И тучи конные, брадатая пехота,
   И пушек медных светлый ряд.

   . . . .
     50
. . . .
   . . . .

На юных ратников завистливо взирали,
Ловили с жадностью мы брани дальный звук,
И, негодуя, мы и детство проклинали,
   И узы строгие наук.

   . . . .
   . . . .
. . . .
     60

И многих не пришло. При звуке песней новых
Почили славные в полях Бородина,
На Кульмских высотах, в лесах Литвы суровых,
   Вблизи Монмартра …

   . . . .

with pillars, palaces and ruined bastions,   30
with marble eulogies and bronze memorials
    to Catherine's eagle champions.

By columns to their fame established
    now sit our great war heroes' ghosts –
look, see the Thunderer, who on Kagúl's banks vanquished
    the Ottomans' unnumbered hosts;
and see the northern fleet's victorious commander,
before whom flames engulfed the air, the water – all;
his loyal brother too, hero of that armada;
    and Navarino's Gannibál...   40

Among such sacred recollections
    I grew up here and came of age.
Dimly, meanwhile, the tide of strife between the nations
    began to thunder and to rage.
Our homeland was beset by bloodshed and commotion;
Russia was stirred to fight: each day massed infantry
and cavalry trooped past (we watched with fierce emotion!),
    and lines of fresh artillery.

. . . .
. . . .   50
. . . .
. . . .

With jealousy we eyed those young recruits, fixated,
and strained an eager ear for distant sounds of war;
our immaturity we all abominated,
    and chafed against our school's strict law.

. . . .
. . . .
. . . .
. . . .   60

Many did not return. They sleep a glorious slumber,
sublimely hymned at last, around Borodinó,
at Kulm, in Lithuania's forests dense and sombre,
    and in Montmartre's *banlieue*...

. . . .   RC

596

* * *

Поедем, я готов; куда бы вы, друзья,
Куда б ни вздумали, готов за вами я
Повсюду следовать, надменной убегая:
К подножию ль стены далекого Китая,
В кипящий ли Париж, туда ли наконец,
Где Тасса не поет уже ночной гребец,
Где древних городов под пеплом дремлют мощи,
Где кипарисные благоухают рощи,
Повсюду я готов. Поедем... но, друзья,
Скажите: в странствиях умрет ли страсть моя?   10
Забуду ль гордую, мучительную деву,
Или к ее ногам, ее младому гневу,
Как дань привычную, любовь я принесу?

597

* * *

Брожу ли я вдоль улиц шумных,
Вхожу ль во многолюдный храм,
Сижу ль меж юношей безумных,
Я предаюсь моим мечтам.

Я говорю: промчатся годы,
И сколько здесь ни видно нас,
Мы все сойдем под вечны своды —
И чей-нибудь уж близок час.

Гляжу ль на дуб уединенный,
Я мыслю: патриарх лесов   10
Переживет мой век забвенный,
Как пережил он век отцов.

Младенца ль милого ласкаю,
Уже я думаю: прости!
Тебе я место уступаю;
Мне время тлеть, тебе цвести.

День каждый, каждую годину
Привык я думой провождать,

596

* * *

I'm ready. Come, my friends, let's travel east or west –
to anywhere at all, wherever you think best.
I'm with you. I intend that haughty miss to jilt.
Let's go to see the wall those distant Chinese built,
or bustling Paris streets – or, better still, the shore
where gondoliers by night sing Tasso's songs no more,
where ash-embedded stones of ancient cities lie,
and where tall cypress groves breathe fragrance to the sky.
I'm game for anywhere. Let's start, then... But, friends, say:
will my emotions die once I go far away?   10
Will I forget the lass who scorns and tortures me?
Or shall I, to appease the girl's hostility,
still need to render her the homage of my love?...   RC

597

* * *

When down the bustling streets I pass,
or in a crowded church I stray,
or share with frenzied youth a glass,
the same old thoughts assert their sway.

The years, I think, are rushing by,
and all our current merry band
will one day in the graveyard lie –
and time for some is near at hand.

When on some lonely oak I gaze,
I muse on how that ancient wood   10
will long outlive my sorry days,
as past our fathers' time it stood.

When I caress an infant's face,
within my mind I say: "Farewell!
I yield to you this precious space:
my time to fade, and yours to swell."

I contemplate each passing year,
each passing day, with bated breath,

Грядущей смерти годовщину
Меж их стараясь угадать.   20

И где мне смерть пошлет судьбина?
В бою ли, в странствии, в волнах?
Или соседняя долина
Мой примет охладелый прах?

И хоть бесчувственному телу
Равно повсюду истлевать,
Но ближе к милому пределу
Мне всё б хотелось почивать.

И пусть у гробового входа
Младая будет жизнь играть,   30
И равнодушная природа
Красою вечною сиять.

598

ГИМН К ПЕНАТАМ

из Саути

Еще одной высокой, важной песни
Внемли, о Феб, и смолкнувшую лиру
В разрушенном святилище твоем
Повешу я, да издает она,
Когда столбы его колеблет буря,
Печальный звук! Еще единый гимн —

Внемлите мне, пенаты: вам пою
Обетный гимн. Советники Зевеса,
Живете ль вы в небесной глубине,
Иль, божества всевышние, всему   10
Причина вы, по мненью мудрецов,
И следуют торжественно за вами
Великий Зевс с супругой белоглавой
И мудрая богиня, дева силы,
Афинская Паллада, — вам хвала.
Примите гимн, таинственные силы!
Хоть долго был изгнаньем удален
От ваших жертв и тихих возлияний,
Но вас любить не остывал я, боги.
И в долгие часы пустынной грусти   20

and wonder, as they disappear,
which date will mark my coming death.   20

And where does Fate intend my end?
At sea... abroad... where battle reigns?
Or will some nearby valley lend
a plot to hold my mute remains?

Though senseless flesh will hardly care
precisely where it goes to rot,
my final sleep I'd like to share
with some once well-belovèd spot.

And let young life in vigour play
before that portalled tomb of mine   30
and heedless nature there, I pray,
in everlasting beauty shine.   JF

598

HYMN TO THE PENATES

from Southey

Phoebus, I pray you, hear yet one more song,
sublime and solemn, then I shall hang up
my lyre, now fallen silent, midst the ruins
of your great sanctuary, so that there,
when tempests shake the columns, it shall make
a mournful music... Yes, one final hymn –

Hearken, Penates, household gods: I sing you
this promised hymn. Whether, as counsellors of Zeus,
you dwell far off in deepest heaven, or
(as sages think) you are the origin   10
of all things – most supreme of deities,
behind whom follow, with respect and pride,
great Zeus himself, his venerable spouse
and the wise goddess, virgin warrior,
Pallas of Athens – praise I render you.
Receive this hymn, you enigmatic powers!
Though I for long was exiled, and unable
to make you offerings and due libations,
I never cooled, gods, in my love for you,
and in long hours of dismal desolation   20

45

Томительно просилась отдохнуть
У вашего святого пепелища
Моя душа — ... зане там мир.
Так, я любил вас долго! Вас зову
В свидетели, с каким святым волненьем
Оставил я ... людское племя,
Дабы стеречь ваш огнь уединенный,
Беседуя с самим собою. Да,
Часы неизъяснимых наслаждений!
Они дают мне знать сердечну глубь,   30
В могуществе и немощах его,
Они меня любить, лелеять учат
Не смертные, таинственные чувства.
И нас они науке первой учат —
Чтить самого себя. О нет, вовек
Не преставал молить благоговейно
Вас, божества домашние...

599

МЕ́ДОК В УАЛЛАХ

из Саути

Попутный веет ветр. — Идет корабль, —
Во всю длину развиты флаги, вздулись
Ветрила все, — идет, и пред кормой
Морская пена раздается. Многим
Наполнилася грудь у всех пловцов.
Теперь, когда свершен опасный путь,
Родимый край они узрели снова;
Один стоит, вдаль устремляя взоры,
И в темных очерках ему рисует
Мечта давно знакомые предметы,   10
Залив и мыс, — пока недвижны очи
Не заболят. Товарищу другой
Жмет руку и приветствует с отчизной,
И Господа благодарит, рыдая.
Другой, безмолвную творя молитву
Угоднику и деве пресвятой,
И милостынь и дальних поклонений
Старинные обеты обновляет,
Когда найдет он всё благополучно.
Задумчив, нем и ото всех далек,   20

my soul kept pleading wearily with you
that I at length might respite find beside
your holy hearth – for there alone is peace.
Yes, I have loved you long! I summon you
to testify to the intense devotion
that's led me to abandon humankind
and tend your sacred flame in solitude,
communing with myself alone. Ah, yes –
what hours of inexpressible delight!
They let me plumb the heart's profundity   30
in all its strength and weaknesses;
they teach me to appreciate and cherish
a sense of mysteries beyond this life.
And the first lesson that they teach is this:
Esteem yourself. No, never, never
have I stopped praying fervently to you,
my household deities…   RC

599

MADOC IN WALES

from Southey

From aft the wind blows. Onward scuds the ship,
penants unfurled in full, and every sail
a-billowing. She scuds on – at her prow
the sea spray spurts aloft. And all the crewmen
now feel emotion brimming in their hearts.
At last their dangerous voyage is completed;
their native country they have glimpsed afresh.
One stands and strains his eyes into the distance,
until, held motionless too long, they start
to ache; meanwhile his memory has traced   10
the hazy lines of once-familiar landmarks –
a headland and a bay. Another sailor
squeezes his comrade's hand, congratulates him
on reaching home, and thanks the Lord in tears.
A third one offers up a wordless prayer
to patron saint and holy Virgin Mary,
renewing vows, made in the distant past,
of almsgivings and distant pilgrimages
if he should find that all is well at home.
Far from the rest, in silent meditation,   20

Сам Ме́док погружен в воспоминаньях
О славном подвиге, то в снах надежды,
То в горестных предчувствиях и страхе.

Прекрасен вечер, и попутный ветр
Звучит меж вервей, и корабль надежный
Бежит, шумя, меж волн. Садится солнце.

600

СОБРАНИЕ НАСЕКОМЫХ

Какие крохотны коровки!
Есть, право, менее булавочной головки.
КРЫЛОВ.

Мое собранье насекомых
Открыто для моих знакомых:
Ну, что за пестрая семья!
За ними где ни рылся я!
Зато какая сортировка!
Вот Глинка — божия коровка,
Вот Каченовский — злой паук,
Вот и Свиньин — российский жук,
Вот Олин — черная мурашка,
Вот Раич — мелкая букашка.
Куда их много набралось!
Опрятно за стеклом и в рамах
Они, пронзенные насквозь,
Рядком торчат на эпиграммах.

10

601

* * *

Когда твои младые лета
Позорит шумная молва,
И ты по приговору света
На честь утратила права,

Один, среди толпы холодной,
Твои страданья я делю
И за тебя мольбой бесплодной
Кумир бесчувственный молю.

Madoc himself is lost in recollections
of glorious deeds, in future aspirations
and in presentiments of woe and horror.

It is a lovely eventide: from aft
the wind hums in the rigging, and the ship
scuds safely through the spray. The sun is setting...   RC

600

AN INSECT COLLECTION

What tiny beasties greet our eyes –
some are less than pinhead-size!
                    KRYLÓV

This insect box – a fine collection –
merits my colleagues' close inspection.
It's colourful – without a doubt.
Where did I dig the rascals out?
And which is which – now, can you guess?
The ladybird? Try Glinka? Yes!
The spider... Kachenóvsky, plainly.
Svinín's the beetle – black, ungainly.
Olin? A tiny ant? – the same!
Raïch – some bug without a name...   10
So many! Lucky lad I am!
Framed under glass in tidy rows,
each insect sits beneath your nose
impaled here on an epigram.   JC

601

* * *

When noisy talk makes you the subject,
at your young age, of unfair blame,
and high society's harsh verdict
brings disrepute upon your name,

among the many void of feeling
it's only I who share your pain
and, to a god who's deaf appealing,
pray for you, even though in vain.

Но свет... Жестоких осуждений
Не изменяет он своих:
Он не карает заблуждений,
Но тайны требует для них.

Достойны равного презренья
Его тщеславная любовь
И лицемерные гоненья:
К забвенью сердце приготовь;

Не пей мутительной отравы;
Оставь блестящий, душный круг;
Оставь безумные забавы:
Тебе один остался друг.

Once it has censured indiscretions,
the world does not withdraw its spite: 10
it only pardons those transgressions
that are committed out of sight.

Show your contempt in equal measure
for their loud-mouthed acclaim and for
their hypocritical displeasure:
best brace yourself to be ignored;

hold those foul vipers in aversion,
avoid the brash, pretentious crew,
avoid their fatuous diversions –
there's one true friend still left to you.   RC

1830

602

ЦИКЛОП

Язык и ум теряя разом,
Гляжу на вас единым глазом:
Единый глаз в главе моей.
Когда б Судьбы того хотели,
Когда б имел я сто очей,
То все бы сто на вас глядели.

603

В АЛЬБОМ КАРОЛИНЫ СОБАНЬСКОЙ

Что в имени тебе моем?
Оно умрет, как шум печальный
Волны, плеснувшей в берег дальный,
Как звук ночной в лесу глухом.

Оно на памятном листке
Оставит мертвый след, подобный
Узору надписи надгробной
На непонятном языке.

Что в нем? Забытое давно
В волненьях новых и мятежных
Твоей душе не даст оно
Воспоминаний чистых, нежных.

Но в день печали, в тишине,
Произнеси его тоскуя;
Скажи: есть память обо мне,
Есть в мире сердце, где живу я.

10

1830

602

CYCLOPS

No power of thought nor speech preserving,
with one eye you I'm now observing:
one eye is all that I've been granted.
If Fate, deciding otherwise,
in me one hundred eyes had planted,
I'd watch you with all hundred eyes.   RC

603

FOR THE ALBUM OF KAROLINA SOBAŃSKA

You want my autograph – but why?
This name will die, a mournful roar
of breaking wave on far-off shore,
or in dark woods a night owl's cry.

My name signed on your album page
will leave a mark that's dead, the same
as when on tombs there's carved a name
in script of a forgotten age.

This name… you'll cease to think of it
when mired in turmoil and dissension,   10
and of our former friendship it
will bring you no fond recollection.

When lonely, though, in misery,
pronounce it then to ease your grief,
and say: "Someone remembers me –
there's still one heart in which I live."   RC

604

ОТВЕТ

Я вас узнал, о мой оракул!
Не по узорной пестроте
Сих неподписанных каракул,
Но по веселой остроте,
Но по приветствиям лукавым,
Но по насмешливости злой
И по упрекам… столь неправым,
И этой прелести живой.
С тоской невольной, с восхищеньем
Я перечитываю вас   10
И восклицаю с нетерпеньем:
Пора! в Москву, в Москву сейчас!
Здесь город чопорный, унылый,
Здесь речи — лед, сердца — гранит;
Здесь нет ни ветрености милой
Ни муз, ни Пресни, ни харит.

605 a

ПУШКИН, ОТ МЕЧТАНИЯ ПЕРЕШЕДШИЙ
К РАЗМЫШЛЕНИЮ

*Не напрасно, не случайно
Жизнь от Бога мне дана.
Не без воли Бога тайной
И на казнь осуждена.*

*Сам я своенравной властью
Зло из темных бездн воззвал,
Сам наполнил душу страстью,
Ум сомненьем взволновал.*

*Вспомнись мне, забвенный мною!
Просияй сквозь сумрак дум, —   10
И созиждется Тобою
Сердце чисто, светел ум.*

Филарет, Митрополит Московский и Коломенский

604

A REPLY

I've recognized you, mystifier! –
not by these scribbled lines, unsigned,
traced by a faux-calligraphier,
but by the wit, acute and kind,
and by the cunning two-edged greeting,
and by the wicked raillery,
and the rebukes I shan't be heeding,
the charm and the vivacity.
I feel such longing, such frustration,
as I reread the lines you've sent,   10
and can't hold back an exclamation:
"To Moscow, then! High time I went!"
Here it's a grim, pretentious city;
here talk is ice, and hearts are stone;
here is no fun – and, more's the pity,
no Muses, Graces, nor your home.   RC

605 a

PUSHKIN, AFTER TURNING FROM FANTASY
TO REPENTANCE

No way chanced, and no way senseless,
life's a gift God's given me.
Nor is death His final sentence
passed upon my destiny.

I, with my own wayward power,
from grim depths drew evil out,
filled my soul with passion's fire,
discomposed my mind with doubt.

Though disowned by me, sustain me,
shine into my thoughts' dark night –   10
then You will create within me
heart that's pure and mind that's bright.

Filarét, Metropolitan of Moscow and Kolómna   RC

605 б

МИТРОПОЛИТУ ФИЛАРЕТУ

В часы забав иль праздной скуки,
Бывало, лире я моей
Вверял изнеженные звуки
Безумства, лени и страстей.

Но и тогда струны лукавой
Невольно звон я прерывал,
Когда твой голос величавый
Меня внезапно поражал.

Я лил потоки слез нежданных,
И ранам совести моей   10
Твоих речей благоуханных
Отраден чистый был елей.

И ныне с высоты духовной
Мне руку простираешь ты,
И силой кроткой и любовной
Смиряешь буйные мечты.

Твоим огнем душа палима
Отвергла мрак земных сует,
И внемлет арфе серафима
В священном ужасе поэт.   20

606

СОНЕТ

Scorn not the sonnet, critic.
WORDSWORTH

Суровый Дант не презирал сонета;
В нем жар любви Петрарка изливал;
Игру его любил творец Макбета;
Им скорбну мысль Камоэнс облекал.

И в наши дни пленяет он поэта:
Вордсворт его орудием избрал,

605 b

FOR METROPOLITAN FILARÉT

In hours of idleness or pleasure
I'd take my lyre, and with its aid
I'd brashly play some flippant measure
that folly, sloth or lust conveyed.

But even then the godless prattle
of strings I'd halt instinctively,
when your majestic voice would startle
my ear with its sonority.

With tears my eyes would soon be flowing:
your gladdening words of fragrant grace,   10
their calming, cleansing oil bestowing,
my smarting conscience healed apace.

And now, though lifted high in spirit,
you place your friendly hand in mine
(such loving power you exhibit!)
and quieten my restless mind.

My soul, now purified with fire,
will earth's dark vanities abhor;
a seraph's harp, a seraphs' choir,
the poet hears with holy awe.   RC

606

SONNET

Scorn not the sonnet, critic.
WORDSWORTH

Unyielding Dante held the sonnet high;
sweet Petrarch with his passion made it warm;
Macbeth's creator loved its playful eye;
Camões draped his sorrows with its form.

In our day, too, it's won the poets' praise:
the noble Wordsworth took it in his arms

Когда вдали от суетного света
Природы он рисует идеал.

Под сенью гор Тавриды отдаленной
Певец Литвы в размер его стесненный   10
Свои мечты мгновенно заключал.

У нас еще его не знали девы,
Как для него уж Дельвиг забывал
Гекзаметра священные напевы.

607

НА БУЛГАРИНА

Не то беда, что ты поляк:
Костюшко лях, Мицкевич лях!
Пожалуй, будь себе татарин, —
И тут не вижу я стыда;
Будь жид — и это не беда;
Беда, что ты Видок Фиглярин.

608

ОЛЕНЬ

Шумит кустарник... На утес
Олень веселый выбегает,
Пугливо он подножный лес
С вершины острой озирает,
Глядит на светлые луга,
Глядит на синий свод небесный
И на днепровские брега,
Венчанны чащею древесной.
Недвижим, строен он стоит
И чутким ухом шевелит …   10

Но дрогнул он — незапный звук
Его коснулся — боязливо
Он шею вытянул и вдруг
С вершины прянул...

when, far away from vain and worldly ways,
he drew us perfect nature and its charms;

and underneath Crimea's distant skies
Mickiewicz dreamt his dreams and heaved his sighs   10
within its close, encompassing embrace.

Our maidens, though, had not yet heard its strains,
till Delvig, too, abandoned for its grace
the sonorous hexameter's refrains.   JF

607

ON BULGÁRIN

A Pole? Indeed! It's no disgrace:
great Mickiewicz – he was one.
So why not join the Tatar race
or call yourself a Jew for fun?
I name you now (poor living lie):
"Vidocq Figlyárin" – fool and spy!   JC

608

A DEER

The bushes rustle… to the ledge
comes bounding forth a sprightly deer,
and shyly from the rock's sharp edge
his eyes across the forest peer;
on glistening fields he gazes down;
the heavens' blue vault above he sees,
the Dnieper too, its forest crown
rimming the riverbank with trees.
Unmoving, poised, there stands the deer,
then flicks his keen, attentive ear …   10

But now he's flinched – a sudden sound
has startled him – and, seized with fear,
he's raised his head, and with a bound
leaps from the crag…   RC

609

К ВЕЛЬМОЖЕ

Послание к Князю Н.Б. Юсупову. Москва, 1830

От северных оков освобождая мир,
Лишь только на поля, струясь, дохнет зефир,
Лишь только первая позеленеет липа,
К тебе, приветливый потомок Аристиппа,
К тебе явлюся я; увижу сей дворец,
Где циркуль зодчего, палитра и резец
Ученой прихоти твоей повиновались
И вдохновенные в волшебстве состязались.

Ты понял жизни цель: счастливый человек,
Для жизни ты живешь. Свой долгий ясный век   10
Еще ты смолоду умно разнообразил,
Искал возможного, умеренно проказил;
Чредою шли к тебе забавы и чины.
Посланник молодой увенчанной Жены,
Явился ты в Ферней — и циник поседелый,
Умов и моды вождь пронырливый и смелый,
Свое владычество на Севере любя,
Могильным голосом приветствовал тебя.
С тобой веселости он расточал избыток,
Ты лесть его вкусил, земных богов напиток.   20
С Фернеем распростясь, увидел ты Версаль.
Пророческих очей не простирая вдаль,
Там ликовало всё. Армида молодая,
К веселью, роскоши знак первый подавая,
Не ведая, чему судьбой обречена,
Резвилась, ветреным двором окружена.
Ты помнишь Трианон и шумные забавы?
Но ты не изнемог от сладкой их отравы:
Ученье делалось на время твой кумир:
Уединялся ты. За твой суровый пир   30
То чтитель промысла, то скептик, то безбожник.
Садился Дидерот на шаткий свой треножник,
Бросал парик, глаза в восторге закрывал
И проповедывал. И скромно ты внимал
За чашей медленной афею иль деисту,
Как любопытный скиф афинскому софисту.

Но Лондон звал твое внимание. Твой взор
Прилежно разобрал сей двойственный собор:

609

TO A GRANDEE

Letter to Prince N.B. Yusúpov. Moscow, 1830

As soon as zephyrs breathe upon the fields and ponds
and liberate the world from icy northern bonds,
as soon as lindens bud and first turn green and fair,
I'll be delighted, Aristippus' gracious heir,
to visit you and see that palace where the brush,
the sculptor's chisel and the builder's compass rush
to serve your learnèd whim, and many a magician
has vied in an inspired creative competition.

You early understood, most fortunate of men,
that life's its own reward. Your long and brilliant span   10
from tender youth you wisely filled with variation;
you sought the possible, caroused in moderation,
and in succession came amusements, titles, fame.
When you, young envoy of a crowned and sceptred dame,
first visited Ferney, that cynic sly and grey,
who boldly ruled the minds and manners of his day,
contented with his sway o'er lands of snow and ice,
was pleased to welcome you in his sepulchral voice.
He lavished on you his abundant stores of mirth
and flattery, the nectar loved by gods on earth.   20
You left Ferney behind and went to see Versailles.
Not casting far ahead the mind's prophetic eye,
all revelled there. A young enchantress on the throne,
not knowing what the Fates had destined, set the tone
of rampant merrymaking, splendour and romance,
and led the giddy court in never-ending dance.
Do you remember Trianon's loud revelry?
Yet its sweet poison couldn't sap your energy,
and learning for a while became your highest aim:
to your secluded and ascetic banquet came   30
devout, then sceptical, then godless Diderot,
who, perching on his shaky tripod, liked to throw
his powdered wig aside, eyes closed in ecstasy,
and sermonize. You drained your wine cup modestly
and listened to an atheist or deist preaching
as would a Scythian an Athenian sophist's teaching.

But London beckoned then, where you would scrutinize
their twofold council's work with penetrating eyes:

Здесь натиск пламенный, а там отпор суровый,
Пружины смелые гражданственности новой.   40

Скучая, может быть, над Темзою скупой,
Ты думал дале плыть. Услужливый, живой,
Подобный своему чудесному герою,
Веселый Бомарше блеснул перед тобою.
Он угадал тебя: в пленительных словах
Он стал рассказывать о ножках, о глазах,
О неге той страны, где небо вечно ясно,
Где жизнь ленивая проходит сладострастно,
Как пылкий отрока восторгов полный сон,
Где жены вечером выходят на балкон,   50
Глядят и, не страшась ревнивого испанца,
С улыбкой слушают и манят иностранца.
И ты, встревоженный, в Севиллу полетел.
Благословенный край, пленительный предел!
Там лавры зыблются, там апельсины зреют…
О, расскажи ж ты мне, как жены там умеют
С любовью набожность умильно сочетать,
Из-под мантильи знак условный подавать;
Скажи, как падает письмо из-за решетки,
Как златом усыплен надзор угрюмой тетки;   60
Скажи, как в двадцать лет любовник под окном
Трепещет и кипит, окутанный плащом.

Всё изменилося. Ты видел вихорь бури,
Падение всего, союз ума и фурий,
Свободой грозною воздвигнутый закон,
Под гильотиною Версаль и Трианон
И мрачным ужасом смененные забавы.
Преобразился мир при громах новой славы.
Давно Ферней умолк. Приятель твой Вольтер,
Превратности судеб разительный пример,   70
Не успокоившись и в гробовом жилище,
Доныне странствует с кладбища на кладбище.
Барон д'Ольбах, Морле, Гальяни, Дидерот,
Энциклопедии скептической причот,
И колкий Бомарше, и твой безносый Касти,
Все, все уже прошли. Их мненья, толки, страсти
Забыты для других. Смотри: вокруг тебя
Всё новое кипит, былое истребя.
Свидетелями быв вчерашнего паденья,
Едва опомнились младые поколенья.   80

resistance on one side to check the other's passion,
the mainsprings of a bold new commonwealth in action.   40

You wearied of the frugal Thames along the way,
and thought of sailing on, when merry Beaumarchais
came bursting on the scene, as eager then to please
and lively as the splendid hero of his plays.
He guessed your secret thoughts: in words that tantalize,
he told of dainty feet and captivating eyes,
the blisses of a land where skies are always azure,
where life is sweetly spent in idleness and pleasure,
as full of rapture as a lad's impassioned dream,
where on their balconies, señoras can be seen   50
to smile invitingly at strangers and not worry
that dalliance may provoke a jealous Spaniard's fury.
Aroused, you headed for Seville and lost no time.
Oh, blessèd southern realm – oh, captivating clime!
There laurels gently wave, and there the orange grows…
Oh, tell me of that land where every woman knows
how piety and passion tenderly combine,
and how, behind her veil, to give a secret sign;
oh, tell me how a note will flutter from the grille,
how, lulled by gold, a watchful aunt will see no ill,   60
and how a lover, in a furtive mantle wrapped,
will wait below the window, tremulous and rapt.

All changed before your eyes. You saw the tempest rage,
reason with Furies leagued, the downfall of an age.
You saw the law raised up by freedom's dread crusade,
Versailles and Trianon beneath the falling blade,
amusements giving way to terror grim and gory,
a world transformed amid the thunder of new glory.
In silence lies Ferney. Voltaire, your former mate,
a stark example of the vagaries of fate,   70
can find no final place to lay his weary bones,
and from one cemetery to another roams.
D'Holbach, Galiani, Diderot and Morellet,
the whole Encyclopedic priesthood in array,
your noseless Casti, caustic Beaumarchais – the lot –
all, all of them are gone. Their passions and their thought
are now forgotten. Look: surrounding you today,
a new and bustling life has swept the old away.
Young generations, after all the storms they've seen,
have scarce recovered from the ruin as they glean   80

Жестоких опытов сбирая поздний плод,
Они торопятся с расходом свесть приход.
Им некогда шутить, обедать у Темиры,
Иль спорить о стихах. Звук новой, чудной лиры,
Звук лиры Байрона развлечь едва их мог.

Один всё тот же ты. Ступив за твой порог,
Я вдруг переношусь во дни Екатерины.
Книгохранилище, кумиры, и картины,
И стройные сады свидетельствуют мне,   90
Что благосклонствуешь ты музам в тишине,
Что ими в праздности ты дышишь благородной.
Я слушаю тебя: твой разговор свободный
Исполнен юности. Влиянье красоты
Ты живо чувствуешь. С восторгом ценишь ты
И блеск Алябьевой и прелесть Гончаровой.
Беспечно окружась Корреджием, Кановой,
Ты, не участвуя в волнениях мирских,
Порой насмешливо в окно глядишь на них
И видишь оборот во всем кругообразный.

Так, вихорь дел забыв для муз и неги праздной   100
В тени порфирных бань и мраморных палат,
Вельможи римские встречали свой закат.
И к ним издалека то воин, то оратор,
То консул молодой, то сумрачный диктатор
Являлись день-другой роскошно отдохнуть,
Вздохнуть о пристани и вновь пуститься в путь.

610

НОВОСЕЛЬЕ

Благословляю новоселье,
Куда домашний свой кумир
Ты перенес — а с ним веселье,
Свободный труд и сладкий мир.

Ты счастлив: ты свой домик малый,
Обычай мудрости храня,
От злых забот и лени вялой
Застраховал, как от огня.

a cruel harvest's fruits, retrieving what remains
and hurrying to count their losses and their gains.
They have no time to dine with women they admire,
hold forth on verse or jest. A new and wondrous lyre,
the lyre of Byron, scarce diverted them at all.

You only are unchanged. I step into your hall,
and Catherine's golden age for me is resurrected.
The volumes, canvases and statues you've collected,
the graceful gardens, tell me vividly that here,
in sweet tranquillity, you hold the Muses dear   90
and live and breathe their arts in noble isolation.
I listen to you speak: your easy conversation
is vibrant still with youth, and beauty's shining flame
as ever warms your heart. In rapture, you acclaim
sublime Alyábyeva, enchanting Goncharóva.
Without a care, among Correggio and Canova,
you stand aloof from all the troubles of the day,
and, casting now and then a mocking glance their way,
you see that all has come around to where it started.

Thus, leaving high affairs, the great of Rome departed   100
for shady marble halls and baths of porphyry
to meet their sunset in the Muses' company.
At times, a general, an orator of fame,
a youthful consul or a grim dictator came
to bask a day or two in comfort far from home,
then, sighing with regret, set off again for Rome.   CC & ER

610

A NEW HOME

Blessed be your new-found habitation,
to which you've brought your cherished toy,
that tiny house – your relaxation,
fond work that brings you peace and joy!

Well done! You've used your model-making,
with the old prudence we admire,
to insure from sloth and troublemaking
your modest dwelling, as from fire.   RC

611

* * *

Надо мной в лазури ясной
Светит звездочка одна,
Справа — запад темно-красный,
Слева — бледная луна.

612

ПОЭТУ

Сонет

Поэт! не дорожи любовию народной.
Восторженных похвал пройдет минутный шум;
Услышишь суд глупца и смех толпы холодной,
Но ты останься тверд, спокоен и угрюм.

Ты царь: живи один. Дорогою свободной
Иди, куда влечет тебя свободный ум,
Усовершенствуя плоды любимых дум,
Не требуя наград за подвиг благородный.

Они в самом тебе. Ты сам свой высший суд;
Всех строже оценить умеешь ты свой труд.   10
Ты им доволен ли, взыскательный художник?

Доволен? Так пускай толпа его бранит
И плюет на алтарь, где твой огонь горит,
И в детской резвости колеблет твой треножник.

613

МАДОННА

Сонет

Не множеством картин старинных мастеров
Украсить я всегда желал свою обитель,
Чтоб суеверно им дивился посетитель,
Внимая важному сужденью знатоков.

611

* * *

Look, a lonely star is shining
up there in the clear blue sky –
west, a crimson sun's declining;
east, a pallid moon mounts high.   RC

612

FOR A POET

Sonnet

When all acclaim you, poet, pay no heed!
The sound of clapping soon will die – instead
you'll hear fools judge, the cold crowd mock your deed:
be calm, austere, with proudly lifted head.

You're king, so dwell alone. Your free path tread
wherever your free mind your steps may lead;
perfect the fruits your secret thoughts have bred,
but ask for no rewards when you succeed.

They are within – where *you*'re the highest judge;
what you esteem excels, though others grudge.   10
Can you your own sharp criticism meet?

You can? Then let the mob besmirch your name,
spit on the altar that enshrines your flame
and, like rough urchins, shake your tripod's feet.   WM & RC

613

MADONNA

Sonnet

I've never wished to adorn my private residence
by hanging wall to wall innumerable old pictures,
and have approving guests repeat remarks and strictures
of pompous connoisseurs in awestruck reverence.

В простом углу моем, средь медленных трудов,
Одной картины я желал быть вечно зритель,
Одной: чтоб на меня с холста, как с облаков,
Пречистая и наш божественный спаситель —

Она с величием, он с разумом в очах —
Взирали, кроткие, во славе и в лучах,   10
Одни, без ангелов, под пальмою Сиона.

Исполнились мои желания. Творец
Тебя мне ниспослал, тебя, моя Мадонна,
Чистейшей прелести чистейший образец.

614

* * *

Полюбуйтесь же вы, дети,
Как в сердечной простоте
Длинный Фирс играет в *эти*,
Те, те, те и те, те, те.

Черноокая Россети
В самовластной красоте
Все сердца пленила *эти*,
Те, те, те и те, те, те.

О, какие же здесь сети
Рок нам стелет в темноте: 10
Рифмы, деньги, дамы *эти*,
Те, те, те и те, те, те.

615

* * *

И вот ущелье мрачных скал
Пред нами шире становится,
Но тише Терек злой стремится,
Луч солнца ярче засиял.

But in my simple home, mid half-done tasks piled high,
one painting I'd have wished my eyes could ever savour –
one canvas, out of which there would, as from the sky,
look down on me the Holy Virgin and our Saviour,

her eyes with dignity, and *his* with shrewdness, bright –
yes, gently they'd look down, suffused in glorious light,   10
with them no angel host, just one tall palm of Zion.

My wish is now fulfilled: God in His bounteousness
has vouchsafed you to me as my Madonna-icon,
the purest paragon of purest loveliness.   RC

614

* * *

Lads, admire the honesty
lanky Firs so staunchly shows
at the games he's playing – *these*,
those, those, those and those, those, those.

Miss Rosseti's jet-black eyes
win the hearts of all the beaux
with her regal beauty – *these*,
those, those, those and those, those, those.

Thus each night can Fate with ease
set more snares than we suppose: 10
rhymes and bets and ladies – *these*,
those, those, those and those, those, those.   RC

615

* * *

This gorge that shadowed crags confine –
look there! – is broadening out before us;
the Terek races now less furious;
once more the sun's rays brighter shine.   RC

616

* * *

Страшно и скучно
Здесь новоселье,
Путь и ночлег.
Тесно и душно.
В диком ущелье —
Тучи да снег.

Солнце не светит,
Небо чуть видно,
Как из тюрьмы.
Солнцу обидно.   10
Путник не встретит
Окроме тьмы
....

617

БЕСЫ

Мчатся тучи, вьются тучи;
Невидимкою луна
Освещает снег летучий;
Мутно небо, ночь мутна.
Еду, еду в чистом поле;
Колокольчик дин-дин-дин...
Страшно, страшно поневоле
Средь неведомых равнин!

«Эй, пошел, ямщик!..» — «Нет мочи
Коням, барин, тяжело;   10
Вьюга мне слипает очи;
Все дороги занесло;
Хоть убей, следа не видно;
Сбились мы. Что делать нам!
В поле бес нас водит, видно,
Да кружит по сторонам.

Посмотри; вон, вон играет,
Дует, плюет на меня;

616

* * *

Frightening and cheerless –
soon we'll be warm, though –
path to an inn!
Thronged here and airless.
Snow and fierce storm, though,
in the ravine.

Heaven is sunless.
As from a dungeon,
sky's but a crack.
Traveller encounters   10
(sun's in high dudgeon!)
nothing but black.

....   JH & RC

617

DEMONS

Clouds are rushing, clouds are writhing –
murky skies, a murky night –
and a ghostly moon in hiding
bathes the flying snow in light.
Through the wilds, I'm riding, riding;
ding-ding-ding, the bell rings on...
and, despite myself, it's frightening
in these endless fields unknown.

"Hey there, driver, let's go faster!"
"'Fraid the horses can't take more;   10
I'm half blinded by the blast, sir,
and the roads are drifted o'er;
for my life, I just can't see 'em –
not a trace is to be found!
Heaven help us, it's a demon
has us going round and round.

"Look, he's playing there, cavorting,
blowing, spitting at me now,

71

Вон — теперь в овраг толкает
Одичалого коня;   20
Там верстою небывалой
Он торчал передо мной;
Там сверкнул он искрой малой
И пропал во тьме пустой».

Мчатся тучи, вьются тучи;
Невидимкою луна
Освещает снег летучий;
Мутно небо, ночь мутна.
Сил нам нет кружиться доле;   30
Колокольчик вдруг умолк;
Кони стали... «Что там в поле?» —
«Кто их знает? пень иль волк?»

Вьюга злится, вьюга плачет;
Кони чуткие храпят;
Вот уж он далече скачет;
Лишь глаза во мгле горят;
Кони снова понеслися;
Колокольчик дин-дин-дин...
Вижу: духи собралися   40
Средь белеющих равнин.

Бесконечны, безобразны,
В мутной месяца игре
Закружились бесы разны,
Будто листья в ноябре...
Сколько их! куда их гонят?
Что так жалобно поют?
Домового ли хоронят,
Ведьму ль замуж выдают?

Мчатся тучи, вьются тучи;   50
Невидимкою луна
Освещает снег летучий;
Мутно небо, ночь мутна.
Мчатся бесы рой за роем
В беспредельной вышине,
Визгом жалобным и воем
Надрывая сердце мне...

then he drives the horses, snorting,
to the gulley's very brow;   20
like a milepost grave and eerie,
he rose up before my face;
then a flash, and I was peering
into naught but empty space."

Clouds are rushing, clouds are writhing –
murky skies, a murky night –
and a ghostly moon in hiding
bathes the flying snow in light.
Horses weary of their circling   30
now stop short, as does the bell.
"What's that shadow out there lurking?"
"Wolf or tree stump – who can tell?"

Snow is raging, snow is howling;
skittish horses snort and blow;
then he bounds off yonder, prowling
in the gloom, his eyes aglow.
We continue on our journey;
ding-ding-ding, the bell proceeds...
Now I see them: spirits hurry   40
to convene in whitening fields.

Demons hideous, assembling
in the moonlight's murky play,
whirl in multitudes, resembling
autumn leaves in wild array...
What drives on these hosts unending?
Why the mournful sounds they make?
Could it be a witch's wedding
or a household spirit's wake?

Clouds are rushing, clouds are writhing –   50
murky skies, a murky night –
and a ghostly moon in hiding
bathes the flying snow in light.
Swarm on swarm, the demons hasten
through the vastness without rest,
and their shrieks and lamentation
rend the heart within my breast...   CC

618

ЭЛЕГИЯ

Безумных лет угасшее веселье
Мне тяжело, как смутное похмелье.
Но, как вино — печаль минувших дней
В моей душе чем старе, тем сильней.
Мой путь уныл. Сулит мне труд и горе
Грядущего волнуемое море.

Но не хочу, о други, умирать;
Я жить хочу, чтоб мыслить и страдать;
И ведаю, мне будут наслажденья
Меж горестей, забот и треволненья: 10
Порой опять гармонией упьюсь,
Над вымыслом слезами оболью сь,
И может быть — на мой закат печальный
Блеснет любовь улыбкою прощальной.

619

КАВКАЗ

Кавказ подо мною. Один в вышине
Стою над снегами у края стремнины;
Орел, с отдаленной поднявшись вершины,
Парит неподвижно со мной наравне.
Отселе я вижу потоков рожденье
И первое грозных обвалов движенье.

Здесь тучи смиренно идут подо мной;
Сквозь них, низвергаясь, шумят водопады;
Под ними утесов нагие громады;
Там ниже мох тощий, кустарник сухой;   10
А там уже рощи, зеленые сени,
Где птицы щебечут, где скачут олени.

А там уж и люди гнездятся в горах,
И ползают овцы по злачным стремнинам,
И пастырь нисходит к веселым долинам,
Где мчится Арагва в тенистых брегах,
И нищий наездник таится в ущельи,
Где Терек играет в свирепом весельи;

618

ELEGY

The giddy, vanished years of mirth and laughter
afflict me like a troubled morning after.
Past sorrow, though, is like a wine to me,
which, aging, only gains in potency.
My path is bleak. The future sea is stormy
and promises but toil and woe before me.

And yet from thoughts of death, my friends, I shrink;
I want to live – to suffer and to think.
Amid the cares, the woes and tribulations,
I know I'll have my share of consolations –   10
at times be drunk on harmony again,
and weep o'er new inventions of the pen.
And love then, as my sorry light grows dimmer,
may flash a tender smile, her parting glimmer.   CC & IZ

619

THE CAUCASUS

The Caucasus stretches below me, and I,
alone on a ledge, survey snowy white vistas:
an eagle lifts off from a peak in the distance
and, motionless, hangs at my height in the sky.
From here I see newly born streamlets emerging,
and snow slides reveal their first ominous stirring.

Processions of storm clouds pass meekly below
as water, cascading, pours through them and crashes
in torrents against the exposed rocky masses;
still lower, sparse mosses and dry bushes grow;   10
and groves, like green canopies, flourish in patches,
where deer frisk and twittering birds fill the branches.

And people nest up on the steep mountain flanks,
and sheep graze the plentiful slopes in contentment;
a shepherd descends to vales shady and pleasant,
where sweeps the Arágva in shadowy banks;
a raider hides deep in a gorge in privation,
where frolics the Terek in savage elation;

Играет и воет, как зверь молодой,
Завидевший пищу из клетки железной;
И бьется о берег в вражде бесполезной,
И лижет утесы голодной волной...
Вотще! нет ни пищи ему, ни отрады:
Теснят его грозно немые громады.

20

620

МОНАСТЫРЬ НА КАЗБЕКЕ

Высоко над семьею гор,
Казбек, твой царственный шатер
Сияет вечными лучами.
Твой монастырь за облаками,
Как в небе реющий ковчег,
Парит, чуть видный, над горами.

Далекий, вожделенный брег!
Туда б, сказав прости ущелью,
Подняться к вольной вышине!
Туда б, в заоблачную келью,
В соседство Бога скрыться мне!..

10

621

ОТВЕТ АНОНИМУ

О, кто бы ни был ты, чье ласковое пенье
Приветствует мое к блаженству возрожденье,
Чья скрытая рука мне крепко руку жмет,
Указывает путь и посох подает;
О, кто бы ни был ты: старик ли вдохновенный,
Иль юности моей товарищ отдаленный,
Иль отрок, музами таинственно храним,
Иль пола кроткого стыдливый херувим, —
Благодарю тебя душою умиленной.

Вниманья слабого предмет уединенный,
К доброжелательству досель я не привык —
И странен мне его приветливый язык.
Смешон, участия кто требует у света!
Холодная толпа взирает на поэта,

10

it frolics and howls like a beast in a cage
that's spotted a morsel of food; and, assailing   20
the close-lying banks with a force unavailing,
it licks at the rocks in insatiable rage...
In vain! It will never be fed or know gladness,
confined by the mute and forbidding stone masses.   CC

620

MONASTERY ON KAZBÉK

Kazbék, your regal tent abides
above your mountain clan, ablaze
with glittering, eternal rays.
Beyond the clouds your cloister hides,
a skyborne ark that seems to soar,
scarce seen, above the mountainsides.

Oh, distant, long-awaited shore!
Now, bidding the ravine farewell,
to freedom's lofty heights I'd fly,
and there, in a celestial cell,   10
take refuge close to God on high!   CC

621

REPLY TO AN UNNAMED WRITER

You are unknown to me. Your kind and charming lines, though,
are welcoming me back to happiness and life;
your hand, too, though unseen, is firmly squeezing mine:
it points the way ahead and offers me a staff.
You are unknown to me – a man of years, inspired?
Some friend of mine when young, from whom I've been estranged?
A lad of wondrous gifts, a Muses' protégé?
Or, from the gentler sex, a shy angelic being?
Whoever you may be, I'm touched – my heartfelt thanks!

A lonely figure now, attracting sparse attention,   10
for long I've been unused to favourable notice –
and compliments to me are now a foreign tongue.
How foolish to expect the public's interest!
Most folk are unconcerned for us these days, regarding

Как на заезжего фигляра: если он
Глубоко выразит сердечный, тяжкий стон,
И выстраданный стих, пронзительно-унылый,
Ударит по сердцам с неведомою силой, —
Она в ладони бьет и хвалит, иль порой
Неблагосклонною кивает головой.   20
Постигнет ли певца незапное волненье,
Утрата скорбная, изгнанье, заточенье, —
«Тем лучше, — говорят любители искусств, —
Тем лучше! наберет он новых дум и чувств
И нам их передаст». Но счастие поэта
Меж ими не найдет сердечного привета,
Когда боязненно безмолвствует оно…

622

ТРУД

Миг вожделенный настал: окончен мой труд многолетний.
    Что ж непонятная грусть тайно тревожит меня?
Или, свой подвиг свершив, я стою, как поденщик ненужный,
    Плату приявший свою, чуждый работе другой?
Или жаль мне труда, молчаливого спутника ночи,
    Друга Авроры златой, друга Пенатов святых?

623

СТИХИ, СОЧИНЕННЫЕ НОЧЬЮ ВО ВРЕМЯ БЕССОННИЦЫ

Мне не спится, нет огня;
Всюду мрак и сон докучный.
Ход часов лишь однозвучный
Раздается близ меня.
Парки бабье лепетанье,
Спящей ночи трепетанье,
Жизни мышья беготня…
Что тревожишь ты меня?
Что ты значишь, скучный шепот?
Укоризна, или ропот   10
Мной утраченного дня?
От меня чего ты хочешь?
Ты зовешь или пророчишь?
Я понять тебя хочу,
Смысла я в тебе ищу…

poets like vagrant clowns – and if a poet should
utter from deep within a heavy, heartfelt sigh,
and if an anguished verse of penetrating sorrow
should strike them to the core with force unfelt before,
they may well clap and pass remarks of praise (or sometimes
shake heads among themselves in mark of disapproval).   20
Then if the poet meets some unforeseen mischance –
a tragic loss, perhaps, or banishment or exile –
"So much the better," say those patrons of the arts.
"So much the better! He'll pick up fresh thoughts and feelings
and pass them on to us." But should good fortune come,
he'll wait in vain for them to voice congratulations,
if bashfully he speaks no word of it himself...   RC

622

WORK

Here is the moment I've craved – my labour of years is accomplished!
   Why, then, this baffling distress secretly troubling my soul?
Am I just standing about, task fulfilled, like a workman unneeded,
   one who has taken his pay, chary of other employ?
Or am I missing my work, that companion in long nights of silence,
   friend of the gold-bedecked Dawn, friend of the gods where I've dwelt? RC

623

VERSES COMPOSED AT NIGHT DURING INSOMNIA

Lamp's gone out, and sleep has fled;
dark brings wearisome delusion.
With monotonous intrusion
clock keeps ticking by my bed.
Dreaded Fate's old-haggish muttering,
slothful night time's restive shuddering,
mouse-like scuttling to and fro...
why do you disturb me so?
What's the message that you're mumbling –
is it a rebuke? Or grumbling   10
over time that I've let go?
What is it from me you're wanting?
Are you calling me or warning?
Tell me clearly, so I may
grasp the sense of what you say...   RC

624

* * *

В начале жизни школу помню я;
Там нас, детей беспечных, было много;
Неровная и резвая семья.

Смиренная, одетая убого,
Но видом величавая жена
Над школою надзор хранила строго.

Толпою нашею окружена,
Приятным, сладким голосом, бывало,
С младенцами беседует она.

Ее чела я помню покрывало   10
И очи светлые, как небеса.
Но я вникал в ее беседы мало.

Меня смущала строгая краса
Ее чела, спокойных уст и взоров,
И полные святыни словеса.

Дичась ее советов и укоров,
Я про себя превратно толковал
Понятный смысл правдивых разговоров,

И часто я украдкой убегал
В великолепный мрак чужого сада,   20
Под свод искусственный порфирных скал.

Там нежила меня теней прохлада;
Я предавал мечтам свой юный ум,
И праздно мыслить было мне отрада.

Любил я светлых вод и листьев шум,
И белые в тени дерев кумиры,
И в ликах их печать недвижных дум.

Всё — мраморные циркули и лиры,
Мечи и свитки в мраморных руках,
На главах лавры, на плечах порфиры —   30

624

* * *

I think of school at life's beginning, where
we lads – a motley family of fresh
and lively pupils – lived without a care.

A woman very meek, in shabby dress,
who had a nonetheless majestic poise,
was there to strictly guide our early steps.

Surrounded by our sprightly throng of boys,
she frequently instructed us and led
discussions in a sweet and pleasant voice.

I see the scarf she wore about her head,   10
recall her gaze, as clear as cloudless skies,
but I gave little thought to what she said.

I shrank before her stern and lovely eyes,
her brow and lips serene, her tone subdued
and words so full of sanctity and wise.

Her counsels and reproaches I eschewed;
their truthfulness and simple clarity
I wilfully, perversely misconstrued.

I often stole away and, breaking free,
took refuge in a garden's gloomy splendour,   20
beneath its man-made cliffs of porphyry.

The shady cool caressed me there; at leisure,
I let my youthful mind pursue its dreams,
and it was idle thought that gave me pleasure.

I loved the sound of leaves and sparkling streams,
and frozen thoughts imprinted on the brows
of marble statues in the shade of trees.

The compasses and lyres beneath dark boughs,
the scrolls and swords in hands of marble white,
the mantled shoulders, heads with laurel crowns –   30

Всё наводило сладкий некий страх
Мне на сердце; и слезы вдохновенья,
При виде их, рождались на глазах.

Другие два чудесные творенья
Влекли меня волшебною красой:
То были двух бесов изображенья.

Один (Дельфийский идол) лик младой
Был гневен, полон гордости ужасной,
И весь дышал он силой неземной.

Другой женообразный, сладострастный,   40
Сомнительный и лживый идеал —
Волшебный демон — лживый, но прекрасный,

Пред ними сам себя я забывал;
В груди младое сердце билось — холод
Бежал по мне и кудри подымал.

Безвестных наслаждений темный голод
Меня терзал — уныние и лень
Меня сковали — тщетно был я молод.

Средь отроков я молча целый день
Бродил угрюмый — всё кумиры сада   50
На душу мне свою бросали тень …

625

К КРИТИКУ

Румяный критик мой, насмешник толстопузый,
Готовый век трунить над нашей томной музой,
Поди-ка ты сюда, присядь-ка ты со мной,
Попробуй, сладим ли с проклятою хандрой.
Смотри, какой здесь вид: избушек ряд убогий,
За ними чернозем, равнины скат отлогий,
Над ними серых туч густая полоса.
Где нивы светлые? где темные леса?
Где речка? На дворе у низкого забора
Два бедных деревца стоят в отраду взора,   10
Два только деревца. И то из них одно

within my heart, these visions would excite
sweet terror; shining tears of inspiration
were born in eyes enchanted by the sight.

Another two miraculous creations
attracted me with their bewitching grace:
two images of demons, evocations.

The Delphic idol had a youthful face,
but wrathful, full of awful pride, exuding
an otherworldly power in his gaze.

The other, womanlike, erotic, drew me   40
to follow an uncertain, false ideal –
bewitching demon, false but rich in beauty.

Before them I'd forget myself and feel
a shiver stand my hair on end and run
all through me, heart pulsating with the thrill.

My thirst for unknown pleasures would become
a torment; indolence and gloom assailed
and manacled me; vainly was I young.

Among the lads, for days on end, I strayed
morose and mute; the statues in the garden   50
upon my soul still cast their haunting shade ...   CC

625

TO A CRITIC

You, critic of my work – complacent, florid, paunchy –
you scoffer, ever prone to mock my downbeat style,
bring yourself over here and take a seat beside me:
let's try to get to grips with this damned downbeat thinking!
Look at this scene: a line of godforsaken shacks,
black earth beyond that slopes away into the distance;
above there loom dense banks of storm clouds leaden-grey.
But sunlit meadowlands, dark forests – where are they?
And where's the brook? Outside, along a sagging fence,
stand two gaunt trees (to bring the eyes relief!),   10
two wretched trees, no more – and one of them already

Дождливой осенью совсем обнажено,
И листья на другом, размокнув и желтея,
Чтоб лужу засорить, лишь только ждут Борея.
И только. На дворе живой собаки нет.
Вот, правда, мужичок, за ним две бабы вслед.
Без шапки он; несет подмышкой гроб ребенка
И кличет издали ленивого попенка,
Чтоб тот отца позвал да церковь отворил.
Скорей! ждать некогда! давно бы схоронил.   20
Что ж ты нахмурился?
                              — Нельзя ли блажь оставить!
И песенкою нас веселой позабавить?...

———————

Куда же ты?
                    — В Москву, чтоб графских именин
Мне здесь не прогулять.
                              — Постой, а карантин!
Ведь в нашей стороне индейская зараза.
Сиди, как у ворот угрюмого Кавказа,
Бывало, сиживал покорный твой слуга;
Что, брат? уж не трунишь, тоска берет — ага!

626 а

НА ГНЕДИЧА

С тобою в спор я не вступаю,
Что жесткое в стихах твоих встречаю;
Я руку наложил,
Погладил — занозил.

626 б

К ПЕРЕВОДУ *ИЛИАДЫ*

Крив был Гнедич поэт, преложитель слепого Гомера,
Боком одним с образцом схож и его перевод.

stands stripped of foliage by autumn's driving rains,
while on the other tree the yellowed leaves hang sodden,
waiting for winter gales to drown them in the mud.
That's all. You'll see no dog or other beast at large –
though (look!) one peasant's there, two wenches coming after.
Hatless, beneath his arm he holds an infant's coffin
and shouts across to where the priest's young son is loafing,
for him to call his dad and open up the church:
"Get on – no time to waste. Should long since have been buried." –   20
But why, friend, do you frown?
                        "Give up this drivel please,
and entertain us with a jolly song instead."

––––––––––

Where are you off to now?
                        "To Moscow. Mustn't miss
Count X's nameday do."
                        But wait – the quarantine!
There's cholera all round – you've surely not forgotten?
Stay put, as just last year your humble servant had to –
stay put for days beyond the Caucasus' grim gateway…
Well, friend, you scoff no more! Who's downbeat now? Aha!   RC

626 a

ON GNEDICH

If fault I find, I'm sure the worst is
  that there's a certain roughness in your verses;
    I smooth a page and catch
    my palm – there, look, a scratch!   RC

626 b

ON THE TRANSLATION OF THE *ILIAD*

Gnedich, with only one eye, was translator of blind poet Homer.
  Likewise the work he achieved only made one of a pair.   RC

627

ЦАРСКОСЕЛЬСКАЯ СТАТУЯ

Урну с водой уронив, об утес ее дева разбила.
  Дева печально сидит, праздный держа черепок.
Чудо! не сякнет вода, изливаясь из урны разбитой;
  Дева, над вечной струей, вечно печальна сидит.

628

ТРИ ГЛУХОГО

Глухой глухого звал к суду судьи глухого,
Глухой кричал: «Моя им сведена корова!» —
«Помилуй, — возопил глухой тому в ответ: —
Сей пустошью владел еще покойный дед».
Судья решил: «Чтоб не было разврата,
Жените молодца, хоть девка виновата».

629

ПРОЩАНИЕ

В последний раз твой образ милый
Дерзаю мысленно ласкать,
Будить мечту сердечной силой
И с негой робкой и унылой
Твою любовь воспоминать.

Бегут меняясь наши лета,
Меняя всё, меняя нас,
Уж ты для своего поэта
Могильным сумраком одета,
И для тебя твой друг угас.

Прими же, дальная подруга,
Прощанье сердца моего,
Как овдовевшая супруга,
Как друг, обнявший молча друга
Пред заточением его.

10

627

A STATUE AT TSÁRSKOYE SELÓ

Dreaming, she let the urn slip, and it broke on the rock into pieces.
   Sitting there sadly, the maid holds but a profitless shard.
Wonder of wonders! The water that spills from the urn never dwindles.
   There, by a stream ever full, ever in sadness she sits.   CC

628

THREE DEAF MEN

Plaintiff and judge were deaf. The former cried:
"That wretched fellow took my cow away!"
The deaf respondent angrily replied,
"This barren plot was ours in Granddad's day."
His Lordship ruled: "For fear of public shame,
the lad must wed – although the girl's to blame."   JC

629

FAREWELL

Rashly in my imagination
I fondle you, dear, one last time,
dream one last dream of exaltation
and with an anxious, sad elation
one last time call your love to mind.

Our years change, racing on. Unsparing,
they change the world – they change us too.
So now a deathly shroud you're wearing –
that's how you seem to your despairing
poet, and dead he'll seem to you.   10

Dear distant friend, my heart is aching –
accept this farewell I now send
like a new widow, heart still breaking,
or one who mutely hugs his shaking
friend to a prison cell condemned.   RC

630

ПАЖ, ИЛИ ПЯТНАДЦАТЫЙ ГОД

C'est l'âge de Chérubin...

Пятнадцать лет мне скоро минет;
Дождусь ли радостного дня?
Как он вперед меня подвинет!
Но и теперь никто не кинет
С презреньем взгляда на меня.

Уж я не мальчик — уж над губой
Могу свой ус я защипнуть;
Я важен, как старик беззубый;
Вы слышите мой голос грубый,
Попробуй кто меня толкнуть.   10

Я нравлюсь дамам, ибо скромен,
И между ими есть одна...
И гордый взор ее так томен,
И цвет ланит ее так тёмен,
Что жизни мне милей она.

Она строга, властолюбива,
Я сам дивлюсь ее уму —
И ужас как она ревнива;
Зато со всеми горделива
И мне доступна одному.   20

Вечор она мне величаво
Клялась, что если буду вновь
Глядеть налево и направо,
То даст она мне яду; право —
Вот какова ее любовь!

Она готова хоть в пустыню
Бежать со мной, презрев молву...
Хотите знать мою богиню,
Мою севильскую графиню?..
Нет! ни за что не назову!   30

630

THE PAGE, OR AT THE AGE OF FIFTEEN

C'est l'âge de Chérubin...

My sixteenth year will soon arrive;
I long to see the joyous day.
Oh, when it comes, I'll truly thrive!
Yet even now no man alive
would cast a mocking glance my way.

I'm not a boy – I twirl the hair
upon my upper lip, you see;
I sport an elder's knowing air
and gravel voice, as you're aware...
So watch your step when you're with me.   10

The ladies like my modest ways,
and one among them steals my breath...
She wields a haughty, languid gaze;
her cheeks with such deep colour blaze
that I for her would suffer death.

She's so commanding and so bold,
she has the most amazing mind –
and jealous – you should hear her scold!
But though you'd find her proud and cold,
alone with me she's warm and kind.   20

She swore with regal wrath last night
that if I ever dared again
to cast my eye to left or right,
she'd give me poison at the sight –
for that's how much she loves her men!

She's ready, scorning worldly shame,
to fly with me to desert cell.
You'd like to know the lady's name,
my countess from the south of Spain?
Oh no, I swear, I'll never tell!   JF

631

ИНЕЗИЛЬЯ

Я здесь, Инезилья,
Я здесь под окном.
Объята Севилья
И мраком и сном.

Исполнен отвагой,
Окутан плащом,
С гитарой и шпагой
Я здесь под окном.

Ты спишь ли? Гитарой
Тебя разбужу.   10
Проснется ли старый,
Мечом уложу.

Шелковые петли
К окошку привесь...
Что медлишь?... Уж нет ли
Соперника здесь?...

Я здесь, Инезилья,
Я здесь под окном.
Объята Севилья
И мраком и сном.   20

632

ДВОЕ РЫЦАРЕЙ

Пред испанкой благородной
Двое рыцарей стоят.
Оба смело и свободно
В очи прямо ей глядят.
Блещут оба красотою,
Оба сердцем горячи,
Оба мощною рукою
Оперлися на мечи.

631

INESILLA

I'm here, Inesilla,
I'm here 'neath your room.
Engulfed lies Sevilla
in slumber and gloom.

Cloak, rapier I'm wearing,
and hat with its plume,
guitar too – and daring
to stand 'neath your room.

You're sleeping? Then waken –
I'll strum my guitar.   10
The old man's awake? Then
he'll learn who we are!

Just hang from your window
a length of silk rope.
You're dawdling within, though –
with no one, I hope!

I'm here, Inesilla,
I'm here 'neath your room.
Engulfed lies Sevilla
in slumber and gloom.   RC

632

TWO KNIGHTS

Lovely lady, Spanish lady,
    now you must decide;
look, two knights have come a-wooing,
    strong in youth and pride.
Leaning on their swords before you,
    famed throughout the land;
both are ardent, gallant, handsome:
    both desire your hand.

Жизни им она дороже
И, как слава, им мила;   10
Но один ей мил — кого же
Дева сердцем избрала?
«Кто, реши, любим тобою?» —
Оба деве говорят
И с надеждой молодою
В очи прямо ей глядят.

633

РИФМА

Эхо, бессонная нимфа, скиталась по брегу Пенея.
　　Феб, увидев ее, страстию к ней воспылал.
Нимфа плод понесла восторгов влюбленного бога;
　　Меж говорливых наяд, мучась, она родила
Милую дочь. Ее прияла сама Мнемозина.
　　Резвая дева росла в хоре богинь-аонид,
Матери чуткой подобна, послушна памяти строгой,
　　Музам мила; на земле Рифмой зовется она.

634

ОТРОК

Невод рыбак расстилал по брегу студеного моря;
　　Мальчик отцу помогал. Отрок, оставь рыбака!
Мрежи иные тебя ожидают, иные заботы:
　　Будешь умы уловлять, будешь помощник царям.

635

МОЯ РОДОСЛОВНАЯ

Смеясь жестоко над собратом,
Писаки русские толпой
Меня зовут аристократом:
Смотри, пожалуй, вздор какой!
Не офицер я, не асессор,
Я по кресту не дворянин,
Не академик, не профессор;
Я просто русский мещанин.

You are dearer far than riches,
   life, or fleeting fame: 10
one – and only one – attracts you:
   which one? Speak his name!
Both beseech you, both implore you:
   "Lady, is it I?"
See them gazing, young and hopeful –
   now you must reply…   JC

633

RHYME

Echo, unable to sleep, was wandering alone by the river.
   Phoebus, that amorous god, spied her and blazed with desire.
Soon the unfortunate nymph grew great with the fruit of his pleasure;
   whispering Naiads heard groans of a mother-to-be.
Lovely the baby she bore: and Memory, mother of Muses,
   fostered the spirited child, bringing her up with her own.
Sharp and retentive the girl (how very like Echo, her mother!),
   friend of the Muses above. Mortals on earth call her "Rhyme".   JC & RC

634

A LAD

Fishing the cold northern sea, a man spread his net on the water,
   helped in the task by his son. Lad, leave the fisher behind!
Nets of another design now await you, new cares to attend to:
   you'll be a fisher of minds, you'll be a helper of kings.   CC

635

MY PEDIGREE

The tribe of Russian scribblers, mocking
a confrère with malignant wit,
calls me "aristocratic". Shocking,
the sheer absurdity of it!
I am no officer, assessor,
seigneur by dint of medals worn,
academician or professor:
a Russian commoner – no more.

Понятна мне времен превратность,
Не прекословлю, право, ей: 10
У нас нова рожденьем знатность,
И чем новее, тем знатней.
Родов дряхлеющих обломок
(И по несчастью не один),
Бояр старинных я потомок;
Я, братцы, мелкий мещанин.

Не торговал мой дед блинами,
Не ваксил царских сапогов,
Не пел с придворными дьячками,
В князья не прыгал из хохлов,   20
И не был беглым он солдатом
Австрийских пудреных дружин;
Так мне ли быть аристократом?
Я, слава Богу, мещанин.

Мой предок Рача мышцей бранной
Святому Невскому служил;
Его потомство гнев венчанный,
Иван IV пощадил.
Водились Пушкины с царями;
Из них был славен не один,   30
Когда тягался с поляками
Нижегородский мещанин.

Смирив крамолу и коварство,
И ярость бранных непогод,
Когда Романовых на царство
Звал в грамоте своей народ,
Мы к оной руку приложили,
Нас жаловал страдальца сын.
Бывало нами дорожили;
Бывало... но — я мещанин.   40

Упрямства дух нам всем подгадил:
В родню свою неукротим,
С Петром мой пращур не поладил
И был за то повешен им.
Его пример будь нам наукой:
Не любит споров властелин.
Счастлив князь Яков Долгорукий,
Умен покорный мещанин.

Unstable, true, are all things human –
a fact I fully understand.   10
Our grandees of today are new men:
the more they're new, the more they're grand.
My failing bloodline's well nigh ended
(fate that for others too impends);
from old boyars I am descended,
yet just a commoner, my friends.

My grandsire was no pancake-frier,
did not grease emperors' boots or mince
cantatas in the palace choir,
or jump from Cossack clerk to prince;   20
he was no pawn on French vacation
from some bepowdered Austrian squad.
So what fits me for noble station?
I am a commoner, thank God.

My forebear Racha marched with Nevsky,
and served him bravely in the north –
and, though an offspring had transgressed, he
was spared by dread Iván IV.
The Pushkins were by tsars befriended,
and more than one earned glory's nod   30
when with our Polish foes contended
the commoner of Nízhgorod.

With strife and intrigue in remission,
and havoc of tempestuous wars,
the people by their free petition
called the Románovs to be tsars.
That roll had our names, too, upon it;
the new tsar did his thanks bestow.
Yes, once our family were honoured –
once… now I am a commoner, though.   40

A fatal penchant for defiance
we all shared: proud and obdurate,
my ancestor refused compliance
to Peter and was hanged for that.
This teaches us important lessons:
a ruler hates one who defies.
Prince Dolgorúky won concessions,
but commoners who yield are wise.

Мой дед, когда мятеж поднялся
Средь петергофского двора,   50
Как Миних, верен оставался
Паденью третьего Петра.
Попали в честь тогда Орловы,
А дед мой в крепость, в карантин,
И присмирел наш род суровый,
И я родился мещанин.

Под гербовой моей печатью
Я кипу грамот схоронил
И не якшаюсь с новой знатью,
И крови спесь угомонил.   60
Я грамотей и стихотворец,
Я Пушкин просто, не Мусин,
Я не богач, не царедворец,
Я сам большой: я мещанин.

Post scriptum

Решил Фиглярин, сидя дома,
Что черный дед мой Ганнибал
Был куплен за бутылку рома
И в руки шкиперу попал.

Сей шкипер был тот шкипер славный,
Кем наша двигнулась земля,   70
Кто придал мощно бег державный
Рулю родного корабля.

Сей шкипер деду был доступен,
И сходно купленный арап
Возрос, усерден, неподкупен,
Царю наперсник, а не раб.

И был отец он Ганнибала,
Пред кем средь чесменских пучин
Громада кораблей вспылала,
И пал впервые Наварин.   80

Решил Фиглярин вдохновенный:
Я во дворянстве мещанин.
Что ж он в семье своей почтенной?
Он?... он в Мещанской дворянин.

My grandsire – when revolt was brewing
at Peterhof, and P. the Third   50
was overthrown – though facing ruin,
stayed true, like Minikh, to his word.
From this the Counts Orlóv gained lustre,
but Granddad they made prisoner;
our fractious kin then lost their bluster,
and I was born a commoner.

Beneath my crested seal now moulders
a stack of parchments, undisturbed;
with our new lords I don't rub shoulders;
my arrogance of blood I've curbed.   60
I'm just a versewright and a bookman;
as Pushkin (not Musín) I'm known;
no plutocrat, no titled footman –
a commoner: great on my own.   WA & RC

Postscript

From home Figlyárin claimed (the trickster!):
my black great-granddad Gannibál,
a boy bought for a flask of liquor,
into a skipper's hands did fall.

This "skipper" was the great shipmaster
by whom our land was commandeered,   70
who set the course it held thereafter,
gripped hard the helm and firmly steered.

The boy pleased well this skipper royal.
The Negro he'd so cheaply bought
reached manhood uncorrupt and loyal –
no slave, but favoured friend at court.

Another Gannibál he fathered,
who helped launch Chesme's cannon shells
that fired and sank the Turks' armada,
then fought till Navarino fell.   80

Figlyárin claimed (with inspiration!)
that I'm a commoner midst lords.
But what of *his* exalted station?
He's just a courtier midst bawds.   RC

636

ЭПИГРАММА

Не то беда, Авдей Флюгарин,
Что родом ты не русский барин,
Что на Парнасе ты цыган,
Что в свете ты Видок Фиглярин:
Беда, что скучен твой роман.

637

ЗАКЛИНАНИЕ

О, если правда, что в ночи,
Когда покоятся живые,
И с неба лунные лучи
Скользят на камни гробовые,
О, если правда, что тогда
Пустеют тихие могилы —
Я тень зову, я жду Леилы:
Ко мне, мой друг, сюда, сюда!

Явись, возлюбленная тень,
Как ты была перед разлукой,
Бледна, хладна, как зимний день,
Искажена последней мукой.
Приди, как дальная звезда,
Как легкий звук иль дуновенье,
Иль как ужасное виденье,
Мне всё равно, сюда! сюда!..

Зову тебя не для того,
Чтоб укорять людей, чья злоба
Убила друга моего,
Иль чтоб изведать тайны гроба,
Не для того, что иногда
Сомненьем мучусь... но, тоскуя,
Хочу сказать, что всё люблю я,
Что всё я твой: сюда, сюда!

10

20

636

EPIGRAM

Flyugárin, here's the sorry truth
(your foreign forebears I'm ignoring):
another's work as yours you're scoring,
you love to ape Vidocq the sleuth,
but – worst of all – your novel's boring.   JC & RC

637

INVOCATION

Oh, if it's true that in the night –
that time when living souls are sleeping,
when from above the moon's dim light˙
across the graveyard stones comes creeping –
oh, if it's true that then appear
dead spirits, silent tombs vacating,
I'll call Leíla's ghost; I'm waiting:
come to me, friend, come near, come near!

Appear, ghost, loved by me of old,
as you were at our valediction,   10
like winter weather, grey and cold,
disfigured by your last affliction;
come, like a star, far off but clear,
like a faint sound, an emanation,
or like some frightening visitation –
no matter how, just come, come near!

I'm summoning you, not for this –
not to expose the shameful history
of why they killed the friend I miss,
nor to explore the grave's grim mystery,   20
nor yet because sometimes a fear
torments me... no, it's that I mourn you
and want to say I still adore you –
I am still yours: come near, come near!   RC

638

ДВА ЧУВСТВА

Два чувства дивно близки нам,
В них обретает сердце пищу:
Любовь к родному пепелищу,
Любовь к отеческим гробам.

На них основано от века
По воле Бога самого
Самостоянье человека,
Залог величия его.

Животворящая святыня!
Земля была б без них мертва,   10
Как ……………… пустыня
И как алтарь без божества.

639

* * *

Когда порой воспоминанье
Грызет мне сердце в тишине,
И отдаленное страданье
Как тень опять бежит ко мне;
Когда людей повсюду видя
В пустыню скрыться я хочу,
Их слабый глас возненавидя, —
Тогда забывшись я лечу
Не в светлый край, где небо блещет
Неизъяснимой синевой,   10
Где море теплою волной
На пожелтелый мрамор плещет,
И лавр и темный кипарис
На воле пышно разрослись,
Где пел Торквато величавый,
Где и теперь во мгле ночной
Далече звонкою скалой
Повторены пловца октавы.

Стремлюсь привычною мечтою
К студеным северным волнам.   20

638

TWOFOLD LOYALTY

We have a twofold loyalty:
from both emotions we are nourished –
our love for dear ones who have perished,
our love for graves where forebears lie.

Upon this twin predisposition,
from start of time, by God's decree,
is based our human free volition,
assuring us of dignity.

O life-bestowing springs of blessing!
Without them dead the earth would be –   10
a wasteland, waterless, depressing,
an altar to no deity.   RC

639

* * *

When sometimes in the silent hours
my heart is gnawed by recollection
and sufferings from the distant past
rush back to engulf me like a shadow,
when seeing people thronging round
I long to hide in solitude,
repelled by their insipid talk –
I'm driven then to seek escape,
not to that land where heavens shine
with an unutterable blueness,   10
where warm sea billows gently plash
against the yellowed marble boulders,
and dark-green cypresses and laurels
grow lush and free across the landscape,
where Tasso sang majestically,
where, as the shade of night descends,
the oarsman's stanzas still re-echo
back from the sounding rocks far off.

No – rather my habitual thoughts
turn towards chilly northern waters.   20

Меж белоглавой их толпою
Открытый остров вижу там.
Печальный остров — берег дикий
Усеян зимнею брусникой,
Увядшей тундрою покрыт
И хладной пеною подмыт.
Сюда порою приплывает
Отважный северный рыбак,
Здесь невод мокрый расстилает
И свой разводит он очаг.   30
Сюда погода волновая
Заносит утлый мой челнок
. . . .

640

МОНОЛОГ БАРОНА

из Скупого рыцаря

Сцена II: Подвал

БАРОН

Как молодой повеса ждет свиданья
С какой-нибудь развратницей лукавой
Иль дурой, им обманутой, так я
Весь день минуты ждал, когда сойду
В подвал мой тайный, к верным сундукам.
Счастливый день! могу сегодня я
В шестой сундук (в сундук еще неполный)
Горсть золота накопленного всыпать.
Не много, кажется, но понемногу
Сокровища растут. Читал я где-то,   10
Что царь однажды воинам своим
Велел снести земли по горсти в кучу,
И гордый холм возвысился — и царь
Мог с вышины с весельем озирать
И дол, покрытый белыми шатрами,
И море, где бежали корабли.
Так я, по горсти бедной принося
Привычну дань мою сюда в подвал,
Вознес мой холм — и с высоты его
Могу взирать на все, что мне подвластно.   20

Amid the ranks of white-capped breakers
I see a bleak and treeless isle.
That mournful island's savage coastline,
constantly drenched in icy spray,
sprouts cranberries in wintry bareness
mid withered tundra vegetation.
A fearless northern fisherman
will sometimes steer his boat this way,
and here he'll spread his sodden nets
and light himself a warming fire.   30
And this is where the gales and seas
now cast my flimsy craft ashore

. . . .   RC

640

THE BARON'S SOLILOQUY

from The Mean-Spirited Knight

Scene 2. A vaulted cellar.

BARON

Like a young playboy waiting for a date
with some seductive creature who's bewitched him,
or with a dumb girl he's led on – I too
have waited all day for the moment when I
could creep down to my vault, to my strong chests.
This is a special day! Today I can
spread a fresh layer of gold that I've amassed
in my sixth chest, the one that's not yet full.
Little it seems, but little it is by little
that treasures grow. I'm sure that I've read somewhere   10
of a king once who put his troops to work
gathering earth by handfuls in a heap,
until a lofty hill rose up, and then
the king could from the top enjoy the view
of white tents stretching far across the plain
and of his fleet riding at sea beyond.
In the same way I've brought by meagre handfuls
regular contributions to this store,
until my hill has risen – and from its top
I can view everything that I control.   20

Что не подвластно мне? как некий демон
Отселе править миром я могу;
Лишь захочу — воздвигнутся чертоги;
В великолепные мои сады
Сбегутся нимфы резвою толпою;
И музы дань свою мне принесут,
И вольный гений мне поработится,
И добродетель и бессонный труд
Смиренно будут ждать моей награды.
Я свистну, и ко мне послушно, робко   30
Вползет окровавленное злодейство,
И руку будет мне лизать, и в очи
Смотреть, в них знак моей читая воли.
Мне всё послушно, я же — ничему;
Я выше всех желаний; я спокоен;
Я знаю мощь мою: с меня довольно
Сего сознанья...

(Смотрит на свое золото.)

                            Кажется, не много,
А скольких человеческих забот,
Обманов, слез, молений и проклятий   40
Оно тяжеловесный представитель!
Тут есть дублон старинный.... вот он. Нынче
Вдова мне отдала его, но прежде
С тремя детьми полдня перед окном
Она стояла на коленях воя.
Шел дождь, и перестал, и вновь пошел,
Притворщица не трогалась; я мог бы
Ее прогнать, но что-то мне шептало,
Что мужнин долг она мне принесла
И не захочет завтра быть в тюрьме.   50
А этот? этот мне принес Тибо —
Где было взять ему, ленивцу, плуту?
Украл, конечно; или, может быть,
Там на большой дороге, ночью, в роще...
Да! если бы все слезы, кровь и пот,
Пролитые за все, что здесь хранится,
Из недр земных все выступили вдруг,
То был бы вновь потоп — я захлебнулся б
В моих подвалах верных... Но пора.

(Хочет отпереть сундук.)

What do I *not* control? Now like some demon
I can be sovereign over all the world;
I need but wish – and palaces will rise;
in my luxuriant gardens bands of nymphs
will gather playfully to bring me pleasure;
the goddesses of art will pay their dues;
free-ranging Genius will be my slave;
Virtue and never-sleeping Industry
will patiently await my recognition.
I'll only whistle, and obediently   30
the very Power of Evil will creep up,
cringe, lick my hand, then look into my eyes,
and in them read the message of my will.
Everything's mine, but I am... nobody's;
I've risen above desire; I am untroubled;
I know my power. But that's enough from me
of introspection...

(He looks at his gold.)

           Yes, it seems so little,
and yet with all its weight it represents
so many human worries, tears and lies –   40
so many prayers, so many curses! I've
a Spanish gold coin – here it is. Just now
a widow paid it back to me; before that,
she'd knelt for half the day outside my window
with three young children, wailing – what a scene!
The rain came down, then stopped and came again –
she kept up her performance though. I could have
chased her away, but something said to me
that she had brought her husband's debt to pay me –
she didn't want to land in jail tomorrow.   50
And this one? This was brought me by Thibault –
where did he get it from, the lazy villain?
Stole it, I'll bet – or maybe he went down
one night to where the high road skirts the wood...
Yes! If the bowels of Earth were suddenly
to throw up all the tears and blood and sweat
shed for these precious treasures that lie here,
there'd be a second Flood – and I should choke
to death down in these strongrooms... Now it's time, though!

(He makes as though to open a chest.)

Я каждый раз, когда хочу сундук   60
Мой отпереть, впадаю в жар и трепет.
Не страх (о нет! кого бояться мне?
При мне мой меч: за злато отвечает
Честной булат), но сердце мне теснит
Какое-то неведомое чувство...
Нас уверяют медики: есть люди,
В убийстве находящие приятность.
Когда я ключ в замок влагаю, то же
Я чувствую, что чувствовать должны
Они, вонзая в жертву нож: приятно   70
И страшно вместе.

(Отпирает сундук.)

                  Вот мое блаженство!

(Всыпает деньги.)

Ступайте, полно вам по свету рыскать,
Служа страстям и нуждам человека.
Усните здесь сном силы и покоя,
Как боги спят в глубоких небесах...
Хочу себе сегодня пир устроить:
Зажгу свечу пред каждым сундуком,
И все их отопру, и стану сам
Средь них глядеть на блещущие груды.

(Зажигает свечи и отпирает сундуки один за другим.)

Я царствую!.. Какой волшебный блеск!   80
Послушна мне, сильна моя держава;
В ней счастие, в ней честь моя и слава!
Я царствую... но кто вослед за мной
Приимет власть над нею? Мой наследник!
Безумец, расточитель молодой,
Развратников разгульных собеседник!
Едва умру, он, он! сойдет сюда
Под эти мирные, немые своды
С толпой ласкателей, придворных жадных.
Украв ключи у трупа моего,   90
Он сундуки со смехом отопрет.
И потекут сокровища мои
В атласные диравые карманы.
Он разобьет священные сосуды,

Whenever I approach one of my chests   60
to open it, I flush and palpitate.
It isn't fear. (Oh no! – what should I fear?
I have my sword by me; my valiant blade
will answer for the treasure.) But a strange
sensation grips my heart that I can't fathom…
The medics tell us that some folk there are
who get a kick from murder. And when I
insert the key into the lock, I feel
the same sensation as must they when they
bury the dagger in their victim: pleasant,   70
but at the same time dreadful.

(He opens the chest.)

                              There! What joy!

(He pours the money in.)

In you go, no more roaming through the world
and pandering to human lusts and needs.
Here you shall sleep the deep sleep of the strong,
a sleep like gods sleep in the farthest heavens…
Today I want to give myself a treat:
I'll light a candle by each treasure chest;
I'll open all of them, and then I'll feast
my eyes on glistening heaps of gold all round me.

(He lights candles and opens each chest in turn.)

I reign supreme!… Oh, what a magic glow!   80
My empire is obedient, secure;
it is my bliss, my honour, and my glory!
I reign supreme… But after me, then who'll
succeed to all this power? My son and heir!
That brainless youth, who sprinkles cash like water,
has playboys and good-timers for his friends!
I'll be no sooner dead than he – yes, he! –
will come down to these peaceful, silent vaults
with his false friends and greedy hangers-on.
He'll filch the bunch of keys off my dead body   90
and with a smirk unlock my treasure chests.
And all my closely guarded wealth will then
stream into satin pockets full of holes.
He'll smash the sacred vessels, and the oil

Он грязь елеем царским напоит —
Он расточит... А по какому праву?
Мне разве даром это все досталось,
Или шутя, как игроку, который
Гремит костьми да груды загребает?
Кто знает, сколько горьких воздержаний, 100
Обузданных страстей, тяжелых дум,
Дневных забот, ночей бессонных мне
Все это стоило? Иль скажет сын,
Что сердце у меня обросло мохом,
Что я не знал желаний, что меня
И совесть никогда не грызла, совесть,
Когтистый зверь, скребущий сердце, совесть,
Незваный гость, докучный собеседник,
Заимодавец грубый, эта ведьма,
От коей меркнет месяц и могилы 110
Смущаются и мертвых высылают?..
Нет, выстрадай сперва себе богатство,
А там посмотрим, станет ли несчастный
То расточать, что кровью приобрел.

О, если б мог от взоров недостойных
Я скрыть подвал! о, если б из могилы
Прийти я мог, сторожевою тенью
Сидеть на сундуке и от живых
Сокровища мои хранить, как ныне!..

641

МОНОЛОГ САЛЕРИ

из Моцарта и Салери

Сцена I

САЛЕРИ

Все говорят: нет правды на земле.
Но правды нет — и выше. Для меня
Так это ясно, как простая гамма.

Родился я с любовию к искусству;
Ребенком будучи, когда высоко
Звучал орган в старинной церкви нашей,
Я слушал и заслушивался — слезы
Невольные и сладкие текли.

kept for anointing kings will soak the floor.
He'll squander... By what rule of law, I ask?
I hardly gained all this without exertion,
or as a pastime, like a gambler who
rattles the dice to rake in piles of money!
There's no one knows what bitter self-denials,   100
what passions held in check, what ruminations,
what anxious days, what long and sleepless nights
all this has cost me. Or will my son assert that
this heart of mine is overgrown with moss
and that I've never known desires, that I've
not even felt the bite of conscience? – conscience,
that sharp-clawed beast that tears the heart... yes, conscience,
that uninvited guest, relentless talker,
who gives you credit, then demands it back,
that witch who makes the moon go dark and stirs   110
the graves and conjures up the dead!...
No: first of all, boy, toil to make your fortune –
and then let's see if the young good-for-nothing
wastes what he's earned by his own sweat and blood.

If only I could hide this vaulted cellar
from all unworthy eyes! If only I
could come back from the grave, a ghostly watchman,
and sitting on a chest preserve my treasures
from living beings, just as I do now!...   RC

641

SALIERI'S SOLILOQUY

from Mozart and Salieri

Scene 1

SALIERI

They all say there's no justice here on earth.
But there's no justice up in heaven either –
that's clear to me, as clear as do-re-mi.

I've had a love of art since I was born.
When I was just a child and high aloft
in our old church the organ notes resounded,
I listened with such rapture that I wept –
I couldn't help it – yes, I wept for pleasure.

Отверг я рано праздные забавы;
Науки, чуждые музыке, были   10
Постылы мне; упрямо и надменно
От них отрекся я и предался
Одной музыке. Труден первый шаг
И скучен первый путь. Преодолел
Я ранние невзгоды. Ремесло
Поставил я подножием искусству;
Я сделался ремесленник: перстам
Придал послушную, сухую беглость
И верность уху. Звуки умертвив,
Музыку я разъял, как труп. Поверил   20
Я алгеброй гармонию. Тогда
Уже дерзнул, в науке искушенный,
Предаться неге творческой мечты.
Я стал творить; но в тишине, но в тайне,
Не смея помышлять еще о славе.
Нередко, просидев в безмолвной келье
Два, три дня, позабыв и сон и пищу,
Вкусив восторг и слезы вдохновенья,
Я жег мой труд и холодно смотрел,
Как мысль моя и звуки, мной рожденны,   30
Пылая, с легким дымом исчезали.
Что говорю? Когда великий Глюк
Явился и открыл нам новы тайны
(Глубокие, пленительные тайны),
Не бросил ли я все, что прежде знал,
Что так любил, чему так жарко верил,
И не пошел ли бодро вслед за ним
Безропотно, как тот, кто заблуждался
И встречным послан в сторону иную?

Усильным, напряженным постоянством   40
Я наконец в искусстве безграничном
Достигнул степени высокой. Слава
Мне улыбнулась; я в сердцах людей
Нашел созвучия своим созданьям.
Я счастлив был: я наслаждался мирно
Своим трудом, успехом, славой; также
Трудами и успехами друзей,
Товарищей моих в искусстве дивном.
Нет! никогда я зависти не знал,
О, никогда! — нижè, когда Пиччини   50
Пленить умел слух диких парижан,
Нижè, когда услышал в первый раз

I quickly gave up juvenile pursuits;
school subjects that weren't relevant to music   10
I hated; proud and stubborn as I was,
I wouldn't study them; I pledged myself
to music, nothing else. I found the first
step hard, the journey trying, but the early
problems I overcame. My hard-won skill
I set up as a pedestal for art –
yes, skilled I made myself: I trained my fingers
to rattle briskly up and down the keys,
my ear to hear true pitch. I butchered music,
dissecting scores like corpses. I worked out   20
my harmonies by algebra. And then,
having perfected my technique, I dared
to indulge in dreams of creativity.
I started to compose, but on the quiet,
in secret, not yet nursing thoughts of fame.
Sometimes, alone in my retreat, I'd sit
for days on end, forgetting sleep and food, but
relishing inspiration's thrills and tears –
and then I'd burn my work and coldly watch
the musical ideas that I'd created   30
flare up, then disappear in puffs of smoke.
What next, then? When that great composer Gluck
came and divulged to us his magic spells
(yes, deep and potent magic), what did I do?
I threw aside all that I'd learnt before,
all that I'd loved, believed in, with such fervour;
I stepped out after Gluck without a qualm,
without a query – like a man who's lost
and someone sends him off the other way.

By strenuous and dogged perseverance   40
at last I made it to the top in music,
an art form without frontiers – and I won
a smiling reputation: with the public
my compositions struck an answering chord.
Now I was happy, and I could enjoy
my work, success and fame in peace – and, too,
the works and the successes of my friends,
comrades in the sublimest of the arts.
I never felt the slightest jealousy,
no, never! – not when Niccolò Piccinni   50
bewitched unruly Paris with his operas,
nor when my ears first heard the opening bars

Я Ифигении начальны звуки.
Кто скажет, чтоб Сальери гордый был
Когда-нибудь завистником презренным,
Змеей, людьми растоптанною, вживе
Песок и пыль грызущею бессильно?
Никто!..
        А ныне — сам скажу — я ныне
Завистник. Я завидую; глубоко,
Мучительно завидую. — О небо!   60
Где ж правота, когда священный дар,
Когда бессмертный гений — не в награду
Любви горящей, самоотверженья,
Трудов, усердия, молений послан —
А озаряет голову безумца,
Гуляки праздного?.. О Моцарт, Моцарт!...

642

ДЕЛЬВИГУ

Мы рождены, мой брат названый,
Под одинаковой звездой.
Киприда, Феб и Вакх румяный
Играли нашею судьбой.

Явилися мы рано оба
На ипподром, а не на торг,
Вблизи Державинского гроба,
И шумный встретил нас восторг.

Избаловало нас начало.
И в гордой лености своей   10
Заботились мы оба мало
Судьбой гуляющих детей.

Но ты, сын Феба беззаботный,
Своих возвышенных затей
Не предавал рукой расчетной
Оценке хитрых торгашей.

В одних журналах нас ругали,
Упреки те же слышим мы:
Мы любим славу да в бокале
Топить разгульные умы.   20

of Gluck's great *Iphigénie en Tauride*.
Who'd say that I, with all my self-respect,
could stoop to be a jealous man, a snake
that's trampled underfoot, but still lives on,
biting the sand and dust in impotence?
No one could say that!

                Yet I'll tell you frankly –
I *am* now jealous, with a jealousy
intense, excruciating... Heaven above!   60
Where is your justice, when you send your sacred
gift, your immortal spark, not to reward
fervent devotion or self-abnegation,
or hard work, or enthusiasm, or prayer –
but as a halo for an idiot,
an idle good-for-nothing?... Mozart, Mozart!...   RC

642

FOR DELVIG

Dear brother, we have shared between us
a single birth star, you and I;
and Phoebus, florid Bacchus, Venus –
all three toyed with our destiny.

We favoured friendly competition
from boyhood, never wrote to sell;
we lived for art, Derzhávin-fashion,
and nothing could our rapture quell.

Too pampered by our first successes
and lulled by wilful laziness,   10
we both were blind to the excesses
that spoil lads prone to rakishness.

You're Phoebus' son – he's your defender:
be bold, then. Your sublime ideas
for profit you did not surrender
in bargains struck with racketeers.

They've flayed us in the various journals;
the same old gripes we hear again:
we're vain, we share that vice infernal
of getting sozzled on champagne.   20

Твой слог могучий и крылатый
Какой-то дразнит пародист,
И стих, надеждами богатый,
Жует беззубый журналист …

643

ГЕРОЙ

Что есть истина?

ДРУГ

Да, слава в прихотях вольна.
Как огненный язык, она
По избранным главам летает,
С одной сегодня исчезает
И на другой уже видна.
За новизной бежать смиренно
Народ бессмысленный привык;
Но нам уж то чело священно,
Над коим вспыхнул сей язык.
На троне, на кровавом поле,   10
Меж граждан на чреде иной
Из сих избранных кто всех боле
Твоею властвует душой?

ПОЭТ

Всё он, всё он — пришлец сей бранный,
Пред кем смирилися цари,
Сей ратник, вольностью венчанный,
Исчезнувший, как тень зари.

ДРУГ

Когда ж твой ум он поражает
Своею чудною звездой?
Тогда ль, как с Альпов он взирает   20
На дно Италии святой;
Тогда ли, как хватает знамя
Иль жезл диктаторский; тогда ль,
Как водит и кругом и вдаль
Войны стремительное пламя,
И пролетает ряд побед
Над ним одна другой вослед;
Тогда ль, как рать героя плещет
Перед громадой пирамид,

Your fervent, lofty style's derided
by mean reviewers and their chums,
and verse we hoped would be applauded
is chewed by hacks with toothless gums ...   RC

643

A HERO

What is truth?

FRIEND

Renown moves freely where she pleases.
Yes, like a tongue of flame she hovers
around the heads of those she chooses:
today she vanishes from one
to glow at once upon another.
The mass of common folk, unthinking,
chase tamely anything that's new;
the brow that *we*, though, count as holy
is that on which this tongue has blazed.
Say then: of those Renown has chosen –   10
on throne, on battlefield, elsewhere
among plain citizenry – who
has won your warmest admiration?

POET

Just one, just one – that warrior-upstart
before whom monarchs did obeisance,
that soldier freely crowned a ruler
who vanished like the dark at dawn.

FRIEND

When does this luminary capture
your notice with his awesome brilliance?
Is it when from the Alps he gazes   20
far down on sacred Italy?
or when he grasps the battle standard,
or the dictator's sceptre? Or
when the man leads the raging fire
of war through lands both near and far,
with victories in quick succession
soaring above him and beyond?
Or when the troops acclaim their hero
beneath the towering pyramids?

Иль как Москва пустынно блещет,   30
Его приемля, — и молчит?

ПОЭТ

Нет, не у Счастия на лоне
Его я вижу, не в бою,
Не зятем кесаря на троне;
Не там, где на скалу свою
Сев, мучим казнию покоя,
Осмеян прозвищем героя,
Он угасает недвижим,
Плащом закрывшись боевым.
Не та картина предо мною!   40
Одров я вижу длинный строй,
Лежит на каждом труп живой,
Клейменный мощною чумою,
Царицею болезней… он,
Не бранной смертью окружен,
Нахмурясь, ходит меж одрами
И хладно руку жмет чуме,
И в погибающем уме
Рождает бодрость… Небесами
Клянусь: кто жизнию своей   50
Играл пред сумрачным недугом,
Чтоб ободрить угасший взор,
Клянусь, тот будет небу другом,
Каков бы ни был приговор
Земли слепой…

ДРУГ

                    Мечты поэта —
Историк строгой гонит вас!
Увы! его раздался глас, —
И где ж очарованье света!

ПОЭТ

Да будет проклят правды свет,
Когда посредственности хладной,   60
Завистливой, к соблазну жадной,
Он угождает праздно! — Нет!
Тьмы низких истин мне дороже
Нас возвышающий обман…
Оставь герою сердце! Что же
Он будет без него? Тиран…

ДРУГ

Утешься…

Or when in desolation Moscow 30
lights up in welcome – and keeps silence?

POET

No, it's not fondled by success,
nor fired by combat, nor enthroned
as Caesar's son-in-law I see him.
Nor do I see him sitting there
upon his rock, by peace tormented,
mocked by the appellation "hero",
huddled beneath his soldier's cloak and
wasting away in idleness.
That's not the picture that confronts me. 40
I do, though, see long rows of beds;
on each there lies a living corpse,
with flesh disfigured by Plague's stigma,
that mighty queen of ailments. He,
not now ringed round with battle dead,
frowns as he walks between the trestles,
grasps the cold hand of Plague in his,
and in those minds about to fail
engenders courage. By the Heavens
I swear: that man who risked his life, 50
in face of hideous infection,
to bring good cheer to eyes grown dim –
I swear, that man is loved by Heaven,
whatever judgement undiscerning
Earth has delivered...

FRIEND

                    Poets' dreams,
dispelled now by the strict historian!
Alas, his verdict's been pronounced.
So where's this world's fond fantasy?

POET

A curse be on the glare of truth
when pointlessly it gratifies 60
cold, jealous mediocrity
that craves for titillation! No:
I prize a falsehood that uplifts us
above a host of shoddy truths.
A hero needs a heart: without one
what will he be? A tyrant only...

FRIEND

Live on in hope!...   / RC

117

644

ОБВАЛ

Дробясь о мрачные скалы,
Шумят и пенятся валы,
И надо мной кричат орлы,
 И ропщет бор,
И блещут средь волнистой мглы
 Вершины гор.

Оттоль сорвался раз обвал,
И с тяжким грохотом упал,
И всю теснину между скал
 Загородил, 10
И Терека могущий вал
 Остановил.

Вдруг, истощась и присмирев,
О Терек, ты прервал свой рев;
Но задних волн упорный гнев
 Прошиб снега...
Ты затопил, освирепев,
 Свои брега.

И долго прорванный обвал
Неталой грудою лежал, 20
И Терек злой под ним бежал,
 И пылью вод
И шумной пеной орошал
 Ледяный свод.

И путь по нем широкий шел:
И конь скакал, и влекся вол,
И своего верблюда вёл
 Степной купец,
Где ныне мчится лишь Эол,
 Небес жилец. 30

AVALANCHE

Here, crashing on the sombre stone,
the surge is spattered into foam;
above the forest's plaintive moan,
    an eagle shrieks,
and, shining through the mist alone,
    rise mountain peaks.

Once, breaking free, a mass of snow
came roaring down some time ago
and choked the narrow gorge below
    with icy waste,   10
and stopped the Terek's mighty flow,
    where once it raced.

Exhausted then, your fury spent,
you ceased your roar, O Terek, yet
the surge behind would not relent
    and pierced the snow...
while you, within your edges pent,
    would overflow.

And long the frozen tunnel lay,
a mound that wouldn't melt away;   20
beneath, the Terek made its way
    without a halt,
and sullenly it washed with spray
    the icy vault.

Above it ran an open road,
where oxen plodded, horses rode,
and merchants of the steppe would goad
    their camels on,
where winds from Aeolus' abode
    now speed alone.   CC

645

СТИХОТВОРЕНИЕ АРХИПА ЛЫСОГО

из Истории села Горюхина

Поэзия некогда процветала в древнем Горюхине. Доныне стихотворения Архипа Лысого сохранились в памяти потомства. В нежности не уступят они эклогам известного Виргилия, в красоте воображения далеко превосходят они идиллии г-на Сумарокова. И хотя в щеголеватости слога и уступают новейшим произведениям наших муз, но равняются с ними затейливостию. и остроумием.

Приведем в пример сие сатирическое стихотворение:

> Ко боярскому двору
> Антон староста идет,
> Бирки в пазухе несет,
> Боярину подает,
> А боярин смотрит,
> Ничего не смыслит.
> Ах ты, староста Антон,
> Обокрал бояр кругом,
> Село по миру пустил,
> Старостиху надарил.

646

ОТРЫВОК

> Не розу Пафосскую,
> Росой оживленную,
> Я ныне пою;
> Не розу Феосскую,
> Вином окропленную,
> Стихами хвалю;
> Но розу счастливую,
> На персях увядшую
> Элизы моей...

645

A VERSE OF ARKHÍP THE BALD

from A History of Goryúkhino Village

Poetry once flourished in ancient Goryúkhino. The verses of Arkhíp the Bald have been preserved in the memory of later generations up to the present. In delicacy they are a match for the *Eclogues* of the renowned Virgil, and in richness of imagination they far outstrip the idylls of Mr Sumarókov. Although they fall short of the latest works of our poets in elegance of style, they equal them in inventiveness and wit.

As an example let us quote these satirical lines:

> To the boyar's manor house
> sly Antón, the elder, goes,
> goes to tell him what he owes;
> records, scratched on wood, he shows.
> Puzzled boyar stands there blinking,
> of what's owed he has no inkling.
> Oh, you rascally Antón,
> you've defrauded everyone –
> boyars, serfs face penury,
> yet your wife's in luxury!

RC

646

A FRAGMENT

> No roses of Paphos,
> dew-dappled and fine,
> in song do I greet;
> no roses of Teos
> all sprinkled with wine,
> in verse do I treat;
> but roses that faded
> with joy on the breast
> of Liza my sweet...

JF

647

ПЕСНЯ МЕРИ

из Пира во время чумы

Было время, процветала
В мире наша сторона:
В воскресение бывала
Церковь божия полна;
Наших деток в шумной школе
Раздавались голоса,
И сверкали в светлом поле
Серп и быстрая коса.

Ныне церковь опустела;
Школа глухо заперта;   10
Нива праздно перезрела;
Роща темная пуста;
И селенье, как жилище
Погорелое, стоит, —
Тихо все. Одно кладбище
Не пустеет, не молчит.

Поминутно мертвых носят,
И стенания живых
Боязливо бога просят
Упокоить души их!   20
Поминутно места надо,
И могилы меж собой,
Как испуганное стадо,
Жмутся тесной чередой!

Если ранняя могила
Суждена моей весне —
Ты, кого я так любила,
Чья любовь отрада мне, —
Я молю: не приближайся
К телу Дженни ты своей,   30
Уст умерших не касайся,
Следуй издали за ней.

И потом оставь селенье!
Уходи куда-нибудь,
Где б ты мог души мученье
Усладить и отдохнуть.

647

MARY'S SONG

from A Feast during the Plague

Time was when our peaceful village
was a happy, thriving place.
Every Sabbath thankful people
filled the kirk to laud God's grace;
in the schoolroom voices rang out –
ditties by our wee bairns sung;
and across the sunlit meadows
steel blades flashed as scythes were swung.

Now the kirk has lost its people;
school is silent, locked for good;   10
fields with uncut corn have ripened;
no one roams the darkened wood.
Derelict now stands the village,
like an empty burnt-out mill.
All is quiet; just the graveyard –
that's not empty, that's not still:

all the time they're bringing bodies;
and with wailing those who live
pray in fear to their Creator
peace unto the dead to give.   20
All the time they need new spaces,
while the tombs of those who sleep
stand together crowding tightly,
like a flock of frightened sheep.

If my springtime's cut off early
blighted by a fate too drear,
you, whom I have loved so dearly,
you, whose love's my only cheer,
keep away from your dead Jenny,
I implore you – don't come near;   30
don't press my cold lips with kisses;
follow far behind my bier.

Then depart this stricken village;
go away, go anywhere
where you may find rest and comfort
and relieve your soul's despair.

И когда зараза минет,
Посети мой бедный прах;
А Эдмонда не покинет
Дженни даже в небесах!   40

648

ПЕСНЯ ПРЕДСЕДАТЕЛЯ

из Пира во время чумы

Когда могущая Зима,
Как бодрый вождь, ведет сама
На нас косматые дружины
Своих морозов и снегов, —
Навстречу ей трещат камины,
И весел зимний жар пиров.

Царица грозная, Чума
Теперь идет на нас сама
И льстится жатвою богатой;
И к нам в окошко день и ночь   10
Стучит могильною лопатой....
Что делать нам? и чем помочь?

Как от проказницы Зимы,
Запремся также от Чумы!
Зажжем огни, нальем бокалы,
Утопим весело умы
И, заварив пиры да балы,
Восславим царствие Чумы.

Есть упоение в бою,
И бездны мрачной на краю,   20
И в разъяренном океане,
Средь грозных волн и бурной тьмы,
И в аравийском урагане,
И в дуновении Чумы.

Всё, всё, что гибелью грозит,
Для сердца смертного таит
Неизъяснимы наслажденья —
Бессмертья, может быть, залог!
И счастлив тот, кто средь волненья
Их обретать и ведать мог.   30

When the plague is past, then, Edmund,
come greet my poor dust so fond;
Jenny will stay true to Edmund
even in the world beyond.   RC

648

SONG OF THE MASTER OF REVELS

from A Feast during the Plague

When mighty Winter, like the head
of a bold army boldly led,
attacks us with her spiky squadrons
of icicles and frost and snow –
the fireplace parries with a crackle,
the festive season's all aglow.

But now the Plague, that dreaded queen,
is marching on us, feared, unseen,
cocksure of an abundant harvest;
and on our windows day and night   10
she taps with her great graveyard shovel...
We're trapped! Who'll help us in our plight?

Just as on winter's tricks before,
so on Queen Plague let's lock our door!
Let's light the torches, fill the glasses,
and drown our minds in jollity,
and, rousing feast and dance to frenzy,
let's hail the Plague Queen's sovereignty!

There is a thrill in waging war,
or treading a dark chasm's door,   20
or tossing on the ocean's fury
mid stormy gloom and seas that drench,
or braving an Arabian sandstorm,
or breathing in the plague's vile stench.

In anything that bids to kill,
there lurks that strangely pleasing thrill
for mortal beings – could this offer
a pledge of immortality?
This thrill if man can find and savour
mid all life's tempests, lucky he!   30

Итак, — хвала тебе, Чума,
Нам не страшна могилы тьма,
Нас не смутит твое призванье!
Бокалы пеним дружно мы
И девы-розы пьем дыханье, —
Быть может... полное чумы!

649

ЦЫГАНЫ

с английского

Над лесистыми брегами,
В час вечерней тишины,
Шум и песни под шатрами,
И огни разложены.

Здравствуй, счастливое племя!
Узнаю твои костры;
Я бы сам в иное время
Провождал сии шатры.

Завтра с первыми лучами
Ваш исчезнет вольный след,
Вы уйдете — но за вами
Не пойдет уж ваш поэт.

Он бродящие ночлеги
И проказы старины
Позабыл для сельской неги
И домашней тишины.

650

ИЗ BARRY CORNWALL

Here's a health to thee, Mary.

Пью за здравие Мери,
Милой Мери моей.
Тихо запер я двери
И один без гостей
Пью за здравие Мери.

So – Plague, it's you we celebrate!
We've no dread of the tomb's dark gate;
your summons causes us no terror.
Let's breathe our girlfriend's fragrant breath,
and drink the foaming cup together –
what if we breathe, and drink, our death!   RC

649

GYPSIES

from the English

Streamside trees have ceased their rustle;
twilight brings her quietude;
round the tents there's song and bustle;
splints are lit to kindle wood.

Greetings, lucky folk, unworried!
I can build a campfire too.
I'd at other times have hurried
off to share that life with you.

Once tomorrow's dawn shall show it-
self, you'll disappear – you're free!   10
Off you'll go, then; but your poet
won't come: him no more you'll see.

Houseless nights he's put behind now,
with his former escapades;
rustic pleasures fill his mind now –
homely evenings, quiet days.   RC

650

FROM BARRY CORNWALL

Here's a health to thee, Mary.

Here's a health to my Mary,
Mary sweetest and best.
I've eased shut the door early;
so, alone, with no guest –
here's a health to my Mary!

Можно краше быть Мери,
Краше Мери моей,
Этой маленькой пери;
Но нельзя быть милей
Резвой, ласковой Мери.   10

Будь же счастлива, Мери,
Солнце жизни моей!
Ни тоски, ни потери,
Ни ненастливых дней
Пусть не ведает Мери.

651

НА ПЕРЕВОД *ИЛИАДЫ*

Слышу умолкнувший звук божественной эллинской речи;
  Старца великого тень чую смущенной душой.

652

ОБЕЩАНИЕ

Для берегов отчизны дальной
Ты покидала край чужой;
В час незабвенный, в час печальный
Я долго плакал пред тобой.
Мои хладеющие руки
Тебя старались удержать;
Томленье страшное разлуки
Мой стон молил не прерывать.

Но ты от горького лобзанья
Свои уста оторвала;   10
Из края мрачного изгнанья
Ты в край иной меня звала.
Ты говорила: «В день свиданья
Под небом вечно голубым,
В тени олив, любви лобзанья
Мы вновь, мой друг, соединим».

Но там, увы, где неба своды
Сияют в блеске голубом,

Prettier than my dear Mary
others, maybe, exist –
prettier, yes, than that fairy.
Sweeter, though, than the rest
must be fun-loving Mary.   10

Be you happy, dear Mary:
in your sunlight I'm blessed!
May no days grey and dreary,
may no loss nor distress
come to trouble sweet Mary.   RC

651

ON THE TRANSLATION OF THE *ILIAD*

Hearing the long-muted sound of Hellas's Heaven-sent language,
   great man of old, to your voice, soul-stirred, my being responds.   RM

652

THE PROMISE

You lived among us, then departed
for your dear homeland far away.
I can't forget how, broken-hearted,
I wept and wept with you that day.
My hands, ice-cold and void of feeling,
strove to detain you forcibly;
with choking cries I kept appealing
"Stay on – prolong my agony!"

You firmly, though, cut short my anguished
kisses and disengaged my hand.   10
You urged: "This land where you've been banished –
now leave it for a brighter land.
And there I'll greet you," you kept saying,
"where skies are ever blue and clear,
where shady olive boughs are swaying.
We'll kiss then once again, my dear."

But there, alas, where sunlight dances
from clear blue skies across the deep,

Где тень олив легла на воды,
Заснула ты последним сном. 20
Твоя краса, твои страданья
Исчезли в урне гробовой —
А с ними поцелуй свиданья...
Но жду его; он за тобой...

653

НА ГРАФИНЮ ПОТЕМКИНУ

Когда Потемкину в потемках
Я на Пречистенке найду,
То пусть с Булгариным в потомках
Меня поставят наряду.

and where the olives spread their branches –
there you now sleep a lasting sleep.   20
Your pain, your loveliness too fleeting,
are gone now to the grave below.
But where's that promised kiss of greeting?…
For that I wait still: that you owe.   RC

653

ON COUNTESS POTYÓMKINA

If only Potyómkina graces my wedding
as Matron of Honour (her absence I'm dreading),
the public can say – and I'll swear that it's true –
"That scribbler Bulgárin writes better than you."   JC

Стихотворения, точно не датируемые

654

ГЛУПЦЫ

Конечно, презирать не трудно
Отдельно каждого глупца,
Сердиться так же безрассудно
И на отдельного страмца.
....

Но что .... чудно —
Всех вместе презирать и трудно —
....

Их эпиграммы площадные,
Из Бьеврианы занятые ...

655

* * *

Когда так нежно, так сердечно,
Так радостно я встретил вас,
Вы удивилися, конечно,
Досадой хладно воружась.

Вечор в счастливом усыпленье
....
Мое живое сновиденье
Ваш милый образ озарил.

Verses without precise dates

654

MORONS

Despising separately each moron
one at a time – that's not too hard;
and at each separate scoundrel for one
to get enraged would be absurd
....

What's harder – which is quite surprising –
is the whole lot to be despising
....

Their epigrams are far from clever,
cribbed from the Marquis de Bièvre ...   RC

655

* * *

We met. I greeted you so gently,
with joy and cordiality;
you were astonished, evidently,
and showed me cold antipathy.

Last night, as I was blithely dreaming,
....
I saw your lovely image gleaming –
a radiant vision, as in life.

С тех пор я .... слезами
Мечту прелестную зову.   10
Во сне был осчастливлен вами
И благодарен наяву.

656

ГОНДОЛА

В голубом небесном поле
Светит Веспер золотой.
Старый дож плывет в гондоле
С догарессой молодой.

Воздух полн дыханьем лавра.
.... морская мгла,
Дремлют флаги Бучентавра,
Ночь безмолвна и тепла.

657

* * *

О нет, мне жизнь не надоела,
Я жить люблю, я жить хочу,
Душа не вовсе охладела,
Утратя молодость свою.
Еще хранятся наслажденья
Для любопытства моего,
Для милых снов воображенья,
Для чувств .... всего.

658

* * *

Друг сердечный мне намедни говорил:
По тебе я, красна девица, изныл,
На жену свою взглянуть я не хочу —
А я всё-таки ...

And now .... with weeping
that charming vision I invoke.   10
You brought me bliss while I was sleeping,
and thankfulness when I awoke.   RC

656

A GONDOLA

A gondola! The evening star
   sees it serenely glide,
bearing the aged doge along –
   a lady at his side...

The warm air's filled with scent of bay,
   .... mists hide the moon;
the *Bucintoro*'s ensigns droop;
   quite still lies the lagoon...   JC & RC

657

* * *

Oh no, I do not find life old:
I love it and would yet live on;
my soul with time has not grown cold,
although its youthful bloom is gone.
There still remain those keen delights
of curiosity of mind,
of inspiration's happy flights,
of feelings .... and of life.   JF

658

* * *

Recently a friend I love said this to me:
"Lovely girl, I've nearly died for love of you;
at my wife no longer do I wish to look –
nonetheless I ..."   RC

Married Life and Final Years

1831–37

1831

659

СТАРОСТЬ

из Бориса Годунова

МНИШЕК

Мы, старики, уж нынче не танцуем,
Музыки гром не призывает нас,
Прелестных рук не жмем и не целуем —
Ох, не забыл старинных я проказ!
Теперь не то, не то, что прежде было:
И молодежь, ей-ей — не так смела,
И красота не так уж весела —
Признайся, друг: все как-то приуныло.
Оставим их; пойдем, товарищ мой,
Венгерского, обросшую травой,
Велим отрыть бутылку вековую
Да в уголку потянем-ка вдвоем
Душистый ток, струю, как жир, густую,
А между тем посудим кой о чем.
Пойдем же, брат.

10

ВИШНЕВЕЦКИЙ

И дело, друг, пойдем.

660

ГРОБНИЦА СВЯТАЯ

Перед гробницею святой
Стою с поникшею главой...
Всё спит кругом; одни лампады
Во мраке храма золотят

1831

659

OLD AGE

from Borís Godunóv

MNISZECH

We old men now no longer join the dancing;
we're not enticed by a mazurka's din;
we no more squeeze and kiss those pretty fingers –
Oh, when I think what pranks we revelled in!
No: things are not the same now as they once were –
youth now, for sure, lacks our audacity,
and beauty's lost its former gaiety...
You must confess, it's all grown rather dreary.
Come, friend, let's leave them; let's go off and ask
my men to dig us out a vintage flask   10
of Magyar wine all overgrown with herbage,
and in some nook we'll make our two hearts glow
with liquor, thick like oil, a fragrant nectar,
and, as we drink, discuss – what? I don't know...
Let's go then, friend.

WIŚNIOWIECKI

                                    That's right, old friend, let's go.   RC

660

A HALLOWED TOMB

I stand before a hallowed tomb
and bow my head amid the gloom...
The temple sleeps, and, softly shining,
suspended vigil lamps alone

Столбов гранитные громады
И их знамен нависший ряд.

Под ними спит сей властелин,
Сей идол северных дружин,
Маститый страж страны державной,
Смиритель всех ее врагов,   10
Сей остальной из стаи славной
Екатерининских орлов.

В твоем гробу восторг живет!
Он русский глас нам издает;
Он нам твердит о той године,
Когда народной веры глас
Воззвал к святой твоей седине:
«Иди, спасай!» Ты встал — и спас...

Внемли ж и днесь наш верный глас,
Встань и спасай царя и нас,   20
О старец грозный! На мгновенье
Явись у двери гробовой,
Явись, вдохни восторг и рвенье
Полкам, оставленным тобой!

Явись и дланию своей
Нам укажи в толпе вождей,
Кто твой наследник, твой избранный!
Но храм — в молчанье погружен,
И тих твоей могилы бранной
Невозмутимый, вечный сон...   30

661

КЛЕВЕТНИКАМ РОССИИ

О чем шумите вы, народные витии?
Зачем анафемой грозите вы России?
Что возмутило вас? волнения Литвы?
Оставьте: это спор славян между собою,
Домашний, старый спор, уж взвешенный судьбою,
Вопрос, которого не разрешите вы.

Уже давно между собою
Враждуют эти племена;

gild regimental colours lining
the soaring colonnades of stone.

That mighty lord lies resting close,
that idol of the northern hosts,
revered defender of the nation,
who put its every foe to flight,   10
the last of Catherine's convocation
of eagles glorious and bright.

A joy within your tomb yet dwells,
and in the people's voice it tells
of how the faith of every Russian
invoked your sainted head of grey,
imploring, "Save us from destruction!"
And you arose and saved the day...

O heed once more our faithful cries!
Save us and save the tsar! Arise!   20
Emerging from your crypt, dread Father,
for but a moment stand beside
the door, and fill with joy and ardour
the regiments you left behind!

Come forth and point to one among
the generals your chosen one
and worthiest of your successors!
But all is quiet. Silence deep
pervades your martial tomb's recesses,
serene in its eternal sleep...   CC

661

FOR RUSSIA'S ACCUSERS

Hold on, you rabble-rousers, what's the hue and cry?
You threaten Russia with anathema, but why?
What got your dander up? Insurgency in Poland?
Keep out of it! This quarrel is one of Slav with Slav –
one weighed upon the scales of destiny and solely
a family dispute that you will not resolve.

For centuries these tribes have clashed,
oft crossing swords with one another,

Не раз клонилась под грозою
То их, то наша сторона.
Кто устоит в неравном споре:
Кичливый лях, иль верный росс?
Славянские ль ручьи сольются в русском море?
Оно ль иссякнет? вот вопрос.

Оставьте нас: вы не читали
Сии кровавые скрижали;
Вам непонятна, вам чужда
Сия семейная вражда;
Для вас безмолвны Кремль и Прага;
Бессмысленно прельщает вас
Борьбы отчаянной отвага —
И ненавидите вы нас...

За что ж? ответствуйте; за то ли,
Что на развалинах пылающей Москвы
Мы не признали наглой воли
Того, под кем дрожали вы?
За то ль, что в бездну повалили
Мы тяготеющий над царствами кумир
И нашей кровью искупили
Европы вольность, честь и мир?

Вы грозны на словах — попробуйте на деле!
Иль старый богатырь, покойный на постеле,
Не в силах завинтить свой измаильский штык!
Иль русского царя уже бессильно слово?
Иль нам с Европой спорить ново?
Иль русский от побед отвык?
Иль мало нас? Или от Перми до Тавриды,
От финских хладных скал до пламенной Колхиды,
От потрясенного Кремля
До стен недвижного Китая,
Стальной щетиною сверкая,
Не встанет русская земля?
Так высылайте ж нам, витии,
Своих озлобленных сынов:
Есть место им в полях России
Среди нечуждых им гробов.

and as they weathered blast on blast,
first one gave way and then the other.   10
Which side will gain ascendancy –
the haughty Pole or stalwart Russian?
Will Slavic tributaries swell the Russian sea?
Or will it dwindle? That's the question.

Leave this to us! You've never read
the bloody annals of our nations.
You do not, cannot comprehend
these old domestic altercations.
Does "Kremlin" mean a thing to you?
Or "Praga"? No, you're captivated   20
by senseless dreams of derring-do,
and we're the target of your hatred…

But why? Is it that we alone,
as Moscow's ruins burned about us, stood defiant
against the brazen will of one
who left you trembling and compliant?
That we, in Europe's hour of need,
cast down that mighty idol into the abyss
and with our very blood redeemed
her honour, liberty and peace?   30

Your words are menacing; let's see if deeds can match them!
Are Izmaíl's great men, abed and out of action,
too feeble to affix their bayonets in haste?
Or is the word of Russia's sovereign uncompelling?
Is this the first of Europe's meddling?
Have we forgotten victory's taste?
Are we too few? Will Russian lands from Perm to Tauris,
from Finland's frigid rocks to sultry, southern Colchis,
and from the shaken Kremlin's walls
to those of an unmoving China,   40
with hackles bristling, weapons shining,
not rise and rally to the cause?
So send your sons, you troublemakers!
Excite their fury, fan the flames!
There's room for them in Russia's acres
beside their countrymen's remains.   CC

662

ИЗ ПИСЬМА К ВЯЗЕМСКОМУ

Любезный Вяземский, поэт и камергер…
(Василья Львовича узнал ли ты манер?
Так некогда письмо он начал к камергеру,
Украшенну ключом за Верность и за Веру).
Так солнце и на нас взглянуло из-за туч!
На заднице твоей сияет тот же ключ.
Ура! хвала и честь поэту-камергеру.
Пожалуй, от меня поздравь княгиню Веру.

663

БОРОДИНСКАЯ ГОДОВЩИНА

Великий день Бородина
Мы братской тризной поминая,
Твердили: «Шли же племена,
Бедой России угрожая;
Не вся ль Европа тут была?
А чья звезда ее вела!..
Но стали ж мы пятою твердой
И грудью приняли напор
Племен, послушных воле гордой,
И равен был неравный спор.   10

И что ж? свой бедственный побег,
Кичась, они забыли ныне;
Забыли русский штык и снег,
Погребший славу их в пустыне.
Знакомый пир их манит вновь —
Хмельна для них славянов кровь;
Но тяжко будет им похмелье;
Но долог будет сон гостей
На тесном, хладном новоселье,
Под злаком северных полей!   20

Ступайте ж к нам: вас Русь зовет!
Но знайте, прошеные гости!
Уж Польша вас не поведет:
Через ее шагнете кости!..»
Сбылось — и в день Бородина

662

FROM A LETTER TO VYÁZEMSKY

My greetings, Vyázemsky, great bard and chamberlain…
(My uncle – you recall his manner? – once began
a letter to a friend with similar address,
who'd come to wear the key for Faith and Faithfulness.)
So on us too the sun from out the clouds has shined!
The same heraldic key now gleams on your behind.
Hurrah! I send you praise that couldn't be sincerer –
and pass my greetings to the faithful Princess Vera.   RC

663

THE ANNIVERSARY OF BORODINÓ

While gathered solemnly to pay
our homage to Borodinó,
we said, "The nations in array
came onward to lay Russia low.
Was not all Europe here that day?
And whose bright star then led the way?
We dug our heels in, dauntless still,
and, bearing up against the might
of tribes that served a haughty will,
we evened that uneven fight.   10

"And now? Their pride has swollen so
that they forget the grim retreat,
the Russian bayonets and snow
that buried all their glory deep.
They long to slake their thirst anew,
for Slavic blood's a heady brew.
But know: the spree will take its toll,
and long their troubled sleep will last
in new-found lodgings cramped and cold
beneath the northern meadow grass.   20

"So Russia bids you to the feast!
But this time, guests, do not suppose
that Poland will escort you east.
The way will lie across her bones!"
And on that day it came to pass

145

Вновь наши вторглись знамена
В проломы падшей вновь Варшавы;
И Польша, как бегущий полк,
Во прах бросает стяг кровавый —
И бунт раздавленный умолк.   30

В боренье падший невредим;
Врагов мы в прахе не топтали,
Мы не напомним ныне им
Того, что старые скрижали
Хранят в преданиях немых;
Мы не сожжем Варшавы их;
Они народной Немезиды
Не узрят гневного лица
И не услышат песнь обиды
От лиры русского певца.   40

Но вы, мутители палат,
Легкоязычные витии,
Вы, черни бедственный набат,
Клеветники, враги России!
Что взяли вы?... Еще ли росс
Больной, расслабленный колосс?
Еще ли северная слава
Пустая притча, лживый сон?
Скажите: скоро ль нам Варшава
Предпишет гордый свой закон?   50

Куда отдвинем строй твердынь?
За Буг, до Ворсклы, до Лимана?
За кем останется Волынь?
За кем наследие Богдана?
Признав мятежные права,
От нас отторгнется ль Литва?
Наш Киев дряхлый, златоглавый,
Сей пращур русских городов,
Сроднит ли с буйною Варшавой
Святыню всех своих гробов?   60

Ваш бурный шум и хриплый крик
Смутили ль русского владыку?
Скажите, кто главой поник?
Кому венец: мечу иль крику?
Сильна ли Русь? Война, и мор,
И бунт, и внешних бурь напор

that Warsaw, as in decades past,
saw Russian flags again break through,
while Poland, like a host in rout,
dropped bloody banners as it flew –
and so the rising sputtered out.   30

The fallen we won't ever injure
or trample in the dust, bereft,
nor will we point a righteous finger
at what, now writ in stone, is left
for silent histories to expound.
We won't burn Warsaw to the ground.
They'll never see the wrathful gaze
of Nemesis – a nation's ire –
or hear a bitter note in lays
composed upon a Russian lyre.   40

But you – your wagging tongues confound
the Chambers' volatile discussion
and recklessly alarm the crowd –
accusers, enemies of Russia!
To what avail? Does Russia still
have "feet of clay", look "weak" or "ill"?
Is northern glory still a thing
of fables and of fantasies?
Will Warsaw soon be issuing
its own imperious decrees?   50

Shall we remove our bastions past
the Bug, the Vorskla – to the sea?
To whom then will Volhynia pass?
To whom Bohdán's old legacy?
And, following the rebels' lead,
will Lithuania secede?
Will Kiev, with its golden domes,
the mother of all cities Russian,
unite the relics of its tombs
with Warsaw's violent convulsion?   60

Is Russia's tsar dismayed at all
to hear your hoarse, hysteric cries?
Who bowed his head and who stood tall?
Do shouts or sabres take the prize?
Is Russia strong? Well, long she bore
rebellion, pestilence and war.

Ее, беснуясь, потрясали —
Смотрите ж: всё стоит она!
А вкруг ее волненья пали —
И Польши участь решена... 70

Победа! сердцу сладкий час!
Россия! встань и возвышайся!
Греми, восторгов общий глас!..
Но тише, тише раздавайся
Вокруг одра, где он лежит,
Могучий мститель злых обид,
Кто покорил вершины Тавра,
Пред кем смирилась Эривань,
Кому суворовского лавра
Венок сплела тройная брань. 80

Восстав из гроба своего,
Суворов видит плен Варшавы;
Вострепетала тень его
От блеска им начатой славы!
Благословляет он, герой,
Твое страданье, твой покой,
Твоих сподвижников отвагу,
И весть триумфа твоего,
И с ней летящего за Прагу
Младого внука своего. 90

664

ЗАПИСКА К А.О. РОССЕТ

Quoique vous connaissiez déjà ces vers, comme je viens d'en envoyer un exemplaire à M-me la comtesse de Lambert, il est juste que vous en ayez un pareil.

От вас узнал я плен Варшавы.
....
Вы были вестницею славы
И вдохновеньем для меня.

Vous aurez ce second vers dès que je vous l'aurai trouvé!

Beset by foreign storms, she reeled.
Behold, she rises undefeated!
The troubled waters have receded,
and Poland's destiny is sealed...   70

O triumph, to the heart so sweet!
O Russia, let glad voices sound!
Arise and take your lofty seat!
But keep the revels low around
the couch where he now convalesces,
avenger of malign offences,
who humbled Yereván and strove
to subjugate the peaks of Taurus,
for whom a triple victory wove
a garland of Suvórov's laurels.   80

Suvórov, rising from his grave,
sees Warsaw captive and contrite.
His shade is quickened by the blaze
of glory he once set alight.
The honoured hero comes to bless
your suffering, your peaceful rest,
the valour of your sons, the tiding
of this, your triumph, and his own
young grandson, at full gallop riding
past Praga with the news for home.   CC

664

A NOTE TO ALEXÁNDRA O. ROSSET

You are already familiar with these poems, but because I have already sent a copy to Countess Lambert, it is only right that you should have one too.

From you I learnt of Warsaw's capture,
....
you filled me with poetic rapture
in bringing me such glorious news.

You will have that second line as soon as I have come up with it for you. RC

665

ЭХО

Ревет ли зверь в лесу глухом,
Трубит ли рог, гремит ли гром,
Поет ли дева за холмом —
   На всякий звук
Свой отклик в воздухе пустом
   Родишь ты вдруг.

Ты внемлешь грохоту громов
И гласу бури и валов,
И крику сельских пастухов —
   И шлешь ответ;   10
Тебе ж нет отзыва... Таков
   И ты, поэт!

666

СКВОРЕЦ

Брадатый староста Авдей
С поклоном барыне своей
Заместо красного яичка
Поднес ученого скворца.
Известно вам: такая птичка
Умней иного мудреца.
Скворец, надувшись величаво,
Вздыхал о царствии небес
И приговаривал картаво:
«Христос воскрес! Христос воскрес!»   10

667

АНАТОЛЬ

Одна стихи ему читала,
И щеки рделися у ней,
И тихо грудь ее дышала:
«Приди, жених души моей,
Тебя зову на томной лире!
Но где найду мой идеал?
И кто поймет меня в сем мире?»
Но Анатоль не понимал...

665

ECHO

Should in dark woods a wild thing cry,
should thunder roar, horns blare nearby,
a girl's voice sing a lullaby –
   to any sound
you instantly give your reply,
   though none's around.

Yes, when you hear the thunder roar,
the crash of waves upon the shore,
a peasant shouting from his door,
   response you send –   10
but get no answer: likewise for
   you, poet-friend!   RC

666

A STARLING

Avdéy, the village elder, owes
an egg for Easter, painted red.
Up to Her Ladyship he goes,
bows and presents a bird instead –
a starling, which, the public knows,
beats every feathered friend for brain.
The clever fowl devoutly shows
contempt for this, our earthly prison –
and then it squawks, and squawks again,
that Christ is risen – "Christ is risen!"   JC

667

ANATOLE

A lone girl reads a young man verses;
her burning cheeks with blushes glow;
her words with sighs she intersperses:
"Oh come, belovèd of my soul,
I call you on my weary lyre.
The perfect man where can I find?
Who will discern what I desire?"
Discern? No. Anatole stays blind...   RC

668

19 ОКТЯБРЯ 1831

Чем чаще празднует лицей
Свою святую годовщину,
Тем робче старый круг друзей
В семью стесняется едину,
Тем реже он; тем праздник наш
В своем веселии мрачнее;
Тем глуше звон заздравных чаш,
И наши песни тем грустнее.

Так дуновенья бурь земных
И нас нечаянно касались,   10
И мы средь пиршеств молодых
Душою часто омрачались;
Мы возмужали; рок судил
И нам житейски испытанья,
И смерти дух средь нас ходил
И назначал свои закланья.

Шесть мест упраздненных стоят,
Шести друзей не узрим боле,
Они разбросанные спят —
Кто здесь, кто там на ратном поле,   20
Кто дома, кто в земле чужой,
Кого недуг, кого печали
Свели во мрак земли сырой,
И надо всеми мы рыдали.

И мнится, очередь за мной,
Зовет меня мой Дельвиг милый,
Товарищ юности живой,
Товарищ юности унылой,
Товарищ песен молодых,
Пиров и чистых помышлений,   30
Туда, в толпу теней родных
Навек от нас утекший гений.

Тесней, о милые друзья,
Тесней наш верный круг составим,
Почившим песнь окончил я,
Живых надеждою поздравим,
Надеждой некогда опять

668

19TH OCTOBER 1831

The more our Lycée comes to hold
its sacred annual celebration,
more timidly we friends of old
assemble as one generation –
more seldom too: our numbers shrink
in feasting that is now more dreary;
and softer do our glasses clink
in singing songs now sad and weary.

Yes, earthly tempests blew their blast
until, too soon, our fate we doubted,   10
so in our youthful feastings past
our spirits were too often clouded.
We grew to manhood; destiny
decreed we share life's tribulation;
Death came to join our company
to make his choice for liquidation.

Six places now deserted stand,
six friends no more shall we be sighting;
they sleep in close or distant land –
some here, some there in field of fighting,   20
some amid aliens, some at home,
some sick, and some in desolation,
borne to their graves in damp earth's gloom,
and each we've mourned with lamentation.

I sense that soon my turn will come –
my dear friend Delvig now is calling,
my friend of youthful days of fun,
my friend of days when fun was palling,
my friend to songs of student cheer,
in feasts and projects shared between us –   30
there midst the shades of near and dear
he calls me, that departed genius.

And now draw close, each loyal friend,
draw close our circle true and loving:
my song of mourning's at an end;
let's wish for hope for us still living,
for hope that we may once more meet

В пиру лицейском очутиться,
  Всех остальных еще обнять
И новых жертв уж не страшиться.   40

669

* * *

Ты просвещением свой разум осветил,
  Ты правды лик увидел,
И нежно чуждые народы возлюбил,
  И мудро свой возненавидел.

Когда безмолвная Варшава поднялась,
  И Польша бунтом опьянела,
И смертная борьба .... началась,
  При клике «Польска не згинела!» —

Когда же Дибич ....
  Пестро парижский пустомеля   10
Ревел на кафедре ....
  Ты пил здоровье Лелевеля.

Ты руки потирал от наших неудач,
  С лукавым смехом слушал вести,
Когда ...... бежали вскачь,
  И гибло знамя нашей чести.

.... Варшавы бунт ....
  .... в дыме
Поникнул ты главой и горько возрыдал,
  Как жид о Иерусалиме.   20

670

ПОДРАЖАНИЯ ДАНТЕ

I

И дале мы пошли — и страх обнял меня.
Бесенок, под себя поджав свое копыто,
Крутил ростовщика у адского огня.

at our next Lycée celebration,
and all those with us warmly greet,
fearing no new annihilation.   AR & RC

669

* * *

You've an enlightened mind: to you Truth's face is known;
    your guide is Reason's revelation;
you've fondly learnt to love all peoples but your own –
    yet cavil at your Russian nation.

When Warsaw all at once rose up, and Polish lands
    rebelled, with rage intoxicated,
and when their fight to death for sovereignty began
    mid cries of "Poland undefeated!" –

and after Dibich .... –
    Then, when that blabberer of drivel   10
in Paris bellowed from his rostrum...
    you toasted Joachim Lelewel.

At our defeats you rubbed your hands in sheer delight,
    greeting the news in gleeful manner
that our troops were ...... in headlong flight,
    dishonoured, having lost their banner.

But when the Poles were crushed ....
    .... in smoke and flame,
you hung your head in shame and bitter lamentation,
    as Jews wept for Jerusalem.   RC

670

IMITATIONS OF DANTE

I

And further on we went – and fear in me rose higher.
A devil imp, his hoof beneath him tightly bending,
roasted a usurer above the hellish fire.

Горячий капал жир в копченое корыто.
И лопал на огне печеный ростовщик.
А я: «Поведай мне: в сей казни что сокрыто?»

Виргилий мне: «Мой сын, сей казни смысл велик:
Одно стяжание имев всегда в предмете,
Жир должников своих сосал сей злой старик

И их безжалостно крутил на вашем свете.»   10
Тут грешник жареный протяжно возопил:
«О, если б я теперь тонул в холодной Лете!

О, если б зимний дождь мне кожу остудил!
Сто на сто я терплю: процент неимоверный!» —
Тут звучно лопнул он — я взоры потупил.

Тогда услышал я (о диво!) запах скверный,
Как будто тухлое разбилось яицо,
Иль карантинный страж курил жаровней серной.

Я, нос себе зажав, отворотил лицо.
Но мудрый вождь тащил меня всё дале, дале —   20
И, камень приподняв за медное кольцо,

Сошли мы вниз — и я узрел себя в подвале.

II

Тогда я демонов увидел черный рой,
Подобный издали ватаге муравьиной —
И бесы тешились проклятою игрой:

До свода адского касалася вершиной
Гора стеклянная, как Арарат, остра —
И разлегалася над темною равниной.

И бесы, раскалив как жар чугун ядра,
Пустили вниз его смердящими когтями;   30
Ядро запрыгало — и гладкая гора,

Звеня, растрескалась колючими звездами.
Тогда других чертей нетерпеливый рой
За жертвой кинулся с ужасными словами.

Into a blackened drain dripped boiling fat unending,
and, cooking in the flames, the man began to burst.
I asked: "Why was such fate decreed for his offending?"

Virgil replied: "My son, his crime was of the worst:
he had but one sole aim in life – that is, extortion.
The old rogue sucked his debtors' fat to slake his thirst

and roasted them alive without the least compunction."   10
And now the one cried out who burned there for his sin:
"If only I had drowned in Lethe's chill oblivion!

If only winter rain could fall and cool my skin!
I'm charged a hundredfold – a rate no knave should call for!"
And here he burst again: I turned my eyes from him.

At that point, with disgust, I smelt the vilest odour,
as if a rotten egg had spattered in my space,
or quarantine police were burning pans of sulphur.

I could but pinch my nose and turn away my face.
But Virgil, my wise guide, kept hurrying me onwards.   20
We grasped a ring of bronze and lifted from its place

a slab of stone that led us to a cellar downwards.

II

And then a pitch-black swarm of demons met my gaze,
as if a cloud of ants had suddenly descended.
I watched the devils play one of their hellish games –

Up to the roof of hell a peak of glass ascended,
a mountain peak as sharp as that of Ararat;
across a dark expanse the base of it extended.

The devils worked to make a cannon ball red-hot,
then sent it rolling down from claws with ordure spattered;   30
the ball bounced on, and thus the mountain's glassy sheet,

with tinkling sound, to jagged stars was shattered.
Then other devils came in an impatient swarm,
upon their victims sprang and words of terror uttered.

Схватили под руки жену с ее сестрой,
И заголили их, и вниз пихнули с криком
И обе сидючи пустились вниз стрелой...

Порыв отчаянья я внял в их вопле диком;
Стекло их резало, впивалось в тело им —
А бесы прыгали в веселии великом.

Я издали глядел — смущением томим.

They seized a woman and her sister by the arm;
they stripped them bare and made them sit with hideous screeching –
on buttocks both slid down, sustaining frightful harm…

Cries of despair I heard amidst their wild beseeching;
the glass cut into them and lodged within their flesh –
and all the devils jumped about with gleeful shrieking.   40

I watched from far – engulfed in doubt and deep distress.   AR & RC

1832

671

* * *

Нет, я не дорожу мятежным наслажденьем,
Восторгом чувственным, безумством, исступленьем,
Стеньем, криками вакханки молодой,
Когда, виясь в моих объятиях змией,
Порывом пылких ласк и язвою лобзаний
Она торопит миг последних содраганий!

О, как милее ты, смиренница моя!
О, как мучительно тобою счастлив я,
Когда, склоняяся на долгие моленья,
Ты предаешься мне нежна без упоенья,   10
Стыдливо-холодна, восторгу моему
Едва ответствуешь, не внемлишь ничему
И оживляешься потом всё боле, боле —
И делишь наконец мой пламень по неволе!

672

МАЛЬЧИКУ

из Катулла

Minister vetuli, puer

Пьяной горечью Фалерна
Чашу мне наполни, мальчик!
Так Постумия велела,
Председательница оргий.
Вы же, воды, прочь теките
И струей, вину враждебной,

1832

671

* * *

No, those wild joys I now renounce without complaint –
the body's fierce desire, delirium, unconstraint,
the groans, the frenzied cries a young bacchante'll make
as, tight within my arms but writhing like a snake,
she scars me with each kiss and sears me with her clasping,
climaxing fast our spasms of shuddering and gasping.

My dear submissive one, how much more I love you!
How painfully intense the joy I feel with you,
when, bending to my long and eager supplication,
you yield yourself to me in gentle resignation;   10
first, frigid and abashed, you show no satisfaction
with my aroused desire, you offer no reaction;
and then you come to life, a little now, then more –
and share at last my fire that left you cold before!   RC

672

FOR A SERVANT BOY

from Catullus

Minister vetuli, puer.

Fill the cup, my boy, with wine,
strong Falernus wine with bite –
so Postumia commands,
mistress of our Bacchic rite.
You, though, waters, flow away,
with your stream that weakens wine –

Строгих постников поите:
Чистый нам любезен Бахус.

673

В АЛЬБОМ А. О. СМИРНОВОЙ

В тревоге пестрой и бесплодной
Большого света и двора
Я сохранила взгляд холодный,
Простое сердце, ум свободный
И правды пламень благородный
И как дитя была добра;
Смеялась над толпою вздорной,
Судила здраво и светло,
И шутки злости самой черной
Писала прямо набело.   10

674

В АЛЬБОМ КНЯЖНЫ А. Д. АБАМЕЛЕК

Когда-то (помню с умиленьем)
Я смел вас нянчить с восхищеньем,
Вы были дивное дитя.
Вы расцвели — с благоговеньем
Вам ныне поклоняюсь я.
За вами сердцем и глазами
С невольным трепетом ношусь
И вашей славою и вами,
Как нянька старая, горжусь.

675

КРАСАВИЦА

в альбом Графини Е.М. Завадовской

Всё в ней гармония, всё диво,
Всё выше мира и страстей;
Она покоится стыдливо
В красе торжественной своей;

succour those who now abstain.
Only Bacchus here must reign.   JF

673

FOR THE ALBUM OF ALEXÁNDRA SMIRNÓVA

Amid the gaudy, vain distraction
of court and high society,
I've always kept a cool dispassion,
a simple heart, a mind that's free –
the noble flame of truth my guide –
and showed the kindness of a child.
I've rendered judgements keen and fitting
and of the petty crowd made light,
the blackest jests at times committing
to paper of the purest white.   CC

674

FOR THE ALBUM OF PRINCESS A.D. ABAMELÉK

Once (this brings back a warm sensation!)
I cradled you in admiration –
a gorgeous baby you were then.
You've blossomed now – in veneration
I greet you, as we meet again.
My heart and eyes fix their attention
on you; I quiver deep inside;
and in both you and your perfection,
like an old nursemaid, I take pride.   RC

675

A BEAUTIFUL WOMAN

for the album of Countess Ye.M. Zavadóvskaya

In her all's heavenly harmony,
in her no wanton worldliness;
she rests serenely, modestly,
triumphant in her loveliness.

Она кругом себя взирает:
Ей нет соперниц, нет подруг;
Красавиц наших бледный круг
В ее сиянье исчезает.

Куда бы ты ни поспешал,
Хоть на любовное свиданье,   10
Какое б в сердце ни питал
Ты сокровенное мечтанье, —
Но, встретясь с ней, смущенный, ты
Вдруг остановишься невольно,
Благоговея богомольно
Перед святыней красоты.

676

К ГРАФИНЕ Н.Л. СОЛЛОГУБ

Нет, нет, не должен я, не смею, не могу
Волнениям любви безумно предаваться;
Спокойствие мое я строго берегу
И сердцу не даю пылать и забываться;
Нет, полно мне любить; но почему ж порой
Не погружуся я в минутное мечтанье,
Когда нечаянно пройдет передо мной
Младое, чистое, небесное созданье,
Пройдет и скроется?... Ужель не можно мне,
Любуясь девою в печальном сладострастье,   10
Глазами следовать за ней и в тишине
Благословлять ее на радость и на счастье,
И сердцем ей желать все блага жизни сей,
Веселый мир души, беспечные досуги,
Всё — даже счастие того, кто избран ей,
Кто милой деве даст название супруги.

677

В АЛЬБОМ

Гонимый рока самовластьем
От пышной далеко Москвы,
Я буду вспоминать с участьем
То место, где цветете вы.

And when she casts her gaze around her,
she finds no rivals there – not one:
she far outshines that set of wan
Petersburg beauties that surround her.

Wherever, friend, you're hurrying,
perhaps to a lovers' assignation,   10
whatever dream you're nurturing
deep down in your imagination –
if you meet her (a sight sublime!),
you'll falter in incomprehension
and, with a worshipper's intention,
kneel pilgrim-like at Beauty's shrine.   RC

676

TO COUNTESS N.L. SOLLOGÚB

I must not, cannot, do not dare
insanely yield to passion's pains;
I guard my inner calm with care
and keep my sober heart in chains.
Though done with love, am I not free
to dream a passing dream at times,
when accidentally I see
a pure, angelic girl go by
and disappear?… And can't I then,
admiring her with longing gaze,   10
pursue her with my eyes and send
a prayer to bless her all her days,
and wish her goodness from above,
and happiness and peace in life –
yes, even joy for him she'll love,
who'll call the charming girl his wife?   JF

677

FOR AN ALBUM

Far from old Moscow and its pleasure,
banished by fate, to live I'm doomed;
but in my heart I'll always treasure
the city where your flower has bloomed.

Столичный шум меня тревожит;
Всегда в нем грустно я живу —
И ваша память только может
Одна напомнить мне Москву.

678

* * *

Я ехал в дальные края;
Не шумных .... жажлал я,
Искал не злата, не честей,
В пыли средь копий и мечей.

———————

Желал я душу освежить,
Бывалой жизнию пожить
В забвенье сладком близ друзей
Минувшей юности моей.

679

В АЛЬБОМ

Долго сих листов заветных
Не касался я пером;
Виноват, в столе моем
Уж давно без строк приветных
Залежался твой альбом.
В именины, очень кстати,
Пожелать тебе я рад
Много всякой благодати,
Много сладостных отрад, —
На Парнасе много грома,
В жизни много тихих дней
И на совести твоей
Ни единого альбома
От красавиц, от друзей.

10

The din of Petersburg distracts me;
to a wretched life I'm here consigned –
the thought of you alone attracts me
and brings dear Moscow back to mind.   RC

678

* * *

I rode to some far-distant land;
no rowdy feasts did I demand –
I sought not gold nor fame's reward
amid the dust with lance and sword.

———————

My soul I thirsted to restore,
to live the life I lived before,
as in some sweet forgetful haze,
beside the friends from bygone days.   JF

679

FOR AN ALBUM

Blank still are your precious pages,
buried in this desk of mine.
Your poor album's lain long ages
empty, uninscribed, unsigned
(sorry! – it quite slipped my mind).
Now your name day's come, my pleasure
is, today, to wish you here
much to cherish, much to treasure,
much to offer you good cheer –
much acclaim for verses written,   10
many days at peace to spend –
and a conscience never smitten
by an album still unpenned,
lent by lover or by friend.   RC

680

ПЕСНЯ СВАДЕБНОГО ХОРА

из Русалки

Сватушка, сватушка,
Бестолковый сватушка!
По невесту ехали,
В огород заехали,
Пива бочку пролили,
Всю капусту полили,
Тыну поклонилися,
Верее молилися:
Верея ль, вереюшка,
Укажи дороженьку   10
По невесту ехати.

Сватушка, догадайся,
За мошоночку принимайся,
В мошне денежка шевелится,
К красным девушкам норовится.

681

ПЕСНЯ НЕИЗВЕСТНОЙ ДЕВУШКИ

из Русалки

По камушкам по желтому песочку
Пробегала быстрая речка,
В быстрой речке гуляют две рыбки,
Две рыбки, две малые плотицы.
А слышала ль ты, рыбка-сестрица,
Про вести-то наши, про речные?
Как вечор у нас красна девица топилась,
Утопая, мила друга проклинала.

680

SONG OF THE WEDDING CHOIR

from Rusálka

Clumsy old matchmaker,
grant us a pardon:
fetching the bride
we got lost in the garden,
soaked all the cabbage;
spilt beer on the floor;
bowed to the fencing,
and prayed to the door.
Dear little doorpost,
do show us the way –   10
to get to the bride, then
we'll bring her today.

Matchmaker, listen! Your money is jingling.
Open your pouch, please… Our fingers are tingling.
Lovely young maidens… Our fingers are tingling.   JC

681

SONG OF AN UNKNOWN GIRL

from Rusálka

Where the stream runs deep and strong
– yellow sand and pebbles, oh –
two small fishes swam along
– yellow sand and pebbles, oh.
Fishes gossiped as they swam
– yellow sand and pebbles, oh –
down the river, near the dam
– yellow sand and pebbles, oh.
She who should have been a bride
– yellow sand and pebbles, oh –   10
broke her heart and drowned and died
– yellow sand and pebbles, oh;
stood in sorrow on the bank
– yellow sand and pebbles, oh –
cursed her lover as she sank
– yellow sand and pebbles, oh!   JC

682

ДВЕ ПЕСНИ РУСАЛОК

из Русалки

I

РУСАЛКИ

Веселой толпою
С глубокого дна
Мы ночью всплываем,
Нас греет луна.
Любо нам порой ночною
Дно речное покидать,
Любо вольной головою
Высь речную разрезать,
Подавать друг дружке голос,
Воздух звонкий раздражать,   10
И зеленый, влажный волос
В нем сушить и отряхать.

ОДНА

Тише, тише! под кустами
Что-то кроется во мгле.

ДРУГАЯ

Между месяцем и нами
Кто-то ходит по земле...

(Прячутся. Князь и другие являются на берег, говорят и уходят.)

II

РУСАЛКИ

Что, сестрицы? в поле чистом
Не догнать ли их скорей?
Плеском, хохотом и свистом
Не пугнуть ли их коней?   20
Поздно. Рощи потемнели,
Холодеет глубина,
Петухи в селе пропели,
Закатилася луна.

682

TWO SONGS OF RUSÁLKAS

from Rusálka

I

THE RUSÁLKAS

> We rise from the deep
> to the warmth of the moon –
> when men are asleep
> is our happy high noon…
> Sweet it is to seek the light,
> break the silent water's face,
> gliding up at dead of night,
> free to splash, to swim, to race.
> Sweet is it to call and cry,
> mock the tinkling, echoing air,
> wring our green and soaking hair,
> comb it well and let it dry.

10

FIRST RUSÁLKA

> Hush! Beware… a man comes creeping –
> trees and darkness hide his face.

SECOND RUSÁLKA

> Be it so! The moon unsleeping
> sees him seek this haunted place…

> *(They hide. The prince and others appear on the bank,
> speak and leave.)*

II

THE RUSÁLKAS

> Sisters, quickly, let's pursue them,
> chuckling, whistling, far and near,
> till our taunts and tricks undo them,
> drive their horses mad with fear.
> Late, too late. The woodlands darken;
> cold and deep the waters run;
> eerie moonlight dwindles… Hearken!
> Now the cock salutes the sun.

20

ОДНА

Погодим еще, сестрица.

ДРУГАЯ

Нет, пора, пора, пора.
Ожидает нас царица,
Наша строгая сестра.

FIRST RUSÁLKA

Sister, still there's time to play…

SECOND RUSÁLKA

Time for all to hide below.
Dawn of day forbids delay –
when the queen commands, we go.

JC

1833

683

ИЗ ГЕДИЛА

Славная флейта, Феон, здесь лежит. Предводителя хоров
  Старец, ослепший от лет, некогда Скирпал родил
И, вдохновенный, нарек младенца Феоном. За чашей
  Сладостно Вакха и муз славил приятный Феон.
Славил и Ватала он, молодого красавца: прохожий!
  Мимо гробницы спеша, вымолви: здравствуй Феон!

684

* * *

Юноша! скромно пируй, и шумную Вакхову влагу
  С трезвой струею воды, с мудрой беседой мешай.

685

ВИНО

из Иона Хиосского

Злое дитя, старик молодой, властелин добронравный,
  Гордость внушающий нам, шумный заступник любви!

1833

683

FROM HEDYLUS

Here lies the flautist of fame and leader of choruses Theon.
Scirpalus, blinded by age, sired him and, being inspired,
called the boy Theon. In time, as Theon reclined with his wine cup,
Bacchus and all the divine Muses he sweetly extolled.
Battalus too, handsome lad, he extolled without stinting. O stranger,
hurrying now past my tomb, stop and say, "Theon, hello!"   CC

684

* * *

Feast, my boy, modestly: mix, with Bacchus's boisterous nectar,
water in sobering streams, discourse befitting the wise.   CC

685

WINE

from Ion of Chios

Child full of mischief; when old, still youthful; a master indulgent;
noisy procurer of love, giving a boost to our pride.   RC

686

ИЗ ГОРАЦИЯ

Царей потомок, Меценат,
Мой покровитель стародавний:

Иные колесницу мчат
В ристалище под пылью славной
И, заповеданной ограды
Касаясь жгучим колесом,
Победной ждут себе награды
И мнят быть равны с божеством.
Другие на свою главу
Сбирают титла знамениты,   10
Непостоянные квириты
Им придают ……… молву.
……………………………

687

ИЗ КСЕНОФАНА КОЛОФОНСКОГО

Чистый лоснится пол; стеклянные чаши блистают;
Все уж увенчаны гости; иной обоняет, зажмурясь,
Ладана сладостный дым; другой открывает амфору,
Запах веселый вина разливая далече; сосуды
Светлой студеной воды, золотистые хлебы, янтарный
Мед и сыр молодой — всё готово; весь убран цветами
Жертвенник. Хоры поют. Но в начале трапезы, о други,
Должно творить возлиянья, вещать благовещие речи,
Должно бессмертных молить, да сподобят нас чистой душою
Правду блюсти: ведь оно ж и легче. Теперь мы приступим: 10
Каждый в меру свою напивайся. Беда не велика
В ночь, возвращаясь домой, на раба опираться; но слава
Гостю, который за чашей беседует мудро и тихо!

686

FROM HORACE

To you, Maecenas, born of kings,
my patron now from long ago.

Some men there are who drive a chariot
beneath the hippodrome's famed dust;
the turning post that's out of bounds
they all but graze with scorching wheels,
expectant of the victor's prize,
and think themselves to be a god.
Other men gather for their names
prestigious titles, when the inconstant   10
citizenry ....
votes to award them rank and fame.
....   RC

687

FROM XENOPHANES OF COLOPHON

Now the immaculate floor has a shine, and the drinking cups glisten;
each of the guests has been garlanded; one, with his eyes growing narrow,
savours the smoky-sweet incense; another cracks open a wine jar,
spreading the mirthful perfume of the grape; ample vessels of water –
cool, crystal clear and refreshing – with golden-brown loaves, amber honey,
freshly made cheese... all is ready, bright flowers adorning the altar.
Song fills the air. But the feast, O my friends, must begin with the fitting
words of good augur, libations and prayers that the blessèd immortals
reckon us worthy, with hearts that are pure, of devoutly upholding
heavenly justice; it's easier then. Now the banquet commences.   10
Each is most welcome to drink his full measure. It's no great dishonour,
heading for home after nightfall, to lean on a slave, but our praises
go to the guest who, while draining his wine cup, speaks wisely and softly! CC

688

ИЗ ЭВБУЛА

Бог веселый винограда
Позволяет нам три чаши
Выпивать в пиру вечернем.
Первую во имя Граций,
Обнаженных и стыдливых,
Посвящается вторая
Краснощекому здоровью,
Третья дружбе многолетней.
Мудрый после третьей чаши
Все венки с главы слагает   10
И творит уж излиянья
Благодатному Морфею.

689

* * *

Царь увидел пред собою
Столик с шахматной доскою.

Вот на шахматную доску
Рать солдатиков из воску
Он расставил в стройный ряд.
Грозно куколки стоят,
Подбоченясь на лошадках,
В коленкоровых перчатках,
В оперенных шишачках,
С палашами на плечах.   10

Тут лохань перед собою
Приказал налить водою;
Плавать он пустил по ней
Тьму прекрасных кораблей,
Барок, каторог и шлюпок
Из ореховых скорлупок —
…………………………
…………………………
А прозрачные ветрильцы
Будто бабочкины крильцы,   20
А веревки ……………

688

FROM EUBULUS

The festive god of grapes and wine
allows us each to drink in toast
three glasses at the evening feast –
the first one in the Graces' name,
those beauties naked and demure;
the second glass we dedicate
to rosy-cheeked good health and cheer;
the third to long-lived friendship's bonds;
but when the third has disappeared,
the wise man lays his garlands down   10
and sings his most effusive song
to blessed Morpheus, god of sleep.   JF

689

* * *

Once a king a table spied
where a chessboard lay spread wide.

On the chessboard thus displayed
waxen soldiers he arrayed,
placing them as well he could
so that firm and fierce they stood –
arms akimbo, all astride
steeds, in cotton gloves attired;
helmets tall with plumes they wore,
broad swords on their shoulders bore.   10

Next he had in front of him
placed a washtub full to brim,
then he launched to float on it
fleets of ships, quite exquisite –
galleys, sloops, all kinds of craft,
out of little nutshells carved –

....
....
sails translucent to the eyes,
like the wings of butterflies;   20
ropes ....   JH & RC

690

ГНЕДИЧУ

С Гомером долго ты беседовал один,
 Тебя мы долго ожидали,
И светел ты сошел с таинственных вершин
 И вынес нам свои скрижали.
И что ж? ты нас обрел в пустыне под шатром,
 В безумстве суетного пира,
Поющих буйну песнь и скачущих кругом
 От нас созданного кумира.
Смутились мы, твоих чуждаяся лучей.
 В порыве гнева и печали   10
Ты проклял ли, пророк, бессмысленных детей,
 Разбил ли ты свои скрижали?
О, ты не проклял нас. Ты любишь с высоты
 Скрываться в тень долины малой,
Ты любишь гром небес, но также внемлешь ты
 Жужжанью пчел над розой алой.
Таков прямой поэт. Он сетует душой
 На пышных играх Мельпомены,
И улыбается забаве площадной
 И вольности лубочной сцены,   20
То Рим его зовет, то гордый Илион,
 То скалы старца Оссиана,
И с дивной легкостью меж тем летает он
 Во след Бовы иль Еруслана.

691

ГУСАР

Скребницей чистил он коня,
А сам ворчал, сердясь не в меру:
«Занес же вражий дух меня
На распроклятую квартеру!

Здесь человека берегут,
Как на турецкой перестрелке,
Насилу щей пустых дадут,
А уж не думай о горелке.

690

FOR GNEDICH

Alone with Homer you did long in converse speak,
  and we as long for you were waiting.
Then, radiant, you descended from the mystic peak
  to bring us slabs of godly writing.
What then? You found us here in desert camp entranced,
  intent on revelry unbridled
while mindlessly we sang wild songs and wildly danced
  around our self-made golden idol.
Abashed we shunned in fear your countenance that shone.
  Possessed by anger and repugnance,   10
did you your children, prophet-like, disown –
  smash hallowed tablets into fragments?
No, you did not disown! You like the heights to leave
  and roam deep woodlands in the gloaming;
you like the thunder's roll on high, but also love
  to hear the bees on roses humming.
A true poet is such. A solemn tragedy
  on stage excites his heart's compassion;
he smiles at horseplay, too, in vulgar comedy
  and folklore's lack of inhibition.   20
Now Rome, now noble Troy, now agèd Ossian's
  grim crags – each one in turn will call him,
and, in between, Bová's and valiant Yeruslán's
  amusing exploits will enthral him.   RC

691

THE HUSSAR

He groomed his horse and, as he did it,
began to bitterly complain:
"Who found me this accursèd billet?
The Evil One must be to blame!

"Here hospitality would rival
a Turkish gunfight; all you get
is soup enough for bare survival.
And vodka? – that you can forget.

Здесь на тебя как лютый зверь
Глядит хозяин, а с хозяйкой...
Небось не выманишь за дверь
Ее ни честью, ни нагайкой.

То ль дело Киев! Что за край!
Валятся сами в рот галушки,
Вином — хоть пару поддавай,
А молодицы-молодушки!

Ей-ей, не жаль отдать души
За взгляд красотки *чернобривой*,
Одним, одним не хороши...»
— А чем же? расскажи, служивый.

Он стал крутить свой длинный ус
И начал: «Молвить без обиды,
Ты, хлопец, может быть, не трус,
Да глуп, а мы видали виды.

Ну, слушай: около Днепра
Стоял наш полк; моя хозяйка
Была пригожа и добра,
А муж-то помер, замечай-ка!

Вот с ней и подружился я;
Живем согласно, так что любо:
Прибью — Марусинька моя
Словечка не промолвит грубо;

Напьюсь — уложит, и сама
Опохмелиться приготовит;
Мигну бывало: Эй, кума! —
Кума ни в чем не прекословит.

Кажись: о чем бы горевать?
Живи в довольстве, безобидно!
Да нет: я вздумал ревновать.
Что делать? враг попутал видно.

Зачем бы ей, стал думать я,
Вставать до петухов? кто просит?
Шалит Марусинька моя;
Куда ее лукавый носит?

"The landlord's manner is as gracious
as any wolf's, and you can tempt   10
his wife with earnest declarations
or crack the whip; she won't relent.

"But Kiev – what a land! – is brimming
with dumplings that drop on your tongue,
with flowing wine, enough to swim in,
and pretty wives so fresh and young!

"By God, you'd give the ghost up gladly
to glimpse their eyes, their raven hair,
but they have just one failing, sadly…"
"What, soldier? Say what happened there!"   20

He twirled his long moustache, contented,
and said, "You're plucky, lad, but you
know nothing – no offence intended –
and I have seen a thing or two.

"Just listen. When our force was stationed
beside the Dnieper, there I knew
a pretty hostess, kind and patient;
her husband then was dead, mind you!

"We hardly could have got on better,
and lived together in accord;   30
my sweet Marúsya, when I beat her,
would never say an ugly word.

"She'd tuck me in when I saw double
and pour a morning-after drink,
and never give me any trouble
when I would beckon her and wink.

"You'd think that I would be contented
to live in harmony. Oh, no,
beset by jealous doubts, I fretted.
The Devil has his ways, you know.   40

"Just why does she, I kept repeating,
get up before the roosters crow?
If my Marúsya isn't cheating,
then where the devil does she go?

Я стал присматривать за ней.
Раз я лежу, глаза прищуря,
(А ночь была тюрьмы черней,
И на дворе шумела буря).

И слышу: кумушка моя
С печи тихохонько прыгнула,   50
Слегка обшарила меня,
Присела к печке, уголь вздула

И свечку тонкую зажгла,
Да в уголок пошла со свечкой,
Там с полки скляночку взяла
И, сев на веник перед печкой,

Разделась донага; потом
Из склянки три раза хлебнула,
И вдруг на венике верхом
Взвилась в трубу — и улизнула.   60

Эге! смекнул в минуту я:
Кума-то, видно, басурманка!
Постой, голубушка моя!..
И с печки слез — и вижу: склянка.

Понюхал: кисло! что за дрянь!
Плеснул я на пол: что за чудо?
Прыгнул ухват, за ним лохань,
И оба в печь. Я вижу: худо!

Гляжу: под лавкой дремлет кот;
И на него я брызнул склянкой —   70
Как фыркнет он! я: брысь!.. И вот
И он туда же за лоханкой.

Я ну кропить во все углы
С плеча, во что уж ни попало;
И всё: горшки, скамьи, столы,
Марш! марш! всё в печку поскакало.

Кой черт! подумал я; теперь
И мы попробуем! и духом
Всю склянку выпил; верь не верь —
Но к верху вдруг взвился я пухом.   80

"I watched her then without her knowing –
and once lay still, my eyes like slits
(outside an angry storm was blowing;
the night was just as black as pitch),

"and heard my lover softly leaping
down off the stove; she patted me,   50
assured herself that I was sleeping,
and, blowing on a coal that she

"then used to light a slender candle,
she took a vial from the shelf,
picked up a ready broom to straddle
and by the stove undressed herself.

"She raised the vial, sure to shake it,
and took three swallows of the brew,
and then, astride her broom, stark naked,
she rose and up the chimney flew.   60

"I figured this out in an instant:
my lover was an infidel!
You wait, my dove, one bloody minute!
And I got off the stove as well.

"I sniffed the vial: sour and nasty!
I spilled some and – fantastic sight! –
the oven fork and tub ran past me
and up the flue. This wasn't right!

"Beneath a bench, the cat was lying;
he snorted when I splashed him too;   70
then, 'Scat!' I said, and he went flying
behind the washtub up the flue.

"I sprinkled drops in all directions,
on everything in sight – a pan,
then tables, cooking pots and benches –
said, 'Forward, march!' And off they ran!

"The deuce, I thought, and had the notion
to try my own wings; sure enough,
no sooner had I downed the potion
than off I flew like so much fluff.   80

Стремглав лечу, лечу, лечу,
Куда, не помню и не знаю;
Лишь встречным звездочкам кричу:
Правей!.. и на земь упадаю.

Гляжу: гора. На той горе
Кипят котлы; поют, играют,
Свистят и в мерзостной игре
Жида с лягушкою венчают.

Я плюнул и сказать хотел…
И вдруг бежит моя Маруся: 90
— Домой! кто звал тебя, пострел?
Тебя съедят! — Но я, не струся:

— Домой? да! черта с два! почем
Мне знать дорогу? — Ах, он странный!
Вот кочерга, садись верьхом
И убирайся, окаянный.

— Чтоб я, я сел на кочергу,
Гусар присяжный! Ах ты, дура!
Или предался я врагу?
Иль у тебя двойная шкура?   100

Коня!— На, дурень, вот и конь. —
И точно; конь передо мною,
Скребет копытом, весь огонь,
Дугою шея, хвост трубою.

— Садись. — Вот сел я на коня,
Ищу уздечки, — нет уздечки.
Как взвился, как понес меня —
И очутились мы у печки.

Гляжу; всё так же; сам же я
Сижу верхом, и подо мною   110
Не конь — а старая скамья:
Вот что случается порою».

И стал крутить он длинный ус,
Прибавя: «Молвить без обиды,
Ты, хлопец, может быть, не трус,
Да глуп, а мы видали виды».

"I flew headlong and kept on flying,
no telling where I might be bound;
I dodged the passing stars while crying,
'Make way!' – then tumbled to the ground.

"I saw a mountain, cauldrons boiling,
heard songs and whistling in the fog;
amid the revels, they were joining
a Jew in marriage to a frog.

"I spat and would have uttered something…
Marúsya ran to me, concerned: 90
'Go home at once, you good-for-nothing!
They'll eat you live!' I, undeterred,

"said, 'How the deuce do you expect me
to get home?' 'He's a funny one,'
she muttered. 'Leave this place directly!
Get on this poker and begone!'

"'You'd ask a sworn hussar to straddle
a poker? Hah! Do you suppose
I've sold my soul? Or does your prattle
mean you've more lives than one to lose?   100

"'I'll have a horse!' Her answer: 'Granted.'
And, sure enough, a fiery mount
before me pawed the ground and panted,
with arching neck and tail stretched out.

"'Get on, you silly fool!' I mounted
and looked for reins, but found none. Then,
borne up and over lands uncounted,
I wound up by the stove again.

"There everything was as it had been,
but I, no longer on a horse,   110
bestrode a bench. Such things do happen,
although not every day, of course."

He twirled his long moustache and ended,
"You may be plucky, lad, but you
know nothing – no offence intended –
and I have seen a thing or two."   CC

692

РИФМАЧАМ

Французских рифмачей суровый судия,
О классик Депрео, к тебе взываю я:

Хотя постигнутый неумолимым роком
В своем отечестве престал ты быть пророком,
Хоть дерзких умников простерлася рука
На лавры твоего густого парика;
Хотя, растрепанный новейшей вольной школой,
К ней в гневе обратил ты свой затылок голый, —
Но я молю тебя, поклонник верный твой,
Будь мне вожатаем. Дерзаю за тобой   10
Занять кафедру ту, с которой в прежни лета
Ты слишком превознес достоинства сонета,
Но где торжествовал твой здравый приговор
Минувших лет глупцам, вранью тогдашних пор.
Новейшие врали вралей старинных стоят —
И слишком уж меня их бредни беспокоят.
Ужели всё молчать, да слушать? О беда!..
Нет, всё им выскажу однажды завсегда.

О вы, которые, восчувствовав отвагу,
Хватаете перо, мараете бумагу,   20
Тисненью предавать труды свои спеша,
Постойте — наперед узнайте, чем душа
У вас исполнена — прямым ли вдохновеньем
Иль необдуманным одним поползновеньем,
И чешется у вас рука по пустякам,
Иль вам не верят в долг, а деньги нужны вам.
Не лучше ль стало б вам с надеждою смиренной
Заняться службою гражданской иль военной,
С хваленым Жуковым табачный торг завесть
И снискивать в труде себе барыш и честь,   30
Чем объявления совать во все журналы,
Вельможе пошлые кропая мадригалы,
Над меньшей собратьей в поту лица острясь,
Иль выше мнения отважно вознесясь,
С оплошной публики (как некие писаки)
Подписку собирать — на будущие враки?...

692

FOR RHYMESTERS

Boileau, I call on you, doyen of classicism,
you, who were stringent judge of second-rate French rhymesters:

Though you've succumbed to Fate the Ineluctable,
and in your land no more are honoured as a prophet;
though connoisseurs (so-called) have dared to lay a hand
upon the wreath of bay that graced your ample wig;
and though, dishevelled by these new freethinking critics,
you've turned your naked head towards them in your wrath –
I, loyal devotee of yours, still do entreat you:
please be my guide; for I'm ascending now the pulpit   10
you used to occupy, from which in bygone years
you preached too fervently the merits of a sonnet,
but where you won acclaim for your just condemnation
of the buffoons you knew (flock of outdated rooks!).
Today's buffoons deserve what you gave those of your day –
their mindless ravings I already find too wearing.
Must I still hold my peace and go on listening? Spare me!
No! I'll now speak my mind to them for good and all.

You, then, ambitious ones, who, eager for adventure,
are grasping well-inked pens and soiling sheets of paper   20
in haste to send your works off to some printing press,
stop! – and before you act consider what it is
that's filled your soul. Can it be real inspiration,
or just a vague desire that you've not yet thought through?
Can that which sets your hand a-tingling just be rubbish,
or are you in deep debt and need some ready money?
Might it perhaps be best to curb your aspirations
and get an army job or join the civil service,
or sell tobacco with that estimable Zhukov,
earning yourself some funds and credit through employment –   30
instead of filling journals with your self-promotion,
churning out hackneyed odes to praise the great and good,
while straining every nerve to mock at lesser folk,
or setting yourself up beyond our expectations
by seeking (like some hacks) subscriptions in advance
from trusting citizens – for future books of trash?...   RC

693

ПОМИНАНИЯ

Сват Иван, как пить мы станем,
Непременно уж помянем
Трех Матрен, Луку с Петром,
Да Пахомовну потом.
Мы живали с ними дружно,
Уж как хочешь — будь что будь —
Этих надо помянуть,
Помянуть нам этих нужно.
Поминать, так поминать,
Начинать, так начинать,   10
Лить, так лить, разлив разливом.
Начинай-ка, сват, пора.
Трех Матрен, Луку, Петра
В первый раз помянем пивом,
А Пахомовну потом
Пирогами да вином,
Да еще ее помянем:
Сказки сказывать мы станем —
Мастерица ведь была
И откуда что брала.   20
А куды разумны шутки,
Приговорки, прибаутки,
Небылицы, былины
Православной старины!..
Слушать, так душе отрадно.
И не пил бы и не ел,
Всё бы слушал да сидел.
Кто придумал их так ладно?
Стариков когда-нибудь
(Жаль, теперь нам не досужно)   30
Надо будет помянуть —
Помянуть и этих нужно...
Слушай, сват, начну первой,
Сказка будет за тобой.

COMMEMORATIONS

Friend Iván, as we start drinking,
we should certainly be thinking
of our late Pakhómovna,
three Matryónas, Pyótr, Luká…
We were friends, the lot of us;
like it, lump it, come what may,
for their souls we now should pray –
pray for them, yes, that's a must.
Call their names, their names, yes, call;
call the names, yes, name them all!   10
Pour the liquor till we're plastered.
You begin, friend – here you are!
Three Matryónas, Pyótr, Luká –
toast them all with beer for starters.
After them Pakhómovna –
drink, and eat pie too, for her;
then for her drink one toast more: it's
then we'll start to tell some stories…
She was such a clever one,
with a word for everyone –   20
all those proverbs, aphorisms,
jokes and jests and witticisms…
and the legends that she told
from the Orthodox of old!…
Listening was such a pleasure.
Never mind the pies and beer,
better just to sit and hear
as she chattered – what a treasure!
To our other chums who've gone
(no time now, it's such a pity)   30
we must drink a toast anon…
No, to toast them now's a duty…
listen: I'll be number one;
friend, have your say when I'm done.   RC

694

ПЛЕТНЕВУ

Ты хочешь, мой наперсник строгий,
Боев парнасских судия,
Чтоб ……… тревогой
…………………………
…… на прежний лад настроя,
Давно забытого героя,
Когда-то бывшего в чести,
Опять на сцену привести.
Ты говоришь: «………….
Онегин жив, и будет он
Еще нескоро схоронен.
О нем вестей ты много знаешь,
И с Петербурга и Москвы
Возьмут оброк его главы...»

10

695

* * *

В славной в Муромском земле,
В Карачарове селе
Жил-был дьяк с своей дьячихой.
Под конец их жизни тихой
Бог отраду им послал —
Сына им он даровал ...

696

* * *

В поле чистом серебрится
Снег волнистый и рябой,
Светит месяц, тройка мчится
По дороге столбовой.

Пой: в часы дорожной скуки,
На дороге, в тьме ночной
Сладки мне родные звуки
Звонкой песни удалой.

694

FOR PLETNYÓV

You're urging me, my friend unsparing,
stern judge of writerly disputes,
that I should .... despairing,
....
retune the strings I'd laid aside
and bring that hero once admired,
that figure from an earlier age,
back once again onto the stage.
You tell me: "..............
Onégin's living; it's too soon   10
to send him downwards to the tomb.
On him you've still much information.
Believe me: in each capital
fresh chapters will be saleable."   RC

695

* * *

Down in Múrom's far-famed lands,
Karachárovo still stands.
In that village scribe and wife
spent far back a tranquil life.
When their life was nearly done,
God bestowed on them a son ...   RC

696

* * *

Silvery snow is blowing, swirling
through the fields – the moon is bright –
while my lonely sleigh is whirling
onward through the dreary night.

Sing! The endless roads oppress me;
darkness lays the spirit low.
Now let happy notes caress me –
rousing songs of long ago.

Пой, ямщик! Я молча, жадно
Буду слушать голос твой.   10
Месяц ясный светит хладно,
Грустен ветра дальный вой.

Пой: «Лучинушка, лучина,
Что же не светло горишь?»
....

697

ОСЕНЬ

Отрывок

Чего в мой дремлющий тогда не входит ум?
ДЕРЖАВИН

I

Октябрь уж наступил — уж роща отряхает
Последние листы с нагих своих ветвей;
Дохнул осенний хлад, дорога промерзает,
Журча еще бежит за мельницу ручей,
Но пруд уже застыл; сосед мой поспешает
В отъезжие поля с охотою своей,
И страждут озими от бешеной забавы,
И будит лай собак уснувшие дубравы.

II

Теперь моя пора: я не люблю весны;
Скучна мне оттепель; вонь, грязь — весной я болен;   10
Кровь бродит; чувства, ум тоскою стеснены.
Суровою зимой я более доволен,
Люблю ее снега; в присутствии луны
Как легкий бег саней с подругой быстр и волен,
Когда под соболем, согрета и свежа,
Она вам руку жмет, пылая и дрожа!

III

Как весело, обув железом острым ноги,
Скользить по зеркалу стоячих, ровных рек!
А зимних праздников блестящие тревоги?...
Но надо знать и честь; полгода снег да снег,   20
Ведь это наконец и жителю берлоги,

Driver, sing! As I lie pining,
let me hear familiar strains,   10
while that chilly moon is shining,
while the moaning wind complains.

Sing: "My little candle glowing,
why don't you more brightly burn?"
....   JC

697

AUTUMN

A fragment

And what does not then come into my drowsing mind?
DERZHÁVIN

I

October has arrived. The grove shakes off the traces
of foliage that cling to naked branches still;
the breath of autumn chills the road as well as glazes
the pond, although the brook still babbles by the mill;
my eager neighbour, with his hunting party, chases
wild game with gusto in his distant fields until
the winter corn is trampled by their frenzied larking,
and noisy dogs awake the sleeping woods with barking.

II

This time of year is mine: the spring I can't abide;
the dreary thaw, the stench, the mud – spring makes me queasy;   10
the blood is restless; yearning grips the heart and mind.
The winter, frosty and austere, has more to please me;
I love its snows; as you and your young lady ride
in moonlit ways, the sleigh sweeps on so free and easy
when, flushed and warm beneath her sable in the chill,
she dares to squeeze your hand, atremble with the thrill!

III

What fun then, shod with blades of iron, to go gliding
along the rivers still and smooth as glass below!
And aren't the holidays resplendent and exciting!
But there's a limit: months of snow and only snow   20
will try the patience of a bear, fed up with hiding

Медведю, надоест. Нельзя же целый век
Кататься нам в санях с Армидами младыми,
Иль киснуть у печей за стеклами двойными.

IV

Ох, лето красное! любил бы я тебя,
Когда б не зной, да пыль, да комары, да мухи.
Ты, все душевные способности губя,
Нас мучишь; как поля, мы страждем от засухи;
Лишь как бы напоить да освежить себя —
Иной в нас мысли нет, и жаль зимы старухи,   30
И, проводив ее блинами и вином,
Поминки ей творим мороженым и льдом.

V

Дни поздней осени бранят обыкновенно,
Но мне она мила, читатель дорогой,
Красою тихою, блистающей смиренно.
Так нелюбимое дитя в семье родной
К себе меня влечет. Сказать вам откровенно,
Из годовых времен я рад лишь ей одной,
В ней много доброго; любовник не тщеславный,
Я нечто в ней нашел мечтою своенравной.   40

VI

Как это объяснить? Мне нравится она,
Как, вероятно, вам чахоточная дева
Порою нравится. На смерть осуждена,
Бедняжка клонится без ропота, без гнева.
Улыбка на устах увянувших видна;
Могильной пропасти она не слышит зева;
Играет на лице еще багровый цвет.
Она жива еще сегодня, завтра нет.

VII

Унылая пора! очей очарованье!
Приятна мне твоя прощальная краса —   50
Люблю я пышное природы увяданье,
В багрец и в золото одетые леса,
В их сенях ветра шум и свежее дыханье,
И мглой волнистою покрыты небеса,
И редкий солнца луч, и первые морозы,
И отдаленные седой зимы угрозы.

inside his narrow den. We can't forever go
on sleighing blithely with enchantresses or lazing
morosely by the stove behind the double glazing.

IV

Ah, Summer, maiden fair, I'd love you were it not
for heat and dust and flies, mosquitoes that beset us.
You sap our mental powers till, overcome and hot,
we suffer like the fields from drought as you torment us,
and cool refreshment's all that occupies our thought;
old lady winter now is missed, a fond remembrance;   30
we saw her off with wine and pancakes and partake
of quantities of ice and ice cream at her wake.

V

It's usual to speak of autumn days severely;
for me, though, gentle reader, autumn is aglow
with quiet beauty – meekly, splendidly endearing.
I'm drawn to her as to a child whose parents show
her no affection. I can tell you quite sincerely
that she alone of all the seasons cheers me so;
she has much good in her; no vain or boastful lover,
I have a dream all mine that gives me cause to love her.   40

VI

How can I put it? She appeals to me, my friend,
perhaps as a consumptive girl whose days are waning
appeals to you at times. Pour soul, to death condemned,
she languishes without a murmur, uncomplaining.
Her withered lips still form a smile, and to the end
her face is brightened by a play of crimson shading;
she doesn't feel the grave's remorseless chasm yawn.
She's still alive today, tomorrow she'll be gone.

VII

O melancholy time! Enchanting to the senses!
My eyes are gladdened by your parting loveliness: 50
the lavish withering of nature, the excesses
of forests richly clad in gold and crimson dress,
their rustling canopies, the gusty breath of freshness,
the hazy, undulating skies, the rare caress
of gentle sun upon my face, the frost's first kisses
and hoary winter's chilling menace in the distance.

VIII

И с каждой осенью я расцветаю вновь;
Здоровью моему полезен русский холод;
К привычкам бытия вновь чувствую любовь:
Чредой слетает сон, чредой находит голод;   60
Легко и радостно играет в сердце кровь,
Желания кипят — я снова счастлив, молод,
Я снова жизни полн — таков мой организм
(Извольте мне простить ненужный прозаизм).

IX

Ведут ко мне коня; в раздолии открытом,
Махая гривою, он всадника несет,
И звонко под его блистающим копытом
Звенит промерзлый дол, и трескается лед.
Но гаснет краткий день, и в камельке забытом
Огонь опять горит — то яркий свет лиет,   70
То тлеет медленно — а я пред ним читаю,
Иль думы долгие в душе моей питаю,

X

И забываю мир — и в сладкой тишине
Я сладко усыплен моим воображеньем,
И пробуждается поэзия во мне:
Душа стесняется лирическим волненьем,
Трепещет и звучит, и ищет, как во сне,
Излиться наконец свободным проявленьем —
И тут ко мне идет незримый рой гостей,
Знакомцы давние, плоды мечты моей.   80

XI

И мысли в голове волнуются в отваге,
И рифмы легкие навстречу им бегут,
И пальцы просятся к перу, перо к бумаге,
Минута — и стихи свободно потекут.
Так дремлет недвижим корабль в недвижной влаге,
Но чу! — матросы вдруг кидаются, ползут
Вверх, вниз — и паруса надулись, ветра полны;
Громада двинулась и рассекает волны.

XII

Плывет. Куда ж нам плыть?...
. . . .   90

VIII

And every year I bloom anew in autumn's rays;
as tonic for my health, the Russian cold's a wonder;
once more I relish the familiar round of days;
sleep finds me in its time, and so, in turn, does hunger;   60
the blood runs joyously and lightly in my veins;
desires brim over; once again I'm happy, younger
and full of life: it's my peculiar organism
(if you'll forgive an out-of-place prosaicism).

IX

I have them bring my horse, and in the wide expanses,
with tossing mane, he bears his rider over ground
that rings aloud beneath each glinting hoof that passes,
as crackling ice and all the frozen vale resound.
The day fades early, and a fire already dances
in its forgotten hearth; it blazes, then dies down   70
and slowly smoulders as I sit and read beside it,
or fall to pondering extended thoughts in quiet.

X

And I forget the world; in sweetest reverie,
I find I'm sweetly lulled by my imagination,
and I feel poetry awakening in me:
my heart is in the grip of lyric excitation;
it throbs with sound, and, as in sleep, it seeks a free
expressive outlet for its inner agitation –
and now I'm visited by swarms of guests unseen,
my old acquaintances, the offspring of my dream.   80

XI

My head is whirling with reflections – bold, exciting –
and rhymes flit eagerly to meet them, row on row;
my fingers seek a pen, the pen a sheet for writing;
another minute and the verses freely flow.
Just so, a tranquil ship at anchor drowses lightly,
but of a sudden sailors scramble to and fro,
aloft, below; the sails take wind, fill out and flutter;
the mighty vessel puts to sea and cleaves the water.

XII

She's under way. Where shall we sail? ......
....   CC

698

* * *

Когда б не смутное влеченье
Чего-то жаждущей души,
Я здесь остался б — наслажденье
Вкушать в неведомой тиши:
Забыл бы всех желаний трепет,
Мечтою б целый мир назвал —
И всё бы слушал этот лепет,
Всё б эти ножки целовал...

699

* * *

Зачем я ею очарован?
Зачем расстаться должен с ней?
Когда б я не был избалован
Цыганской жизнию моей.

———————

Она глядит на вас так нежно,
Она лепечет так небрежно,
Она так тонко весела,
Ее глаза так полны чувством,
Вечор она с таким искусством
Из-под накрытого стола
Мне свою ножку подала.

10

700

ЦЫГАНОЧКА

Колокольчики звенят,
Барабанчики гремят,
  А люди-то, люди —
  Ой, люшеньки-люли!
  А люди-то, люди
На цыганочку глядят.

698

* * *

But for my soul's obscurely asking
and pining for I know not what,
stay I would here for ever, basking
in bliss at this forgetful spot.
Desire's vain tremors never missing,
I'd count the world a dreamy wisp,
those slender feet forever kissing,
forever hearing that sweet lisp...   WA

699

* * *

Why is it that she charms me so?
Why is it she and I must part?
If only I could overthrow
the habits of my gypsy heart!...

———————

She looks at you with tender passion,
she chatters in such careless fashion,
her subtle mirth is meant to tease,
her lovely eyes so warm and shining.
And then last night, as we were dining,
beneath the table with such ease   10
she slid her foot between my knees!   JF

700

GYPSY GIRL

Little bells go *ting, ting, ting*,
little drums go *dring, dring, dring*,
    while people, the people –
    oy, lyoo-pippy leeple! –
    while people, the people
watch the gypsy dance and sing.

А цыганочка то пляшет,
В барабанчики то бьет,
Голубой ширинкой машет,
Заливается-поет: 10
«Я плясунья, я певица,
Ворожить я мастерица».

701

* * *

Чу, пушки грянули! крылатых кораблей
Покрылась облаком станица боевая,
Корабль вбежал в Неву — и вот среди зыбей
Качаясь плавает, как лебедь молодая.

Ликует русский флот. Широкая Нева
Без ветра, в ясный день глубоко взволновалась.
Широкая волна плеснула в острова ...

702

ВОЕВОДА

Польская баллада

Поздно ночью из похода
Воротился воевода.
Он слугам велит молчать;
В спальню кинулся к постеле;
Дернул полог... В самом деле!
Никого; пуста кровать.

И, мрачнее черной ночи,
Он потупил грозны очи,
Стал крутить свой сивый ус...
Рукава назад закинул,   10
Вышел вон, замок задвинул;
«Гей, ты, кликнул, чертов кус!

А зачем нет у забора
Ни собаки, ни затвора?
Я вас, хамы! — Дай ружье;

Now the little Gypsy's whirling,
now she beats her little drum,
now a bright blue scarf she's twirling,
singing till the heartstrings thrum.   10
"Singing, dancing, I'm excelling –
brilliant too at fortune-telling."   RC

701

* * *

The cannon have just fired! The combat-ready flock
of battleships, wings spread, is veiled behind a cloud.
A new ship has been launched in the Nevá, and there
she floats swell-swayed, as would a new-fledged swan.

The Russian fleet resounds with cheers. The broad Nevá
has crested, though the day is windless, calm and bright;
and a broad wave has splashed against the islands' shores ...   RC

702

THE WARLORD

A Polish ballad

Late at night a lord comes riding...
Watch him, through the castle striding
(see the servants shake with dread):
first, the bedroom... well suspected!
Next, the curtains... as expected,
no one there – an empty bed!

Lord of Poland's plains, victorious,
shrewd in love, in battle glorious,
twirls his grey moustache, and then
tests the lock, his eyes half closing,   10
and, filled now with dark supposing,
bellows, "Are you dogs or men?

"You – my serf – suggest a reason
why the door stands wide... What treason
chained the guard-dogs?... Stupid brute!

Приготовь мешок, веревку,
Да сними с гвоздя винтовку.
Ну, за мною!.. Я ж ее!»

Пан и хлопец под забором
Тихим крадутся дозором,   20
Входят в сад — и сквозь ветвей,
На скамейке у фонтана,
В белом платье, видят, панна
И мужчина перед ней.

Говорит он: «Всё пропало,
Чем лишь только я, бывало,
Наслаждался, что любил:
Белой груди воздыханье,
Нежной ручки пожиманье...
Воевода всё купил.   30

Сколько лет тобой страдал я,
Сколько лет тебя искал я!
От меня ты отперлась.
Не искал он, не страдал он;
Серебром лишь побряцал он,
И ему ты отдалась.

Я скакал во мраке ночи
Милой панны видеть очи,
Руку нежную пожать;
Пожелать для новоселья   40
Много лет ей и веселья,
И потом навек бежать.»

Панна плачет и тоскует,
Он колени ей целует,
А сквозь ветви те глядят,
Ружья на земь опустили,
По патрону откусили,
Вбили шомполом заряд.

Подступили осторожно.
«Пан мой, целить мне не можно, —   50
Бедный хлопец прошептал: —
Ветер, что ли; плачут очи,
Дрожь берет; в руках нет мочи,
Порох в полку не попал». —

Did we try to fool our betters?
Bring a musket, knife and fetters;
let me teach you how to shoot..."

Lord and lad go scouting, keeping
stealthy lookout, slowly creeping   20
through the trees at dead of night.
In the grove, despising danger,
stands a young unhappy stranger,
sits a lady dressed in white.

Now he whispers: "All is perished –
all the love I vainly cherished,
all the happiness I sought...
Tender touch of gentle fingers
(how the sad remembrance lingers!...) –
All I've lost the baron's bought.   30

"Through the years I wooed you plainly,
through the years I served you vainly:
all my yearning passed you by.
Did the baron's heart lie bleeding?
Silver coins rang loudly, pleading.
You accepted. Tell me why...

"Through the darkness I have ridden,
ever faithful, still unbidden,
all to kiss your tender hand...
May my sorrows touch you never!   40
Soon I'll say farewell for ever;
soon I'll seek a foreign land."

While he kneels before her, sighing,
hears her long and bitter crying,
lurking spies prepare the gun.
Pour the powder, killing's fuel,
load the bullet, round and cruel,
ramrod home! – the job is done.

"Master, please, why did you choose me?...
I'm a wretched shot – excuse me..."   50
the scared servant tries to say.
"Eyes are stinging, hands are shaking –
what a noise the wind is making...
half the powder's blown away."

«Тише ты, гайдучье племя!
Будешь плакать, дай мне время!
Сыпь на полку... Наводи...
Цель ей в лоб. Левее... выше.
С паном справлюсь сам. Потише;
Прежде я; ты погоди».   60

Выстрел по саду раздался.
Хлопец пана не дождался;
Воевода закричал,
Воевода пошатнулся...
Хлопец видно промахнулся:
Прямо в лоб ему попал.

703

БУДРЫС И ЕГО СЫНОВЬЯ
Литовская баллада

Три у Будрыса сына,
    как и он, три литвина.
Он пришел толковать с молодцами.
    «Дети! седла чините,
    лошадей проводите,
Да точите мечи с бердышами.

Справедлива весть эта:
    на три стороны света
Три замышлены в Вильне похода.
    Паз идет на поляков,   10
    а Ольгерд на прусаков,
А на русских Кестут воевода.

Люди вы молодые,
    силачи удалые
(Да хранят вас литовские боги!),
    Нынче сам я не еду,
    вас я шлю на победу;
Трое вас, вот и три вам дороги.

Будет всем по награде:
    пусть один в Новеграде   20
Поживится от русских добычей.

"Quiet, you whining fool! Tomorrow
be prepared to taste some sorrow.
Check the powder: take your aim…
Left a little… see the beauty?
Higher… Kill her. Do your duty.
Leave the other… he's my game."   60

Then a sudden shot resounded.
Both the lovers stood dumbfounded;
someone shrieked and fell down dead.
Yes, the lad was primed and ready,
held the musket straight and steady –
shot his master through the head.   JC

703

BUDRYS AND HIS SONS

A Lithuanian ballad

With three sons to his name,
Lithuanians (the same),
Budrys came to the youngsters, then said he:
"Sharpen axes and swords, boys;
have them fetch you your horses;
get your saddles all mended and ready.

"Against three different lands
three campaigns we have planned
here in Vilnius: we need to make war. So,
son Olgérd, attack Prussia;   10
son Kestút , invade Russia;
and son Paz lead your men against Warsaw.

"You're all strapping and young,
and as strong as they come.
(Guard them well, Lithuanian deities!)
I myself shall not go –
be victorious, though.
You are three: fight with threefold audacity.

"For each son there's a prize:
one for Nóvgorod vies,   20
and will win from that city great plunder.

Жены их, как в окладах,
в драгоценных нарядах;
Домы полны; богат их обычай.

А другой от прусаков,
от проклятых крыжаков,
Может много достать дорогого,
Денег с целого света,
сукон яркого цвета;
Янтаря — что песку там морского.   30

Третий с Пазом на ляха
пусть ударит без страха:
В Польше мало богатства и блеску,
Сабель взять там не худо;
но уж верно оттуда
Привезет он мне на дом невестку.

Нет на свете царицы
краше польской девицы.
Весела — что котенок у печки —
И как роза румяна,
а бела, что сметана;   40
Очи светятся будто две свечки!

Был я, дети, моложе,
в Польшу съездил я тоже
И оттуда привез себе жонку;
Вот и век доживаю,
а всегда вспоминаю
Про нее, как гляжу в ту сторонку».

Сыновья с ним простились
и в дорогу пустились.
Ждет, пождет их старик домовитый,   50
Дни за днями проводит,
ни один не приходит.
Будрыс думал: уж, видно, убиты!

Снег на землю валится,
сын дорогою мчится,
И под буркою ноша большая.
«Чем тебя наделили?
что там? Ге! не рубли ли?»
— «Нет, отец мой; полячка младая».   60

There the merchants' successes
   buy the women fine dresses,
and their dwellings are rich beyond wonder!

   "Then, Olgérd, from the Prussians
   (Devil take those knight-ruffians)
you can win yourself treasures galore:
   gold from north and from south,
   and luxuriant cloth –
and there's amber like sand on the shore.   30

   "To the Poles the third goes –
   Paz, don't spare them your blows.
In resources their land's not excelling;
   take their swords – no bad thing –
   and be certain to bring
me a daughter-in-law for my dwelling.

   "Than those maidens no queen
   has a charm more serene:
they're content as a cat by the stove is.
   Like two candle flames gleam   40
   their bright eyes; smooth as cream
is their skin, and their cheeks glow like roses.

   "When a youngster like you,
   boys, I rode out there too,
found a good Polish missus and brought her;
   now with years I've declined,
   but still call her to mind
every time that I look to that quarter."

So the three go their ways,
   while the old fellow stays;   50
waiting, waiting, he keeps the fires burning;
   but so many days fled
   that his sons he thought dead,
for not one of them yet was returning.

Snow has spread like a quilt;
   a son gallops full tilt –
in his cloak holds a bundle quite massive.
   "Well then, what was your share?
   Is it roubles in there?"
"Father, no: it's a young Polish lassie."   60

Снег пушистый валится;
всадник с ношею мчится,
Черной буркой ее покрывая.
«Что под буркой такое?
Не сукно ли цветное?»
— «Нет, отец мой; полячка младая.»

Снег на землю валится,
третий с ношею мчится,
Черной буркой ее прикрывает.
Старый Будрыс хлопочет   70
и спросить уж не хочет,
А гостей на три свадьбы сзывает.

704

ПЕТЕРБУРГ

Вступление в Медного всадника

На берегу пустынных волн
Стоял *он*, дум великих полн,
И вдаль глядел. Пред ним широко
Река неслася; бедный чёлн
По ней стремился одиноко.
По мшистым, топким берегам
Чернели избы здесь и там,
Приют убогого чухонца;
И лес, неведомый лучам
В тумане спрятанного солнца,   10
Кругом шумел.
                          И думал он:
Отсель грозить мы будем шведу,
Здесь будет город заложен
На зло надменному соседу.
Природой здесь нам суждено
В Европу прорубить окно,1
Ногою твердой стать при море.
Сюда по новым им волнам
Все флаги в гости будут к нам,
И запируем на просторе.   20

Прошло сто лет, и юный град,
Полнощных стран краса и диво,

Downy snow forms a quilt;
comes a horseman full tilt,
and a bundle beneath his cloak has he.
   "So what's that you've got there?
   Is it cloth rich and fair?"
"Father, no: it's a young Polish lassie."

Snow has quilted the track.
With a cloak-covered sack
the third son at a gallop is heading.
   But old Budrys, on fire,   70
   doesn't wait to enquire –
summons guests to his sons' triple wedding.   JH & RC

704

ST PETERSBURG

Introduction to The Bronze Horseman

On shores where lonely waters lapped,
stood *he*, in thoughts momentous rapt,
and peered afar. Before his gaze,
a broad expanse of river swept,
a skiff forlornly rode the waves,
and, dark against the mossy ground,
the scattered hovels that were found
gave refuge to the wretched Finn.
Unfathomed by a sun that in
the mist lay hidden, woods profound   10
about him murmured.
              Then he thought:
It's here, a menace to the Swede,
we'll found a city, so to thwart
our haughty neighbour and his breed;
and here, at nature's own behest,
we'll hew a window on the West,
stand fast, one foot upon the shore;
and, greeting every flag that flies
on waves they've never plied before,
we'll revel under spacious skies.   20

A hundred years passed onward then
as to the North's delight and wonder,

Из тьмы лесов, из топи блат
Вознесся пышно, горделиво;
Где прежде финский рыболов,
Печальный пасынок природы,
Один у низких берегов
Бросал в неведомые воды
Свой ветхой невод, ныне там
По оживленным берегам   30
Громады стройные теснятся
Дворцов и башен; корабли
Толпой со всех концов земли
К богатым пристаням стремятся;
В гранит оделася Нева;
Мосты повисли над водами;
Темно-зелеными садами
Ее покрылись острова,
И перед младшею столицей
Померкла старая Москва,   40
Как перед новою царицей
Порфироносная вдова.

Люблю тебя, Петра творенье,
Люблю твой строгий, стройный вид,
Невы державное теченье,
Береговой ее гранит,
Твоих оград узор чугунный,
Твоих задумчивых ночей
Прозрачный сумрак, блеск безлунный,
Когда я в комнате моей   50
Пишу, читаю без лампады,
И ясны спящие громады
Пустынных улиц, и светла
Адмиралтейская игла,
И, не пуская тьму ночную
На золотые небеса,
Одна заря сменить другую
Спешит, дав ночи полчаса
Люблю зимы твоей жестокой
Недвижный воздух и мороз,   60
Бег санок вдоль Невы широкой,
Девичьи лица ярче роз,
И блеск, и шум, и говор балов,
А в час пирушки холостой
Шипенье пенистых бокалов
И пунша пламень голубой.

from murky wood and marshy fen,
a city grew in pride and splendour.
Where once the godforsaken Finn,
pathetic, nature's poor relation,
alone beside the water's brim
cast weathered nets in desolation,
now palaces stand side by side
along the bustling riverside, 30
and graceful spires rise over these,
while vessels crowding in to berth
from every corner of the earth
lie off the richly laden quays.
Nevá has decked herself in stone;
above her, bridges hang suspended;
the islands now are overgrown
with shady gardens green and tended.
Old Moscow pales beside her rival;
a dowager in purple, she 40
gives way before the new arrival,
who mounts the throne in majesty.

I love you, work of Peter's making,
so graceful and austere in tone,
Nevá imperiously taking
her course by splendid banks of stone,
the lacework of your iron railing,
the moonless sheen of pensive night,
the twilight luminous, unfailing.
Retiring to my room, I write 50
without a lamp's illumination,
and see, in clear delineation,
each sleeping edifice and, higher,
the glowing Admiralty spire!
And never giving darkness leave
to mount the golden skies and lour,
the morning hastens to relieve
the evening after half an hour.
I love your winter's cruel ways –
the air so still, the waters frozen, 60
the river swept by racing sleighs
and girlish faces bright as roses,
the glitter of the balls, the gossip,
and late, at bachelors' soirées,
the froth of effervescent goblets
and flowing punch's azure blaze.

Люблю воинственную живость
Потешных Марсовых полей,
Пехотных ратей и коней
Однообразную красивость,   70
В их стройно зыблемом строю
Лоскутья сих знамен победных,
Сиянье шапок этих медных,
На сквозь простреленных в бою.
Люблю, военная столица,
Твоей твердыни дым и гром,
Когда полнощная царица
Дарует сына в царской дом,
Или победу над врагом
Россия снова торжествует,   80
Или, взломав свой синий лед,
Нева к морям его несет
И, чуя вешни дни, ликует.

Красуйся, град Петров, и стой
Неколебимо как Россия,
Да умирится же с тобой
И побежденная стихия;
Вражду и плен старинный свой
Пусть волны финские забудут
И тщетной злобою не будут   90
Тревожить вечный сон Петра!...

705

СУМАСШЕСТВИЕ

Не дай мне бог сойти с ума.
Нет, легче посох и сума;
    Нет, легче труд и глад.
Не то, чтоб разумом моим
Я дорожил; не то, чтоб с ним
    Расстаться был не рад:

Когда б оставили меня
На воле, как бы резво я
    Пустился в темный лес!
Я пел бы в пламенном бреду,   10
Я забывался бы в чаду
    Нестройных, чудных грез.

I love the animated muster
of forces on the Field of Mars,
the stepping horses, men in arms,
their uniformity and lustre,   70
the ranks, unfurling in the wind,
of tattered flags that won their day,
the glinting hats of brass, undimmed
though pierced by gunfire in the fray.
I love, war capital, your fortress,
the smoke and thunder of each gun
saluting when the northern empress
delivers to her house a son,
or when, another victory won,
the Russians lift triumphant voices,   80
or when Nevá, now breaking free,
conveys her deep-blue ice to sea
and, catching wind of spring, rejoices.

Increase in beauty, Peter's child,
and stand, like Russia, firm, unyielding!
May seas with you be reconciled,
your victory at last conceding.
Let Finnish waters set aside
a hatred born of long subjection,
lest they, with futile insurrection,   90
disturb the tsar's eternal rest!   CC

705

INSANITY

Dear God, don't let me go insane!
Better a beggar's bag and cane,
    or hunger and travail.
It isn't that I prize my mind,
and thoughts of losing it, I find,
    are not without appeal.

If left to wander as I would,
I'd plunge into a murky wood
    and roam among the trees.
I'd sing delirious refrains   10
and lose myself within a haze
    of strange, disjointed dreams.

И я б заслушивался волн,
И я глядел бы, счастья полн,
　　В пустые небеса;
И силен, волен был бы я,
Как вихорь, роющий поля,
　　Ломающий леса.

Да вот беда: сойди с ума,
И страшен будешь как чума;　　　　20
　　Как раз тебя запрут,
Посадят на цепь дурака
И сквозь решетку как зверка
　　Дразнить тебя придут.

А ночью слышать буду я
Не голос яркий соловья,
　　Не шум глухой дубров —
А крик товарищей моих
Да брань смотрителей ночных
　　Да визг, да звон оков.　　　　30

706

КУМИРЫ

　　　Толпа глухая,
Крылатой новизны любовница слепая,
Надменных баловней меняет каждый день,
И катятся стуча с ступени на ступень
Кумиры их, вчера увенчанные ею.

707

* * *

Воды глубокие
Плавно текут.
Люди премудрые
Тихо живут.

I'd listen raptly to the waves,
and, full of happiness, I'd gaze
   at empty skies, and oh,
how powerful I'd be and free,
a whirlwind ravaging the lea
   and laying forests low!

But once you're quite bereft of sense,
they'll fear you like the pestilence   20
   and lock you up, poor fool.
Behind the bars, chained hand and foot,
you'll be subjected, like a brute,
   to taunts and ridicule.

The night will resonate no more
with murmurs of the forest or
   the nightingale's refrains.
Amid the cries of comrades near
and curses of the guards, I'll hear
   the clanking of my chains.   CC

706

IDOLS

      The populace, unheeding,
who undiscerningly adore things new and fleeting,
their bragging favourites exchange from day to day;
then, thumping as they fall, the images that they
revered the day before roll down from stair to stair.   RC

707

* * *

Placidly flowing
are streams that run deep;
those who're most knowing
to placid ways keep.   RC

1834

708

* * *

Я возмужал среди печальных бурь,
И дней моих поток, так долго мутный,
Теперь утих дремотою минутной
И отразил небесную лазурь.

Надолго ли?... а кажется прошли
Дни мрачных бурь, дни горьких искушений.

709

ПЕСНИ ЗАПАДНЫХ СЛАВЯН

I. ВИДЕНИЕ КОРОЛЯ

Король ходит большими шагами
Взад и вперед по палатам;
Люди спят — королю лишь не спится:
Короля султан осаждает,
Голову отсечь ему грозится
И в Стамбул отослать ее хочет.

Часто он подходит к окошку;
Не услышит ли какого шума?
Слышит, воет ночная птица,
Она чует беду неминучу,
Скоро ей искать новой кровли
Для своих птенцов горемычных.
Не сова воет в Ключе-граде,
Не луна Ключ-город озаряет,
В церкви божией гремят барабаны,

1834

708

* * *

I've persevered amid the tempest's blast,
and now the turbid current of my life
has found a quiet haven from the past,
reflecting in its depths the azure sky.

But will it stay?... I'd like to think they're gone,
those days of storm, of dark and bitter longing...   JF

709

BALLADS OF THE WESTERN SLAVS

I. THE KING'S VISION

The king walks with wide-striding paces
up and down through the length of his chambers.
All now sleep – but the king is not sleeping:
the sultan has newly besieged him,
and he threatens to cut the king's head off
and send it to Istanbul for a trophy.

The king keeps approaching the window:
will he hear any sound, any signal?
But he hears just a night bird now crying:
she senses the woes that are nearing;   10
she'll soon need a new roof to nest in,
new shelter for chicks that are helpless.
But there's no owl that cries in Ključ city,
and there's no moon to shine on Ključ city.
Loud drums in the church are now beating,

Вся свечами озарена церковь.
Но никто барабанов не слышит,
Никто света в церкви божией не видит,
Лишь король то слышал и видел.

Из палат своих он выходит   20
И идет один в божию церковь.
Стал на паперти, дверь отворяет…
Ужасом в нем замерло сердце,
Но великую творит он молитву
И спокойно в церковь божию входит.

Тут он видит чудное виденье:
На помосте валяются трупы,
Между ими хлещет кровь ручьями,
Как потоки осени дождливой.
Он идет, шагая через трупы,   30
Кровь по щиколку ему досягает…

Горе! в церкви турки и татары
И предатели, враги богумилы.
На амвоне сам султан безбожный,
Держит он наголо саблю,
Кровь по сабле свежая струится
С вострия до самой рукояти.
Короля незапный обнял холод:
Тут же видит он отца и брата.
Пред султаном старик бедный справа,   40
Униженно стоя на коленах,
Подает ему свою корону;
Слева, также стоя на коленах,
Его сын, Радивой окаянный,
Бусурманскою чалмою покрытый
(С тою самою веревкою, которой
Удавил он несчастного старца),
Край полы у султана целует,
Как холоп, наказанный фалангой.

И султан безбожный, усмехаясь,   50
Взял корону, растоптал ногами,
И промолвил потом Радивою:
«Будь над Боснией моей ты властелином,
Для гяур-християн беглербеем».
И отступник бил челом султану,
Трижды пол окровавленный целуя.

and the building is lit up by candles.
But nobody hears the drums rolling,
and nobody sees the lights glimmer;
just the king hears the drum, sees the candles.

So forth from his chambers he ventures   20
to walk to the church unattended.
He opens the door in the porchway...
His heart nearly dies with the horror,
but a vehement prayer he gives voice to
and calmly steps in through the entrance.

There a vision he sees quite appalling:
dead bodies lie thick on the paving,
with blood flowing round them in rivers
like torrents of rain in the autumn.
On he walks, stepping over the corpses,   30
and the blood nearly reaches his ankles...

What horror!... In the church Turks and Tatars
and enemy Bogomil traitors!
Near the altar the impious sultan
stands, with sabre unsheathed held before him;
fresh blood down the sabre is streaming
from tip of the blade to the handle.
The king is gripped tight by a coldness.
He sees now his father and brother:
close by, to the right of the sultan   40
the old one is brokenly kneeling
and offers his crown in obeisance;
to the left, and in like manner kneeling,
is his son, Radivoj the accursèd,
head wrapped in an infidel turban
(and holding the rope with which earlier
he'd strangled his piteous father),
now kissing the hem of the sultan,
like a slave bastinadoed for misdeeds.

Then the impious sultan, with laughter,   50
stamped a foot on the crown that he'd taken,
and young Radivoj he commanded:
"Now that Bosnia is mine, be its ruler,
be the governor of infidel Christians."
The traitor bowed low to the sultan,
thrice kissing the still-bloodied floor stones.

И султан прислужников кликнул
И сказал: «Дать кафтан Радивою!
Не бархатный кафтан, не парчовый,
А содрать на кафтан Радивоя 60
Кожу с брата его родного».
Бусурмане на короля наскочили,
Донага всего его раздели,
Атаганом ему кожу вспороли,
Стали драть руками и зубами,
Обнажили мясо и жилы,
И до самых костей ободрали,
И одели кожею Радивоя.

Громко мученик господу взмолился:
«Прав ты, боже, меня наказуя! 70
Плоть мою предай на растерзанье,
Лишь помилуй мне душу, Иисусе!»
При сем имени церковь задрожала,
Всё внезапно утихнуло, померкло, —
Всё исчезло — будто не бывало.

И король ощупью в потемках
Кое-как до двери добрался
И с молитвою на улицу вышел.
Было тихо. С высокого неба
Город белый луна озаряла. 80
Вдруг взвилась из-за города бомба,
И пошли бусурмане на приступ.

II. ЯНКО МАРНАВИЧ

Что в разъездах бей Янко Марнавич?
Что ему дома не сидится?
Отчего двух ночей он сряду
Под одною кровлей не ночует?
Али недруги его могучи?
Аль боится он кровомщенья?

Не боится бей Янко Марнавич
Ни врагов своих, ни кровомщенья,
Но он бродит, как гайдук бездомный,
С той поры, как Кирила умер. 10

В церкви Спаса они братовались,
И были по Богу братья;

The sultan then summoned his servants.
"Radivoj's to be given a kaftan –
not figured in silk nor of velvet,
but a kaftan of skin you shall make him,   60
one torn from the flesh of his brother."
The infidels leapt from the platform
and stripped the king bare of his clothing;
then with sabres they slashed at his body
and with hands and with teeth tore its covering,
flaying skin from raw sinew and muscle,
exposing the bones as they did so.
Then they dressed Radivoj in the kaftan.

The king-martyr prayed loud to his Saviour:
"O Lord, you are right to chastise me   70
and to give up my flesh to tormentors,
but spare my soul, Jesus, I beg you!"
At this name the whole church started shaking;
all went suddenly silent and darkened –
all vanished, like dreams fly on waking.

Then, feeling his way in the darkness,
the king somehow groped to the doorway
and saying a prayer left the building.
It was quiet. From the night sky above him
the moon shone down bright on the city,   80
then suddenly boomed an explosion:
the heathens had started their onslaught.   AR & RC

II. JANKO MARNAVIĆ

Why's he roaming, Bey Janko Marnavić?
Why at home does he not take some respite?
And why does he for two nights together
not under the same roof lie sleeping?
Are there powerful foes that pursue him?
Or is he at risk in a blood feud?

Not at risk, not Bey Janko Marnavić –
he fears neither foes nor a blood feud;
but he's lived on the run like an outlaw
from the time of the death of Kirila.   10

In St Saviour's they'd vowed to be brothers –
and brothers in God they were truly –

Но Кирила несчастливый умер
От руки им избранного брата.

Веселое было пированье,
Много пили меду и горелки;
Охмелели, обезумели гости,
Два могучие беи побранились.

Янко выстрелил из своего пистоля,
Но рука его пьяная дрожала.   20
В супротивника своего не попал он,
А попал он в своего друга.
С того времени он, тоскуя, бродит,
Словно вол, ужаленный змиею.

Наконец он на родину воротился
И вошел в церковь святого Спаса.
Там день целый он молился Богу,
Горько плача и жалостно рыдая.
Ночью он пришел к себе на дом
И отужинал со своей семьею,   30
Потом лег и жене своей молвил;
«Посмотри, жена, ты в окошко.
Видишь ли церковь Спаса отселе?»
Жена встала, в окошко поглядела
И сказала: «На дворе полночь,
За рекою густые туманы,
За туманом ничего не видно».
Повернулся Янко Марнавич
И тихонько стал читать молитву.

Помолившись, он опять ей молвил: 40
«Посмотри, что ты видишь в окошко?»
И жена, поглядев, отвечала:
«Вижу, вон, малый огонечек
Чуть-чуть брезжит в темноте за рекою».
Улыбнулся Янко Марнавич
И опять стал тихонько молиться.

Помолясь, он опять жене молвил:
«Отвори-ка, женка, ты окошко:
Посмотри, что там еще видно?»
И жена, поглядев, отвечала: 50
«Вижу я на реке сиянье,
Близится оно к нашему дому».

but death came to hapless Kirila
at the hand of the brother he'd chosen.

The feasting was merry and mirthful;
mead and vodka were drunk by the glassful,
and the drink made men tipsy and heedless,
and two mighty Beys picked a quarrel.

Yanko fired from his full-loaded pistol,
but drunk was his hand, and it trembled.   20
He missed as he fired at his rival,
and instead the lead lodged in his brother.
Since then in deep grief he has wandered,
like an ox that a viper has bitten.

At last he came home to his birthplace
and went into the Church of St Saviour.
All day there he stood to God praying,
weeping bitterly, piteously sobbing,
then back he came home towards nightfall,
took his seat with the family for supper,   30
then lay by his wife in bed, saying:
"Dear wife, please now look through the window.
Can you see hence the Church of St Saviour?"
His wife rose and looked through the window,
and said: "Outside it's dark, towards midnight.
Thick mist now hangs over the river,
and through the thick mist I see nothing."
On his side then turned Janko Marnavić,
and started to say a prayer softly.

When he'd done, to his wife he repeated: 40
"Tell me, wife, what you see through the window."
His wife looked once more, and then answered:
"I see a small light in the distance,
just a glimmer out there past the river."
He smiled then, did Janko Marnavić,
and started again to pray softly.

When he'd prayed, then a third time he asked her:
"Little wife, please now open the window,
and tell me what more you can see there."
His wife looked a third time, then answered: 50
"I see on the river a radiance,
and it's coming this way ever closer."

Бей вздохнул и с постели свалился.
Тут и смерть ему приключилась.

III. БИТВА У ЗЕНИЦЫ-ВЕЛИКОЙ

Радивой поднял желтое знамя:
Он идет войной на бусурмана.
А далматы, завидя наше войско,
Свои длинные усы закрутили,
На бекрень надели свои шапки
И сказали: «Возьмите нас с собою:
Мы хотим воевать бусурманов».
Радивой дружелюбно их принял
И сказал им: «Милости просим!»

Перешли мы заповедную речку,   10
Стали жечь турецкие деревни,
А жидов на деревьях вешать.
Беглербей со своими бошняками
Против нас пришел из Банялуки;
Но лишь только заржали их кони
И на солнце их кривые сабли
Засверкали у Зеницы-Великой,
Разбежались изменники далматы;
Окружили мы тогда Радивоя
И сказали: «Господь Бог поможет,   20
Мы домой воротимся с тобою
И расскажем эту битву нашим детям».
Стали биться мы тогда жестоко,
Всяк из нас троих воинов стоил;
Кровью были покрыты наши сабли
С острия по самой рукояти.
Но когда через речку стали
Тесной кучкою мы переправляться,
Селихтар с крыла на нас ударил
С новым войском, с конницею свежей.   30
Радивой сказал тогда нам: «Дети,
Слишком много собак-бусурманов,
Нам управиться с ними невозможно.
Кто не ранен, в лес беги скорее
И спасайся там от Селихтара».
Всех-то нас оставалось двадцать,
Все друзья, родные Радивою,
Но и тут нас пало девятнадцать.
Закричал Георгий Радивою:

With a sigh the Bey fell from the bedstead.
Death had come, and his life now was ended.   RC

III. THE BATTLE AT GREAT ZENICA

Radivoj raised the bright-yellow banner,
all set to wage war on the Muslims.
The Dalmatians, on seeing our soldiers,
twirled tighter their lengthy moustaches,
and tilting their caps at an angle,
said: "Let us support you in battle:
we too wish to combat the Muslims."
Radivoj was well pleased by their offer,
and said with a smile: "You are welcome!"

We crossed the prohibited river,   10
setting fire to the infidel homesteads
and hanging the Jews from the tree boughs.
The Pasha with his Bosniak horsemen
rode out from Banja Luka against us;
But just as their horses neared, neighing,
and scimitars shimmered and sparkled
in the rays of the sun by Zenica,
the traitorous Dalmatians fast scattered;
Radivoj we then quickly encircled,
and said: "It is God who will help us,   20
we'll bring you safe home soon among us
and relive this day with our children."
Upon which we pitched into battle,
with each man worth three as he duelled;
our sabres were gory and bloodstained
from blade tip right down to the handle.
But then when we came to the river
and together began to crowd over,
the Pasha's commander outflanked us
with troops that were new, and fresh horses.   30
Radivoj therefore turned and addressed us:
"My lads, there are too many Muslims:
the dogs have us fully outnumbered.
Let him who's not wounded seek safety
and flee from the foe to the forest."
Our numbers were now down to twenty,
Radivoj's loyal friends and close kinsmen,
but nineteen then fell as we faltered,
and Đorđe, Radivoj's sole companion,

«Ты садись, Радивой, поскорее   40
На коня моего вороного;
Через речку вплавь переправляйся,
Конь тебя из погибели вымчит».
Радивой Георгия не послушал,
Наземь сел, поджав под себя ноги.
Тут враги на него наскочили,
Отрубили голову Радивою.

IV. ФЕОДОР И ЕЛЕНА

....
....
Стамати был стар и бессилен,
А Елена молода и проворна;
Она так-то его оттолкнула,
Что ушел он охая да хромая.
Поделом тебе, старый бесстыдник!
Ай да баба! отделалась славно!

Вот Стамати стал думать думу:
Как ему погубить бы Елену?   10
Он к жиду лиходею приходит,
От него он требует совета.
Жид сказал: «Ступай на кладбище,
Отыщи под каменьями жабу
И в горшке сюда принеси мне».

На кладбище приходит Стамати,
Отыскал под каменьями жабу
И в горшке жиду ее приносит.
Жид на жабу проливает воду,
Нарекает жабу Иваном   20
(Грех велик христианское имя
Нарещи такой поганой твари!).
Они жабу всю потом искололи,
И ее—ее ж кровью напоили;
Напоивши, заставили жабу
Облизать поспелую сливу.

И Стамати мальчику молвил:
«Отнеси ты Елене эту сливу
От моей племянницы в подарок».
Принес мальчик Елене сливу,   30
А Елена тотчас ее съела.

cried aloud: "Radivoj, mount up quickly,   40
take your seat on my raven-black stallion;
he shall swim with you over the river,
and shall carry you fast out of danger."
Radivoj did not heed Đorđe's counsel,
but sat on the ground to recover.
There the enemy pounced as he rested;
Radivoj's head was struck from his body.   AR

IV. TODOR AND JELENA

....
....
Stamati was ageing and weakly;
Jelena was youthful and agile.
She pushed him away once in anger,
and off he went grumbling and limping.
Serves him right, then, the shameless old shambler!
Well done, girl, to get rid of that one!

But Stamati was planning and plotting:
how best to put paid to Jelena?   10
He turned to a Jew that he knew of
to ask for his aid and his counsel.
The Jew told him: "Go to the graveyard,
and find a toad under a gravestone,
then bring it to me in a pitcher."

Stamati set out for the graveyard.
He found a toad under a gravestone
and returned with it shut in a pitcher.
The Jew filled the pitcher with water
and named the fat toad in it Jovan   20
(a sin for a creature so pagan
to be given a name that is Christian!).
They pricked the toad's body all over,
made it drink of the blood that flowed from it,
then they took the toad out of the pitcher,
and gave it a ripe plum for licking.

Stamati now summoned a servant.
"Now take this ripe plum to Jelena,
a gift from my niece it is, tell her."
The lad took the plum to Jelena,   30
and she at once seized it and ate it.

Только съела поганую сливу,
Показалось бедной молодице,
Что змия у ней в животе шевелится.
Испугалась молодая Елена;
Она кликнула сестру свою меньшую.
Та ее молоком напоила,
Но змия в животе всё шевелилась.

Стала пухнуть прекрасная Елена,
Стали баить: Елена брюхата.   40
Каково-то будет ей от мужа,
Как воротится он из-за моря!
И Елена стыдится и плачет,
И на улицу выдти не смеет,
День сидит, ночью ей не спится,
Поминутно сестрице повторяет:
«Что скажу я милому мужу?»

Круглый год проходит, и — Феодор
Воротился на свою сторонку.
Вся деревня бежит к нему на встречу,   50
Все его приветно поздравляют;
Но в толпе не видит он Елены,
Как ни ищет он ее глазами.
«Где ж Елена?» наконец он молвил;
Кто смутился, а кто усмехнулся,
Но никто не отвечал ни слова.

Пришел он в дом свой — и видит,
На постеле сидит его Елена.
«Встань, Елена», говорит Феодор.
Она встала, — он взглянул сурово.   60
«Господин ты мой, клянусь Богом
И пречистым именем Марии,
Пред тобою я не виновата,
Испортили меня злые люди».

Но Феодор жене не поверил:
Он отсек ей голову по плечи.
Отсекши, он сам себе молвил:
«Не сгублю я невинного младенца,
Из нее выну его живого,
При себе воспитывать буду.   70
Я увижу, на кого он походит,

As soon as the poor girl had swallowed
the ripe plum, it seemed that inside her
she had a snake writhing and twisting.
Jelena was now very frightened;
she called her young sister to help her,
who fed her warm milk to relieve her,
but still the snake writhed in her stomach.

The lovely Jelena grew swollen.
Folk started to say: "She's expecting!   40
She'll have to explain to her husband,
as soon as he's back from his travels."
Jelena was shamefaced and weeping;
she dared not walk out on the roadway,
sat around all day, lay all night sleepless.
She was constantly asking her sister:
"What on earth shall I tell my dear husband?"

A year passed – then finally Todor
came back to the homeland he'd yearned for.
All the villagers ran out to meet him,   50
made him welcome and gave him their greetings;
but wherever he looked in the mêlée,
he failed to see his Jelena.
"Where's Jelena?" he finally asked them.
Some blushed, others smiled at him wryly,
but none of them answered his question.

He came to his house, and then saw her
sitting there on a bed, his Jelena.
"Jelena, stand up," said her husband.
She stood – and he looked at her grimly.   60
"My master, I beg you to listen:
I swear before God and Our Lady,
that I stand here quite guiltless before you;
I fell for the schemes of bad people."

Todor could not believe his wife's protests:
so he severed her head from her shoulders.
Having done so, he uttered this promise:
"I shall spare the poor baby she carries,
and take him alive from her body;
I shall raise him and keep him beside me.   70
Then I'll see who it is he resembles.

Так наверно отца его узнаю
И убью своего злодея».

Распорол он мертвое тело.
Что ж! — на место милого дитяти,
Он черную жабу находит.
Взвыл Феодор: «Горе мне, убийце!
Я сгубил Елену понапрасну:
Предо мной она была невинна,
А испортили ее злые люди».   80

Поднял он голову Елены,
Стал ее целовать умиленно,
И мертвые уста отворились,
Голова Елены провещала:
«Я невинна. Жид и старый Стамати
Черной жабой меня окормили».
Тут опять уста ее сомкнулись,
И язык перестал шевелиться.

И Феодор Стамати зарезал,
А жида убил, как собаку,   90
И отпел по жене панихиду.

V. ВЛАХ В ВЕНЕЦИИ

Как покинула меня Парасковья,
И как я с печали промотался,
Вот далмат пришел ко мне лукавый:
«Ступай, Дмитрий, в морской ты город,
Там цехины, что у нас каменья.

Там солдаты в шелковых кафтанах,
И только что пьют да гуляют;
Скоро там ты разбогатеешь
И воротишься в шитом долимане
С кинжалом на серебряной цепочке.   10

И тогда-то играй себе на гуслях;
Красавицы побегут к окошкам
И подарками тебя закидают.
Эй, послушайся! отправляйся морем;
Воротись, когда разбогатеешь».

I'll be certain to spot the child's father,
and then I'll put paid to the blackguard."

He cut open his wife's lifeless body,
but there, in the place of a baby,
he found a black toad in her belly.
Todor cried out in anguish: "I'm finished!
I've murdered Jelena for nothing:
she *did* stand there guiltless before me –
she *did* fall for schemes of bad people."   80

He picked up the head of Jelena,
and tenderly started to kiss it;
her lips, though dead, opened before him,
and forth from her head he heard spoken:
"I am guiltless. The Jew and Stamati –
they used a black toad to destroy me."
Her mouth then shut tight as beforehand,
and the tongue ceased all movement inside it.

Todor then plunged his knife in Stamati,
put the Jew, like a dog, to death too, and   90
had a requiem sung for Jelena.   AR & RC

V. A SLAV IN VENICE

When my darling Paraskeva had left me
and from sorrow I'd squandered my money,
a crafty Dalmatian approached me.
"To the great marine city go, Dmitar.
Gold coins there are common as pebbles.

"There soldiers dress up in silk kaftans,
and spend their time idling and drinking.
You'll soon win there riches aplenty,
and stroll in a finely trimmed dolman,
with a knife on a chainlet of silver.   10

"And then you must play on your gusli –
have pretty girls run to their windows
and throw you down showers of presents.
So do as I say: take a ship there
and come back home once you are wealthy."

Я послушался лукавого далмата.
Вот живу в этой мраморной лодке.
Но мне скучно, хлеб их мне, как камень,
Я неволен, как на привязи собака.

Надо мною женщины смеются,   20
Когда слово я по-нашему молвлю;
Наши здесь язык свой позабыли,
Позабыли и наш родной обычай;
Я завял, как пересаженный кустик.

Как у нас бывало кого встречу,
Слышу: «Здравствуй, Дмитрий Алексеич!»
Здесь не слышу доброго привета,
Не дождуся ласкового слова;
Здесь я точно бедная мурашка,
Занесенная в озеро бурей.   30

VI. ГАЙДУК ХРИЗИЧ

В пещере, на острых каменьях
Притаился храбрый гайдук Хризич.
С ним жена его Катерина,
С ним его два милые сына,
Им нельзя из пещеры выдти.
Стерегут их недруги злые.
Коли чуть они голову подымут,
В них прицелятся тотчас сорок ружей.
Они три дня, три ночи не ели,
Пили только воду дождевую,   10
Накопленную во впадине камня.
На четвертый взошло красно солнце,
И вода во впадине иссякла.
Тогда молвила, вздохнувши, Катерина:
«Господь Бог! помилуй наши души!»
И упала мертвая на землю.
Хризич, глядя на нее, не заплакал,
Сыновья плакать при нем не смели;
Они только очи отирали,
Как от них отворачивался Хризич.   20
В пятый день старший сын обезумел,
Стал глядеть он на мертвую матерь,
Будто волк на спящую козу.
Его брат, видя то, испугался.
Закричал он старшему брату:

I heeded the crafty Dalmatian.
Now I live on this raft built of marble,
but it's irksome; their food's hard and tasteless;
I'm a prisoner, a dog on a tether.

The women all look round and mock me   20
when I speak any words in my own tongue;
our folk have forgotten their language
and remember our customs no longer;
I wilt like a shrub that's transplanted.

At home folk I met used to greet me,
"Good day to you, Dmitar Aleksejić!"
But here I get no kindly greeting,
no word of affection or friendship;
I'm like a poor ant in this city,
blown in the lagoon by a tempest.   RC

VI. HRIZIĆ THE HAJDUK

In a cavern, among the sharp boulders,
brave Hrizić the hajduk had hidden.
His wife Katarina was with him –
the two sons he loved were with him also.
They dared not go forth from the cavern,
for enemy forces were watching.
If a head of just one should appear there,
it would bring to the aim forty rifles.
Three days and three nights they ate nothing,
for drinking they'd rainwater only,   10
from rocks where it lay in a hollow.
The sun on the fourth day rose brightly
and dried up the rain in the hollow.
Then spoke with a sigh Katarina:
"Lord God, on our souls grant thy mercy!"
Then she fell to the ground cold and lifeless.
Hrizić shed, though, no tear as he watched her,
and his sons dared not weep in his presence;
they just wiped the tears from their eyelids
when Hrizić was no longer looking.   20
On the fifth day one lad lost his senses –
started eyeing the corpse of his mother
as a wolf eyes a goat that is sleeping.
The younger lad looked on with horror.
He cried out at once to his brother:

235

«Милый брат! не губи свою душу;
Ты напейся горячей моей крови,
А умрем мы голодною смертью,
Станем мы выходить из могилы
Кровь сосать наших недругов спящих».   30
Хризич встал и промолвил: «Полно!
Лучше пуля, чем голод и жажда».
И все трое со скалы в долину
Сбежали, как бешеные волки.
Семерых убил из них каждый,
Семью пулями каждый из них прострелен;
Головы враги у них отсекли
И на копья свои насадили, —
А и тут глядеть на них не смели.
Так им страшен был Хризич с сыновьями.   40

VII. ПОХОРОННАЯ ПЕСНЯ

Иакинфа Маглановича

С Богом, в дальнюю дорогу!
Путь найдешь ты, слава Богу.
Светит месяц; ночь ясна;
Чарка выпита до дна.

Пуля легче лихорадки;
Волен умер ты, как жил.
Враг твой мчался без оглядки;
Но твой сын его убил.

Вспоминай нас за могилой,
Коль сойдетесь как-нибудь;   10
От меня отцу, брат милый,
Поклониться не забудь!

Ты скажи ему, что рана
У меня уж зажила;
Я здоров, — и сына Яна
Мне хозяйка родила.

Деду в честь он назван Яном;
Умный мальчик у меня;
Уж владеет атаганом
И стреляет из ружья.   20

"Brother dear, keep your soul from transgression.
Quench your thirst from my blood that runs hot still,
and then let us die of starvation.
We'll return from the grave to wreak vengeance,
sucking blood from our foes as they slumber."   30
Then Hrizić arose and said: "Come now!
Let a bullet outstrip thirst and hunger!"
All three then emerged from the cavern,
running down like mad wolves to the valley.
They each of them felled seven foemen,
but each of them met seven bullets.
Then the enemy troops cut their heads off
and lifted them high on their pikestaffs.
Even now, though, to watch them folk dared not –
they so dreaded the family Hrizić.   AR & RC

VII. FUNERAL SONG

by Jakint Maglanović

God be with you as you leave us,
He will guide you, true believer.
Clear are moon and starlit sky –
quaffed life's liquor, glass drained dry.

Gunfire's easier than infection;
free in life, in death you're free.
Foe? He fled without reflection;
slain, though, by your son was he.

Think of us in death, dear brother,
if our father you should see.   10
As you run to greet each other,
pass a greeting on from me.

Say: my wound is healed already,
I'm again a healthy man –
riding, standing, firm and steady.
And a son was born me – Jan.

Granddad Jan the boy's called after;
he's a smart and able one;
with a yataghan he's master,
matchless marksman with a gun.   20

Дочь моя живет в Лизгоре;
С мужем ей не скучно там.
Тварк ушел давно уж в море;
Жив иль нет, — узнаешь сам.

С Богом, в дальнюю дорогу!
Путь найдешь ты, слава Богу.
Светит месяц; ночь ясна;
Чарка выпита до дна.

VIII. МАРКО ЯКУБОВИЧ

У ворот сидел Марко Якубович;
Перед ним сидела его Зоя,
А мальчишка их играл у порогу.
По дороге к ним идет незнакомец,
Бледен он и чуть ноги волочит,
Просит он напиться, ради Бога.
Зоя встала и пошла за водою,
И прохожему вынесла ковшик,
И прохожий до дна его выпил,
Вот, напившись, говорит он Марке: 10
«Это что под горою там видно?»
Отвечает Марко Якубович:
«То кладбище наше родовое».
Говорит незнакомый прохожий:
«Отдыхать мне на вашем кладбище,
Потому что мне жить уж не долго».
Тут широкий розвил он пояс,
Кажет Марке кровавую рану.
«Три дня, — молвил, — ношу я под сердцем
Бусурмана свинцовую пулю.   20
Как умру, ты зарой мое тело
За горой, под зеленою ивой.
И со мной положи мою саблю,
Потому что я славный был воин».

Поддержала Зоя незнакомца,
А Марко стал осматривать рану.
Вдруг сказала молодая Зоя:
«Помоги мне, Марко, я не в силах
Поддержать гостя нашего доле».
Тут увидел Марко Якубович,   30
Что прохожий на руках ее умер.

Daughter lives now in Lizgorje,
married well there, not a doubt.
Sailor Tvark's another story;
dead or living, you'll find out.

God be with you as you leave us,
He will guide you, true believer.
Clear are moon and starlit sky –
quaffed life's liquor, glass drained dry.   RC

VIII. MARKO JAKUBOVIĆ

By the gate there sat Marko Jakubović,
and in front of him sat his wife Zoja,
while their little son played in the doorway.
A stranger came towards them on the roadway,
all pale, scarce dragging foot forward;
he begged them in God's name for water.
Zoja rose and went off to fetch water,
and brought a jug back for the stranger,
and the stranger drained the jug to the bottom.
Having drunk, he then turned towards Marko.   10
"What is that I see there by the hillside?"
Then Marko Jakubović gave answer:
"That's the graveyard where our loved ones lie buried."
The stranger replied then to Marko:
"I must rest then myself in your graveyard,
for my life here is now nearly over."
And the broad belt he wore he unfastened,
and showed a raw wound there to Marko.
"Near my heart," he said, "lodged is a bullet
of lead that was fired by a heathen.   20
When I die, you must bury my body
by the hill there beneath the green willow,
and lay this good sabre beside me,
as I've been a right valorous warrior."

Zoja came to support the weak stranger,
while Marko examined the shot wound.
Young Zoja then suddenly shouted:
"Help, Marko, I'm no longer able
to hold up our visitor further."
It dawned then on Marko Jakubović   30
that the traveller had died as they held him.

Марко сел на коня вороного,
Взял с собою мертвое тело
И поехал с ним на кладбище.
Там глубокую вырыли могилу
И с молитвой мертвеца схоронили.
Вот проходит неделя, другая,
Стал худеть сыночек у Марка;
Перестал он бегать и резвиться,
Всё лежал на рогоже да охал. 40
К Якубовичу калуер приходит, —
Посмотрел на ребенка и молвил:
«Сын твой болен опасною болезнью;
Посмотри на белую его шею:
Видишь ты кровавую ранку?
Это зуб вурдалака, поверь мне».

Вся деревня за старцем калуером
Отправилась тотчас на кладбище;
Там могилу прохожего разрыли,
Видят, — труп румяный и свежий, — 50
Ногти выросли, как вороньи когти,
А лицо обросло бородою,
Алой кровью вымазаны губы, —
Полна крови глубокая могила.
Бедный Марко колом замахнулся,
Но мертвец завизжал и проворно
Из могилы в лес бегом пустился.
Он бежал быстрее, чем лошадь,
Стременами острыми язвима;
И кусточки под ним так и гнулись, 60
А суки дерев так и трещали,
Ломаясь, как замерзлые прутья.

Калуер могильною землею
Ребенка больного всего вытер,
И весь день творил над ним молитвы.
На закате красного солнца
Зоя мужу своему сказала:
«Помнишь? ровно тому две недели,
В эту пору умер злой прохожий».

Вдруг собака громко завыла, 70
Отворилась дверь сама собою,
И вошел великан, наклонившись,

Marko mounted his raven-black stallion,
and, taking the dead body with him,
he bore it across to the graveyard.
There they dug a deep grave by the willow,
and with prayers gave the dead man a burial.
A week then went by, then another,
and Marko's small son began sickening;
no more was he active or playful,
but lay on the matting and whimpered.   40
A monk came to see Jakubović –
he looked at the child, then asserted:
"The boy's ill with a dangerous illness;
take a look at his neck and its whiteness:
do you see that small patch red and bloody?
That's a vampire's tooth mark, believe me."

The monk then set off, and the village
all followed behind to the graveyard.
They dug up the grave of the traveller
and found the corpse ruddy and healthy;   50
his nails had grown long, like a crow's claws,
his face was now bushy and bearded,
and his lips were deep crimson with blood smears –
deep blood filled the grave at the bottom.
Poor Marko held a stake up to smite him,
but the corpse gave a screech and then nimbly
leapt up and ran off to the forest,
so fast he'd have outrun a stallion
that a sharply spurred rider was goading.
As he ran he bent bushes beneath him   60
and snapped with loud cracks the tree branches,
as if they were frost-bitten brushwood.

The monk dug some earth from the graveside,
took the child and smeared him all over,
then intoned prayers above him till evening.
As the red sun was setting at nightfall,
Zoja suddenly said to her husband:
"It's exactly a fortnight – remember? –
since that odious traveller expired."

A dog then they heard howling loudly;   70
the door of its own accord opened,
and in came a giant, who stooping

Сел он, ноги под себя поджавши,
Потолка головою касаясь.
Он на Марка глядел неподвижно,
Неподвижно глядел на него Марко,
Очарован ужасным его взором;
Но старик, молитвенник раскрывши,
Запалил кипарисную ветку,
И подул дым на великана.   80
И затрясся вурдалак проклятый,
В двери бросился и бежать пустился,
Будто волк, охотником гонимый.

На другие сутки в ту же пору
Пес залаял, дверь отворилась,
И вошел человек незнакомый.
Был он ростом, как цесарский рекрут.
Сел он молча и стал глядеть на Марко;
Но старик молитвой его прогнал.

В третий день вошел карлик малый, —   90
Мог бы он верьхом сидеть на крысе,
Но сверкали у него злые глазки.
И старик в третий раз его прогнал,
И с тех пор уж он не возвращался.

IX. БОНАПАРТ И ЧЕРНОГОРЦЫ

«Черногорцы? что такое? —
Бонапарте вопросил: —
Правда ль: это племя злое,
Не боится наших сил?

Так раскаятся ж нахалы:
Объявить их старшинам,
Чтобы ружья и кинжалы
Все несли к моим ногам».

Вот он шлет на нас пехоту
С сотней пушек и мортир,   10
И своих мамлюков роту,
И косматых кирасир.

Нам сдаваться нет охоты, —
Черногорцы таковы!

sat down with his legs folded under,
while his head was still touching the ceiling.
He stared hard at Marko, unmoving;
Marko stared back – he too was unmoving,
bewitched by the glare of the giant.
But then the monk opened his prayer book,
set fire to a spray of fresh cypress
and blew the thick smoke at the giant.   80
The vampire, now cursed, started trembling;
he rushed to the door and fled swiftly,
like a wolf that is hounded by hunters.

At sundown the following evening,
again the dog barked, the door opened,
and a man who was new to them entered.
His build was like that of a soldier.
He sat and stared quietly at Marko,
but the monk prayed once more and expelled him.

The next day there entered a midget –   90
a rat could have served as his charger,
but his eyes, though so tiny, flashed evil.
The old man a third time expelled him;
since then he has never returned there.   RC & AR

IX. BONAPARTE AND THE MONTENEGRINS

"Montenegrins? Who the devil?…"
once enquired Napoleon.
"Aren't they people wild and evil,
shrugging off the wars I've won?

"Let the rascals show submission.
Pass this word to their elite:
'All your arms and ammunition
come and lay here at my feet.'"

Now he sends to our location
cannon, mortars by the score,   10
Mamelukes in close formation,
and cuirassiers galore.

"Give in? That's not our intention!"
all we Montenegrins say.

Для коней и для пехоты
Камни есть у нас и рвы...

Мы засели в наши норы
И гостей незваных ждем, —
Вот они вступили в горы,
Истребляя всё кругом.   20

. . . .

Идут тесно под скалами.
Вдруг, смятение!.. Глядят:
У себя над головами
Красных шапок видят ряд.

«Стой! пали! Пусть каждый сбросит
Черногорца одного.
Здесь пощады враг не просит:
Не щадите ж никого!»

Ружья грянули, — упали
Шапки красные с шестов: 30
Мы под ними ниц лежали,
Притаясь между кустов.

Дружным залпом отвечали
Мы французам. — «Это что? —
Удивясь, они сказали; —
Эхо, что ли?» Нет, не то!

Их полковник повалился.
С ним сто двадцать человек.
Весь отряд его смутился,
Кто, как мог, пустился в бег.   40

И французы ненавидят
С той поры наш вольный край
И краснеют, коль завидят
Шапку нашу невзначай.

X. СОЛОВЕЙ

Соловей мой, соловейко,
Птица малая лесная!
У тебя ль, у малой птицы,

Thwarting hostile intervention,
rocks and gullies block their way.

Well concealed, we lie in waiting
for our uninvited guests...
Now they're here, our hills invading,
homes destroyed, our folk distressed!   20

....

Through the mountains they're advancing
rank on rank; then, seized with dread,
they all notice, upwards glancing,
ledges lined with caps of red.

"Halt! Take aim! Let each man slaughter
Montenegrins, one for one.
Here foes never ask for quarter;
so, I tell you, give them none!"

Rifles thundered, red caps tumbled
down to earth by bullets flung –   30
we, though, lay there, still unhumbled,
under poles where caps had hung.

With one volley we responded –
called then to the French, "What's that?"
They cried back to us, confounded,
"Our guns' echo?" No, not that!

One of us felled their commander;
with him six score men lay dead.
Now his whole division floundered,
and, as best they could, they fled.   40

Since that time the French have hated
this dear land where we've lived free,
and they redden, shamed, frustrated,
if by chance our caps they see.   RC

X. A NIGHTINGALE

Nightingale, my nightingale, oh,
little bird who loves the woodlands!
You, my little woodland songster

245

Незаменные три песни,
У меня ли, у молодца,
Три великие заботы!
Как уж первая забота —
Рано молодца женили;
А вторая-то забота —
Ворон конь мой притомился;
Как уж третья-то забота —
Красну-девицу со мною
Разлучили злые люди.
Вы копайте мне могилу
Во поле, поле широком,
В головах мне посадите
Алы цветики-цветочки,
А в ногах мне проведите
Чисту воду ключевую.
Пройдут мимо красны девки,
Так сплетут себе веночки.
Пройдут мимо стары люди,
Так воды себе зачерпнут.

10

20

XI. ПЕСНЯ О ГЕОРГИЕ ЧЕРНОМ

Не два волка в овраге грызутся,
Отец с сыном в пещере бранятся.
Старый Петро сына укоряет:
«Бунтовщик ты, злодей проклятый!
Не боишься ты Господа Бога,
Где тебе с султаном тягаться,
Воевать с белградским пашою!
Аль о двух головах ты родился?
Пропадай ты себе, окаянный,
Да зачем ты всю Сербию губишь?»
Отвечает Георгий угрюмо:
«Из ума, старик, видно, выжил,
Коли лаешь безумные речи».
Старый Петро пуще осердился,
Пуще он бранится, бушует.
Хочет он отправиться в Белград,
Туркам выдать ослушного сына,
Объявить убежище сербов.
Он из темной пещеры выходит;
Георгий старика догоняет:
«Воротися, отец, воротися!
Отпусти мне невольное слово».

10

20

have just three songs never changing.
I, a poor young lad, for my part,
have three overwhelming troubles.
Here's the first one of these troubles –
I was married off too early;
and the second of my troubles –
my black stallion is exhausted;   10
then the third one of these troubles:
that fair maid that I'm in love with –
evil folk have made her hate me.
Dig me, then, in open country –
dig a grave for me to lie in;
at the head plant flowers for me,
pretty blossoms, scarlet blossoms;
at the foot bring water to me,
channel pure spring water to me.
When the lovely girls come past me,   20
they will plait themselves sweet garlands;
when the older folk come past me,
they will draw themselves fresh water.   RC

XI. BALLAD OF BLACK ĐORĐE

Are two wolves fighting there in the gully?
No: it's father and son in the cavern
who are brawling. Old Petar is shouting:
"You're a damnable rebel, an outlaw –
you've no fear of the Lord God Almighty.
Are you mad... to make war on the Sultan
and to march on Belgrade, on the Pasha?
What's possessed you that you are so reckless?
Be off with you, impious scoundrel!
Why bring ruin to the whole land of Serbia?"   10
Then Đorđe replies to him gruffly:
"You're out of your senses, old gaffer,
to bark out such senseless opinions."
Old Petar grows even more angry;
he protests even louder and blusters:
he'll set off for Belgrade, he's decided,
to inform on his son's insurrection
and reveal the Serb fighters' hideout.
He goes out from the dark of the cavern,
but the son overtakes his old father: 20
"Come back here, come back, Father, I beg you.
Forgive the rash words I have spoken."

Старый Петро не слушает, грозится —
«Вот ужо, разбойник, тебе будет!»
Сын ему вперед забегает,
Старику кланяется в ноги.
Не взглянул на сына старый Петро.
Догоняет вновь его Георгий
И хватает за сивую косу.
«Воротись, ради Господа Бога: 30
Не введи ты меня в искушенье!»
Отпихнул старик его сердито
И пошел по белградской дороге.
Горько, горько Георгий заплакал,
Пистолет из-за пояса вынул,
Взвел курок, да и выстрелил тут же.
Закричал Петро, зашатавшись:
«Помоги мне, Георгий, я ранен!»
И упал на дорогу бездыханен.
Сын бегом в пещеру воротился;   40
Его мать вышла ему на встречу.
«Что, Георгий, куда делся Петро?»
Отвечает Георгий сурово:
«За обедом старик пьян напился
И заснул на белградской дороге».
Догадалась она, завопила:
«Будь же богом проклят ты, черный,
Коль убил ты отца родного!»
С той поры Георгий Петрович
У людей прозывается Черный.   50

XII. ВОЕВОДА МИЛОШ

Над Сербией смилуйся ты, Боже!
Заедают нас волки янычары!
Без вины нам головы режут,
Наших жен обижают, позорят,
Сыновей в неволю забирают,
Красных девок заставляют в насмешку
Распевать зазорные песни
И плясать бусурманские пляски.
Старики даже с нами согласны:
Унимать нас они перестали, —   10
Уж и им нестерпимо насилье.
Гусляры нас в глаза укоряют:
«Долго ль вам мирволить янычарам?
Долго ль вам терпеть оплеухи?

But old Petar, not listening, threatens:
"On your head be it, bandit and outlaw!"
Then the son runs ahead of his father,
and kneels down at the feet of his father;
on goes Petar, ignoring his son now,
but Đorđe again overtakes him
and grabs his grey hair to restrain him.
"Come back, in God's name, to the cavern,   30
and don't put more strain on my patience."
Petar pushed him away in his anger
and made for Belgrade on the highway.
Bitter, bitter the tears shed by Đorđe!
From his gun belt he pulled out a pistol,
cocked his weapon and there and then fired it.
Petar shouted out, staggering forward:
"Help me, Đorđe, please help me, I'm injured…"
Then he fell on the roadway unbreathing.
The son then ran back to the cavern,   40
and his mother came forward to meet him.
"Well, Đorđe, what's become of your father?"
And Đorđe replied to her grimly:
"The old man got too drunk after dinner
and fell asleep on the road to Belgrade there."
But she realized, and cried out in anguish:
"May God curse you, you blackest of villains,
for committing your own father's murder!"
And from then on has Đorđe Petrović
been called Karađorđe – "Black Đorđe".   RC

XII. MILOŠ THE WARLORD

Have compassion, O God, on our Serbia!
Like wolves, the Sultan's guardsmen devour us.
They slaughter our innocent people;
our wives they insult and dishonour;
our sons they round up and take captive;
our pretty young girls they make sport of,
and have them sing songs that are shameful
and dance for them heathenish dances.
Our old men now share our revulsion,
and try to restrain us no longer –   10
they too find the violence appalling.
The eyes of old minstrels reproach us:
"How long will you yield to oppressors –
how long will you let them abuse you?

Или вы уж не сербы, — цыганы?
Или вы не мужчины, — старухи?
Вы бросайте ваши белые домы,
Уходите в Велийское ущелье, —
Там гроза готовится на турок,
Там дружину свою собирает   20
Старый сербин, воевода Милош.»

XIII. ВУРДАЛАК

Трусоват был Ваня бедный:
Раз он позднею порой,
Весь в поту, от страха бледный,
Чрез кладбище шел домой.

Бедный Ваня еле дышет,
Спотыкаясь, чуть бредет
По могилам; вдруг он слышит,
Кто-то кость, ворча, грызет.

Ваня стал; — шагнуть не может.
Боже! думает бедняк,   10
Это верно кости гложет
Красногубый вурдалак.

Горе! малый я не сильный;
Съест упырь меня совсем,
Если сам земли могильной
Я с молитвою не съем.

Что же? вместо вурдалака —
(Вы представьте Вани злость!)
В темноте пред ним собака
На могиле гложет кость.   20

XIV. СЕСТРА И БРАТЬЯ

Два дубочка выростали рядом,
Между ими тонковерхая елка.
Не два дуба рядом выростали,
Жили вместе два братца родные:
Один Павел, а другой Радула.
А меж ими сестра их Елица.
Сестру братья любили всем сердцем,
Всякую ей оказывали милость;

Or are you not Serbs now, but Gypsies,
not men any more, but old women?
Abandon your fine whitewashed houses
and leave for the gorge up by Velje.
For the Turks now a storm there is brewing,
and fighters are there being gathered   20
by old Miloš, our Serbian warlord."   RC

XIII. A VAMPIRE

Poor young Jova's pluck is failing.
He's returning home quite late;
sweating, and with visage paling,
he goes through the graveyard gate.

Poor young Jova, almost fainting,
stumbles on past tombs of stone,
when he hears the sound of grunting
and of someone chewing bone.

Jova stops, no closer drawing.
"Oh my God!" runs through his head.   10
"Those are bones a vampire's gnawing,
with his lips all bloody red.

"It's the end! I'm small and weakly,
me he'll certainly devour;
I must take some grave soil quickly
and then eat it with a prayer."

But (and think how Jova's angry!)
that's no vampire in the gloom –
nothing but a dog who's hungry,
gnawing bones upon a tomb.   AR

XIV. SISTER AND BROTHERS

Two young oak trees had grown up together,
and between them a slender-topped fir tree.
No, not oaks were they, grown up together,
but two brothers who lived with each other:
one was Pavle, the other Radule,
and between them their sister Jelica.
Their fair sister the brothers loved dearly,
and they showed her all manner of kindness;

Напоследок ей нож подарили
Золоченый в серебряной оправе.   10

Огорчилась молодая Павлиха
На золовку, стало ей завидно
Говорит она Радуловой любе:
«Невестушка, по Богу сестрица!
Не знаешь ли ты зелия такого,
Чтоб сестра омерзела братьям?»
Отвечает Радулова люба:
«По Богу сестра моя, невестка,
Я не знаю зелия такого;
Хоть бы знала, тебе б не сказала;   20
И меня братья мои любили,
И мне всякую оказывали милость».

Вот пошла Павлиха к водопою,
Да зарезала коня вороного
И сказала своему господину:
«Сам себе на зло сестру ты любишь,
На беду даришь ей подарки:
Извела она коня вороного».
Стал Елицу допытывать Павел:
«За что это? скажи Бога ради».   30
Сестра брату с плачем отвечает:
«Не я, братец, клянусь тебе жизнью,
Клянусь жизнью твоей и моею».
В ту пору брат сестре поверил.

Вот Павлиха пошла в сад зеленый,
Сивого сокола там заколола
И сказала своему господину:
«Сам себе на зло сестру ты любишь,
На беду даришь ты ей подарки:
Ведь она сокола заколола».   40
Стал Елицу допытывать Павел:
«За что это? скажи Бога ради».
Сестра брату с плачем отвечает:
«Не я, братец, клянусь тебе жизнью,
Клянусь жизнью твоей и моею!»
И в ту пору брат сестре поверил.

Вот Павлиха по вечеру поздно
Нож украла у своей золовки
И ребенка своего заколола

then at length the two gave her a dagger
all gilded in a casing of silver.   10

Pavle's wife Pavlovica grew bitter
at her sister-in-law out of envy;
so she spoke to the wife of Radule:
"My dear sister in God, we are kindred:
do you know of a poison that's able
to make loathsome a sister to her brothers?"
And Radule's wife gave her this answer:
"Dear sister in God, yes, we're kinsfolk,
but a poison of that kind I know not;
if I knew, I would surely not tell you,   20
for my brothers have loved me so truly
and have shown me all manner of kindness."

Pavlovica now went to the horse pond
and slew the black stallion that drank there.
She said then to Pavle her husband:
"To your hurt you show love to your sister;
those gifts that you give her bring trouble:
that woman has killed the black stallion."
Then did Pavle close-question his sister:
"In God's name, say: why did you do this?"   30
She answered her brother with weeping:
"Not I it was, brother, that did it;
on your life, and on mine too, I swear it!"
That time did her brother believe her.

Pavlovica now went to the garden
and stabbed the grey falcon that perched there;
she said then to Pavle her husband:
"To your hurt you show love to your sister;
those gifts that you give her bring trouble:
that woman has stabbed the grey falcon."   40
Then Pavle close-questioned his sister:
"In God's name, say: why did you do this?"
She answered her brother with weeping:
"Not I it was, brother, that did it;
on your life, and on mine too, I swear it!"
That time too her brother believed her.

Pavlovica now, late in the evening,
stole her sister-in-law's gilded dagger,
and she stabbed her own child as he lay there,

В колыбельке его золоченой.   50
Рано утром к мужу прибежала,
Громко воя и лицо терзая.
«Сам себе на зло сестру ты любишь,
На беду даришь ты ей подарки:
Заколола у нас она ребенка.
А когда еще ты мне не веришь,
Осмотри ты нож ее злаченый».
Вскочил Павел, как услышал это,
Побежал к Елице во светлицу:
На перине Елица почивала,   60
В головах нож висел злаченый.
Из ножен вынул его Павел, —
Нож злаченый весь был окровавлен.
Дернул он сестру за белу руку:
«Ой, сестра, убей тебя Боже!
Извела ты коня вороного
И в саду сокола заколола,
Да за что ты зарезала ребенка?»
Сестра брату с плачем отвечает:
«Не я, братец, клянусь тебе жизнью,   70
Клянусь жизнью твоей и моею!
Коли ж ты не веришь моей клятве,
Выведи меня в чистое поле,
Привяжи к хвостам коней борзых,
Пусть они мое белое тело
Разорвут на четыре части».
В ту пору брат сестре не поверил;
Вывел он ее в чистое поле,
Привязал ко хвостам коней борзых
И погнал их по чистому полю.   80
Где попала капля ее крови,
Выросли там алые цветочки;
Где осталось ее белое тело,
Церковь там над ней соорудилась.

Прошло малое после того время,
Захворала молодая Павлиха.
Девять лет Павлиха всё хворает, —
Выросла трава сквозь ее кости,
В той траве лютый змей гнездится,
Пьет ей очи, сам уходит к ночи.   90
Люто страждет молода Павлиха;
Говорит она своему господину:
«Слышишь ли, господин ты мой, Павел,

fast asleep in his rich gilded cradle.   50
In the morning she ran to her husband,
loudly wailing, with face full of torment.
"To your hurt you show love to your sister;
those gifts that you give her bring trouble:
with her dagger she has now stabbed our baby –
and if you mistrust what I tell you,
then examine with care her gold dagger."
Jumping up at her words when he heard them,
Pavle ran to the room of Jelica:
on her bed there his sister was sleeping,   60
at the bedhead there hung the gold dagger.
Pavle pulled out the knife from its casing –
the gold blade was all covered in bloodstains.
Then he seized the white arm of his sister.
"Oh, may God take your life for this, sister!
By the horse pond you've killed the black stallion,
in the garden you've stabbed the grey falcon,
but why have you now slain the baby?"
She answered her brother with weeping:
"Not I it was, brother, that did it;   70
on your life, and on mine too, I swear it!
If my oath does not seem to you truthful,
then take me to the broad open meadow,
and tie me to the tails of swift horses:
let them pull my white body asunder,
let them tear it apart in four pieces."
But her brother no longer believed her;
To the broad open meadow he took her,
tied her fast to the tails of swift horses,
then drove them across the broad meadow.   80
Wherever a drop of her blood fell,
there grew from the earth crimson flowers;
and where came to rest her white body,
a church was erected above her.

Not long after all this had happened,
Pavlovica, though young, became poorly;
nine years she lay ill, not recovering –
till weeds sprouted up round her body,
and there lurked in the weeds a cruel serpent,
and it drank from her eyes until nightfall;   90
so most cruelly did Pavlovica suffer.
Then finally she said to her husband:
"Are you hearing me, Pavle, my master?

Сведи меня к золовкиной церкви,
У той церкви авось исцелюся».
Он повел ее к сестриной церкви,
И как были они уже близко,
Вдруг из церкви услышали голос:
«Не входи, молодая Павлиха,
Здесь не будет тебе исцеленья».   100
Как услышала то молодая Павлиха,
Она молвила своему господину:
«Господин ты мой! прошу тебя Богом,
Не веди меня к белому дому,
А вяжи меня к хвостам твоих кóней
И пусти их по чистому полю».
Своей любы послушался Павел,
Привязал ее к хвостам своих кóней
И погнал их по чистому полю.
Где попала капля ее крови,   110
Выросло там тернье да крапива;
Где осталось ее белое тело,
На том месте озеро провалило.
Ворон конь по озеру выплывает,
За конем золоченая люлька,
На той люльке сидит сокол-птица,
Лежит в люльке маленький мальчик;
Рука матери у него под горлом,
В той руке теткин нож золоченый.

XV. ЯНЫШ КОРОЛЕВИЧ

Полюбил королевич Яныш
Молодую красавицу Елицу,
Любит он ее два красные лета,
В третье лето вздумал он жениться
На Любусе, чешской королевне.
С прежней любой идет он проститься.
Ей приносит с червонцами черес,
Да гремучие серьги золотые,
Да жемчужное тройное ожерелье;
Сам ей вдел он серьги золотые,   10
Навязал на шею ожерелье,
Дал ей в руки с червонцами черес,
В обе щеки поцеловал молча
И поехал своею дорогой.
Как одна осталася Елица,
Деньги наземь она пометала,

Take me down to the church of your sister;
at that church, maybe, I shall find healing."
To the church of his sister he took her,
and when they had nearly arrived there,
they heard from the church a voice speaking:
"Do not enter the church, Pavlovica;
for in this place you will not find healing.   100
Pavlovica, on hearing this message,
then turned to her husband and begged him:
"My master, in God's name I ask you,
to the church of white stone do not take me;
but tie me to the tails of your horses –
let them loose then across the broad meadow."
Then Pavle obeyed his wife's wishes;
he tied her to the tails of his horses
and drove them across the broad meadow.
Wherever a drop of her blood fell,   110
there grew from the earth thorns and nettles,
and where came to rest her white body,
on that spot a lake flooded over.
On the lake there swam up a black stallion,
and behind it a cradle of gilt work;
on the cradle a falcon was perching,
and a small boy lay there in the cradle;
his mother's hand was beneath the boy's gullet,
and the hand held his aunt's gilded dagger.   RC & AR

XV. PRINCE YANYSH

Now it chanced that the king's son, Prince Yanysh,
fell in love with the lovely Yelitsa.
For two happy summers he loved her;
in the third he decided to marry
a Czechian princess named Lyubusa.
So he went to take leave of his first love.
He brought her a pouch of gold ducats,
and rich golden earrings that jangled,
and pearls on a triple-strung necklace.
He himself decked her ears with the earrings,   10
and around her neck fastened the necklace;
in her hand put the pouch of gold ducats;
on each cheek gave a kiss without speaking,
and set off once more on his journey.
When Yelitsa was left there without him,
to the ground she cast down all the ducats;

257

Из ушей выдернула серьги,
Ожерелье надвое разорвала,
А сама кинулась в Мораву.
Там на дне молодая Елица   20
Водяною царицей очнулась
И родила маленькую дочку,
И ее нарекла Водяницей.

Вот проходят три года и боле,
Королевич ездит на охоте,
Ездит он по берегу Моравы;
Захотел он коня вороного
Напоить студеною водою.
Но лишь только запененную морду
Сунул конь в студеную воду,   30
Из воды вдруг высунулась ручка:
Хвать коня за узду золотую!
Конь отдернул голову в испуге,
На узде висит Водяница,
Как на уде пойманная рыбка, —
Конь кружится по чистому лугу,
Потрясая уздой золотою;
Но стряхнуть Водяницы не может.
Чуть в седле усидел королевич,
Чуть сдержал коня вороного,   40
Осадив могучею рукою.
На траву Водяница прыгнула.
Говорит ей Яныш королевич:
«Расскажи, какое ты творенье:
Женщина ль тебя породила,
Иль богом проклятая Вила?»
Отвечает ему Водяница:
«Родила меня молодая Елица.
Мой отец Яныш королевич,
А зовут меня Водяницей».   50
Королевич при таком ответе
Соскочил с коня вороного,
Обнял дочь свою Водяницу
И, слезами заливаясь, молвил:
«Где, скажи, твоя мать Елица?
Я слыхал, что она потонула».
Отвечает ему Водяница:
«Мать моя царица водяная;
Она властвует над всеми реками,
Над реками и над озерами;   60

from her ear lobes she pulled out the earrings;
from her neck tore the necklace and broke it;
then she leapt in the river Morava.
In its depths the young maiden Yelitsa   20
reawoke as the queen of the waters;
she gave birth to a baby, a daughter,
with the name "Child of Water, Vodyanitsa".

So three years passed by, even longer,
then Prince Yanysh one day rode out hunting,
rode out hunting beside the Morava.
Yanysh wanted to give his black stallion
a drink of the cool river water.
When the horse thrust his hot, foaming muzzle
down to drink in the cool river water,   30
a small hand rose up out of the water
and grasped hold of the steed's golden bridle.
The black horse reared its head in a panic –
to the reins Vodyanitsa was hanging
like a fish that's been hooked by an angler.
The black steed galloped round in the meadow,
shaking hard as he could his gold harness,
but he failed to shake off Vodyanitsa.
Though the prince with strong arm pulled the bridle,
he could scarcely sit safe in the saddle –   40
he could scarcely control the black stallion.
On the grass now leapt down Vodyanitsa,
and Yanysh the king's son addressed her:
"Explain to me, what creature are you?
Were you born of a mother, a woman,
or are you a spirit, a demon?"
To the prince answered young Vodyanitsa:
"I was born of my mother Yelitsa,
with a king's son, Prince Yanysh, for father,
and I'm called by the name Vodyanitsa."   50
As soon as the prince heard this answer,
down at once he jumped off the black stallion
and embraced his young child Vodyanitsa,
and with tears in his eyes he addressed her:
"Tell me, where is your mother Yelitsa?
I have heard that she drowned in the river."
Vodyanitsa then gave him this answer:
"My mother is queen of fresh waters;
her dominion extends to all rivers;
all rivers and lakes are her kingdom;   60

Лишь не властвует она синим морем,
Синим морем властвует Див-Рыба».
Водянице молвил королевич:
«Так иди же к водяной царице
И скажи ей: Яныш королевич
Ей поклон усердный посылает
И у ней свидания просит
На зеленом берегу Моравы.
Завтра я заеду за ответом».
Они после того расстались.   70

Рано утром, чуть заря зарделась,
Королевич над рекою ходит;
Вдруг из речки, по белые груди,
Поднялась царица водяная
И сказала: «Яныш королевич,
У меня свидания просил ты:
Говори, чего еще ты хочешь?»
Как увидел он свою Елицу,
Разгорелись снова в нем желанья,
Стал манить ее к себе на берег.   80
«Люба ты моя, млада Елица,
Выдь ко мне на зеленый берег,
Поцелуй меня по-прежнему сладко,
По-прежнему полюблю тебя крепко».
Королевичу Елица не внимает,
Не внимает, головою кивает:
«Нет, не выду, Яныш королевич,
Я к тебе на зеленый берег.
Слаще прежнего нам не целоваться,
Крепче прежнего меня не полюбишь.   90
Расскажи-ка мне лучше хорошенько,
Каково, счастливо ль поживаешь
С новой любой, молодой женою?»
Отвечает Яныш королевич:
«Против солнышка луна не пригреет,
Против милой жена не утешит».

XVI. КОНЬ

«Что ты ржешь, мой конь ретивый,
Что ты шею опустил,
Не потряхиваешь гривой,
Не грызешь своих удил?
Али я тебя не холю?

the blue seas, though, are not her dominion:
they are ruled by the King of the Fishes."
Then the Prince said to young Vodyanitsa:
"Will you go to the queen of fresh waters
and say that the prince wants to send her
his respects, which are heartfelt and earnest?
Will you ask that she grant him a meeting
on the bank of the river Morava?
I shall call for an answer tomorrow."
And with that prince and water sprite parted.   70

Next morning, when the sky had scarce reddened,
the prince walked along by the river.
Then all of a sudden before him,
white-breasted, half-rose from the river
the freshwater queen. She said, "Yanysh,
you have asked for a meeting here with me:
is there anything more you are wanting?"
As soon as he saw his Yelitsa,
once more his desires were rekindled,
and he beckoned her out of the river.   80
"Dear Yelitsa, my own little loved one,
step here on the grass where I'm standing –
come and kiss me as sweetly as ever;
I shall love you as strongly as ever."
But Yelitsa refused what he asked her –
she refused him and, shaking her head, said:
"No, Yanysh, I'll not leave the river,
not step on the grass where you're standing.
We'll not kiss now more sweetly than ever –
you'll not love me more strongly than ever.   90
Instead, you'd do better to tell me:
are you happy? What life are you living
with your new love, the young wife you've married?"
And Prince Yanysh, the king's son, gave answer:
"Never moonlight shall warm like the sunshine –
never wife shall delight like a sweetheart."   RC & AR

XVI. THE STEED

"Why d'you neigh, my lively stallion?
Why d'you hang your neck so low,
proudly shake your mane no longer,
keenly champ your bit no more?
Don't I cosset and caress you,

Али ешь овса не вволю?
Али сбруя не красна?
Аль поводья не шелковы,
Не серебряны подковы,
Не злачены стремена?»   10

Отвечает конь печальный:
«Оттого я присмирел,
Что я слышу топот дальный,
Трубный звук и пенье стрел;
Оттого я ржу, что в поле
Уж не долго мне гулять,
Проживать в красе и в холе,
Светлой сбруей щеголять;
Что уж скоро враг суровый
Сбрую всю мою возьмет   20
И серебряны подковы
С легких ног моих сдерет;
Оттого мой дух и ноет,
Что наместо чапрака
Кожей он твоей покроет
Мне вспотевшие бока».

710

ПОКОЙ И ВОЛЯ

Пора, мой друг, пора! покоя сердце просит —
Летят за днями дни, и каждый час уносит
Частичку бытия, а мы с тобой вдвоем
Предполагаем жить, и глядь — как раз — умрем.
На свете счастья нет, но есть покой и воля.
Давно завидная мечтается мне доля —
Давно, усталый раб, замыслил я побег
В обитель дальнюю трудов и чистых нег.

711

НА МИЦКЕВИЧА

Он между нами жил
Средь племени ему чужого, злобы
В душе своей к нам не питал, и мы

feed you all the oats you wish,
deck you in the finest trappings,
fit you out with reins of silk,
have you shod with silver horseshoes,
hung with stirrups forged of gold?"   10

Sadly then the steed gave answer:
"This is why I seem depressed:
I can hear a distant marching,
bugles bray and arrows sing.
This is why I neigh: I've not long
freely now to roam the fields,
live with beauty and in comfort,
show off all my gleaming gear;
very soon a savage foe will
take the trappings that were mine,   20
prize the gorgeous silver horseshoes
from the hooves that ran so fast.
This too makes my spirit suffer:
when to serve him I begin,
my perspiring flanks he'll cover
with a cloth made from your skin."   RC

710

PEACE AND INDEPENDENCE

It's time, my dear, it's time! For peace my heart's appealing –
day chases after day; each passing hour is stealing
a scrap of what we are. We're planning, you and I,
together to live on. Reflect, though: soon we'll die.
On earth here there's no bliss. But peace and independence
there are; long in my dreams I've craved such an existence –
yes, long back, weary serf, I thought of taking flight
to a refuge far away of work and pure delight.   RC

711

ON MICKIEWICZ

He lived among us here,
amid folk alien to him. He nursed
no malice in his heart towards us. We

263

Его любили. Мирный, благосклонный,
Он посещал беседы наши. С ним
Делились мы и чистыми мечтами
И песнями (он вдохновен был свыше
И с высока взирал на жизнь). Нередко
Он говорил о временах грядущих,
Когда народы, распри позабыв,   10
В великую семью соединятся.
Мы жадно слушали поэта. Он
Ушел на запад — и благословеньем
Его мы проводили. Но теперь
Наш мирный гость нам стал врагом — и ядом
Стихи свои, в угоду черни буйной,
Он напояет. Издали до нас
Доходит голос злобного поэта,
Знакомый голос!.. Боже! освяти
В нем сердце правдою твоей и миром   20
И возврати ему...

712

ПОСЛЕДНИЙ ДЕНЬ ПОМПЕИ

Везувий зев открыл — дым хлынул клубом — пламя
Широко развилось, как боевое знамя.
Земля волнуется — с шатнувшихся колонн
Кумиры падают! Народ, гонимый страхом,
Под каменным дождем, под воспаленным прахом,
Толпами, стар и млад, бежит из града вон.

713

КЛАДБИЩЕ

Стою печален на кладбище.
Гляжу кругом — обнажено
Святое смерти пепелище
И степью лишь окружено.
И мимо вечного ночлега
Дорога сельская лежит,
По ней рабочая телега
.... изредка стучит.

for our part loved him. In good will and peace
he used to join in our debates. Together
we shared our musings and our poetry
good-heartedly (sublime his inspiration –
sublime his outlook too on life). Quite often
he used to speak of times he saw ahead
when nations would forget their rivalries   10
and join themselves in one great family.
We hung upon the poet's words. Then he
left Russia for the west, and at our parting
we blessed him on his way. Our erstwhile guest, though,
that man of peace, has now turned foe – to please
a mob that thirsts for war he steeps his verse
in poison. Now from far away there comes
to us a poet's voice that's full of rancour –
a voice we knew so well!… O God, endue
his heart with peace and with your truth and justice;
restore to him, we pray…   RC

712

THE LAST DAY OF POMPEII

Vesuvius gapes and spews dense clouds of smoke, extending
great coils of flame that billow like a battle ensign.
Chaos prevails below: tall columns topple down;
townsfolk, convulsed with fear as each fond idol crashes,
both old and young, beneath the incandescent ashes
and stones that fall like rain, rush frenzied from the town.   RC

713

A GRAVEYARD

I stand among the graves and mourn,
I look about… and think of ends.
The sacred ashes lie forlorn,
and all around the steppe extends.
A country road lies near at hand,
and now and then I hear the sound
of wagon wheels against the sand
as they go past the hallowed ground.

Одна равнина справа, слева.
Ни речки, ни холма, ни древа.
Кой-где чуть видятся кусты.
Немые камни и могилы
И деревянные кресты
Однообразны и унылы.

714

ГЕОРГИЙ ЧЕРНЫЙ

Менко Вуич грамоту пишет
Георгию, своему побратиму:
«Берегися, Черный Георгий,
Над тобой подымается туча,
Ярый враг извести тебя хочет,
Недруг хитрый, Милош Обренович
Он в Хотин подослал потаенно
Янка младшего с Павлом...
....

Осердился Георгий Петрович,
Засверкали черные очи,
Нахмурились черные брови ...

715

ПЕСНЯ КОСАРЕЙ

из Сцен из рыцарских времен

Ходит во́ поле коса,
Зелена́я полоса
    Вслед за ней ложится.
Ой, ходи, моя коса.
    Сердце веселится.

Bare fields are all the eye can see –
no brook, no hill, no lonely tree.   10
Among the graves and silent stones
a few scant bushes dot the land,
and wooden crosses, row on row,
monotonous and mournful stand.   JF

714

BLACK ĐORĐE

Menko Vujić is writing a message,
he is writing to his blood-brother Đorđe:
"Black Đorđe, Karađorđe, be careful!
Above you dark storm clouds are gathering.
A formidable foe means to kill you:
your sly enemy Miloš Obrenović.
To Khotín he has just sent in secret
both Janko the younger and Pavle…"
…………………………………

Then Đorđe Petrović grew angry;
his black eyes then were flashing in fury;   10
his black eyebrows were puckered in scowling …   RC

715

HARVESTERS' SONG

from Scenes from the Age of Chivalry

Now the scythe goes down the field,
and the long green swathe must yield,
    lying there behind it.
Oi, my scythe, cut down the field,
    happy hearts will bind it.   MH

716

ПЕСНЯ ФРАНЦА

из Сцен из рыцарских времен

Воротился ночью мельник...
— Женка! Что за сапоги?
— Ах ты, пьяница, бездельник!
Где ты видишь сапоги?
Иль мутит тебя лукавый?
Это ведра. ¾ Ведра? право? —
Вот уж сорок лет живу,
Ни во сне, ни на яву
Не видал до этих пор
Я на ведрах медных шпор.   10

716

FRANZ'S SONG

from Scenes from the Age of Chivalry

Home he comes, one night, the miller.
"Wifey! Whose great boots are those?"
"Ah, you drunken, idle fellow,
seeing boots now, I suppose!
Has the Evil One bemused you?
They're my buckets." "Buckets? Truly?
Well, I'm forty, no mistake,
but in dreams or wide awake
I've not seen one pail like yours.
Buckets!… And with fine brass spurs!"

MH

1835

717

ИЗ АНАКРЕОНА

Ода LV

Узнают коней ретивых
По их выжженным таврам,
Узнают парфян кичливых:
По высоким клобукам;
Я любовников счастливых
Узнаю по их глазам:
В них сияет пламень томный —
Наслаждений знак нескромный.

718

ИЗ АНАКРЕОНА

Ода LVI

Поредели, побелели
Кудри, честь главы моей,
Зубы в деснах ослабели,
И потух огонь очей.
Сладкой жизни мне не много
Провожать осталось дней:
Парка счет ведет им строго,
Тартар тени ждет моей.
Не воскреснем из-под спуда,
Всяк навеки там забыт:
Вход туда для всех открыт —
Нет исхода уж оттуда.

1835

717

FROM ANACREON

Ode LV

Mettled steeds you'll recognize
by the brand that's scorched their hides;
Parthian lords you'll recognize
by their turbaned heads held high.
I, though, always recognize
happy lovers by their eyes:
in them glows a languid fire –
mark of gratified desire.   RC

718

FROM ANACREON

Ode LVI

Thin my hair's become and grey,
once the glory of my head;
teeth are loosened with decay;
fire that lit my eyes is dead.
Time now left for joy is brief;
Fate a stringent limit sets,
and she'll grant me no relief.
Hades now my ghost awaits.
Resurrection – there is none:
from extinction no escaping;   10
for us all death's door is gaping –
no way back for anyone.   RC

719

ИЗ АНАКРЕОНА

Ода LVII

Что же сухо в чаше дно?
Наливай мне, мальчик резвый,
Только пьяное вино
Раствори водою трезвой.
Мы не скифы, не люблю,
Други, пьянствовать бесчинно:
Нет, за чашей я пою
Иль беседую невинно.

720

* * *

Юношу, горько рыдая, ревнивая дева бранила;
    К ней на плечо преклонен, юноша вдруг задремал.
Дева тотчас умолкла, сон его легкий лелея.
    И улыбалась ему, тихие слезы лия.

721

АСАНАГАНИЦА

Что белеется на горе зеленой?
Снег ли то, али лебеди белы?
Был бы снег — он уж бы растаял,
Были б лебеди — они б улетели.
То не снег и не лебеди белы,
А шатер Аги Асан-аги.
Он лежит в нем, весь люто изранен.

Посетили его сестра и матерь,
Его люба не могла, застыдилась.
Как ему от боли стало легче,
Приказал он своей верной любе:
«Не ищи меня в моем белом доме,
В белом доме, ни во всем моем роде».
Как услышала мужнины речи,
Запечалилась бедная Кадуна.

10

719

FROM ANACREON

Ode LVII

Look, we've let the cup go dry!
Come, my lad, and pour me more,
but dilute the drunken wine –
sober water also pour.
We're not Scythians. I dislike
drunken orgies, friends, I swear:
no, I sing when drinking wine,
or in harmless talk I share.   JF

720

* * *

Bitterly sobbing, the maid was still jealously hurling reproaches,
   when, of a sudden, the lad, head on her shoulder, dozed off.
Instantly quiet, the maid, taking care not to trouble his slumber,
   smiled at him gently, her eyes silently welling with tears.   CC

721

THE WIFE OF HASSAN-AGA

What shows white on the green of the hillside?
Is it snow? Is it swans in white plumage?
If snow, it should all have now melted;
if swans, they'd have all taken wing now.
It's not snow, it's not swans in white plumage,
It's the tent of the aga Hassan-Aga.
In the tent he lies seriously wounded.

His sister and his mother came to see him;
his wife, though, stayed away because of shyness.
The aga, when from pain he found some comfort,   10
to his wife, still fond and faithful, sent this order:
"Don't come to find me in my white stone mansion,
not in my mansion nor among my kinsfolk."
Now when the lady heard her husband's orders,
poor woman, she was overcome with sorrow.

Она слышит, на двор едут кони;
Побежала Асан-агиница,
Хочет броситься, бедная, в окошко,
За ней вопят две милые дочки:
«Воротися, милая мать наша,   20
Приехал не муж Асан-ага,
А приехал брат твой Пинторович».
Воротилась Асан-агиница,
И повисла она брату на шею —
«Братец милый, что за посрамленье!
Меня гонят от пятерых деток» ...

722

ИЗ ГОРАЦИЯ

Кто из богов мне возвратил
Того, с кем первые походы
И браней ужас я делил,
Когда за призраком свободы
Нас Брут отчаянный водил,
С кем я тревоги боевые
В шатре за чашей забывал
И кудри, плющем увитые,
Сирийским мирром умащал?

Ты помнишь час ужасный битвы,   10
Когда я, трепетный квирит,
Бежал, нечестно брося щит,
Творя обеты и молитвы?
Как я боялся! как бежал!
Но Эрмий сам незапной тучей
Меня покрыл и вдаль умчал
И спас от смерти неминучей.

А ты, любимец первый мой,
Ты снова в битвах очутился...
И ныне в Рим ты возвратился   20
В мой домик темный и простой.
Садись под сень моих пенатов.
Давайте чаши. Не жалей
Ни вин моих, ни ароматов.
Венки готовы. Мальчик! лей.
Теперь не кстати воздержанье:

She then heard horses entering the courtyard;
she ran, the wife of the aga Hassan-Aga,
and meant to throw herself from out the window.
Behind her cried aloud her two small daughters:
"Come back, dear mother, come back from the window,   20
it's not your husband who has come, the aga,
the one who's come is Uncle Pintorović."
Back turned the wife of the aga Hassan-Aga,
and flung her arms around her brother's collar.
"Dear brother, this is such humiliation!
They'll separate me from my five young children." ...   RC

722

FROM HORACE

Which god has given back the friend
with whom I shared the expedition's
ordeals when reckless Brutus led
our forces on towards ghostly visions
of freedom shimmering ahead –
with whom I drowned my apprehension
in cups of wine we drained at ease,
with fragrant Syrian myrrh to freshen
our curls entwined with ivy leaves?

Do you recall the battle's welter,   10
when I – no soldier – fled the field,
ingloriously dropped my shield
and uttered vows and prayers for shelter?
Oh, how I ran in fright that day!
But, in a sudden cloud descending,
swift Hermes whisked me far away
and rescued me from death impending.

Then you, my dear first friend, were thrown
into more battles fraught with danger...
Now back in Rome, don't be a stranger   20
to this, my dim and humble home.
Recline here, by my gods protected.
Bring out the cups. Don't spare my store
of choicest wines and oils sweet-scented.
The wreathes are ready. Come, boy, pour!
This is no time for moderation:

Как дикий скиф хочу я пить.
Я с другом праздную свиданье,
Я рад рассудок утопить.

723

ПОЛКОВОДЕЦ

У русского царя в чертогах есть палата:
Она не золотом, не бархатом богата;
Не в ней алмаз венца хранится за стеклом:
Но сверху донизу, во всю длину, кругом,
Своею кистию свободной и широкой
Ее разрисовал художник быстроокий.
Тут нет ни сельских нимф, ни девственных мадон,
Ни фавнов с чашами, ни полногрудых жен,
Ни плясок, ни охот, — а всё плащи, да шпаги,
Да лица, полные воинственной отваги.   10
Толпою тесною художник поместил
Сюда начальников народных наших сил,
Покрытых славою чудесного похода
И вечной памятью двенадцатого года.

Нередко медленно меж ими я брожу
И на знакомые их образы гляжу,
И, мнится, слышу их воинственные клики.
Из них уж многих нет; другие, коих лики
Еще так молоды на ярком полотне,
Уже состарелись и никнут в тишине   20
Главою лавровой...
               Но в сей толпе суровой
Один меня влечет всех больше. С думой новой
Всегда остановлюсь пред ним — и не свожу
С него моих очей. Чем долее гляжу,
Тем более томим я грустию тяжелой.

Он писан во весь рост. Чело, как череп голый,
Высоко лоснится, и, мнится, залегла
Там грусть великая. Кругом — густая мгла;
За ним — военный стан. Спокойный и угрюмый,
Он, кажется, глядит с презрительною думой.   30
Свою ли точно мысль художник обнажил,
Когда он таковым его изобразил,
Или невольное то было вдохновенье, —
Но Доу дал ему такое выраженье.

I'll drink a Scythian's share of wine.
To greet a friend, in celebration,
I'll drown my reason for a time.   CC

723

A GENERAL

The palace of the tsar contains a splendid chamber.
It's not adorned with gold, nor decked with velvet hangings;
no diamond crown is there kept safe behind a glass;
but on both sides, above, below, for all its length,
an artist skilled, alert, with brushstrokes free and bold
has decorated it with samples of his work.
Here are no rustic nymphs, no virginal madonnas,
no fauns with drinking cups, no ample-breasted matrons,
no hunts, no dancing scenes – just cloaks and swords galore
and faces that, each one, express a soldier's courage.   10
The painter in this room has placed in close array
the senior officers that led our nation's forces,
flaunting the honours won in their superb campaign,
a lasting record of the feats of 1812.

I often slowly browse among those works of art,
I gaze at countenances I have known so well,
seeming to hear their shouts across the battlefield.
Many are now no more – and others there, whose features
still look so young upon the richly painted canvas,
have now grown old and let their laurelled heads droop down,   20
their voices hushed with age...
                              But in this stern-faced throng
one more than all the rest draws me, and with new thoughts
I stand in front of him each time – I cannot tear
my eyes away from him: the longer I stay looking,
the more weighed down I feel with melancholy thoughts.

He's painted at full length. His hairless brow atop
shines like a naked skull; therein, it seems to me,
there lurks a heavy grief. Thick clouds hang dark behind;
beyond him soldiers camp. Quiet and grim he stands,
eyeing the world as though in scornful contemplation.   30
The artist, when he drew his subject in this way,
was it a well-considered view that he was giving –
or was he guided by unconscious inspiration?
That was, in any case, the expression that Dawe gave him.

О вождь несчастливый!.. Суров был жребий твой:
Всё в жертву ты принес земле тебе чужой.
Непроницаемый для взгляда черни дикой,
В молчанье шел один ты с мыслию великой,
И в имени твоем звук чуждый не взлюбя,
Своими криками преследуя тебя,   40
Народ, таинственно спасаемый тобою,
Ругался над твоей священной сединою.
И тот, чей острый ум тебя и постигал,
В угоду им тебя лукаво порицал...
И долго, укреплен могущим убежденьем,
Ты был неколебим пред общим заблужденьем;
И на полу-пути был должен наконец
Безмолвно уступить и лавровый венец,
И власть, и замысел, обдуманный глубоко, —
И в полковых рядах сокрыться одиноко.   50
Там, устарелый вождь, как ратник молодой,
Искал ты умереть средь сечи боевой.
Вотще! Преемник твой стяжал успех, сокрытый
В главе твоей. — А ты, непризнанный, забытый
Виновник торжества, почил — и в смертный час
С презреньем, может быть, воспоминал о нас!

О люди! Жалкий род, достойный слез и смеха!
Жрецы минутного, поклонники успеха!
Как часто мимо вас проходит человек,
Над кем ругается слепой и буйный век,   60
Но чей высокий лик в грядущем поколенье
Поэта приведет в восторг и в умиленье!

724

ТУЧА

Последняя туча рассеянной бури!
Одна ты несешься по ясной лазури.
Одна ты наводишь унылую тень,
Одна ты печалишь ликующий день.

Ты небо недавно кругом облегала,
И молния грозно тебя обвивала;
И ты издавала таинственный гром
И алчную землю поила дождем.

Unhappy general! Your destiny was harsh:
to a country alien to you you gave your all.
The undiscerning mob found you inscrutable.
Thinking great thoughts you used to stride on silently;
the nation that you strove, unspeaking, to protect,
disliking the strange vowels that sounded in your name,   40
kept chasing after you to bait you with their shouts,
taunting the greying head they should have reverenced.
And he, whose ready mind could grasp how right you were,
feigned disaccord with you to gratify your critics.
But you, long-fortified with resolute conviction,
remained unshaken by prevailing misconceptions.
At length, in mid-campaign, you were obliged to forfeit,
with no word of complaint, the honour of your post,
your power, and your plan so thoughtfully devised –
and vanish, lonely man, among the regiments.   50
There – ageing general alongside young recruit –
seeking to die, you rushed into the bloody carnage.
In vain! The winning plan, kept secret in your head,
was seized upon by your successor. As for you,
author of victory, you died ignored, forgotten,
maybe in your last hour remembering us with scorn.

Pathetic human race, provoking tears and scoffing!
You sacrifice what is and deify your hopes.
How often you let pass one whom the present age,
blind and tumultuous, denounces with abuse,   60
but whose nobility in each new generation
will move a poet's heart to love and exaltation!   RC

724

THE CLOUD

Last cloud of a storm that is scattered and over,
alone in the skies of bright azure you hover,
alone with sad shadows you float on your way,
alone you throw gloom on the joy of the day.

By you all the heaven was lately confounded;
you were with the hideous lightning surrounded,
you rang the mysterious thunderclap out,
you rained on the earth that was thirsting in drought.

Довольно, сокройся! Пора миновалась,
Земля освежилась, и буря промчалась,   10
И ветер, лаская листочки древес,
Тебя с успокоенных гонит небес.

725

НА КНЯЗЯ ДОНДУКОВА-КОРСАКОВА

В Академии наук
Заседает князь Дундук.
Говорят, не подобает
Дундуку такая честь;
Почему ж он заседает?
Потому что жопа есть.

726

РОДРИГ

Чудный сон мне Бог послал —
С длинной белой бородою
В белой ризе предо мною
Старец некий предстоял
И меня благословлял.
Он сказал мне: «Будь покоен,
Скоро, скоро удостоен
Будешь царствия небес.
Скоро странствию земному
Твоему придет конец.   10
Уж готовит ангел смерти
Для тебя святой венец...
Путник, ляжешь на ночлеге,
В гавань, плаватель, войдешь.
Бедный пахарь утомленный,
Отрешишь волов от плуга
На последней борозде.
Ныне грешник тот великий,
О котором предвещанье
Слышал ты давно —   20
....
Грешник долгожданный
Наконец к тебе придет

Enough, and begone! 'Tis no time for your power.
The earth is refreshed now, and finished the shower,   10
and the breeze that caresses the leaves as it flies
will chase you away from the quieted skies.   MB

725

ON PRINCE M.A. DUNDUKÓV-KÓRSAKOV

Dundúk has gained a chair
at Russia's highest school.
Some people say "Unfair!",
while others whisper "Fool…"
"So why Dundúk?" you cry.
His bottom fits – that's why!   JC

726

RODERICK

Strange the dream that God has sent me!
In the dream there came a priest:
long and white his flowing beard –
white too was his holy vestment.
There he stood before me, blessed me
and addressed me, "Be at peace.
Very soon you will be deemed
fit to enter Heaven's kingdom –
very soon will come an end
to your earthly pilgrimage.   10
Even now death's angel holds
in readiness your sacred crown.
Traveller, you shall be at rest;
sailor, harbour shall be yours;
and, poor weary ploughman, you shall
loose your oxen from the plough,
having cut the final furrow.
Now the man, that great transgressor –
he of whom a prophecy
long ago you heard…   20
…………………………
that transgressor long-awaited
will at last now come to you,

Исповедовать себя
И получит разрешенье,
И заснешь ты вечным сном».

Сон отрадный, благовещный—
Сердце жадное не смеет
И поверить и не верить.
Ах, ужели в самом деле   30
Близок я к моей кончине?
И страшуся и надеюсь,
Казни вечныя страшуся,
Милосердия надеюсь:
Успокой меня, Творец.
Но твоя да будет воля,
Не моя. —
            Кто там идет?..

727

ИЗ ПОЭМА САУТИ
РОДРИК, ПОСЛЕДНИЙ ИЗ ГОТОВ

I
На Испанию родную
Призвал мавра Юлиан.
Граф за личную обиду
Мстить решился королю.

Дочь его Родрик похитил,
Обесчестил древний род;
Вот за что отчизну предал
Раздраженный Юлиан.

Мавры хлынули потоком
На испанские брега.   10
Царство готфов миновалось,
И с престола пал Родрик.

Готфы пали не бесславно:
Храбро билися они,
Долго мавры сомневались,
Одолеет кто кого.

come to make you his confession;
he'll receive his absolution,
you'll have rest for evermore."

Dream that brings relief and joy!
But my parched soul hardly dares
to believe or disbelieve it.
Can it really now be true   30
that my end is near at hand?
I am fearful, I am hopeful –
fearful of eternal torment,
hopeful of divine compassion.
Grant my spirit peace, Creator.
But Thy will be done, I pray –
Thine, not mine...

                  Who is that coming?   RC

727

FROM SOUTHEY'S
RODERICK, LAST OF THE GOTHS

I

Into Spain, his native country,
Julian enticed the Moors,
meaning thus to punish Roderick
for a private injury.

For the king had raped his daughter,
and had shamed his ancient house.
That is why the count in anger
had betrayed his fatherland.

So the Moorish hordes had flooded
north across to Spanish shores,   10
bringing down the Gothic kingdom
and its king from off his throne.

Gothic troops died undishonoured:
bravely they had fought the fight.
Long the Moorish chiefs had doubted
who would triumph over whom.

Восемь дней сраженье длилось;
Спор решен был наконец:
Был на поле битвы пойман
Конь любимый короля;   20

Шлем и меч его тяжелый
Были найдены в пыли.
Короля почли убитым,
И никто не пожалел.

Но Родрик в живых остался,
Бился он все восемь дней —
Он сперва хотел победы,
Там уж смерти лишь алкал.

И кругом свистали стрелы,
Не касаяся его,   30
Мимо дротики летали,
Шлема меч не рассекал.

Напоследок, утомившись,
Соскочил с коня Родрик,
Меч с запекшеюся кровью
От ладони отклеил,

Бросил об земь шлем пернатый
И блестящую броню.
И спасенный мраком ночи
С поля битвы он ушел.   40

II

От полей кровавой битвы
Удаляется Родрик;
Короля опередила
Весть о гибели его.

Стариков и бедных женщин
На распутьях видит он;
Все толпой бегут от мавров
К укрепленным городам.

Все, рыдая, молят Бога
О спасенье христиан,   50
Все Родрика проклинают;
И проклятья слышит он.

Eight long days the battle lasted
till the conflict was resolved.
Then the king's beloved stallion
on the battlefield was caught.   20

Helmet too and heavy sabre
were discovered in the mud.
Roderick, though, was unlamented,
thought to be among the slain.

But the king in fact was living.
He had fought through all eight days.
At the start he'd hoped to conquer,
latterly just longed for death.

All around him arrows whistled –
none of them, though, touched the king;   30
every javelin flew past him;
sword blades glanced from off his helm.

In the end, from sheer exhaustion,
Roderick jumped from off his horse,
tugged his sword, with gore now sticky,
from his palm and let it fall,

threw to earth his feathered helmet
and his bright enamelled mail –
then in cover of night's darkness
from the battlefield he fled.   40

II

Far away did Roderick hasten
from that scene of bloody strife,
but the baleful news spread faster
that he was already dead.

Agèd men and widowed women
at each crossroads he beheld,
fleeing from the Moors for refuge
into walled and gated towns.

All were sobbing, all imploring
God to rescue Christian Spain –   50
all on Roderick heaped their curses,
and those curses Roderick heard.

И с поникшею главою
Мимо их пройти спешит,
И не смеет даже молвить:
Помолитесь за него.

Наконец на берег моря
В третий день приходит он.
Видит темную пещеру
На пустынном берегу.   60

В той пещере он находит
Крест и заступ — а в углу
Труп отшельника и яму,
Им изрытую давно.

Тленье трупу не коснулось,
Он лежит окостенев,
Ожидая погребенья
И молитвы христиан.

И с мольбою об усопшем
Схоронил его король,   70
И в пещере поселился
Над могилою его.

Он питаться стал плодами
И водою ключевой;
И себе могилу вырыл,
Как предшественник его.

Короля в уединенье
Стал лукавый искушать,
И виденьями ночными
Краткий сон его мутить.   80

Он проснется с содроганьем,
Полон страха и стыда;
Упоение соблазна
Сокрушает дух его.

Хочет он молиться Богу
И не может. Бес ему
Шепчет в уши звуки битвы
Или страстные слова.

So with lowered head he hurried
past these sad and angry folk –
did not even dare to tell them:
"Pray for your defeated king!"

Then at last he reached the sea coast
on the third day of his flight,
and espied a gloomy cavern
down beside the empty shore.   60

In the cavern he discovered
crucifix and spade; beyond
lay a hermit's corpse, and by it,
dug long back, an empty grave.

No decay had touched the body,
which was resting, rigid now,
waiting to be given burial
and a Christian requiem.

Soon, with prayers for the departed,
Roderick had the corpse interred,   70
and within the hermit's cavern
made his home above the tomb.

He began to feed on berries
and drink water from a spring,
and, just like his predecessor,
dug himself a burial space.

In that wilderness the Devil
came to tempt the lonely king,
and with nightly apparitions
to disturb his fitful sleep.   80

He'd awake with fits of shaking,
overcome by fear and shame,
as the frenzy of seduction
threatened to engulf his soul.

He to pray to God kept yearning,
but he could not. Satan hissed
in his ear the cries of battle,
or the words seducers use.

Он в унынии проводит
Дни и ночи недвижим,
Устремив глаза на море,
Поминая старину.

III

Но отшельник, чьи останки
Он усердно схоронил,
За него перед Всевышним
Заступился в небесах.

В сновиденье благодатном
Он явился королю,
Белой ризою одеян
И сияньем окружен.

И король, объятый страхом,
Ниц повергся перед ним,
И вещал ему угодник:
«Встань — и миру вновь явись.

Ты венец утратил царский,
Но Господь руке твоей
Даст победу над врагами,
А душе твоей покой».

Пробудясь, господню волю
Сердцем он уразумел,
И, с пустынею расставшись,
В путь отправился король.

728

СТРАННИК

из Беньяна

I

Однажды странствуя среди долины дикой,
Незапно был объят я скорбию великой
И тяжким бременем подавлен и согбен,
Как тот, кто на суде в убийстве уличен.
Потупя голову, в тоске ломая руки,
Я в воплях изливал души пронзенной муки
И горько повторял, метаясь как больной:
«Что делать буду я? Что станется со мной?»

In remorse and deep dejection
day and night alone he sat   90
motionless, observed the seascape
and thought back upon the past.

III

But the hermit, whose dead body
Roderick gently had interred,
interceded in the heavens
with the Lord for Roderick's soul.

In a life-restoring vision
he appeared before the king,
clothed in robe of dazzling whiteness,
radiating heavenly light.   100

Roderick, overcome with terror,
fell down prostrate to the ground,
but the saintly hermit told him:
"Stand, go back into the world!

"You have forfeited your kingship,
but the Lord is granting you
triumph over your opponents
and serenity within."

Coming to himself now, Roderick
took to heart God's will for him,   110
parted from his lonely refuge
and set off upon his way.   RC

728

THE PILGRIM

from Bunyan

I

One day I wandered through a dreary dale,
when suddenly my heart began to fail.
A heavy burden made me gasp for breath,
as when some murderer hears the doom of death.
I bowed my head, I wrung my hands in grief;
my soul cried out – in pain beyond relief –
sobbing and moaning, racked with feverish fear:
"What shall I do? Where flee? For surely doom is near!"

II

И так я, сетуя, в свой дом пришел обратно.
Уныние мое всем было непонятно.　　　　　　　　　10
При детях и жене сначала я был тих
И мысли мрачные хотел таить от них;
Но скорбь час от часу меня стесняла боле;
И сердце наконец раскрыл я по неволе.
«О горе, горе нам! Вы, дети, ты жена! —
Сказал я, — ведайте; моя душа полна
Тоской и ужасом, мучительное бремя
Тягчит меня. Идет! уж близко, близко время:
Наш город пламени и ветрам обречен;
Он в угли и золу вдруг будет обращен　　　　20
И мы погибнем все, коль не успеем вскоре
Обресть убежище; а где? о горе, горе!»

III

Мои домашние в смущение пришли
И здравый ум во мне расстроенным почли.
Но думали, что ночь и сна покой целебный
Охолодят во мне болезни жар враждебный.
Я лег, но во всю ночь всё плакал и вздыхал
И ни на миг очей тяжелых не смыкал.
Поутру я один сидел, оставя ложе.
Они пришли ко мне; на их вопрос я то же,　　30
Что прежде, говорил. Тут ближние мои,
Не доверяя мне, за должное почли
Прибегнуть к строгости. Они с ожесточеньем
Меня на правый путь и бранью и презреньем
Старались обратить. Но я, не внемля им,
Всё плакал и вздыхал, унынием тесним.
И наконец они от крика утомились
И от меня, махнув рукою, отступились
Как от безумного, чья речь и дикий плач
Докучны, и кому суровый нужен врач.　　　　40

IV

Пошел я вновь бродить — уныньем изнывая
И взоры вкруг себя со страхом обращая,
Как раб, замысливший отчаянный побег,
Иль путник, до дождя спешащий на ночлег.
Духовный труженик — влача свою веригу,
Я встретил юношу, читающего книгу.
Он тихо поднял взор — и вопросил меня,
О чем, бродя один, так горько плачу я?

II

Lamenting thus, I hurried home again;
no one could understand my inner pain.   10
I spoke but little – watched the children play –
and tried to hide my gloomy thoughts away;
but hour by hour I felt the pain increase,
until my heart refused to hold its peace.
"Woe to us all! Dear children! Darling wife!"
I cried. "Know this! My soul is full of strife
and fear! A grievous burden weighs me down:
the hour is close at hand – unhappy town!
Too soon in roaring flame shall all be burnt,
through fire and wind to dust and ashes turned…   20
And all are doomed to perish in a day
unless we flee… But where? Oh grief!… I dare not stay!"

III

My household then conferred in great alarm –
perhaps some inner shock had done me harm?
Sweet sleep, the gentle healer – so they said –
would still the hammers working in my head…
Seeking for rest, I groaned and sighed and wept,
all the tormented night I never slept.
At dawn I rose and sat alone. Once more
they sought me out – I answered as before.   30
My worthy kinsmen, baffled and perplexed,
thought fit to turn to drastic measures next:
threat, and contempt and insult… thus they tried
to put me right! Heedless, I sobbed and cried,
until my weeping wore their patience down.
They gave me up for lost – a tedious clown,
a wretched lunatic, whose endless whining
deserved the sternest measures, called for close confining.

IV

Again in deepest gloom I wandered wide,
casting affrighted looks on either side,   40
like some poor serf, resolved on desperate flight,
or weary traveller, dreading rain and night.
I dragged my chains of penance, sore and bleeding,
until I met a youth intent on reading.
He raised his eyes and gently asked me why
I wandered up and down…what made me cry

И я в ответ ему: «Познай мой жребий злобный:
Я осужден на смерть и позван в суд загробный —⁣   50
И вот о чем крушусь: к суду я не готов,
И смерть меня страшит.» — «Коль жребий твой таков, —
Он возразил, — и ты так жалок в самом деле,
Чего ж ты ждешь? зачем не убежишь отселе?»
И я: «Куда ж бежать? какой мне выбрать путь?»
Тогда: «Не видишь ли, скажи, чего-нибудь» —
Сказал мне юноша, даль указуя перстом.
Я оком стал глядеть болезненно-отверстым,
Как от бельма врачом избавленный слепец.
«Я вижу некий свет», — сказал я наконец.⁣   60
«Иди ж, — он продолжал; — держись сего ты света;
Пусть будет он тебе единственная мета,
Пока ты тесных врат спасенья не достиг;
Ступай!» — И я бежать пустился в тот же миг.

V

Побег мой произвел в семье моей тревогу,
И дети и жена кричали мне с порогу,
Чтоб воротился я скорее. Крики их
На площадь привлекли приятелей моих;
Один бранил меня, другой моей супруге
Советы подавал, иной жалел о друге,⁣   70
Кто поносил меня, кто на смех подымал,
Кто силой воротить соседям предлагал;
Иные уж за мной гнались; но я тем боле
Спешил перебежать городовое поле,
Дабы скорей узреть, оставя те места,
Спасенья верный путь и тесные врата.

729

ТРИ НАБРОСКА О ПРОДОЛЖЕНИИ
ЕВГЕНИЯ ОНЕГИНА

а. Плетневу

Ты мне советуешь, Плетнев любезный,
Оставленный роман наш продолжать
И строгий век, расчета век железный,
Рассказами пустыми угощать.
Ты думаешь, что с целию полезной
Тревогу славы можно сочетать,

so bitterly? "Oh, hard and heavy curse!"
I answered. "Doomed to fearful death, and worse –
beyond the grave – and fearing endless woe:
behold me, unprepared..." "If this be so,"   50
the youth replied, "if such must be your fate,
why do you linger here? Why hesitate?"
"Is there a way?" I asked. "Then tell me where!"
"Surely you see..." he said. "Look over there!"
He pointed far away – I blinked and stared
like some poor wretch with vision half impaired.
"I see a glimmering light!" I said at last.
"Then go, good friend, and hold that vision fast,
seek for the narrow gate of life and light!
Begone!" So there and then I fixed my thoughts on flight.   60

V

News of my plan to flee spread far and wide:
around the gate my wife and children cried,
"Come back! Come back!" Their sorry shrieks brought out
a crowd of anxious friends who milled about
the village square. While one – sincere and sad –
counselled my wife, another called me mad;
some cursed, some laughed, some held me up to coarse
abuse, or planned to hold me down by force;
a few pursued, prepared to seize and bind me...
But soon I left our village fields behind me,   70
eager to find the path to sure salvation,
and pass the narrow gate, beyond all condemnation.   JC

729

THREE DRAFTS ABOUT CONTINUING
EUGENE ONÉGIN

a. for Pletnyóv

Pletnyóv, my friend, I hear your exhortation:
"Resume the novel you had set aside,
and entertain this iron-hearted nation
with chapters new (however slight inside)."
You judge that the desire for approbation
with profit-making can be unified,

И что .... нашему собрату
Брать с публики умеренную плату.
Ты говоришь: пока Онегин жив,
Дотоль роман не кончен — нет причины   10
Его прервать... к тому же план счастлив —

б. Друзьям

Вы за «Онегина» советуете, други,
Приняться мне опять в осенние досуги.
Вы говорите мне: он жив и не женат.
Итак, еще роман не кончен — это клад:
Вставляй в просторную, вместительную раму
Картины новые — открой нам диораму:
Привалит публика, платя тебе за вход —
(Что даст еще тебе и славу и доход).
Пожалуй, я бы рад —
               Так некогда поэт...

г. Друзьям

В мои осенние досуги,
В те дни, как любо мне писать,
Вы мне советуете, други,
Рассказ забытый продолжать.
Вы говорите справедливо,
Что странно, даже неучтиво
Роман не конча перервать,
Отдав уже его в печать,
Что должно своего героя
Как бы то ни было женить,   10
По крайней мере уморить,
И лица прочие пристроя,
Отдав им дружеский поклон,
Из лабиринта вывесть вон.

Вы говорите: «Слава Богу,
Покамест твой Онегин жив,
Роман не кончен — понемногу
Иди вперед; не будь ленив.
Со славы, вняв ее призванью,
Сбирай оброк хвалой и бранью   20
Рисуй и франтов городских
И милых барышень своих,
Войну и бал, дворец и хату,

and that for our *Onégin* it is honest
to charge the public prices more than modest.
You say that, while Onégin's living on,
the novel's still not finished; there's no reason 10
for breaking off; the plot's a clever one... RC

b. for friends

So it's your wish, my friends, that I be undertaking,
these idle autumn days, fresh work on my *Onégin*.
You keep reminding me, "He's unwed and alive,
and so the novel's still unfinished. Write and thrive!
You've made yourself a frame that's wide enough and spacious:
new artwork mount in it; with vivid scenes dismay us;
the public flocking in will pay an entrance fee –
in consequence both fame and profit you will see."
Well, maybe. I'd be glad...
"A poet once, you know..." RC

c. for friends

In my autumnal hours of leisure,
these days when writing seems no chore,
you tell me, friends, I should find pleasure
in turning to my tale once more.
"How odd," you comment, "did it look,
how rude, to interrupt the book
without the end so much as hinted,
and when it was already printed!
Its hero should deserve the grace
of somehow getting himself married, 10
or at the least of being buried.
Please give each character a space,
then wish them all a fond adieu
and each one from the maze bring through."

You say: "Thank God and all that's holy!
While your Onégin still survives,
the tale's unfinished. Fast or slowly,
get on with it – no shutting eyes!
And, having heard the call of fame,
take what you're owed in praise or blame. 20
Portray the fops you've met in town,
the girls whose charms you've noted down,
wars, dances, palaces, a shack,

Чердак, и келью, и харем
И с нашей публики меж тем
Бери умеренную плату,
За книжку по пяти рублей —
Налог не тягостный, ей-ей».

730

* * *

К кастрату раз пришел скрыпач,
Он был бедняк, а тот богач.
«Смотри, сказал певец безмудый, —
Мои алмазы, изумруды —
Я их от скуки разбирал.
А! кстати, брат, — он продолжал, —
Когда тебе бывает скучно,
Ты что творишь, сказать прошу.»
В ответ бедняга равнодушно:
— Я? я муде себе чешу.   10

731

* * *

Как редко плату получает
Великий добрый человек
....
.... в кой-то век
За все заботы и досады
И — то дивиться всякий рад! —
Берет достойные награды
Или достоин сих наград.

732

МИХАЙЛОВСКОЕ

... Вновь я посетил
Тот уголок земли, где я провел
Изгнанником два года незаметных.
Уж десять лет ушло с тех пор — и много

a garret, hermit's cell, harem,
and charge a payment that will seem
not too high to take folk aback –
five roubles for the book, let's say,
not an outrageous price to pay."   RC

730

* * *

Once to a rich castrato's door
there came a fiddler, who was poor.
"See these," the ball-less wonder fluted,
"my gems, of value undisputed,
which boredom drove me to sort through...
But tell me," he piped up anew,
"my friend, when feeling bored and sated,
what do *you* do, when all else palls?"
At which the poor one calmly stated:
"Me? I'm content to scratch my balls."   JD

731

* * *

How seldom, friend, a good great man inherits
honour and wealth with all his worth and pains!
It sounds like stories from the land of spirits
if any man obtain that which he merits
or any merit that which he obtains.

SAMUEL TAYLOR COLERIDGE

732

MIKHÁYLOVSKOYE

... I'm visiting again
this corner of the earth where once I spent
two years of exile in obscurity.
A decade more has passed since then – and many

Переменилось в жизни для меня,
И сам, покорный общему закону,
Переменился я — но здесь опять
Минувшее меня объемлет живо,
И, кажется, вечор еще бродил
Я в этих рощах...
                    Вот опальный домик, 10
Где жил я с бедной нянею моей.
Уже старушки нет — уж за стеною
Не слышу я шагов ее тяжелых,
Ни кропотливого ее дозора.

Вот холм лесистый, над которым часто
Я сиживал недвижим — и глядел
На озеро, воспоминая с грустью
Иные берега, иные волны...
Меж нив златых и пажитей зеленых
Оно синея стелется широко; 20
Через его неведомые воды
Плывет рыбак и тянет за собой
Убогий невод. По брегам отлогим
Рассеяны деревни — там за ними
Скривилась мельница, насилу крылья
Ворочая при ветре...
               На границе
Владений дедовских, на месте том,
Где в гору подымается дорога,
Изрытая дождями, три сосны
Стоят — одна поодаль, две другие 30
Друг к дружке близко, — здесь, когда их мимо
Я проезжал верхом при свете лунном,
Знакомым шумом шорох их вершин
Меня приветствовал. По той дороге
Теперь поехал я, и пред собою
Увидел их опять. Они всё те же,
Всё тот же их знакомый уху шорох —
Но около корней их устарелых
(Где некогда всё было пусто, голо)
Теперь младая роща разрослась, 40
Зеленая семья; кусты теснятся
Под сенью их как дети. А вдали
Стоит один угрюмый их товарищ
Как старый холостяк, и вкруг него
По-прежнему всё пусто.
                  Здравствуй, племя

a change has taken place in how I live;
and I, obedient to the law of nature,
myself have changed – now that I'm here again, though,
the past enfolds me in its warm embrace;
it seems but yesterday that I was roaming
around these woods…
                              Yes, here's my home of exile,   10
where I and my poor nanny lived together.
She's here no more – no longer through the wall
can I now hear her footsteps' heavy tread,
as she so zealously patrolled the house.

There is the wooded hill on which I used
often to sit unstirring, and look out
across the lake, recalling from the past
in sorrow other shores and other waters…
The lake, a sheet of indigo, spreads wide
among green pasturelands and golden cornfields;   20
over the unfathomed surface of the lake
there rows a fisherman who drags behind him
a patched-up net. Along the sloping shore
lie scattered settlements, and there beyond them
a crooked windmill stands, whose creaking sails
turn stiffly in the breeze.
                              At the far edge
of Grandfather's estate you reach a spot
where the main road, deep-rutted by the rains,
begins to climb uphill; nearby you'll see
three pines, the one apart, the others standing   30
quite close, like an old couple; it was here,
whenever I was riding on my horse
by moonlight, I would hear the treetops rustle
in friendly greeting. This time, as I rode
along that way, I saw them once again,
those same three pines; again I heard the same
familiar sound of rustling in their treetops –
but down around their gnarled and ancient roots,
where everything before was bare and empty,
a copse of fresh young pines has sprouted up,   40
a green-clad family, the saplings clustering,
like children, down below. But farther off
their fellow pine yet stands morose and lonely,
like some old bachelor, and round him still
the ground lies vacant.
                              Greetings, family,

Младое, незнакомое! не я
Увижу твой могучий поздний возраст,
Когда перерастешь моих знакомцев
И старую главу их заслонишь
От глаз прохожего. Но пусть мой внук   50
Услышит ваш приветный шум, когда,
С приятельской беседы возвращаясь,
Веселых и приятных мыслей полон,
Пройдет он мимо вас во мраке ночи
И обо мне вспомянет.

733

ВЛАСТЬ КРАСОТЫ

Я думал, сердце позабыло
Способность легкую страдать,
Я говорил: тому, что было,
Уж не бывать! уж не бывать!
Прошли восторги, и печали,
И легковерные мечты...
Но вот опять затрепетали
Пред мощной властью красоты.

734

БЕДНОСТЬ

из Барри Корнуолла

О бедность! затвердил я наконец
Урок твой горький! Чем я заслужил
Твое гоненье, властелин враждебный,
Довольства враг, суровый сна мутитель?..
Что делал я, когда я был богат,
О том упоминать я не намерен:
В молчании добро должно твориться,
Но нечего об этом толковать.
Здесь пищу я найду для дум моих,
Я чувствую, что не совсем погиб   10
Я с участью моей...

of unknown youngsters! I'll not live to see
the time when you're mature and standing strong,
when you shall have outgrown my good old friends
and screened their ageing heads from prying eyes
of travellers. My grandson, though, I hope,   50
may hear your rustled greeting when at night,
after an evening chatting with some friends,
full of a sense of comradeship and joy,
he passes you all by along the road
and thinks of me...   RC

733

BEAUTY'S POWER

To ache with love, I thought, downhearted,
I've lost my old propensity.
"All that which used to be," I'd started
to sigh, "no more will ever be.
Love's joys and pains – they've stopped occurring,
those dreams too easy to believe…"
But now once more I feel them stirring –
so much can Beauty's power achieve!   RC

734

POVERTY

from Barry Cornwall

O Poverty! At last I've learnt by heart
your bitter lesson. How did I deserve
your harassment, you heartless autocrat,
foe of contentment, sleep's disquieter?
All that I did when I was still a rich man
I've no intention of rehearsing now –
we should keep silent on the good we do.
But there's no point in talking on like this:
it must bring food for thought to me alone.
My conscience tells me that I've fallen less low   10
than have my fortunes...   RC

735

* * *

Если ехать вам случится
От Тригорского на Псков,
Там, где Луговка струится
Меж отлогих берегов, —
От большой дороги справа,
Между полем и селом,
Вам представится дубрава,
Слева сад и барский дом.

Летом, в час, как за холмами
Утопает солнца шар,   10
Дом облит его лучами,
Окна блещут как пожар,
И, ездой скучая, мимо
.... развлечен,
Путник смотрит невидимо
На семейство, на балкон.

736

НА ВЫЗДОРОВЛЕНИЕ ЛУКУЛЛА

подражание латинскому

Ты угасал, богач младой!
Ты слышал плач друзей печальных.
Уж смерть являлась за тобой
В дверях сеней твоих хрустальных.
Она, как втершийся с утра
Заимодавец терпеливый,
Торча в передней молчаливой,
  Не трогалась с ковра.

В померкшей комнате твоей
Врачи угрюмые шептались.   10
Твоих нахлебников, цирцей
Смущеньем лица омрачались;
Вздыхали верные рабы
И за тебя богов молили,
Не зная в страхе, что сулили
  Им тайные судьбы.

735

* * *

If your carriage should be going
from Trigórskoye to Pskov,
you'll the Lúgovka glimpse flowing
past steep banks; there do glance off
to the rightward of the roadway –
field and village lie each side –
then you'll see, past grove of oak, a
manor house with park beside.

As the sun to the horizon
sinks in summertime, its rays   10
bathe the house in golden light and
set the window panes ablaze.
Traveller, far it is you've ridden,
wearied by monotony –
now you'll see, though you're still hidden,
friends upon the balcony.   RC

736

ON THE RECOVERY OF LUCULLUS

after the Latin

You ebbed away, young man of wealth!
You heard friends weeping as you lay.
Outside your crystal entryway,
the caller at the door was Death,
a creditor who sidled early
into your hall, said not a word,
but waited patiently and sternly
    and wouldn't be deterred.

Grim doctors spoke in voices muted
within your chamber hushed and dim.   10
The hangers-on and Circes brooded,
their faces clouded by chagrin.
Your faithful slaves heaved sighs, afraid
of what their destinies concealed,
and so, with all their hearts, they prayed
    the gods that you'd be healed.

А между тем наследник твой,
Как ворон к мертвечине падкой,
Бледнел и трясся над тобой,
Знобим стяжанья лихорадкой.   20
Уже скупой его сургуч
Пятнал замки твоей конторы;
И мнил загресть он злата горы
  В пыли бумажных куч.

Он мнил: «Теперь уж у вельмож
Не стану няньчить ребятишек;
Я сам вельможа буду тож;
В подвалах, благо, есть излишек.
Теперь мне честность — трын-трава!
Жену обсчитывать не буду,   30
И воровать уже забуду
  Казенные дрова!»

Но ты воскрес. Твои друзья,
В ладони хлопая ликуют;
Рабы как добрая семья
Друг друга в радости целуют;
Бодрится врач, подняв очки;
Гробовый мастер взоры клонит;
А вместе с ним приказчик гонит
  Наследника в толчки.   40

Так жизнь тебе возвращена
Со всею прелестью своею;
Смотри: бесценный дар она;
Умей же пользоваться ею;
Укрась ее; года летят,
Пора! Введи в свои чертоги
Жену красавицу — и боги
  Ваш брак благословят.

737

ИЗ БИБЛЕЙСКОЙ КНИГИ ИУДИФЬ

Когда владыка ассирийский
Народы казнию казнил,
И Олоферн весь край азийский
Его деснице покорил, —
Высок смиреньем терпеливым

But like a raven quick to feed
on carrion, your heir, it's said,
then hovered, ashen, by your bed
and trembled, feverish with greed.   20
By then, his stingy sealing wax
had fouled your office locks – a sign
of all the gold he thought to mine
   in dusty paper stacks.

"No more," he thought, "will any see
me doting on the spawn of lords;
I too will be a rich grandee,
my cellars piled with wealth in hoards.
Now honesty comes easily!
I won't short-change my wife or, prone   30
to pilfer in necessity,
   steal firewood from the Crown!"

But you've arisen. At the sight,
your friends all clap in exultation;
the slaves, like loving family, hasten
to kiss each other in delight;
the doctor's face looks reassured;
the coffin maker and the heir
are both, with prodding from the steward,
   sent packing in despair.   40

You're given back your life, replete
with all its sweetness and its joy,
a priceless gift that you must treat
with care and put to good employ;
adorn it now; the years fly by;
it's time you bring a lovely wife
within your halls; the gods on high
   will bless your married life.   CC

737

FROM THE BOOK OF JUDITH

Now when Assyria's great king
had wreaked destruction on the nations
and Holophernes had subjected
all Asia to the great king's rule,
Israel, strong in faith in God,

И крепок верой в бога сил,
Перед сатрапом горделивым
Израил выи не склонил;
Во все пределы Иудеи
Проникнул трепет. Иереи   10
Одели вретищем алтарь.
Народ завыл, объятый страхом,
Главу покрыв золой и прахом,
И внял ему всевышний царь.

Притек сатрап к ущельям горным
И зрит: их узкие врата
Замком замкнуты непокорным;
Стеной, как поясом узорным,
Препоясáлась высота.
И над тесниной торжествуя,   20
Как муж на страже, в тишине
Стоит, белеясь, Ветилуя
В недостижимой вышине.

Сатрап смутился изумленный —
И гнев в нем душу помрачил...
И свой совет разноплеменный
Он — любопытный — вопросил:
«Кто сей народ? и что их сила,
И кто им вождь, и отчего
Сердца их дерзость воспалила,   30
И их надежда на кого?...»
И встал тогда сынов Аммона
Военачальник Ахиор
И рек — и Олоферн со трона
Склонил к нему и слух и взор.

738

ВДОХНОВЕНИЕ

из Египетских ночей

> *Поэт сам избирает предметы для своих песен;*
> *толпа не имеет права управлять его вдохновением.*

Поэт идет — открыты вежды,
Но он не видит никого;
А между тем за край одежды

awesome in patient lowliness,
refused to grovel in abasement
before the overbearing satrap.
Throughout the territory of Judah
God's people trembled; temple priests   10
draped sackcloth on the holy altar;
a frightened nation cried to heaven,
and smeared their heads with dust and ashes.
The Lord Almighty heard their prayer.

The satrap marched against the uplands;
the narrow mountain pass, he saw,
was barricaded by the rebels;
the heights were girdled by a wall
like a well-wrought, well-fastened belt.
Rising triumphantly above,   20
impregnable upon the summit,
like a good husband on the watch,
there stood Bethulia, tranquil, radiant.

The satrap was surprised, perplexed,
his judgement darkened by his anger...
Unsure of what to do, he questioned
his council, drawn from many nations:
"Who is this people? What's their strength?
Who's leading them? What gives to them
the boldness that inflames their hearts?   30
On whose help have they set their hope?"
Then up stood Achior, commander
of the auxiliaries from Ammon;
he spoke – and from his throne the satrap,
Lord Holophernes, watched and listened...   RC

738

INSPIRATION

from Egyptian Nights

> *A poet chooses the subjects of his songs himself;*
> *the public has no right to direct his inspiration.*

There was a poet on his way –
with open eyes, but seeing no one.
Another man, though, passing by

Прохожий дергает его...
«Скажи: зачем без цели бродишь?
Едва достиг ты высоты,
И вот уж долу взор низводишь
И низойти стремишься ты.
На стройный мир ты смотришь смутно;
Бесплодный жар тебя томит;   10
Предмет ничтожный поминутно
Тебя тревожит и манит.
Стремиться к небу должен гений;
Обязан истинный поэт
Для вдохновенных песнопений
Избрать возвышенный предмет».

Зачем крутится ветр в овраге,
Подъемлет лист и пыль несет,
Когда корабль в недвижной влаге
Его дыханья жадно ждет?   20
Зачем от гор и мимо башен
Летит орел, тяжел и страшен,
На чахлый пень? Спроси его.
Зачем арапа своего
Младая любит Дездемона,
Как месяц любит ночи мглу?
Затем, что ветру и орлу
И сердцу девы нет закона.
Таков поэт: как Аквилон
Что хочет, то и носит он —   30
Орлу подобно, он летает
И, не спросясь ни у кого,
Как Дездемона избирает
Кумир для сердца своего.

739

ПИР ПЕТРА ПЕРВОГО

Над Невою резво вьются
Флаги пестрые судов;
Звучно с лодок раздаются
Песни дружные гребцов;
В царском доме пир веселый;
Речь гостей хмельна, шумна;
И Нева пальбой тяжелой
Далеко потрясена.

took hold of his lapel and asked him:
"You're wandering aimlessly – why so?
You've hardly made it to the heights,
when – there! – you're looking down already
and hastening to descend once more.
This handsome world you view but dimly;
the fire within you burns in vain;   10
themes that attract and exercise you
are always insignificant.
True genius should aim for heaven:
for poetry to be inspired
a real poet needs to choose
themes that are lofty and sublime."

Why does the wind whirl in the gully,
whipping up leaves and clouds of dust,
when ships becalmed upon the ocean
impatiently await its breath?   20
Why does an eagle, mighty, fearsome,
fly from the crags past lofty towers
to a rotten tree stump? Ask him, then!
Why does the youthful Desdemona
bestow her love on black Othello,
just as the moon, too, loves black night?
The reason is that wind and eagle
and a girl's heart obey no rule.
So too a poet: like the gale
he gathers anything he wants;   30
he flies, like the eagle, where he will;
and freely, asking no one's leave,
like Desdemona, he insists
on choosing the idol he's to love.   RC

739

THE FEAST OF PETER I

Ship flags, flourishing their colours
o'er Nevá, catch wind and play.
Boatmen's songs rise up in chorus
and resound above the spray.
In the tsar's house there is feasting,
tipsy guests are in good cheer,
and the cannon fire, unceasing,
shakes the river far and near.

Что пирует царь великий
В Питербурге-городке?
Отчего пальба и клики
И эскадра на реке?
Озарен ли честью новой
Русский штык иль русский флаг?
Побежден ли швед суровый?
Мира ль просит грозный враг?

Иль в отъятый край у шведа
Прибыл Брантов утлый бот,
И пошел навстречу *деда*
Всей семьей наш юный флот,
И воинственные внуки
Стали в строй пред стариком,
И раздался в честь Науки
Песен хор и пушек гром?

Годовщину ли Полтавы
Торжествует государь,
День, как жизнь своей державы
Спас от Карла русский царь?
Родила ль Екатерина?
Именинница ль она,
Чудотворца-исполина
Чернобровая жена?

Нет! Он с подданным мирится;
Виноватому вину
Отпуская, веселится;
Кружку пенит с ним одну;
И в чело его целует,
Светел сердцем и лицом;
И прощенье торжествует,
Как победу над врагом.

Оттого-то шум и клики
В Питербурге-городке,
И пальба и гром музыки
И эскадра на реке;
Оттого-то в час веселый
Чаша царская полна,
И Нева пальбой тяжелой
Далеко потрясена.

Why is Peter making merry
in the town of Petersburg?   10
Why are warships at the ready?
Why are shouts and cannon heard?
Have new honours cast a glow on
Russian flags and bayonets?
Is the beaten Swedish foeman
making peace instead of threats?

Or is Brandt's frail boat now sailing
into parts won from the Swede,
while our youthful fleet is hailing
the old "grandsire" they succeed,   20
and the warlike clan, converging,
fall in line before their sire,
and, in tribute then to Learning,
songs resound and cannons fire?

Are they marking the occasion
of Poltáva and its strife,
when the tsar, from Charles' invasion,
saved his country's very life?
Is today his Catherine's name day?
Is that wondrous titan proud   30
of a child born to his lady
fair of face and raven-browed?

No! He's pardoning offences,
with a subject making up.
As he does, his mirth's infectious,
and they raise a foaming cup.
The offender's brow he kisses,
heart and countenance aglow,
and he celebrates forgiveness
like a victory o'er the foe.   40

That's why lively songs and clamour
fill the town of Petersburg,
why the warships stand at anchor
and why cannon fire is heard.
That's why Peter's cup is brimming
at this hour of festive cheer,
and the cannon's mighty dinning
shakes the river far and near.   CC

740

ПОДРАЖАНИЕ АРАБСКОМУ

Отрок милый, отрок нежный,
Не стыдись, навек ты мой;
Тот же в нас огонь мятежный,
Жизнью мы живем одной.
Не боюся я насмешек:
Мы сдвоились меж собой,
Мы точь-в-точь двойной орешек
Под единой скорлупой.

741

* * *

На это скажут мне с улыбкою неверной:
— Смотрите, вы поэт уклонный, лицемерный,
Вы нас морочите — вам слава не нужна,
Смешной и суетной вам кажется она;
Зачем же пишете? — Я? для себя. — За что же
Печатаете вы? — Для денег. — Ах, мой Боже!
Как стыдно! — Почему ж? ………………

742

ИЗ СЕРПСКОГО

— Не видала ль, девица,
  Коня моего?
— Я видала, видела
  Коня твоего.
— Куда, красна девица,
  Мой конь пробежал?
  — Твой конь пробежал
На Дунай реку —
    Бежа твой конь,
    Тебя проклинал,
    Тебя проклинал

…………………………

740

AFTER THE ARABIC

Charming lad, so young and tender,
mine for ever, have no shame;
rebels both, we won't surrender,
life has made us both the same.
I don't mind the constant mocking:
two can bear it twice as well;
we're twin walnuts interlocking,
wrapped inside a single shell.   JF

741

* * *

Then folk will say to me, amused but misbelieving,
"Poet, take care! You'll seem dishonest and misleading.
Don't try to fool us – if you've no desire for fame,
and if it's as absurd and pointless as you claim,
why do you write then?" "For myself." "And yet you even
publish your work – what for?" "For money." "God in heaven –
how sordid!" "But why so?"..........................   RC

742

FROM THE SERBIAN

"Pretty maiden, have you seen,
    have you seen my steed?"
"Yes I saw him, yes I've seen,
    I have seen your steed."
"Pretty maiden, whither's run,
    whither's run my steed?"
    "All the way he's run
    to the Danube's shore.
        Your steed as he ran
        heaped curses on you,   10
        heaped curses on you."

....   RC

743

* * *

Сей белокаменный фонтан,
Стихов узором испещренный,
Сооружен и изваян
....
Железный ковшик ...
.... цепью прицепленный
Кто б ни был ты: пастух, ...
Рыбак иль странник утомленный,
Приди и пей ....

744

* * *

Еще в ребячестве, бессмысленный и злой,
Я встретил старика с плешивой головой,
С очами быстрыми, зерцалом мысли зыбкой,
С устами, сжатыми наморщенной улыбкой ...

743

* * *

This fountain of the whitest stone,
engraved so skilfully with verses,
is built and carved to stand alone
....
A bowl of iron ....
.... by iron chain is tethered.
Whoso you are – a shepherd ....
fisherman, traveller tired and weathered,
come near and drink...............   RC

744

* * *

When I was still a boy, unruly and unwise,
I met a bald old man with ever-darting eyes
mirroring thoughts that sparked with novelty and guile,
his mouth and lips compressed to form a puckered smile ...   RC

1836

745

ИЗ ЯНА ПОТОЦКОГО

Альфонс садится на коня;
Ему хозяин держит стремя.
«Сеньор, послушайтесь меня:
Пускаться в путь теперь не время.
В горах опасно, ночь близка,
Другая вента далека.
Останьтесь здесь: готов вам ужин;
В камине разложен огонь;
Постеля есть — покой вам нужен,
А к стойлу тянется ваш конь».   10
— «Мне путешествие привычно
И днем и ночью — был бы путь, —
Тот отвечает, — неприлично
Бояться мне чего-нибудь.
Я дворянин, — ни черт, ни воры
Не могут удержать меня,
Когда спешу на службу я».
И дон Альфонс коню дал шпоры,
И едет рысью. Перед ним
Одна идет дорога в горы   20
Ущельем тесным и глухим.

Вот выезжает он в долину;
Какую ж видит он картину?
Кругом пустыня, дичь и голь...
А в стороне торчит глаголь,
И на глаголе том два тела
Висят. Закаркав, отлетела
Ватага черная ворон,
Лишь только к ним подъехал он.
То были трупы двух гитанов,   30

316

1836

745

FROM JAN POTOCKI

Alphonse leapt up astride his horse;
the landlord held the stirrup for him,
and said: "Señor, hear my advice:
now's not a time to start a journey:
the hills are dangerous, night is falling,
the nearest inn is far away.
Stay here. I have your supper ready;
a fire is burning in the hearth;
there is a bed – you need a rest;
your horse is straining for the stable."   10
The other answered: "I am used
to travelling by day or night.
Where there's a path, I'd be ashamed
to show a dread of anything.
A nobleman I am. No bandit,
no fiend can ever hold me back,
when I am bound for urgent duty."
Alphonse then spurred his horse, and off
they trotted. On ahead there lay
the one road leading through the mountains,   20
along a dark and narrow gorge.

Alphonse emerged into a valley,
astonished at the scene he saw –
all round a wasteland, wild and bare,
but on one side there loomed a gallows,
and on the gallows there were hanging
two bodies; black crows in a flock
cawed loudly and flew off as soon
as Don Alphonse drew near the place.
These were the corpses of *gitanos*,   30

Двух славных братьев-атаманов,
Давно повешенных и там
Оставленных в пример ворам.
Дождями небо их мочило,
А солнце знойное сушило,
Пустынный ветер их качал,
Клевать их ворон прилетал.
И шла молва в простом народе,
Что, обрываясь по ночам,
Они до утра на свободе   40
Гуляли, мстя своим врагам.

Альфонсов конь всхрапел и боком
Прошел их мимо, и потом
Понесся резво, легким скоком,
С своим бесстрашным седоком.

746

ЧИЖИК

Забыв и рощу и свободу,
Невольный чижик надо мной
Зерно клюет и брызжет воду,
И песнью тешится живой.

747

ЛЕИЛА

От меня вечор Леила
Равнодушно уходила.
Я сказал: «Постой, куда?»
А она мне возразила:
«Голова твоя седа».
Я насмешнице нескромной
Отвечал: «Всему пора!
То, что было мускус темный
Стало нынче камфора».
Но Леила неудачным   10
Посмеялася речам
И сказала: «Знаешь сам:
Сладок мускус новобрачным,
Камфора годна гробам».

two well-known robber chieftains, brothers,
who had been hanged there long before,
left to admonish other bandits;
they had been wetted by the rains,
parched by the torrid sun of summer,
swung by the winds of that bleak spot,
while ravens flew to peck their bones.
And simple people heard it said
that they descended of a night
and, free till morning came, roamed wide   40
to wreak revenge upon their foes.

Alphonse's horse let out a snort,
sidled past slowly, nostrils flaring,
then bounded briskly onwards, bearing
his rider, who still flinched at naught.   RC

746

A SISKIN

Of trees and liberty it thinks
no more, my cage bird overhead,
but pecks its grain and sips and prinks,
and sings a lively song instead.   JH

747

LEILA

Yesterday, as dark was falling,
Leila turned as if withdrawing.
"Wait," I said, "don't rush away."
In a tone aloof and taunting,
she replied, "Your head is grey."
Such presumption I refuted.
"All things in their time!" I said.
"Hair as dark as musk, transmuted,
takes on camphor's hue instead."
Leila laughed at my expression's   10
infelicity and said,
"Musk, as I need hardly mention,
sweetly scents the wedding bed.
Camphor's balm is for the dead."   CC

748

Д. В. ДАВЫДОВУ

при посылке Истории пугачевского бунта

Тебе певцу, тебе герою!
Не удалось мне за тобою
При громе пушечном, в огне
Скакать на бешеном коне.
Наездник смирного Пегаса,
Носил я старого Парнаса
Из моды вышедший мундир:
Но и по этой службе трудной,
И тут, о мой наездник чудный,
Ты мой отец и командир.   10
Вот мой Пугач: при первом взгляде
Он виден — плут, казак прямой;
В передовом твоем отряде
Урядник был бы он лихой.

749

ХУДОЖНИКУ

Грустен и весел вхожу, ваятель, в твою мастерскую:
  Гипсу ты мысли даешь, мрамор послушен тебе:
Сколько богов, и богинь, и героев!.. Вот Зевс Громовержец,
  Вот из подлобья глядит, дуя в цевницу, сатир.
Здесь зачинатель Барклай, а здесь совершитель Кутузов.
  Тут Аполлон — идеал, там Ниобея — печаль...
Весело мне. Но меж тем в толпе молчаливых кумиров —
  Грустен гуляю: со мной доброго Дельвига нет;
В темной могиле почил художников друг и советник.
  Как бы он обнял тебя! как бы гордился тобой!   10

750

ИУДА

подражание итальянскому

Как с древа сорвался предатель ученик,
Диявол прилетел, к лицу его приник,
Дхнул жизнь в него, взвился с своей добычей смрадной
И бросил труп живой в гортань геенны гладной...

748

FOR D.V. DAVÝDOV

on sending him The History of the Pugachóv Rebellion

For you – my bard, my hero dashing!
Through flying bullets, cannon crashing
I've not been privileged to speed
behind you on a fiery steed.
I've worn, while riding acquiescent
old Pegasus, the obsolescent
Parnassian uniform with pride –
but even in that hard vocation
you, genius of equitation,
are my commander and my guide.   10
Well, here's my *Pugachóv*, who's clearly
a Cossack true, and rogue writ large;
for his élan you'd prize him dearly
as sergeant in a mounted charge.   JD

749

FOR AN ARTIST

Gladly, but grieving within, I enter, skilled sculptor, your workshop:
    clay comes alive in your hands; marble submits to your power!
Gods are here, goddesses, heroes galore!… Look, Zeus, god of thunder;
    also a satyr I see, sly-looking, piping his flute.
Here's the commencer Barkláy, and there's the completer Kutúzov.
    Phoebus is here in his pride; there is Niobe in tears.
Truly I'm glad to have come! As I stroll past these taciturn statues
    I am in grief nonetheless – missing good Delvig, my pal:
artists' adviser and friend, he's at rest now beneath a dark tombstone.
    You he'd have warmly embraced – you he'd have proudly admired!   RC

750

JUDAS

after the Italian

When, choking, from the tree the false disciple drooped,
a wingèd fiend swooped down and to his visage stooped,
blew breath into the corpse, snatched off the stinking spoil
and cast him down within the hungry maw of Sheol…

Там бесы, радуясь и плеща, на рога
Прияли с хохотом всемирного врага
И шумно понесли к проклятому владыке,
И Сатана, привстав, с веселием на лике
Лобзанием своим насквозь прожег уста,
В предательскую ночь лобзавшие Христа.   10

751

* * *

Напрасно я бегу к сионским высотам,
Грех алчный гонится за мною по пятам...
Так, ноздри пыльные уткнув в песок сыпучий,
Голодный лев следит оленя бег пахучий.

752

МИРСКАЯ ВЛАСТЬ

Когда великое свершалось торжество,
И в муках на кресте кончалось божество,
Тогда по сторонам животворяща древа
Мария-грешница и пресвятая дева
Стояли, бледные, две слабые жены,
В неизмеримую печаль погружены.

Но у подножия теперь креста честного,
Как будто у крыльца правителя градского,
Мы зрим — поставленных на место жен святых
В ружье и кивере два грозных часовых.   10
К чему, скажите мне, хранительная стража? —
Или распятие казенная поклажа,
И вы боитеся воров или мышей? —
Иль мните важности придать царю царей?
Иль покровительством спасаете могучим
Владыку, тернием венчанного колючим,
Христа, предавшего послушно плоть свою
Бичам мучителей, гвоздям и копию?
Иль опасаетесь, чтоб чернь не оскорбила
Того, чья казнь весь род Адамов искупила,   20
И, чтоб не потеснить гуляющих господ,
Пускать не велено сюда простой народ?

There demons, catching him with joy upon their horns,
greeted the foe of all with cheers and loud guffaws
and bore him rowdily to their accursèd master;
then Satan left his throne, his face alight with laughter,
and placed a scorching kiss upon the traitor's lips –
lips that on that dread night on Christ had placed a kiss.   RC

751

* * *

In vain I seek to flee to Zion's lofty height:
rapacious Sin pursues, alert to track my flight...
Thus, gritty nostrils thrust in yielding sandy hollows,
a shy deer's pungent spoor a hungry lion follows.   BD

752

WORLDLY POWER

When the great day of sacrifice at last was ending
and God in agony was dying on the cross,
on either side still stood two women frail and pallid,
the Mary who had sinned and Mary, sinless mother –
they stood beside the cross, the life-bestowing tree,
both plunged in depths of grief beyond all fathoming.

Today, though, stationed by a ceremonial cross,
instead of those two holy women we behold
two fearsome sentinels, with tall peaked caps and muskets,
as though on duty by the city governor's gates.   10
Explain to me: why are they posted here on guard?...
Or is the crucifix state property perhaps,
and needs, you think, to be kept safe from thieves or mice?
Or do you mean to enhance the King of Kings' prestige?
Or will you safeguard by this strict security
the Lord Christ, who endured the crown of piercing thorns
and who of his free will surrendered his own body
to the tormentor's lash, to nails and javelin?
Or are you nervous that the rabble will offend
the one who by his death redeemed the human race   20
and, so that crowds don't get in strolling gentry's way,
have common folk now been required to keep away?   RC

753

ПРАВА

из Пиндемонти

Не дорого ценю я громкие права,
От коих не одна кружится голова.
Я не ропщу о том, что отказали боги
Мне в сладкой участи оспоривать налоги,
Или мешать царям друг с другом воевать;
И мало горя мне, свободно ли печать
Морочит олухов, иль чуткая цензура
В журнальных замыслах стесняет балагура.
Всё это, видите ль, *слова, слова, слова.*
Иные, лучшие мне дороги права;   10
Иная, лучшая потребна мне свобода:
Зависить от властей, зависить от народа —
Не всё ли нам равно? Бог с ними. Никому
Отчета не давать, себе лишь самому
Служить и угождать; для власти, для ливреи
Не гнуть ни совести, ни помыслов, ни шеи;
По прихоти своей скитаться здесь и там,
Дивясь божественным природы красотам,
И пред созданьями искусств и вдохновенья
Трепеща радостно в восторгах умиленья —   20
Вот счастье! вот права...

754

МОЛИТВА

Отцы пустынники и жены непорочны,
Чтоб сердцем возлетать во области заочны,
Чтоб укреплять его средь дольних бурь и битв,
Сложили множество божественных молитв;
Но ни одна из них меня не умиляет,
Как та, которую священник повторяет
Во дни печальные Великого поста;
Всех чаще мне она приходит на уста
И падшего крепит неведомою силой:

Владыко дней моих! дух праздности унылой,   10
Любоначалия, змеи сокрытой сей,
И празднословия не дай душе моей.

753

RIGHTS

from Pindemonte

I set no value on those loud-contested "rights"
that send into a spin the heads of many folk.
It's no complaint of mine that heaven has denied
to me the happy lot of wrangling over taxes
or of restraining kings from warring with each other.
Nor does it vex me much if an unbridled press
pulls wool across fools' eyes or if a zealous censor
obstructs a poor buffoon in publishing his journal:
such matters – do you see? – are all just "words, words, words".
It's other, better rights that I esteem the most,   10
a better liberty that's requisite to me.
A subject of the tsar, a subject of the people –
is it not all the same to us? God, rid us of them!
Render account to none; owe no one but yourself
favours or services; and do not bend your conscience
or mind or neck to those in power or their flunkies.
Roam freely here or there just as the fancy takes you,
be awed by the divine exquisiteness of Nature,
and tremble joyously in transports of emotion
at works that human art and spirit have created –   20
that's pleasure, those are rights!...   RC

754

A PRAYER

The hermit monks and nuns of long ago
composed a multitude of godly prayers
to help their souls soar up to realms unseen
or lend them strength midst deadly storm and strife.
None of those prayers, though, moves me like the one
the priest repeats each solemn day of Lent:
it comes to me more often than the rest,
and, when I fall, gives me new power to rise.

"Lord of my days," it goes, "keep from my soul   10
moody inertia, thoughtlessness of speech,
and the unconscious wish to dominate;

Но дай мне зреть мои, о боже, прегрешенья,
Да брат мой от меня не примет осужденья,
И дух смирения, терпения, любви
И целомудрия мне в сердце оживи.

755

КЛАДБИЩА

Когда за городом, задумчив, я брожу
И на публичное кладбище захожу,
Решетки, столбики, нарядные гробницы,
Под коими гниют все мертвецы столицы,
В болоте кое-как стесненные рядком,
Как гости жадные за нищенским столом,
Купцов, чиновников усопших мавзолеи,
Дешевого резца нелепые затеи,
Над ними надписи и в прозе и в стихах
О добродетелях, о службе и чинах;   10
По старом рогаче вдовицы плач амурный,
Ворами со столбов отвинченные урны,
Могилы склизкие, которы также тут
Зеваючи жильцов к себе на утро ждут, —
Такие смутные мне мысли всё наводит,
Что злое на меня уныние находит.
Хоть плюнуть да бежать...

                              Но как же любо мне
Осеннею порой, в вечерней тишине,
В деревне посещать кладбище родовое,
Где дремлют мертвые в торжественном покое.   20
Там неукрашенным могилам есть простор;
К ним ночью темною не лезет бледный вор;
Близ камней вековых, покрытых желтым мохом,
Проходит селянин с молитвой и со вздохом;
На место праздных урн и мелких пирамид,
Безносых гениев, растрепанных харит
Стоит широко дуб над важными гробами,
Колеблясь и шумя...

but grant me, God, awareness of my faults;
let me not cause my neighbour to offend;
and stir to life within my ready heart
meekness and patience, purity and love." RC

755

CEMETERIES

When lost in thought, I wander from the town
and to the public cemetery come –
the railings, pillars, tombstones neat and pretty,
beneath which rot the dead of all the city,
packed side by side within the spongy sward
like greedy guests about a sparse-set board,
the mausoleums of men of solid station,
preposterously designed by third-rate masons,
each with inscriptions, carved in prose and verse,
which all their virtues, service, ranks rehearse;   10
a widow's paean to the man she cheated;
pillars, robbed of their urns, forlornly fluted;
damp graves, awaiting with a weary yawn,
the tenants scheduled for tomorrow's morn...
I'm troubled by such thoughts of human folly
that I fall prey to spleen and melancholy
and want to spit and run...
                              Yet how I love
on autumn evenings, when the sky above
sleeps like the dead in solemn quietude,
to walk in the ancestral solitude   20
of our poor village graveyard, where there's space,
the tombs are simple, and a thief's whey face
does not intrude to rob when night is drear,
but the good villager a passing prayer
murmurs and sighs as he goes by these stones,
ancient and plain, with lichen overgrown,
and in the place of urns and pyramids,
of noseless Muses, unkempt caryatids,
an oak tree spreads o'er venerable graves
and rustles fluttering leaves...   AS

756

ИЗ ЮВЕНАЛА

От западных морей до самых врат восточных
Не многие умы от благ прямых и прочных
Зло могут отличить… рассудок редко нам
Внушает …………………

———————

«Пошли мне долгу жизнь и многие года!»
Зевеса вот о чем и всюду и всегда
Привыкли вы молить — но сколькими бедами
Исполнен долгий век! Во-первых, как рубцами,
Лицо морщинами покроется — оно
………………………… превращено.   10

757

КНЯЗЮ КОЗЛОВСКОМУ

Ценитель умственных творений исполинских,
Друг бардов английских, любовник муз латинских,
Ты к мощной древности опять меня манишь,
Ты снова мне ………………………… велишь.
Постясь с … мечтой и бедным идеалом,
Я приготовился бороться с Ювеналом,
Чьи строгие стихи, неопытный поэт,
Стихами перевесть я было дал обет.
Но, развернув его суровые творенья,
Не мог я одолеть пугливого смущенья…   10
Стихи бесстыдные приапами торчат,
В них звуки странною гармонией трещат —
Картины …………… латинского разврата
…………………………

758

НА СТАТУЮ ИГРАЮЩЕГО В СВАЙКУ

Юноша, полный красы, напряженья, усилия чуждый,
Строен, легок и могуч, — тешится быстрой игрой!
Вот и товарищ тебе, дискобол! Он достоин, клянуся,
Дружно обнявшись с тобой, после игры отдыхать.

756

FROM JUVENAL

From oceans of the west to the eastern gates of dawn
few minds can tell apart what's well and truly good
from what is evil... We are seldom helped by reason
....

"I beg you, send to me long life and many years!"
That is your constant prayer, at all times, everywhere,
to mighty Zeus. And yet a long life by the end
is fraught with troubles! First, wrinkles will mask your face
like scars, and it will be ....
.... transformed.   RC

757

FOR PRINCE KOZLÓVSKY

You connoisseur of works of intellectual giants,
you friend to English bards, you fan of Latin poets,
again you're urging me to read great ancient writers,
again you're bidding me ....
With fasting, with faint hopes, with modest aspirations,
I had prepared myself to strive with Juvenal;
raw poet that I am, I was about to promise
to translate into verse the stinging lines he wrote.
But when I had perused his bitter compositions,
I could not help but feel embarrassed and unnerved...   10
His poetry is stiff with crude obscenities,
his verses crackle with uncouth disharmonies,
his pictures of .... depravity in Rome
....   RC

758

ON A STATUE OF A SVAYKA PLAYER

Glowing with beauty, a lad, well proportioned, as strong as he's agile,
    moving with effortless grace, joins in a vigorous game!
You've got a friend now, Discobolus! Here's a companion who's worthy –
    first of a manly embrace, then a good rest from the game.   CC

759

НА СТАТУЮ ИГРАЮЩЕГО В БАБКИ

Юноша трижды шагнул, наклонился, рукой о колено
Бодро оперся, другой поднял меткую кость.
Вот уж прицелился... прочь! раздайся, народ любопытный,
Врозь расступись; не мешай русской удáлой игре.

760

19 ОКТЯБРЯ 1836

Была пора: наш праздник молодой
Сиял, шумел и розами венчался,
И с песнями бокалов звон мешался,
И тесною сидели мы толпой.
Тогда, душой беспечные невежды,
Мы жили все и легче и смелей,
Мы пили все за здравие надежды
И юности и всех ее затей.

Теперь не то: разгульный праздник наш
С приходом лет, как мы, перебесился   10,
Он присмирел, утих, остепенился,
Стал глуше звон его заздравных чаш;
Меж нами речь не так игриво льется.
Просторнее, грустнее мы сидим,
И реже смех средь песен раздается,
И чаще мы вздыхаем и молчим.

Всему пора: уж двадцать пятый раз
Мы празднуем лицея день заветный.
Прошли года чредою незаметной,
И как они переменили нас!   20
Недаром — нет! — промчалась четверть века!
Не сетуйте: таков судьбы закон;
Вращается весь мир вкруг человека, —
Ужель один недвижим будет он?

Припомните, о други, с той поры,
Когда наш круг судьбы соединили,
Чему, чему свидетели мы были!
Игралища таинственной игры,

759

ON A STATUE OF A BABKI PLAYER

Taking three paces, the lad, leaning forward with spirited vigour,
    rested one hand on his knee; one held the straight-flying bone.
Now he takes aim… Step aside! Make way, all you curious gawkers;
    don't interrupt the intent play of this bold Russian game.   CC

760

19TH OCTOBER 1836

When we were young still, our reunion time
was bright and boisterous, garlanded with flowers;
we sat in close companionship for hours,
the clink of glasses chimed with song and rhyme.
In blithe audacity we all were living
in those days, hearts possessed by foolish dreams;
we drank to the successes we were craving,
to boyish hopes, to all our eager schemes.

No more! That life so wild and dissolute,
now that we've altered with the years, is ended;   10
we're calmer, quieter now, our manners mended,
the clink of toasting glasses is subdued;
our voices with less merriment are ringing;
we sit more soberly, with ampler space;
more rarely laughter interrupts our singing;
more frequently we sigh and hold our peace.

Time passes: since the birth of the Lycée
this is the five-and-twentieth celebration.
Years have slipped by since that inauguration –
and what a change in us we see today!   20
But from these fleeting years we should be learning,
not grieving! Nature's law should be well known:
the universe around us keeps on turning,
we humans cannot stay unchanged alone.

Remember, friends, what happened since the day
when fate brought us together, all us youngsters –
those great events of which we were spectators!
Like toys with which unmindful children play,

Металися смущенные народы;
И высились и падали цари;   30
И кровь людей то Славы, то Свободы,
То Гордости багрила алтари.

Вы помните: когда возник лицей,
Как царь для нас открыл чертог царицын,
И мы пришли. И встретил нас Куницын
Приветствием меж царственных гостей, —
Тогда гроза двенадцатого года
Еще спала. Еще Наполеон
Не испытал великого народа —
Еще грозил и колебался он.   40

Вы помните: текла за ратью рать,
Со старшими мы братьями прощались
И в сень наук с досадой возвращались,
Завидуя тому, кто умирать
Шел мимо нас... и племена сразились,
Русь обняла кичливого врага,
И заревом московским озарились
Его полкам готовые снега.

Вы помните, как наш Агамемнон
Из пленного Парижа к нам примчался.   50
Какой восторг тогда пред ним раздался!
Как был велик, как был прекрасен он,
Народов друг, спаситель их свободы!
Вы помните — как оживились вдруг
Сии сады, сии живые воды,
Где проводил он славный свой досуг.

И нет его — и Русь оставил он,
Взнесенну им над миром изумленным,
И на скале изгнанником забвенным,
Всему чужой, угас Наполеон.   60
И новый царь, суровый и могучий,
На рубеже Европы бодро стал,
И над землей сошлися новы тучи,
И ураган их ....

nations were thrust aside by fierce assaulters;
monarchs arose, and monarchs tumbled down;   30
and streams of human blood stained red the altars
to pride, to liberty and to renown.

Remember: our Lycée, new home for each,
was given by the tsar palatial quarters.
On our first day Kunítsyn, he who taught us,
made the tsar's guests and us a welcome speech.
Quiescent still at that time was the tempest
of Eighteen Twelve; Napoleon had still
our valiant Russian nation not yet tested;
he'd threatened, but not yet affirmed his will.   40

Remember how the lines of soldiers passed –
we cheered and waved farewell to older brothers,
then came back, vexed, to one class or another,
jealous of those we'd watched as they marched past...
to death. The nations' armies then contended –
Russia lured on her overweening foes,
and burning Moscow's crimson flames portended
the ruin ready for them in the snows.

Remember how the triumph we desired
was won. Our High Lord, after Paris' capture,   50
returned to us mid such acclaim, such rapture!
What a great man he'd proved, so much admired,
well loved abroad, deliverer of nations!
Remember how this whole place sprang to life,
these parks and fountains, thronged with celebrations,
while he enjoyed a glorious relief.

The Russia that at death he left behind
he had raised high above a world astonished;
Napoleon had died, forgotten, banished,
upon his rock, estranged from humankind.   60
Then a new emperor, forceful and demanding,
took a firm stand at Europe's boundary;
above the land clouds gathered, storms portending;
a hurricane ....   RC

761

ПАМЯТНИК

Exegi monumentum

Я памятник себе воздвиг нерукотворный,
К нему не заростет народная тропа,
Вознесся выше он главою непокорной
    Александрийского столпа.

Нет, весь я не умру — душа в заветной лире
Мой прах переживет и тленья убежит —
И славен буду я, доколь в подлунном мире
    Жив будет хоть один пиит.

Слух обо мне пройдет по всей Руси великой,
И назовет меня всяк сущий в ней язык,   10
И гордый внук славян, и финн, и ныне дикий
    Тунгуз, и друг степей калмык.

И долго буду тем любезен я народу,
Что чувства добрые я лирой пробуждал,
Что в мой жестокий век восславил я свободу
    И милость к падшим призывал.

Веленью божию, о муза, будь послушна,
Обиды не страшась, не требуя венца,
Хвалу и клевету приемли равнодушно,
    И не оспоривай глупца.   20

761

MONUMENT

I have set up a monument

I've raised my monument without a master builder;
no public footpath leads there, overgrown with weeds;
defiantly it towers above the granite pillar
    that honours Alexander's deeds.

I'll not all die: in my impassioned verse my spirit
shall outlive my remains and never know decay,
and I shall be renowned as long as on this planet
    a single poet sees the day.

Throughout great Russia's lands will spread my reputation,
and all its many tongues will learn to speak my name,   10
not just proud Slavs, but Finns, Kalmyks – nomadic nation –
    and the Tungús, as yet untamed.

By my compatriots for long I'll be befriended
because to noble thoughts I've stirred them by my word,
because in this harsh age for freedom I've contended –
    sought mercy, too, for those who've erred.

Obey the call of God, I charge you, Inspiration:
don't fear abuse and don't demand a victor's crown;
receive with unconcern both praise and defamation,
    and don't pick quarrels with a clown.   RC

Index of Proper Names
of Mythological and Historical
Characters and Places

Minor personalities and places that Pushkin mentions only once are often explained in the note to the poem in which the name occurs; otherwise relevant information is given in the alphabetical index below. The numbers in square brackets against names refer to the poems in which they are mentioned. An "n" following the number indicates a mention in the Notes only.

Adrianople (now Edirne): A city in European Turkey about 250 kilometres from Istanbul. It was briefly occupied by the Russians during the Russo-Turkish War of 1828–29. On 2nd September 1829 the Treaty of Adrianople was signed there, under which territories to the west and east of the Black Sea were transferred to Russian control and Greece was guaranteed its independence. [578n, 593, 594n]

Aeolus (Russian: *Eol*): Greek god of the winds. [5, 644]

Alexander I (1777–1825): Grandson of Catherine the Great; ruling member of the Románov dynasty for most of Pushkin's youth. Alexander succeeded his father, the militaristic Emperor Paul, in 1801, initiating reforms especially of education and freedom of expression that led many to hope for wider political and social reforms later. He reigned as emperor throughout the Napoleonic Wars, in which he alternately opposed and cooperated with the French. He took personal command of the Russian forces against the French at the Battle of Austerlitz in 1805 and was widely regarded as having contributed by his misjudgements to Russia's defeat. Thereafter an uneasy peace between the two empires, formalized in the Treaty of Tilsit in 1807, was broken by Napoleon's invasion of Russia and occupation of Moscow in 1812. The climax of Alexander's reign was his final victory over Napoleon: as supreme commander of the Russian and allied armies he drove Napoleon back across Europe to France, forcing him to abdicate and occupying Paris in 1814. He then persuaded the victorious allies to pursue a policy of peace and reconciliation with France. In Paris again after Napoleon's final defeat at Waterloo in 1815, Alexander concluded the so-called Holy Alliance with the leaders of Austria and Prussia. The parties to the Alliance committed themselves to ideals of "justice, love and peace" in internal and external affairs, though in practice they interpreted these aims as covering the suppression of democratic, secular and nationalist

337

movements across continental Europe. After lengthy absences from Russia over three years, Alexander returned in triumph towards the end of 1815. In 1818 he spent from January to June touring Russian territories (including Poland); in a famous speech in Warsaw on 15th March, when opening the new Polish parliament, he promised to extend constitutional government to the rest of the Russian Empire. After two months back in St Petersburg, he set off in August on another visit to western Europe, the centrepiece of which was attendance at the Congress of Aachen from 30th September to 22nd November – where, though Alexander repeated informally his promise of constitutional government for Russia, the Holy Alliance confirmed its reactionary and authoritarian policies. Thereafter Alexander became increasingly pietistic and mystical in his personal life, reactionary in foreign affairs and cautious and conservative in domestic policy, where his failure to implement any meaningful reforms, even those promised, disappointed and alienated progressive elements in Russian society. Hence Pushkin's criticisms of him from the late 1810s onwards – which, together with Pushkin's generally freethinking attitude, provoked the Tsar to banish him first to a government posting in southern Russia and later to house arrest at Mikháylovskoye.

[22, 25, 44, 103, 127, 145n, 164, 177, 180n, 186n, 219, 222n, 223, 253n, 271n, 310, 341, 356, 366, 371, 400, 413, 414, 446, 580, 723, 760, 761]

Alexander Nevsky: Prince and Saint (1220–63): ruler of several Russian principalities; renowned for his victories as Prince of Nóvgorod the Great over Swedish and German armies. [16, 635]

Anacreōn: Anacreon of Teos was a Greek lyric poet who flourished in the late sixth century BC. His work – typically light, playful verses about wine, love and old age – was very popular in the ancient world and much imitated then and subsequently. He is said to have lived to an advanced age and to have possessed an unusually deep drinking cup.

[21, 34, 40, 46, 50, 91, 367, 646, 717, 718, 719]

Aphroditē: Greek goddess of love and beauty, equated with the Roman goddess Venus; sometimes also called Cypris (*Kiprída* in Russian). In classical mythology Aphroditē (whose name means "risen from the foam") was said to have emerged from the sea near the Cypriot city of Paphos, where there was a celebrated temple to her. She is also sometimes referred to as "Cytherea" (Russian: *Tsiteréya*), because there was a famous shrine to her on the Greek island of Cythera. In classical mythology Aphroditē was married to the lame blacksmith god Hephaestus (equated with the Roman god Vulcan) but had extramarital affairs with other gods.

[624, 642, 722n]

Apollō: In classical mythology son of Zeus and Leto, god of (among other things) the arts, such as music, poetry and drama, and of the sun; also known as Phoebus and Helios. One of his exploits was to slay the monstrous serpent Python, who had guarded Delphi before Apollo made it his sanctuary. [591, 598, 624, 633, 642, 749]

Aquilo(n): In Roman mythology, the god personifying the north wind, and particularly the cold north-easterly gales that sometimes struck the Mediterranean during winter. [356, 408, 738]

Arágva: A river of Georgia, rising on the southern slopes of the Caucasus. [563, 619]

Aras (Russian: *Aráks*): a river that rises in the mountains of eastern Turkey (not far from Erzurum) and whose waters drain eastwards into the Caspian Sea south of Baku. [572]

Aristippus of Cyrēnē (late fifth and early fourth century BC): Pupil of Socrates, philosopher and precursor of Epicurus, who taught that pleasure should be the aim of life and reputedly led a life of luxury and sensuality. [89, 346, 443, 609]

Armida: The beautiful enchantress in Tasso's epic *Gerusalemme liberata* ("The Liberation of Jerusalem", 1575). [553, 609, 697]

Arpa (Russian: *Arpacháy*): Another name for the Akhuryan river, a tributary of the Aras. At the time of Pushkin's journey to Erzurum the Arpa formed part of the border between the Russian and Turkish Empires.

[572]

Athenaeus (fl. *c.*200 AD): A Greek author from Egypt, who was an industrious collector of excerpts and anecdotes from ancient literature which he incorporated into a lengthy symposium entitled *Deipnosophistai* ("The Intelligentsia at Dinner" or "Table Talk"), a copy of which Pushkin possessed in a French edition that translated the whole work, including poetic excerpts, into prose. Not knowing Greek himself, Pushkin relied on this work for his versions of several Greek epigrams composed at the turn of 1832–33. [683, 684, 685, 687, 688]

Athēnē: In Greek mythology virgin goddess of wisdom and war, often portrayed as a warrior. She was the patron goddess of the city of Athens. Equated with the Roman Minerva. [598]

Augustus (63 BC–14 AD): Ruled as first emperor of Rome from 27 BC till his death. Born Gaius Octavius Thurinus, he was great-nephew of Julius Caesar. When Caesar was assassinated in 44 BC, Octavius was nominated in Caesar's will as his adopted son and heir and took the name Gaius Julius Caesar Octavianus (anglicized as Octavian). Having defeated his last rivals for power, Mark Antony and Cleopatra, in 31 BC, he emerged as leader of the Roman state, within a few years accepting the titles of *Imperator* and *Augustus*. Among the many other initiatives of his reign, Augustus tried to raise the standards of personal morality and strengthen family values in Rome, a policy that led to the disgrace and exile both of his own daughter Julia on charges of adultery and of the leading poet of the time Ovid, whose *Art of Love* had offended the Emperor. Augustus was declared "divine" by the Roman senate on his death, but even earlier he had accepted divine honours in other parts of the Roman Empire. [253, 292, 360, 591n, 722n]

Aurora (Russian: *Avróra*): Roman goddess of the dawn. [374, 622]

Bacchus: Greek god of wine and drunkenness, also called Dionysus and (by the Romans) Liber. He was normally accompanied by an unruly retinue of satyrs, fauns, maenads and other votaries, intoxicated or possessed, playing loud music. Though he was normally imagined as a peace-loving, though boisterous, eternally young adolescent, one myth has him leading a campaign eastwards, as far as India, and, after a bloodless victory, returning in a triumphal procession, riding in a chariot drawn by tigers and noisily attended by his usual retinue.   [642, 672, 683, 684]

Barclay de Tolly: See next entry.

Barkláy-de-Tolli (or Barclay de Tolly): Prince Mikhaíl Bogdánovich (1761–1818): member of a Baltic German family of Scottish descent, who from adolescence followed a distinguished career in the Russian army. Commander-in-chief of the Russian forces at the outset of the Napoleonic invasion of 1812, he doggedly pursued a scorched earth strategy to draw the invaders ever further from base and lengthen their supply lines. Forced by the impatience of his colleagues and the public to take a stand against Napoleon at Smolénsk, he failed to halt Napoleon's advance, leading to his vilification as a foreigner and coward. Yielding to the public outcry, Alexander I demoted Barclay de Tolly and appointed Kutúzov as commander-in-chief in his place. Kutúzov, however, adopted the same strategy of withdrawal, which eventually succeeded in weakening Napoleon and compelling his disastrous retreat. The outcome restored Barclay de Tolly's reputation and popularity, and after Kutúzov's death in 1813 he was again appointed commander-in-chief of the armies that drove Napoleon back to France and occupied Paris.   [723, 749]

Beaumarchais, Pierre-Augustin Caron de Beaumarchais (1732–99): Among many other activities, author of the celebrated comedies *The Barber of Seville* (1775) and *The Marriage of Figaro* (1783), both set in Spain and with a common hero, the resourceful Sevillian barber Figaro. [609, 630]

Bessarabia: A territory, with boundaries similar to those of modern Moldova, running north from the Danube delta and the Black Sea coast between the Rivers Prut and Dniester. Formerly part of Turkish-controlled Moldavia, it was annexed by Russia in 1812. Its capital (as Moldova's) was Kishinyóv (modern Chişinău).   [472, 528n, 649n]

Boileau-Despréaux, Nicolas (1636–1711): French poet, satirist and literary critic. Pushkin did not share his fondness for the sonnet form, but admired him for upholding classical standards in poetry and for campaigning against stupid and shoddy writing, such as that of Chapelain. A bizarre story, perhaps apocryphal, circulated after Boileau's death to the effect that, when playing outdoors as a child, he fell over, uncovering his lower body; a turkey then pecked at his private parts, maiming him for life.   [60, 68, 98, 130, 682]

Borodinó: Village about 140 kilometres west of Moscow, site in 1812 of one of the largest and bloodiest battles of the Napoleonic Wars, where the

Russians made a last, unsuccessful attempt to halt Napoleon's advance before abandoning the city. However, because the Russian army, unde-feated, managed to withdraw in order, Russians subsequently looked back proudly to Borodinó as the turning point in the war.

[25, 44, 595, 663]

de Bourrienne, Louis Antoine Fauvelet (1769–1834): originally a close friend and associate of Napoleon, who later fell out of favour on account of fraudulent activities. After the Bourbon Restoration he re-emerged as a politician of ultra-royalist views. Ten volumes of memoirs about Napoleon were published under his name in 1829–30, but were soon discredited as biased and untrustworthy and are now believed to have been largely ghost-written by a journalist Maxime de Villemarest.   [643]

Bová: Prince Bová was a well-known character of popular Russian literature and ersatz-folklore (actually of foreign literary origin). His father's mur-derer Dodón married his wicked mother Militrísa and imprisoned the prince, who later escaped and embarked on all kinds of heroic exploits.

[22, 690]

Bowles, Reverend William Lisle (1762–1850): English poet who featured in the anthology *The Poetical Works of Millman, Bowles, Wilson, and Barry Cornwall* (Paris, 1829), a volume owned and well used by Pushkin.

[649n]

Brutus, Marcus Junius (78?–42 BC): Fought to defend the Roman Republic against the arbitrary personal rule of Julius Caesar and his successors. He was one of Caesar's assassins in 43 BC. A year later, after his republican army was defeated by Octavian and Antony at Philippi, he committed suicide.   [223, 254, 341, 722]

Bulgárin, Faddéy Venedíktovich (1789–1859): A man of Polish-Belorussian birth, who was brought to St Petersburg as a child, trained as a cadet, then served for a while as a junior officer in the Russian army, before returning to Poland. After the Russian alliance with Napoleon following the Peace of Tilsit (1807) Bulgárin enlisted with the French army and fought with the French during the last phase of the Napoleonic Wars, then settled once more in Poland. In 1819 he finally took up residence in St Petersburg, gaining entry to the literary world there and becom-ing a prolific author, journalist, editor and critic. After the accession of Nicholas I and the suppression of the Decembrist uprising in 1825, Bulgárin began to work as an agent for the secret police. From the later 1820s he was an increasingly bitter literary rival and personal enemy of Pushkin. Pushkin had various nicknames for him, such as (Vidocq) Figlyárin.   [607, 625n, 635, 636, 642, 653]

Byron, Lord (1788–1824): Renowned British romantic and satirical poet, much admired both in Britain and on the Continent. Pushkin became acquainted with his work from 1820 (mostly through French trans-lations) and was much influenced by him. Byron travelled widely in southern Europe and the Near East, and after scandal drove him from

Britain in 1816, he spent most of his remaining years in northern Italy; his travels coloured much of his poetry, and this is reflected in Pushkin's writings of the early 1820s about the Caucasus and the Crimea. Byron died of a fever in Greece in April 1824, while supporting the Greek struggle for independence from the Turks, a cause that he had publicised in his poetry and that endeared him to progressives throughout Europe.

[309, 357, 367, 418, 423, 454, 497, 510, 594, 609]

de Camões, Luís Vaz (c.1524–80): National poet of Portugal, author (among much other poetry) of the Portuguese national epic *The Lusiads*, which presents the hero, the explorer Vasco da Gama, as both a propagator of Christianity in the East and as journeying under the protection of the goddess Venus. Camões was said to have ended his life in poverty.

[7, 22, 606]

Canova, Antonio (1757–1822): A much-admired Italian sculptor.

[510, 609]

Casti, Giovanni Battista (1724–1803): An Italian poet, satirist and librettist of comic operas, who served at Catherine the Great's court in the late 1770s. The loss of his nose was apparently due to syphilis. [609]

Catherine II, "The Great" (1729–96): Reigned as empress from 1762. Her reign was popularly remembered in Russia as a period of stability, military triumph and enlightenment. Russian forces waged a series of successful wars, defeating Turkish armies, destroying the Turkish fleet and annexing Turkish-controlled territories (including the Crimea); Russian armies also suppressed Poland's struggles for independence. At home Catherine promoted education, patronized poetry and the other arts and encouraged contacts with thinkers in Western Europe, corresponding herself with Voltaire among others. In 1767 she convened a national legislative commission to recodify Russian law, and she personally composed beforehand a lengthy "Instruction" (*Nakáz*), based on French enlightenment ideas but adapted to Russian autocracy, setting out the principles to be followed. She was famous for her intelligence, her charm and her successive lovers. In November 1796 Catherine suffered a severe stroke while sitting on the toilet; she died the next day without recovering her faculties.

[25, 46n, 310, 371, 375, 475, 595, 609, 635n]

Catullus, Gaius Valerius (c.84–c.54 BC): Roman lyric poet. [672]

Circe (Greek *Kirkē*; Russian *Tsirtséya*): In Greek mythology (she is mentioned in Homer's *Odyssey*) a seductive sorceress who lived on a remote island and bewitched stranded sailors, turning them into animals. Pushkin sometimes used the name for any flirtatious young woman.

[186, 736]

Coleridge, Samuel Taylor (1772–1834): Poet and philosopher, with Wordsworth and Southey one of the English "Lake Poets". [731]

Cornwall, Barry (pseudonym of Bryan Waller Proctor, 1787–1874): English poet who featured in the anthology *The Poetical Works of Millman,*

Bowles, Wilson, and Barry Cornwall (Paris, 1829), a volume owned and well used by Pushkin. Cornwall's *Dramatic Scenes* (1819), reprinted in that volume, served as a model for Pushkin's *Little Tragedies*.
[650, 665n, 734]

Correggio (Antonio Allegri da Correggio, 1489–1534): Famous Italian painter. [5, 609]

Crimea: A peninsula on the northern side of the Black Sea, narrowly linked to Southern Russia. Known as Tauris by the Greeks (*Tavrída* in Russian), it was occupied from the thirteenth century by the Tatars – who, from early in the fifteenth century, established a khanate there under Turkish protection, ruled from the khans' palace at Bakhchisaráy. The Tatars used the Crimea as a base for raids on Poland, Ukraine and Russia. In 1783 Catherine the Great supressed the khanate and annexed the Crimea to the Russian Empire. [354n, 375, 382n, 428n, 429n, 542, 606]

Dante Alighieri (*c.*1265–1321): Pre-eminent Italian poet, author of the *Divine Comedy*, describing a journey through Hell, Purgatory and Paradise; also of numerous sonnets and shorter poems.
[418, 569, 606, 670n]

Davýdov, Denís Vasílyevich (1784–1839): A cousin of Alexándr and Vasíly L. Davýdov (Nos. 249, 258, 266 and 346). Denís Davýdov was an officer in the hussars, famous as a "hussar-poet" celebrating the hedonism and bravado of military life. He also played an energetic and effective part in the Napoleonic Wars, in particular leading groups of mounted "partisans", who harried Napoleon's army as it retreated from Russia in 1812. Subsequently he became something of a celebrity in Russian society. In 1821 he published a prose treatise on the *Theory of Partisan Operations*. Denís Davýdov is thought to have been the model for Vasíly Denísov in Tolstoy's *War and Peace*. Pushkin met him in Kiev in February 1821 and remained his friend and admirer. [276, 303, 748]

Dawe, George (1781–1829): A British portrait painter who worked in Russia from 1819 to 1829. He was recruited by Alexander I to paint over 300 portraits of Russian heroes of the Napoleonic Wars, which are still displayed in the War Gallery of the Winter Palace. [512, 723]

Delvig, Baron Antón Antónovich (1798–1831): Descendant of a Baltic German family; a minor poet and one of Pushkin's closest friends at school and after. Delvig visited the exiled Pushkin at Mikháylovskoye in April 1825. Delvig admired and imitated the poetry of classical Greece and Rome, and he and Pushkin shared the belief that poets should write for poetry's sake, unswayed by commercial considerations. These fastidious literary views were derided by the more populist and market-conscious writers of the late 1820s and early 1830s, such as Bulgárin and his allies, as snobbish and elitist. Delvig died suddenly in January 1831, leaving Pushkin grief-stricken.
[7n, 24, 42, 43, 109, 222, 252, 366, 446,
490n, 497, 562, 606, 607n, 642, 668, 749]

Derzhávin, Gavriíl Románovich (1743–1816): The greatest Russian poet of the eighteenth century. He traced his ancestry back in the fifteenth century to a Tatar prince who converted to Christianity and gave his allegiance to the Grand Prince of Muscovy. Among Derzhávin's many compositions were odes to Catherine the Great and to eminent Russian military figures, including Alexéi Orlóv, Rumyántsev and Suvórov. In Catherine he praised the personification of enlightened monarchy, contrasting her with the greedy and self-seeking grandees of her court. In the early 1800s the quality of his writing declined with senility. He was present at the reading of the fifteen-year-old Pushkin's 'Recollections in Tsárskoye Seló' (No. 25 in Vol. 1) at the Lycée in January 1815 and, visibly moved, praised it highly. He died in July of the following year.

[7, 21, 25, 30, 46, 68n, 145n, 298, 310, 371, 375, 544n, 642, 697, 761n]

D'Holbach, Baron Paul-Henri Thiry (1723–89): German-born naturalized French philosopher and writer of strongly atheistic views, host of a salon in Paris frequented by Enlightenment figures, friend of Diderot and contributor to the *Encyclopédie*. [609]

Dibich (Diebitsch), Field Marshal Count Iván Ivánovich (1785–1831): A German soldier who from 1801 served with distinction in the Russian army. In 1830 he was appointed to lead the Russian forces in crushing the Polish uprising and initially suffered some reverses. Before the end of the campaign he died of cholera. [669]

Diderot, Denis (1713–84): Eminent French philosopher and writer, a catholic in his youth, who then moved via deism to atheism. Diderot was a prominent figure in the Age of the Enlightenment, who played a leading part in editing and contributing to the famous *Encyclopédie*. He visited St Petersburg for a few months in the early 1770s as a guest of Catherine the Great and was appointed her librarian. [609]

Dnieper: A major southward-flowing river of central European Russia and the Ukraine that passes Kiev and empties into the Black Sea.

[608, 691]

Dolgorúky, Prince Yakov Fyódorovich (1639–1720): Companion of Tsar Peter the Great, renowned for his independence and directness.

[474, 475, 635]

Don: One of the great rivers of Russia, rising two hundred kilometres south of Moscow and flowing south into the Black Sea through the Sea of Azov. Its middle and lower reaches were settled by Cossacks, who regularly served with the Russian army in time of war. Among other produce, the Don basin was famous for its wines. [14, 571, 572]

Dórokhov, Rufín Ivánovich (1801–52): An army officer whom Pushkin met and befriended during his visit to the Caucasus in 1829. Dórokhov was an amiable rake who liked dining, gambling, womanizing and duelling; he also drew caricatures and wrote verse. [583]

Edirne: See Adrianople

Erzurum (Russian: *Arzrúm*): A city in the mountains of eastern Turkey, near the watershed of the Aras and Euphrates rivers. It was temporarily captured by the Russian army under General Paskévich during the campaign of 1829. Pushkin was with the Russian army at the time and recorded the event in his travelogue *Journey to Arzrúm* (published 1836).
[566n, 567n, 569n, 570, 593]

Euphratēs (Russian: *Yevfrát*): One of the great rivers of Mesopotamia, with headwaters in the mountains of eastern Turkey near Erzurum.
[567, 572]

Evxín: The Russian form of Euxine, ancient name of the Black Sea. [593]

Faun: See Satyr.

Fazil Khan Sheyda (1784–1852): Court poet to the Shah of Persia. Pushkin met him in the Caucasus in May 1829 when he was on his way with a Persian delegation to St Petersburg to make amends for the murder of Russian envoys by a Teheran mob four months earlier. [565]

Figlyárin: Pushkin's satirical nickname (in Russian *figlyár* means "clown", "charlatan") for Faddéy Bulgárin. [607, 635, 636]

Galiani, Abbé Ferdinando (1728–87): Neapolitan economist and writer and friend of Diderot, who served in the Neapolitan embassy in Paris in the decade after 1759. [609]

Gannibál, Abrám Petróvich (*c.*1693–1781): Pushkin's maternal great-grandfather. See *Introduction: Family, Birth and Childhood* on p. XIII.
[366, 380, 595n, 635]

Gannibál, Brigadier Iván Abrámovich (1735–1801): Son of the above and Pushkin's great-uncle on his mother's side. He followed a career in naval artillery. During the Russo-Turkish War of 1768–74 he joined the naval Archipelago Expedition of 1769–70; he took a leading part in the capture of the Turkish fort of Navarino on the western coast of Greece in April 1770 and participated a few months later in the destruction of the Turkish fleet at the battle of Chesme. [595, 635]

Glinka, Fyódor Nikoláyevich (1786–1880): Army officer who had fought in the Napoleonic Wars and by 1821 was working on the staff of the governor of St Petersburg. A humane and idealistic man, he was a poet (among his works were metrical versions of the Psalms), a political radical, a member of the Green Lamp club and an associate of future Decembrists. Glinka had been on friendly terms with Pushkin during his early years in St Petersburg and supported him during the events in 1820 that led to his exile. Pushkin liked and admired him as a man, but thought little of him as a poet. After the failure of the Decembrist uprising in 1825 Glinka was arrested, dismissed from army service and placed under police supervision far from St Petersburg. [296, 398, 600]

Glinka, Mikhaíl Ivánovich (1804–57): Eminent Russian composer. He set some of Pushkin's lyrics to music, as well as producing an operatic version of his fairy-tale epic *Ruslán and Lyudmíla*. [631n]

Gnedich, Nikolái Ivánovich (1786–1833): As a boy Gnedich caught small-pox and lost the sight of one eye. In adulthood he became a versatile writer, poet and translator of Latin and Greek poetry and other sup-posed classics including the works of Ossian. He was also a theatre buff, who attended meetings of the Green Lamp club during Pushkin's early St Petersburg years (1817–20). An early admirer of Pushkin as a poet, Gnedich was shocked by the government's decision to banish him from St Petersburg in 1820 and took on the editing of *Ruslan and Lyudmila* in Pushkin's absence. The copies he sent to Pushkin on publication in summer 1820 did not reach Pushkin in Moldavia till March the following year. Between 1809 and its publication in 1829 Gnedich concentrated his efforts on producing a Russian translation of Homer's *Iliad* in dactylic hexameters, the metre of the original, an achievement that earned him the acclaim of his literary contemporaries   [253,626,651,690]

Golítsyn, Prince Sergéi Grigóryevich (1803–68): tall friend of Pushkin's, gambler, nicknamed Firs.   [614]

Goncharóva, Natálya Nikoláyevna: See Púshkina, Natálya Nikoláyevna.

Graces (Russian: *Kharíty*): In classical mythology, three goddesses personi-fying charm, grace and beauty.   [374, 423, 484, 510, 688]

Green Lamp: An unofficial club of young theatre and literature buffs in St Petersburg to which Pushkin belonged during 1819; its members included Nikíta Vsévolozhsky (in whose house they normally met), Barkóv, Engelhardt, Mansúrov, F. Glinka, Yúryev and Yakov Tolstóy. The club also served as a forum for drinking, partying, entertaining girls and discussing radical ideas on political, social and religious topics. "Green" signified hope, and "Lamp" enlightenment. It ceased to meet from autumn 1820, but the news took some time to reach Pushkin in Kishinyóv.   [192, 193n, 206n, 236, 626a n.]

Hades: In classical mythology, a name for Pluto, god of the underworld; also for his realm, the abode of the dead.   [355, 374, 718]

Hafez of Shiraz (1315–90): preeminent Persian mystic and poet. [565,567]

Hermēs: in Greek mythology, a god, often shown wearing a winged helmet, who often served as messenger and errand-boy of the other gods. He was father of Pan. Equated with the Roman god Mercury. [18, 34, 46, 722]

Homer (early 1st millennium BC): Semi-legendary Greek epic poet, author of the *Iliad* and the *Odyssey* about the war between Greeks and Trojans and its aftermath; he was said to have been blind.

[22, 30, 253, 297, 355n, 534, 626, 651, 690, 722n]

Horace (Quintus Horatius Flaccus) (65–8 BC): Roman lyric poet and sati-rist of famously genial and pleasure-loving disposition, with a liking for country life; a friend of Virgil. As a young Roman studying in Greece, he had joined the republicans under Brutus and Cassius in the civil war that followed the murder of Julius Caesar. At the battle of Philippi (42 BC), however, at which Octavian and Antony crushed the republicans, he had on his own testimony taken fright, thrown away his shield and fled the battlefield. Pardoned by Octavian (later Augustus), of whom thereafter he was a loyal supporter and encomiast, he came under the patronage of Augustus's associate, the proverbially wealthy Maecenas.

[30, 38, 42, 53, 105, 203, 346, 560, 591, 688, 722, 761]

Iván IV "The Terrible" (1530–84): Reigned as Tsar of Muscovy from 1633 until his death. He was notorious for sadistic cruelty against his enemies. [61, 477, 570n, 635]

Juvenal (fl. c.100 AD): Roman writer of satires harshly critical of contemporary society. [7, 21, 33, 74, 432, 756, 757]

Kachenóvsky, Mikhaíl Trofímovich (1775–1842): Professor of fine arts and archaeology at Moscow University, historian, journalist and critic, hailing from a Russianized Greek family. He edited the bi-monthly review *Vestnik Yevrópy* (*Herald of Europe*) between 1805 and 1830. His intemperate criticisms had given rise to a fierce quarrel with the satirist Iván Dmítriev, who had responded with a rude epigram in 1806. Partly as a result, and as a traditionalist himself, Kachenóvsky remained hostile to the progressive group of writers headed by the writer and historian Nikolái Karamzín, to which Dmítriev belonged. When the first part of Karamzín's *History of the Russian State* was published in 1818 to general acclaim, Kachenóvsky challenged many of Karamzín's statements in intemperate language, infuriating Karamzín's friends, who encouraged the young Pushkin to respond. Literary warfare continued for many years between Kachenóvsky and Pushkin and his friends.

[158, 255, 256, 265, 275n, 347, 422, 425, 426, 559, 561, 574, 575, 577, 600]

Kagúl: A small river in southern Moldova that flows into the lower Danube. In July 1770 on the Kagúl Russian armies under Count Pyótr Rumyántsev won an important victory over the Turks. [25, 175, 266n, 300, 595]

Karadžić, Vuk Stefanović (1787–1864): Eminent Serbian philologist, anthropologist and reformer of the Serbian language, famous also as a collector of Serbian folk tales and folk songs, some of which Pushkin translated into Russian verse. [709n, 709 X, 709 XIV, 743]

Karađorđe ("Black George", born Đorđe Petrović, 1768–1817): Serbian rebel, who fought for Serbian independence from the Ottoman Empire during the First Serbian Uprising of 1804–13 and became for a while head of the revolutionary Serbian state. When the uprising was quashed, Karađorđe took refuge in Russian territory and settled with his family in Bessarabia. Two years after the Second Serbian Uprising of 1815 he tried to return to Serbia, but the new Serbian leader Miloš Obrenović, fearing a potential rival who would inflame relations with Turkey, had him murdered. Karađorđe's widow and family continued to live in northern Bessarabia. Though widely revered as a Serbian patriot, Karađorđe was a violent and fierce-tempered man, who, in addition to other atrocities, killed his father in a quarrel and had his brother executed for criminal conduct, earning his mother's curse. [233, 709 XI, 714]

Kazbék: A peak on the southern side of the Caucasus range; high on its slopes stand a church and (it is said) a former hermitage.   [469, 620]

Khotín (Hotín): A fortress and town in Bessarabia on the right bank of the Dniester River in what is now western Ukraine.   [714]

Khvostóv, Count Dmitry Ivánovich (1757–1835): Prolific poet of little talent, member of traditionalist literary circle, senator, often mocked by Pushkin and other younger poets, sometimes nicknamed Grafóv ("Count-y"), Svistóv ("Whistler") or Khlystóv ("Lasher"). Among much other work, he translated Racine's tragedy *Andromaque* (1667) into Russian.   [7, 30n, 46, 52, 60, 219, 261, 310, 405, 423, 447, 584]

Kiprída: See Aphroditē.

Kórsakov, Nikolái Alexándrovich (1800–20): A classmate of Pushkin's at the Lycée; he wrote poetry, played the guitar and composed music. After graduation he entered the diplomatic service. In 1819 he was posted to Italy; he died of consumption in Florence the following year. His epitaph, which he composed himself shortly before he died, read:

> Háste to your native land, you traveller passing by –
> a wretched fate it is far from your friends to die!

[42n, 446, 668n]

Kościuszko, Tadeusz (1746–1817): Patriotic Polish-Lithuanian statesman and general, who led a Polish uprising against the partition of Poland and Russian occupation in 1794; the Russians captured Kościuszko in October of that year and the following month crushed the Polish rebels in a savage battle in Praga, a suburb of Warsaw.   [375n, 376, 607]

Krylóv, Iván Andréyevich (1769–1844): Russian playwright, poet and writer of fables in the style of La Fontaine. One of his plays, the mock-tragedy *Podshchípa* (1797–99), satirized classical drama, transferring the tragic Muse's attributes, the buskin and dagger, to the Muse of comedy.   [30, 600]

Kulm: Now Chlumec, a town in northern Bohemia (Czechia) where Russian forces, with their Austrian and Prussian allies, inflicted a major defeat on Napoleon in August 1813.   [44, 595]

Kutúzov, Field-Marshal Prince Mikhaíl Illariónovich (1745–1813): Pre-eminent Russian military leader, promoted general under Catherine the Great in 1784, who distinguished himself in the wars against Turkey and Napoleon. During Napoleon's invasion of Russia in 1812 Kutúzov was appointed commander-in-chief of the Russian armies in succession to Barclay de Tolly. After the hard-fought but indecisive Battle of Borodinó on the approaches to Moscow, Kutúzov decided to fall back beyond the city, abandoning it to Napoleon. Soon afterwards, helped by the devastation of the Russian countryside and the onset of winter, he succeeded in driving the enfeebled French army back out of Russia.   [25, 660, 723, 749]

Lelewel, Joachim (1786–1861): A Polish writer and academic of nationalist views who took a leading part in the Polish uprising of 1830–31; after its suppression he fled to Paris, from where he continued for two years to agitate for Polish independence and issue anti-Russian propaganda. Expelled by the French in 1833, he settled in Belgium. [669]

Lēthē: In classical mythology, a river of the underworld, whose waters were supposed to bring forgetfulness. *Lēthē* is Greek for "oblivion". [355, 405, 416, 417, 670]

Lomonósov, Mikhaíl Vasílyevich (1711–65): Lomonósov was born into a peasant family near Kholmogóry on the lower reaches of the Northern Dviná River in northern Russia. As a boy he used to go fishing with his father on the White Sea. At the age of nineteen he left home for Moscow. Educated in Moscow, Kiev, St Petersburg and Germany he became the first great Russian polymath; he was also the first significant Russian poet in the European tradition, noted particularly for his odes, which led to him being called "the Russian Pindar". He was also known for his fiery temper, which brought him into conflict with the rival poet Sumarókov, amongst others. [7, 46, 68, 634, 739n]

Maecenas, Gaius (d. 8 BC): A Roman statesman, descended from the ancient Etruscan aristocracy. He was a trusted friend and associate of Octavian (later the Emperor Augustus) from the beginning of his career. Enormously rich, he famously sponsored Roman writers, notably the poets Horace and Virgil. [688]

Marie-Antoinette, Queen (1755–93): Frivolous and pleasure-loving wife of King Louis XVI of France, a woman of obstinately reactionary views, guillotined like her husband during the French Revolution. [609]

Mars: God of war in ancient Rome. [704]

Melétsky (Nelédinsky-Melétsky), **Prince Yury Alexándrovich** (1751–1828): Soldier, courtier and writer of ballads and love poetry, admired by Pushkin and the Arzamás group of writers. [92, 583]

Melpomenē: One of the nine Muses, patroness of tragic drama. [30, 172, 690]

Mérimée, Prosper (1803–70): Eminent French writer, author (among much else) of a literary hoax *La Guzla, ou Choix de Poésies Illyriques recueillies dans la Dalmatie, le Bosnie, la Croatie et L'Herzogowine* (1827), largely composed by himself, on which Pushkin drew for his *Songs of the Western Slavs*. Merimée knew and translated Russian, and his novella *Carmen* (1845), on which Bizet's opera was based, was influenced by Pushkin's *Gypsies*. [362n, 709]

Mickiewicz, Adam (1798–1855): Pre-eminent Polish poet and patriot, born in ancient Lithuania, which had already become part of the Russian Empire. In 1824, for subversive activities in support of Polish independence, he was exiled to central Russia and spent five years mostly in St Petersburg and Moscow, becoming a popular figure in literary circles. He spent a large part of 1825 in the Crimea, which he commemorated in his

Crimean Sonnets (1826). Late in 1826 he made Pushkin's acquaintance in Moscow, and they continued to meet there and in St Petersburg as friends and mutual admirers. Mickiewicz was allowed to leave Russia in 1829. Russia's suppression of the Polish uprising in 1831 left him bitterly critical of the Russian government and its apologists; in 1833 he published some savagely anti-Russian poetry and spent most of the rest of his life in western Europe supporting the cause of Polish independence from exile.   [542, 552, 606, 607, 702n, 711]

Mikháylovskoye: Pushkin's mother's country estate in the province of Pskov in western Russia, about 350 kilometres south of St Petersburg. Pushkin often visited it both before and after his years at the Imperial Lycée. He was banished there by government order between August 1824 and September 1826 and continued to visit it from time to time thereafter.   *passim*

Miloš: See Obrenović.

Milton, John (1610–74): English poet and statesman. His most celebrated epic *Paradise Lost* tells of Satan's struggle with God for the future of mankind; Pushkin may well have read a French translation of it as a boy.
                                                                              [5n., 22, 606n]

Minikh (Münnich), **Field Marshal Count Khristofór Antónovich** (1683–1767): Soldier and military engineer of German origin, he was recruited to the Russian service by Peter I and enjoyed increasing authority under him and his immediate successors; he fell from favour under Elizabeth, however, and was exiled for many years to Siberia. The Germanophile Peter III recalled him in 1762 and despite Peter's death soon after he continued to serve under Catherine II.   [635]

Minin, Kuzmá (d. 1616): A merchant of Nizhny Nóvgorod, who played a leading part in the nationalist uprising of 1611–12 that freed Moscow from Polish occupation and led to the establishment of the Románov dynasty.   [137, 635]

Molière (Jean-Baptiste Poquelin, 1622–73): Pre-eminent French dramatist, renowned for his comedies.   [1, 30, 249n, 262n, 635n]

Montmartre: Hill and district just north of Paris, around which in March 1814 the Russians and their allies fought a final battle against Napoleon's forces before occupying the city.   [595]

Morellet, Abbé André (1727–1819): French economist and writer, contributor to the *Encyclopédie*. [609]

Morpheus: Greek god of dreams and sleep.   [82, 688]

Mozart, Wolfgang Amadeus (1756–91): Renowned composer. One of his operas was *The Marriage of Figaro*, based on Beaumarchais's play. In his later years he lived and worked in Vienna, where his spontaneous brilliance excited (it was said) the jealousy of the popular Italian composer Salieri, who also worked there.   [630n, 641]

Murom: A city and region to the east of Moscow associated with the exploits of various legendary Russian folk heroes, notably Ilyá of Murom.
                                                                           [61n, 71, 695]

Muses: In Greek mythology, nine sisters, daughters of Zeus and Mnemosyne (Memory), the virginal goddesses of the arts.   *passim*

Nadézhdin, Nikolái Ivánovich (1804–56): Son of a priest and educated in a seminary, at the age of twenty-two he gave up a religious vocation and embarked on a career in academia and journalism in Moscow under the tutelage of Pushkin's *bête noir* Mikhaíl Kachenóvsky. Having followed Kachenóvsky in publishing hostile reviews of some of Pushkin's work, he too became a target of Pushkin's epigrams. He also began to write verse in a clumsy and archaistic style similar to that of Count Dmitry Khvostóv, whose protégé he also became.   [573, 574, 575, 584, 591]

Naiads: In Greek mythology nymphs of springs, rivers and lakes. [25, 633]

Napoleon Bonaparte (1769–1821): Napoleon rose to prominence in France during the 1790s in the aftermath of the French Revolution. Virtually the whole of his career was taken up with wars in Europe and the Middle East. During 1796–98 he led French armies in an invasion and temporary occupation of Italy. In 1798 and 1799 he led a French expedition that temporarily occupied Egypt and parts of Palestine. Returning to Paris in the autumn of 1799, he seized dictatorial power as First Consul in 1799 and in the following year crossed the St Bernard Pass to defeat the Austrians and reoccupy Italy. He crowned himself emperor in 1804. In 1805 he defeated Russian and Austrian armies at the Battle of Austerlitz. In 1807, after further victories over Prussian and Russian armies, Napoleon and Alexander I met at Tilsit on the River Neman. The Peace of Tilsit that they negotiated confirmed Russia's western borders but conceded control over most of central Europe to the French. In 1810 Napoleon married the Archduchess Marie Louise, daughter of Francis II Emperor of Austria and erstwhile Holy Roman Emperor. The Peace of Tilsit lasted until 1812. In that year Napoleon invaded Russia and advanced on Moscow with an army drawn from across Europe. At Borodinó he fought an indecisive but costly battle with a Russian army under Kutúzov, who then withdrew beyond the city. Napoleon proceeded to occupy Moscow, which was set on fire by its defenders, forcing him to make a disastrous retreat across war-ravaged and wintry terrain. Thereafter he was driven back across Europe by Russian and allied armies, who invaded France and occupied Paris in 1814. Napoleon abdicated and was exiled to the Italian island of Elba, which he was allowed to rule, retaining the title of emperor. Early in 1815, however, he escaped from Elba, returned to France and reoccupied Paris. In June, after "a hundred days" of freedom, he was defeated by British and allied forces at Waterloo and finally exiled to the remote Atlantic island of Saint Helena, where he died on 2nd May (Western calendar) 1821 and where he was initially buried.

[22, 25, 35, 44, 46, 63, 145, 289, 341, 349,
357, 595, 643, 661, 663, 709 IX, 723, 760]

Nashchókin, Pavel Vóïnovich (1801–54): A close friend of Pushkin's in Moscow during his post-exile years; Pushkin often stayed with him when visiting Moscow. He was an inveterate gambler at cards. Another of his hobbies was the creation of a miniature fully furnished toy house, progress on which is also mentioned in letters of Pushkin's from Moscow in 1831 and 1836. [610]

Navarino: A Turkish fort on the west coast of the Greek Peloponnese, captured by the Russians in April 1770 and held by them for a couple of months during their naval expedition to Greece and the Aegean. [595]

Nelédinsky: See Melétsky

Nemesis: In Greek mythology, a goddess personifying indignation and retribution. [418, 663]

Nevá: The river, issuing into the Baltic through the Gulf of Finland, on the delta of which St Petersburg stands. *passim*

Nicholas I (1796–1855): Nicholas succeeded his older brother Alexander as tsar at the end of 1825 and was immediately confronted with an uprising of liberal army officers and intellectuals (the "Decembrist uprising") demanding fundamental political reforms. Nicholas rigorously suppressed the uprising, having five of the leading participants hanged and many others exiled to Siberia. Following his coronation in Moscow the following August, Nicholas summoned Pushkin from exile in Mikháylovskoye and, after interviewing him, ordered his release, undertaking personal responsibility for the censorship of his work and for authorizing its publication. When a cholera epidemic reached Moscow from the east in September 1830 Nicholas immediately travelled there from St Petersburg to control the situation and reassure the inhabitants, a courageous action for which he won much praise. In defence of the Russian Empire he ruthlessly crushed the Polish uprising of 1830–31, provoking the hostility of much of western Europe.

[461n, 463n, 474, 506, 544n, 643, 663, 739n, 760]

Niobē: In classical mythology Niobe, a mother, by a unwise boast angered Apollo and Artemis, who killed all her children. The grieving Niobe was turned to stone, which continued to exude tears. [749]

Obrenović, Miloš (1780–1860): A major figure in the Serbian struggle for independence from Turkey at the beginning of the nineteenth century. He was leader of the Second Uprising in 1815–17, afterwards becoming prince of a semi-autonomous Serbia. Originally an associate of Karađorđe, he later became his rival, fell out with him and finally engineered his murder. [709 XII, 714]

Olég, Prince (reigned 879–912): Olég was a semi-legendary figure in the lore of early Russia. Historically he was a Varangian (Russian: *varyág*) or Viking, one of the Scandinavian adventurers who invaded western Russia and founded its ruling dynasties in the ninth century. Olég ruled Nóvgorod from 879, then occupied Kiev in 882, making it the capital of Rus. Olég waged war with the Khazárs, a semi-nomadic nation from the region north of the Caspian, who controlled much of what is now southern Russia. In 907 Olég led an expedition against Constantinople and hung his shield on the city gates as a token of victory. He concluded an advantageous peace with Constantinople in 911, just before his death in 912, and was succeeded by Igor, for whom he had ruled as regent.

[305, 578]

Olénina, Anna ("Annette") Alexéyevna (1808–88): Daughter of Alexéi N. Olénin, President of the St Petersburg Academy of Fine Arts and Director of the Public Library. Pushkin was much in love with her in mid-1828, and in August proposed marriage to her, but her parents refused him.

[512, 513n, 515, 521, 522, 531, 532, 538, 585]

Olin, Valerián Nikoláyevich (c.1788–1841): Prolific writer of little talent and little success. [600]

Olympus: Highest mountain in Greece, often capped with cloud and believed in ancient times to be the home of the gods. It was also a base for Greek partisans in their struggles against Turkish occupying forces culminating in the Greek War of Independence (1821–29). [594]

Orlóv, Count Alexéi Grigóryevich (1737–1809): He and his brothers Grigóry and Fyódor took a leading part in the coup d'état of 1762 that brought Catherine the Great to power; they all held prominent positions in her administration during the early years of her reign. In 1770 Alexéi was Russian Commander-in-Chief at the victorious naval battle of Chesme off the Aegean coast of Turkey, when the Turkish fleet was set on fire and annihilated. [25, 375, 595, 635]

Orlóv, Count Fyódor Grigóryevich (1741–96): With his brothers Grigóry and Alexéi he took an active part in the coup d'état of 1762 that brought Catherine the Great to power, and for some years thereafter enjoyed her favour and trust. In 1769–70 he took part under Alexéi in the successful Russian naval expedition against the Turks in the Aegean archipelago and eastern Mediterranean, conducting himself with heroism at the battle of Chesme and winning an engagement against a Turkish fleet at Hydra off the Peloponnese. [595, 635]

Orlóv, Count Grigóry Grigóryevich (1734–83): Brother of Alexéi and Fyódor – see above. Grigóry led the *coup d'état* that brought Catherine the Great to the throne in place of her husband in 1762. He was her lover both before and for some years after the coup and was awarded many honours and influential appointments by her. In 1771 Catherine sent him to Moscow to deal with a serious outbreak of the plague and attendant disorders, and his effective response earned him great credit.

[595, 635]

Ósipova, Praskóvya Alexándrovna (1781–1859): Twice-married mistress of Trigórskoye, neighbouring estate to the Pushkins' Mikháylovskoye. She had five children by her first husband (Nikolái I. Vulf, d. 1813) and two by her second (Iván S. Ósipov, died 1824). She was the aunt of Anna Kern. She was always on friendly terms with Pushkin, who was a frequent visitor to Trigórskoye during his exile at Mikháylovskoye. She also owned an estate at Malínniki between Moscow and St Petersburg, where she sometimes stayed, and which Pushkin visited several times between 1828 and 1833.   [139, 369, 386, 437, 455]

Ossian: Ossian, son of Fingal, was a figure from Celtic legend: in youth a mighty warrior, he became in later life a blind minstrel who composed and sang poetry about the exploits of the Celtic kings and warriors of Ireland and Scotland. Translations of his supposed poetry by the Scotsman James Macpherson in the 1760s were later exposed as a fraud. Nonetheless, they had a widespread influence on European culture into the nineteenth century.   [8, 10, 149n, 690]

Ovid (Publius Ovidius Naso, 43 BC–17 or 18 AD): Roman poet who wrote brilliant, witty and often erotic verse. One of his most famous works, his *Ars amatoria*, or *Art of Love*, offended the Emperor Augustus, who was trying to raise standards of sexual morality in Rome. For this, and for an unspecified misdemeanour (possibly to do with his relations with the Emperor's disgraced daughter Julia), Augustus exiled him from Rome in 8 AD; Ovid was sent to the distant frontier of the Roman Empire at Tomis on the shore of the Black Sea (modern Constanţa in Romania), just across the Danube delta from Bessarabia, where Pushkin was exiled from 1820 to 1823. There Ovid spent the last eight years of his life complaining of the harsh conditions and begging Augustus to be allowed back to Rome, where his wife and daughter remained. The poems and verse epistles he wrote at this time are collected in his *Tristia* ("Hardships") and *Epistulæ ex Ponto* ("Letters from the Black Sea"). The reprieve he requested was never granted, and he was buried in exile.   [21, 71, 150n, 253, 265, 292, 298, 360, 366, 367n, 761n]

Pallas: see Athene.

Paphos: In Cyprus, site of a celebrated shrine of Aphroditē.   [482, 646]

Parca: A Roman goddess of fate.   [623, 718]

Parnassus: A mountain in central Greece associated with Apollo and the Muses, and so with poetry. The Castalian spring, sacred to the Muses, rose on the mountain's slopes.

[7, 21, 24, 30, 42, 46, 52, 68, 71, 74/75, 92, 100, 225, 310, 421, 431, 447, 679, 748]

Paskévich, Field Marshal Count Iván Fyódorovich (1782–1856): Fought in the Napoleonic and Turkish wars between 1806 and 1814, but rose to leadership during the trans-Caucasian wars against Persia and Turkey in 1826–29, in both of which he won significant victories, capturing Yereván (capital of modern Armenia) from Persia and leading Russian armies into the mountains of eastern Turkey. He triumphed a third time when appointed by Nicolas I in 1831 to crush the Polish uprising. The Tsar subsequently made him viceroy of Poland.   [663]

Pegasus: In Greek mythology, a winged horse, a blow from whose hoof created the spring of Hippocrene that was sacred to the Muses. Because

of Pegasus's association with the Muses, his name symbolized poetic
inspiration.   [5, 7, 30, 52, 71, 74/75, 310, 460, 748]
Penātēs: in Roman mythology originally gods of the larder, then of the
household and home.   [598, 622]
Periclēs (*c.*495–429 BC): Pre-eminent orator and statesman in democratic
Athens.   [223, 423, 594]
Perún: In Slavic mythology the highest of the gods, god of thunder and
lightning, equivalent to the Greek Zeus.   [25, 305, 595]
Peter I, "the Great" (1672–1725): Reigned as tsar from 1682. In adulthood,
he transformed Russia from a largely isolated and tradition-bound state
that saw its cultural and religious origins in Byzantium to a westward-
looking European power. In the Great Northern War between Russia
and Sweden from 1700 to 1721 Peter succeeded in extending Russian
territory to the Baltic, in quashing a Ukrainian revolt under Mazépa and
in inflicting a decisive defeat on Swedish forces led by King Charles X
(Battle of Poltáva, 1709). In 1703 Peter founded St Petersburg, making
it his new capital city from 1713. He combined immense energy and
a ruthless determination with a convivial personality and a boundless
curiosity and openness to new ideas and technology. It was he who
stood godfather to Pushkin's African ancestor Gannibál and furthered
his career.   [366, 380, 414, 474, 543b, 635, 704, 739]
Petrarch (Francesco Petrarca, 1304–74): Eminent Italian lyric poet, writer
and scholar. He famously addressed ardent love poems to a beautiful
woman named Laura, whom he admired only from a distance.
                    [322, 606]
Petrović, Đorđe: See Karađorđe.
Phoebus: See Apollo.
Pindus: A mountain range in Greece associated with the Muses, and so
with poetry. It also provided bases for Greek partisans in their strug-
gles against Turkish occupying forces culminating in the Greek War of
Independence (1821–29)   [7, 39, 42, 46, 52, 68, 92, 182, 475, 594]
Pletnyóv, Pyótr Alexándrovich (1791–1865): Critic, poet, teacher and
publisher. He gained the reputation of a meticulous editor. In 1822
he published a volume of verses by Pushkin's uncle Vasíly, including
his most popular poem, *A Dangerous Neighbour*. At the end of 1824
he undertook the publication of the first chapter of Pushkin's *Eugene
Onégin*, which came out in February the following year. He went on to
publish other chapters of *Eugene Onégin* as Pushkin completed them,
as well as other works of Pushkin, and the two became firm friends. The
dedication of Chapters Four and Five of *Eugene Onégin*, which Pushkin
composed in 1827, and which has subsequently headed the complete
work, was originally addressed to Pletnyóv by name.   [378, 694, 729]
Polevóy, Nikolái Alexéyevich (1796–1846): Poet, writer, historian, critic
and magazine editor. He earned Pushkin's disgust first by attacking the
historical work of Nikolái Karamzín and then by advertising for advance

subscriptions to his own, in Pushkin's view much inferior, twelve-volume *History of the Russian People*, of which he only published six (1829–33).
[405, 559n, 692]

Pushchin, Iván Ivánovich (1798–1859): Pushchin was the first boy that Pushkin met when he joined the Imperial Lycée in 1811, and they became close friends. Pushchin was known at school for his studiousness. On 11th January 1825 Pushchin visited Pushkin during his exile at Mikháylovskoye; it was the last time they met. For his part in the Decembrist uprising at the end of 1825, Pushchin was condemned to penal servitude in Siberia for life, returning only in 1856.
[24n, 29n, 51, 120, 122, 136n, 446, 473, 501n, 576n, 722n]

Pushchin, Mikhaíl Ivánovich (1800–69): Younger brother of Iván Pushchin (above), who also became a friend of Pushkin's. Having successfully pursued a military career since his teens, Mikhaíl Pushchin was accused of Decembrist sympathies after the 1825 uprising, was briefly imprisoned for a time in the Peter and Paul Fortress in St Petersburg, then demoted and posted to serve with the army in the Caucasus. Pushkin spent time with him there during his 1829 visit.
[576n]

Pushkin, Lev Sergéyevich (1805–52): Alexander Pushkin's younger brother. Lev gave up formal education early in 1821, without completing his course. Pushkin took a close interest in his brother during his years in the South. Lev was staying at Mikháylovskoye during the first months of his brother's exile there, leaving for St Petersburg early in November. Subsequently Pushkin often used him for carrying out errands in the capital. From the later 1820s he served in the Russian army in the Caucasus and elsewhere.
[318, 364, 365, 366, 379, 388, 566n]

Pushkin, Vasíly Lvovich (1766–1830): Alexander Pushkin's uncle, he served in the army until the age of thirty-one. A wit and minor poet, his most notable work was a popular and racy poem entitled *Opásny soséd* (*A Dangerous Neighbour*, 1811). Recognizing his teenage nephew's poetic talent, he introduced him to leading writers such as Zhukóvsky, Karamzín and Vyázemsky. He became prominent in the progressive literary group Arzamás and, being the oldest member, was in March 1816 appointed their "elder". In a letter of April of that year he wrote to Pushkin: "You're Sergéi Lvovich's son – and my brother through Apollo."
[30, 59n, 60, 74, 75, 115, 310, 378, 392, 443, 662]

Púshkina, Natálya Nikoláyevna (*née* Goncharóva, 1812–63): Pushkin's wife, famous for her beauty. Pushkin first met her in Moscow at the end of 1828 and began to court her in the spring of 1829 at the start of his journey southwards to the Caucasus. The courtship continued spasmodically in later 1829 and 1830; they were engaged on 6th May 1830 and married on 18th February 1831.
[563n, 581, 596, 609, 613, 621n, 653, 671, 710]

Raïch, Semyón Yegórovich (1792–1855): Teacher, poet, translator and editor, cool towards Pushkin.
[600]

Rigas, Konstantinos Feraios (1757–98): Greek nationalist and revolution-ary thinker, writer and poet, who campaigned for Greek independence from Turkey. [594]

Riznić, Amalia (1801–25): Amalia Riznić (*née* Ripp), was a girl of Austro-Italian parentage from Vienna. She was married off in 1820 to Jovan Riznić (1792–1861), a native of Trieste of Serb extraction. Riznić had strong business interests in Odessa and settled there, taking Russian citizenship in 1822. In the spring of 1823 Riznić brought his attractive young wife to Odessa, where Pushkin met them soon after his arrival from Kishinyóv. Amalia's marriage was a loveless one, at least on her part, and the free-living Amalia surrounded herself with a swarm of young admirers, including Pushkin. Pushkin's relationship with Amalia was an intense affair of infatuation, jealousy, self-deception, estrange-ment and reconciliation. Amalia developed a serious chest complaint, and in May 1824 her husband sent her back to Trieste, ostensibly for health reasons, so that she could benefit from the Italian climate. The parting, recalled by Pushkin years later, was an emotional and painful one. Afterwards Pushkin came to believe that her husband had sent her away because of her affairs (she had had other lovers too), and he suffered acute jealousy from the belief that she had betrayed him with a rival. In Italy Amalia's chest trouble grew worse, and she died in Trieste in June 1825. The news only reached Pushkin in July the following year.
[327n, 328n, 337n, 339n, 354, 357n, 358n, 458, 514n, 637, 652]

Rossini, Gioachino (1792–1868): Famous Italian operatic composer. He was a favourite of Pushkin's. [354, 564]

Rosset, Alexándra Ósipovna: See Smirnóva.

Rumyántsev, Count Pyótr Alexándrovich (1725–96): Eminent Russian general, who defeated the Turks at the Battle of Kagúl in 1770. He was subsequently awarded the surname Zadunáysky in honour of his subsequent campaign beyond the Danube (*Dunáy* in Russian).
[25, 175, 595]

Saadi of Shiraz (1210–*c*.1291): A celebrated Persian poet and writer.
[542, 565, 740]

Saint-Priest (Russian: *Sen-Prí*), **Count Emmanuíl Kárlovich** (1806–28): Son of a French émigré, famous for his caricatures. [583]

Salieri, Antonio (1750–1825): Italian musician and composer, who spent most of his career in Vienna, where he became a powerful figure in the musical world and (it was reported) became fiercely jealous of Mozart.
[641]

Satyrs (called "Fauns" by the Romans): Mischievous spirits of woods and hills and patrons of lust and revelry, fond of playing their pipes; imag-ined as partly human in form, but with ears, horns and legs of a goat.
[5, 18, 94, 150, 207, 723, 749]

Scott, Sir Walter (1771–1832): Prolific Scottish novelist and poet.
[535, 608]

Scythia: In ancient times a name for the lands north of the Black Sea, later populated by Slavs. Scythians were regarded by the Greeks as barbarians and drunkards. [609, 640n, 719, 722]

Shakespeare, William (1564–1616): Pre-eminent English poet, writer of many plays (including *Macbeth* and *Hamlet*) and sonnets.
[564, 606, 753n]

Smirnóva, Alexándra Ósipovna (née Rosset, 1809–82): Born in Odessa to a family of French extraction and educated in St Petersburg. At the age of 17 she became a maid of honour at court. A St Petersburg beauty of wit and intelligence, she had many admirers, including Prince Pyótr Vyázemsky, Prince Sergéi Golítsyn and Pushkin; Tsar Nicholas himself and his brother Grand Duke Mikhaíl Pávlovich were said to have been her lovers. She married Nikolái Smirnóv in January 1832.
[521, 585, 614, 664, 673]

Sobańska, Karolina (1795–1885): Aristocratic Polish beauty and adventuress, whom Pushkin first met in Kiev in 1821, and with whom he flirted again in Odessa in 1823. Having left her husband, Sobańska was living openly, in defiance of convention, as mistress of a senior and influential Russian general and working with him, under cover, for Russian intelligence. She and Pushkin met again in St Petersburg in the winter of 1829–30, when he once more fell briefly in love with her. She collected autographs of celebrities. [601, 603]

Sobolévsky, Sergéi Alexándrovich (1803–70): Witty versifier, epigrammatist and bibliophile, friend and admirer of Pushkin, fond of good food.
[467, 709n]

Sōcratēs (469–399 BC): famous Athenian philosopher. He left no writings, but his life and conversations were well recorded by Plato and others.
[89, 568n]

Southey, Robert (1774–1843): English writer and member, with Wordsworth and Coleridge, of the "Lake Poets". [598, 599, 726, 727]

Sumarókov, Alexándr Petróvich (1717–77): Prolific poet, playwright and literary critic of mediocre talent, whose arrogant and captious personality brought him into conflict not only with the much-esteemed Mikhaíl Lomonósov, but also with Catherine the Great. His plays were weak adaptations of classical French dramas such as Racine's.
[68, 645]

Suvórov, Count Alexándr Vasílyevich (1730–96): Eminent Russian general who distinguished himself in the wars of the late eighteenth century against Turkey, Poland and revolutionary France. In 1794 he led the Russian forces in the successful storming of Warsaw. [25, 663]

Svinín, Pavel Petróvich (1787–1839): Minor literary figure, not highly esteemed by Pushkin. [600]

Svistóv: See Khvostóv.

Tartarus: In classical mythology, another name for Hades, the abode of the dead. [355, 718]

Tasso, Torquato (1544–95): Italian poet, most famous for his epic *Gerusalemme liberata* ("The Liberation of Jerusalem", 1575), eight-line stanzas from which ("octaves") were said to be a popular source of lyrics for the songs of Venetian gondoliers. After a brilliant beginning, his difficult temperament and the onset of mental illness alienated him from his patrons and led to periods of incarceration and wanderings.
[30, 495, 510, 544, 553, 598, 606n, 639, 697n]

Tavrída: Russianized form of Tauris, an ancient Greek name for the Crimea.
[375, 606, 661]

Temíra: Conventional name for a girlfriend in poetry.
[32, 40, 52, 115, 609]

Teos: Greek city in Ionia, birthplace of the poet Anacreon. [646]

Terek: A river that rises high on the northern slopes of the Caucasus range and, after plunging northwards through mountain gorges, flows east into the Caspian. The Georgian Military Highway, along which Pushkin travelled to and from Georgia in 1829, followed the valley of the Terek through the mountains. [592, 615, 619, 644]

Thermopylae: A narrow passage on the eastern Greek mainland between mountains and sea that links northern and southern Greece. It was the scene of heroic fighting by Greek defenders both against Persian invaders in 480 BC and against Turkish oppressors in 1821. [594]

Tizengáuzen, Countess Yekaterína Fyódorovna (1806–88): Widowed daughter of Yelizavéta Khitrovó and granddaughter of Field Marshal Prince Kutúzov. She, her mother and younger sister were close Petersburg friends of Pushkin. [602]

Trigórskoye: A country estate belonging to Praskóvya Ósipova; it adjoined the Pushkins' estate of Mikháylovskoye and was often visited by Pushkin while he was there.
[139, 365, 366n, 385n, 386n, 392, 402n, 437, 439n, 456n, 457n, 460, 735]

Tsárskoye Seló ("Tsars' Village", originally *Sárskoye Seló*): An estate about twenty kilometres south of St Petersburg containing palaces, notably the huge Catherine Palace, and a large park. The complex, begun in 1711 for Peter the Great's wife Catherine I, became a favourite summer residence of later Russian monarchs such as Catherine the Great. The park contained paths, gardens, woods, canals, cascades, lakes, fountains and statuary, as well as columns, gateways, follies and pavilions commemorating Russian military victories and other successes. It was in a wing of the Catherine Palace that Alexander I in 1811 established the Imperial Lycée (high school) to prepare selected sons of noble families for careers in the public service. From the Lycée the boys had access to the park and its monuments. There were also villas in the area used, especially in the summer, by courtiers and gentry. Pushkin and his wife lived there for five months in the summer and autumn of 1831, shortly after their marriage. [176, 265, 375, 446, 501n, 595]

Tver: Chief city of the eponymous province, situated on the road between Moscow and St Petersburg. It was in Tver Province that Pushkin's Mikháylovskoye neighbour Praskóvya Ósipova and her Vulf relations owned estates at which Pushkin sometimes called when travelling between the two capitals. [585, 586, 587n]

Tyrtaeus (fl. mid-7th century BC): Early Greek poet and author of rousing martial verses. [594]

Ushakóva, Yekaterína Nikoláyevna (1809–72): A young woman from a Moscow family that Pushkin often visited when he was in the city; he fell in love with her during his stay in Moscow in 1826–27 and remained on friendly terms with her until his marriage. [483, 486, 585, 604]

Ushakóva, Yelizavéta Nikoláyevna (1810–72): Sister of Yekaterína (see above), also the object of Pushkin's friendly attentions. In 1830 she married Sergéi D. Kiselyóv, brother of Pavel and Nikolái.
[532n, 553, 585, 604n]

Uvárov, Count Sergéi Semyónovich (1786–1855): Distinguished classical scholar, and from 1818 President of the St Petersburg Academy of Sciences (from 1818) and of the Imperial Russian Academy (from 1831). A man of strongly conservative political views, he was appointed Minister of National Education by Nicholas I in 1833; he was author of the slogan "Orthodoxy, Autocracy, Nationhood", which became the three governing principles of Nicholas's reign. Despite his qualities as a scholar and administrator, certain scandals circulated over his conduct: Uvárov was said to have ingratiated himself with the Minister for Finance in the early 1820s by running errands for his children; when Count Dmitry Sheremétev (1803–71), a rich and as yet unmarried relative of his wife's, fell seriously ill during 1835, Uvárov, misled by a false report of his death, sealed up the man's property in the expectation of shortly inheriting it; it was said that Uvárov had profited personally from the firewood provided for the winter heating of the Academy and other government premises under his control; and when Uvárov appointed Prince Dondukóv-Kórsakov as his vice-president at the St Petersburg Academy, it was interpreted by some as a favour to an erstwhile homosexual lover.
[725n, 736]

Velyásheva, Yekaterína Vasílyevna (1813–65): A niece of Praskóvya Ósipova, one of the girls in the Vulf/Ósipov families to attract Pushkin's attention at one time or another on his visits to the families' estates in Tver Province, when travelling between Moscow and St Petersburg. [586]

Venus (Roman goddess of love): See Aphroditē.

Versailles: The huge palace and park of the French monarchs outside Paris, created by Louis XIV in the seventeenth century. [609]

Vidocq, Eugène François (1775–1857): A disreputable French criminal, then police informer, who later became first head of the French state security police (the *Sûreté Nationale*). Pushkin used his surname as a nickname for his *bête noire* Faddéy Bulgárin. [607, 636]

Virgil (Publius Vergilius Maro, 70–19 BC): Pre-eminent poet of ancient Rome, author of the epic *Aeneid*, the heroic story of the end of the Trojan War, Aeneas's escape by sea, his visit to the underworld and his invasion of Italy. Virgil also wrote a collection of ten short pastoral poems known as the *Eclogues*, set against a background of idealized rusticity. Dante, in his *Inferno*, later imagines Virgil as his guide in his journey to hell.

[22, 30, 34, 346, 355n, 494, 645, 670]

Voltaire (François-Marie Arouet, 1694-1778): French writer, poet, dramatist, essayist and philosopher, much admired in freethinking circles for his independence of mind and anticlericalism. He was regarded as a heretic in Catholic circles, but cultivated by progressive-minded rulers such as Frederick the Great of Prussia (with whom, however, he later fell out) and Catherine the Great of Russia, who conducted a lengthy correspondence with him. Voltaire was a favourite author of Pushkin, who modelled *The Monk* (No. 5 in Vol. 1) and *Bová* (No. 22 in Vol. 1) on his bawdy and irreverent mock-epic (banned in Russia) about Joan of Arc, *La Pucelle d'Orléans*. His satirical novel *Candide* was also a favourite book. Compelled by controversy for much of his life to move from place to place, in 1758 he settled in an estate at Ferney on the French-Swiss border. After his death in Paris his body, denied a church interment, was buried secretly, while his heart and brain were embalmed elsewhere; during the Revolution his remains were in 1791 ceremonially transferred to the Panthéon in Paris. Pushkin seemed to be aware of reports that after the Bourbon restoration in 1814 the remains were moved again.

[2n, 5, 22, 30, 53, 71n, 89, 110, 113n, 152n, 158n, 257n, 281n, 310, 375, 399, 418n, 451, 484n, 609, 744n]

Vorontsóva, Countess Yelizavéta ("Elise") Xavéryevna (*née* Branicka, 1792–1880): From a rich and aristocratic Polish family with an estate in the Ukraine, in 1819 she married Count M.S. Vorontsóv, who later served as Governor-General of New Russia, resident in Odessa, with Pushkin as one of his officials. Famous for her beauty, charm and intelligence, she first met Pushkin in Odessa in September 1823 and had an affair with him during his last months there in 1824. Just before they parted for the last time, Vorontsóva gave Pushkin a heavy gold signet ring set with a large red cornelian inscribed (in mirror image) in antique Hebrew characters, which Pushkin treasured as a talisman and wore until his death. He also sometimes used the ring to seal his letters. Vorontsóva is said to have possessed a similar ring, with which she sealed letters she sent to Pushkin in Mikháylovskoye – letters that she instructed him to destroy as soon as he had read them.

[350, 351, 355, 357n, 358n, 359n, 383, 390, 395n, 406n, 438, 629]

Vrévskaya, Yevpráxiya: See Vulf, Yevpráxiya.

Vulf, Anna Nikoláyevna (1799–1857): Eldest daughter of Praskóvya Ósipova by her first husband. Her relationship with Pushkin was often close. In February 1826 Pushkin sent her for her name day the recently published collection of his poems with the message "To the dear name-day girl Anna Nikoláyevna Vulf, from her most humble well-wisher Alexander Pushkin". But she was fonder of him than he was of her, and his attitude to her was often ironical and even harsh.

[365n, 402, 403, 424, 434, 435n]

Vulf, Anna ("Netty") **Nikoláyevna** (1799–1835): Niece of Praskóvya Ósipovna by her first husband and first cousin of her namesake above. Netty's father's estate was at Bernóvo in the province of Tver, and Pushkin visited her there in the autumn of 1829 on his way from Moscow to St Petersburg. [585]

Vulf, Yevpráxiya ("Zizí" or "Zina") **Nikoláyevna** (1809–83): Youngest daughter of Praskóvya Ósipova, Pushkin's neighbour at Mikháylovskoye, by her first husband. In 1831 she married Baron B.A. Vrevsky; the couple maintained friendly relations with Pushkin in his final years.

[365n, 436, 456, 460, 735]

Vyázemskaya, Princess Vera Fyódorovna (1790–1886): Mother of Pavel and wife of Pyótr Vyázemsky (see below). She shared her husband's close friendship with Pushkin. She was in Odessa in the summer of 1824 at the time of Pushkin's affair with Elise Vorontsóva and his enforced departure for Mikháylovskoye, and she and her husband often saw Pushkin during his visits to Moscow from 1826 onwards. She was to have been matron of honour at Pushkin's wedding in 1831, but fell ill shortly beforehand.

[654n, 662]

Vyázemsky, Prince Pyótr Andréyevich (1792–1878): Poet, critic, controversialist and humourist, known for his sharp wit; member of the progressive literary group Arzamás, where he was given the nickname *Asmodéy* (Asmodaeus). He first got to know Pushkin during Pushkin's Lycée years, and they remained close friends for the rest of the younger poet's life.

[30, 59, 74, 234, 275, 398n, 443n, 443, 447, 448, 459, 465n, 479n, 512n, 521, 526n, 545n, 662]

Wilson, John (1785–1854): Scottish writer, dramatist and poet who featured in the anthology *The Poetical Works of Millman, Bowles, Wilson, and Barry Cornwall* (Paris, 1829), a volume owned and well used by Pushkin. He wrote the play *The City of the Plague* (1816), one scene of which Pushkin translated as his *Feast during the Plague*. [647, 648]

Wordsworth, William (1770–1850): Famous English romantic poet. [606]

Yákovleva, Arína Rodiónovna (1758–1828): A peasant woman, serf of Pushkin's mother's family. Though given her freedom in 1799, she preferred to stay on with the Pushkins and nursed the three children. She and Alexander were especially close, and she acted as his fond companion and housekeeper during his exile at Mikháylovskoye.

[380n, 393, 409, 466, 732]

Yeruslán: Yeruslán Lazarévich was a legendary Russian folk hero who encountered a warrior's severed head on a battlefield of corpses and won a special sword. The story was one source on which Pushkin drew for his *Ruslán and Lyudmíla*. [690]

Yesakóv, Semyón Semyónovich (1798–1831): One of Pushkin's classmates at the Imperial Lycée. He entered the army and rose to the rank of colonel, but committed suicide while on service in Poland, apparently because of a costly professional misjudgement. [104, 668n]

Yusúpov, Prince Nikolái Borísovich (1750–1831): Diplomat and statesman. Well travelled, well connected and extremely rich, he had amassed a vast art collection in his sumptuous palace at Archángelskoye near Moscow. On visits to Europe he had visited the court of Louis XVI and Marie-Antoinette at Versailles and made the acquaintance of Voltaire and other luminaries such as Diderot, Rousseau and Beaumarchais. [609]

Zakrévskaya, Agraféna Fyódorovna (*née* Tolstáya, 1800–79): Wife of Arsény A. Zakrévsky (1783–1865), who, from being Governor-General of Finland, was in 1828 promoted Minister of Internal Affairs. His wife, admired for her beauty by Pushkin for a while in the summer of 1828, was an emotional and capricious woman, notorious in St Petersburg society for her unconventional lifestyle and extravagant and unpredictable behaviour. [525, 529, 530, 601]

Zeus: In Greek mythology, king of the gods and master of human destiny; notorious for his extramarital love affairs. As god of storms and thunder he was prone to punish those who angered him by hurling a thunderbolt. He was equated with the Roman Jupiter or Jove.
[354, 423, 534, 598, 749, 756]

Zhukóvsky, Vasíly Andréyevich (1783–1852): Respected romantic poet and man of letters, who translated much western European poetry, including English and especially German works, into Russian. He first met Pushkin in 1815 and was astonished at his poetic talent, becoming in due course his mentor and lifelong friend. Zhukóvsky's style was normally restrained and mild, but in 1812 he had written some uncharacteristically martial poems such as 'Song of a Bard over the Grave of Russian Victors' and 'A Poet in the Camp of Russian Warriors'. He was a leading member of the progressive literary society Arzamás. He was also close to the imperial court, teaching Russian to the young wife of the future emperor Nicholas I and becoming in due course tutor to Nicholas's son, the future Alexander II. Zhukóvsky acted as Pushkin's literary executor after his death.
[12, 21, 25, 43, 59n, 68, 73n, 149n,
154, 179n, 196, 220, 367, 666n]

Zoïlus (4th–3rd century BC): A Greek philosopher notorious for his carping criticism of Homer and other well-regarded writers. Pushkin applies his name to any pedantic or malicious critic.
[68, 158, 253, 347, 454, 559, 574, 577]

Notes

The names marked in bold are included in Index of Proper Names.

THE CAUCASUS AND COURTSHIP (1829–30)

563 First published at the end of 1830. The poem was first drafted, in a longer form, on 15th May on Pushkin's arrival at Geórgievsk in the north Caucasus. This final version reflects his arrival in Georgia ten days later, and was apparently addressed to **Natálya Goncharóva**, his future wife, whom he had begun to court that spring in Moscow at the start of his journey southwards.

564 First published in 1830. The poem, dated 22nd May, when Pushkin had reached Vladikavkáz, reflects a real-life encounter between the poet and a Kalmyk girl as he approached the north Caucasus ten days earlier. The Kalmyks (or Kalmuks) were a widely dispersed nomadic people of Mongolian extraction, one branch of which roamed the area to the west and northwest of the Caspian Sea.
l. 12 De Vigny's books: Pushkin refers specifically to *Cinq Mars*, a historical novel by the French writer Alfred de Vigny (1797–1863), published in 1826, of which he had a low opinion. *l. 16 Arias by Rossini*: Pushkin mentions 'Ma dov'è', an aria written for male voice, from Act I, Sc. 9, of **Rossini**'s opera *La donna del lago* (1819).

565 Pushkin met the Persian poet **Fazil Khan** on 24th May as they travelled through the Caucasus in opposite directions. He drafted this poem in Tbilisi a few days later, but it was left unfinished and unpublished.

566 First published at the end of 1831. In the summer of 1829 Pushkin travelled across the Caucasus to visit his brother **Lev** and some other friends who were serving in the Russian army during the Russo-Turkish war. Pushkin caught up with them as they advanced into north-eastern Turkey to seize **Erzurum** and witnessed an engagement at Sagan-lu in mid-June, which prompted this poem.
Delibásh: A Turkish term meaning literally "daring head", used to denote Turkish cavalrymen.

567 Dated 5th July 1829, while Pushkin was in **Erzurum**, and first published at the turn of the year, the poem seems to refer to fighting between Russian and Turkish forces witnessed by Pushkin during the Russian campaign in June to capture the city (which lies close to the headwaters of one branch of the **Euphrates**). Pushkin presents

the poem as a translation from the Persian poet **Hafez**, probably (as elsewhere) to distance himself from authorship for personal or censorship reasons; although the poem reflects Hafez's style, no direct source has been found for it in his work. Pushkin's autograph is subtitled "Sheyer 1. For Fargat-Bek". *Sheyer* is Azerbaijani for "poem", and Fargat-Bek was an officer in the Russian army's first Muslim cavalry regiment, which had been recruited in Karabákh, a district of Azerbaijan already under Russian control and famous for its horses and horsemen. *l. 4 your daring warrior horde*: In Russian "the horde from Karabákh". *l. 6 Azrael*: In Islamic tradition, the angel of death.

568   A fragment written in mid-July 1829 and unpublished in Pushkin's lifetime. The historical Crito was a wealthy Athenian friend and disciple of the philosopher **Socrates**, but Pushkin may be using the name fictionally: we do not know how he planned to develop the poem. *l. 6 Ceramicus*: Kerameikós ("the Potters' Quarter") in Greek, a district of ancient Athens, northwest of the Acropolis. *l. 9 a girl (or nymph?)*: Pushkin simply refers to a "nymph": we do not know if he meant an exceptionally attractive human girl or a being from Greek mythology.

569   Unpublished in Pushkin's lifetime. The poem was written in mid-July 1829 in **Erzurum**, while Pushkin was visiting the Russian army there. The morning and evening reveilles reminded Pushkin of his schooldays at the Imperial Lycée at **Tsárskoye Seló** between 1811 and 1817: from there he would have heard the regular reveilles from the nearby guards' barracks, as well as the frequent sound of soldiers marching from St Petersburg to fight in the Napoleonic Wars.

570   Drafted in **Erzurum** around 18th July 1829, and apparently intended as the opening of a longer work. Pushkin later revised the first 29 lines (as printed here) and published them in Chapter 5 of his *Journey to Erzurum* (1836), where he jokingly presented them as the work of an erstwhile Turkish janizary called Aminoğlu. Pushkin's original is fully rhymed to an irregular pattern.

The poem refers to the recent janizaries' revolt in Istanbul. The janizaries were originally an elite corps of trained and disciplined Turkish soldiers enjoying considerable privileges, which they defended jealously, and became a force in Turkish society strongly resistant to reform. With time, too, they became increasingly corrupt, ineffective and resented. In 1826, determined to modernize the Turkish army, Sultan Mahmud II (1784–1839) disbanded the janizaries and brutally suppressed their subsequent mutiny; thousands died when their barracks were set on fire, and many others were executed. Mahmud's reforms were slow to reach distant outposts such as Erzurum, however, where reactionary attitudes and practices persisted for a while. Pushkin puts the words of his poem into the mouth of a surviving janizary of the old school. *ll. 34–35 From Ruse fort... Izmir... Trabzon... Tulcea*: All cities across the then Turkish Empire. Ruse (Russian: *Rushchuk*) is on the lower Danube in modern Bulgaria; Izmir (Smyrna) is a port city in western Anatolia; Trabzon (Trebizond) is in northern Turkey on the Black Sea coast; and Tulcea is now a Romanian city in the Danube delta. *ll. 40–43 sharp spikes... turning black*: Pushkin has largely borrowed these lines from his description of Tsar **Iván the Terrible**'s treatment of his enemies – see III, 477, ll. 20–23. *l. 43 The Sultan's rage*: Sultan Mahmud II – see above.

571   Unpublished in Pushkin's lifetime. Written on his way back home from **Erzurum** in mid-September 1829. Escorted earlier in the journey by **Don** Cossacks returning from the front, Pushkin had heard them discussing what to do with their wives if they found they had given birth during their husbands' absence.

572   First published in 1831. Written in mid-September while Pushkin was travelling through the Cossack lands on the **Don** on his way home from the Caucasus. The poem portrays the return home of Don Cossack horsemen who had been away in Transcaucasia and Turkey fighting for Russia in the recent wars with Persia and Turkey. *l. 7 Aras... Euphrates*: The Cossack troops would have seen both rivers during their invasion of eastern Turkey that summer. *l. 11 River Arpa*: The returning Cossacks would cross the Arpa on leaving Turkey for Russian territory.

573   Written after mid-July 1829; first published in 1836. The verse is directed at **Nikolái Nadézhdin**, who had published a critical review of Pushkin's *Poltáva* under the epigraph: "Undertake work that is not beyond your powers". In response Pushkin here relates (with some adaptation) an anecdote told by the Roman writer Pliny the Elder (*Natural History* 35:36) about the Greek painter Apelles (4th century BC – reputedly the greatest painter of antiquity). According to Pliny, when a cobbler criticized Apelles's depiction of a leg as well as shoes Apelles protested: *Ne supra crepidam sutor judicaret* ("A cobbler shouldn't pass judgement above the shoe").

574   Written after mid-July 1829 and unpublished in Pushkin's lifetime. Earlier in the year **Nadézhdin**, **Mikhaíl Kachenóvsky**'s protégé both at his journal and at Moscow University, had published a critical review of Pushkin's narrative poem *Poltáva* ending with the sentence: "I comfort myself at least with this thought: if the bard of *Poltáva* takes it into his head to target me with an epigram, that will be for me an uncovenanted pleasure." *l. 1 Old Zoïlus*: I.e. Kachenóvsky, target of a number of Pushkin's previous epigrams.

575   Written after mid-July 1829 and unpublished in Pushkin's lifetime. *l. 1 at an unenlightened publication*: In Russian "at an altogether un-European publication". **Nadézhdin** had come to work

in Moscow on **Kachenóvsky**'s journal *Vestnik Yevropy* ("Herald of Europe"). *l. 2 hack*: Kachenóvsky. In the first three lines the translator has replaced Pushkin's tetrameters with pentameters.

576 Unpublished in Pushkin's lifetime. The two epigrams refer to illustrations for Pushkin's verse novel *Eugene Onégin* by Alexándr V. Notbek (1802–66), which were printed in the 1829 issue of the *Nevsky Almanac*, a literary magazine which Pushkin disliked. During his visit to the Caucasus in 1829 Pushkin scribbled several satirical epigrams captioning the illustrations in a copy of the almanac belonging to his friend **Mikhaíl I. Pushchin**, who was serving in the army there. Pushchin subsequently lost the copy but partially remembered two of the epigrams.

576a The first epigram refers to *Eugene Onégin* I, 48: Notbek's illustration depicts Pushkin and Onégin leaning on the granite parapet above the Nevá in St Petersburg, with their backs to the Peter and Paul Fortress across the river. *l. 1 the Bridge Kokúshkin*: Not the bridge across the Nevá visible in the engraving, but a smaller bridge across the Griboyédov Canal, nearly two kilometres away. *l. 6 fateful Power's citadel*: The Peter and Paul Fortress, where **Mikhaíl Pushchin** had been imprisoned after the Decembrist uprising in 1825. *l. 8 don't spit… in the well:* A Russian saying: Pushkin is apparently suggesting that one shouldn't, like the figures in the illustration, show disrespect to the Fortress, in case, like Pushchin, one ended up there.

576b The second epigram (the first four lines of which **Pushchin** could not remember) refers to *Eugene Onégin* III, 32: the relevant engraving shows the weary Tatyána in a flimsy nightdress sitting by her writing table at dawn; she has spent the night penning her love letter to Onégin, which she holds in her fingers.

577 Written between August and October 1829 and first published the same year. *ll. 1–2 Zoïlus' face… I bruised*: A reference to various epigrams, notably Nos. 559 and 561 in Vol. 3, that Pushkin had previously fired at **Mikhaíl Kachenóvsky** under different pseudonyms, including **Zoïlus**. The translation replaces Pushkin's trochaic rhythm with iambics.

578 Written in Moscow between late September and early October 1829 and first published at the turn of the year. *l. 1* **Olég**: Prince of ancient Rus. *l. 2 Constantine's great city*: Constantinople, traditionally called Tsargrád in Russian. Previously Byzantium, it was made second capital of the Roman Empire by the Emperor Constantine the Great (r. 306–37 AD) and renamed after him. After the collapse of the western Roman Empire in the 5th century, Constantinople became sole capital of the eastern Empire and a predominantly Greek city till its conquest in 1453 by the Turks, who called it Istanbul. *l. 9 Bloodshed and war are here again now*: The second stanza refers to the Russo-Turkish War of 1828–29, in

which Russia won important victories on both the eastern front (in Transcaucasia and north-eastern Turkey, where Pushkin had witnessed operations in the summer of 1829) and on the western front, where Russian forces had captured **Adrianople** in European Turkey. In the Peace of Adrianople of September 1829 Russia won important concessions from Turkey, but some in Russia considered the treaty premature and felt that Russia should have persevered with its long-term aspiration of capturing Istanbul itself. Pushkin's original is fully rhymed.

579   A fragment, unpublished in Pushkin's lifetime, written between late September and early October 1829.

580   Written on 21st September 1828 or 1829, and unpublished in Pushkin's lifetime. The poem refers to a celebrated bust of Tsar **Alexander I** carved in 1820 by the Danish sculptor Bertel Thorvaldsen (1770–1844), who worked mainly in Rome, though he returned home during 1819–20. At the end of 1828 Pushkin had jotted down the following note:

> Thorvaldsen, while carving the bust of a well-known personage, was surprised at the odd dichotomy in the otherwise handsome countenance – the upper part frowning and threatening, the lower expressing a constant smile. Thorvaldsen disliked it: "*Questa è una brutta figura*" – "This is a nasty face" (Italian).

l. 8 harlequin: Harlequin was a clown of volatile temperament in traditional Italian pantomime, usually dressed in a diamond-patterned costume of contrasting colours.

581   Begun probably in early October 1829 and completed the following year; first published in 1831. *l. 1 roam the world round*: Pushkin is no doubt thinking of his journeys to the Caucasus in 1829 and to Bóldino in 1830; he also travelled between Moscow and St Petersburg in the winter of 1829–30. *l. 24 Yard's superb repasts*: A Frenchman called Tranquille Yard (Russian *Trankel Yar*) had opened a fashionable restaurant in Moscow in 1826. *l. 26 down Myasnítskaya*: A street in the centre of Moscow.

582   Pushkin wrote this in October-November 1829 and prepared it for publication, but it was never published in his lifetime. He later reworked and shortened the poem for inclusion in his drama (never finished) *Scenes from the Age of Chivalry* (1834–35). *l. 31 Ave, Mater Dei*: "Hail, Mother of God" (Latin). *l. 37 Lumen cæli, sancta Rosa!*: "Light of heaven, sacred Rose!" (Latin). Pushkin's original is fully rhymed.

583   Written during the summer or autumn of 1829 and first published in 1830. The addressee is almost certainly Rufín Ivánovich **Dórokhov**. The translation replaces Pushkin's trochaic rhythm with iambics.

584   First published in 1830. Svistóv (l. 1) is Pushkin's nickname for Count **Dmitri Khvostóv**, and the "heir apparent" (l. 7) is his protégé **Nikolái Nadézhdin**. *l. 5 great poet-counsellor*: I.e. Count Khvostóv, who was a leading figure in the group of traditionalist Russian writers known as the "Forum (*Beséda*) for Lovers of the Russian Language".

585   Written by Pushkin when visiting friends in **Tver** province between mid-October and early November. Unpublished in Pushkin's lifetime. *l. 1 Netty*: one of the cousins of **Anna N. Vulf**. *l. 3 R and O*: Probably **Alexándra Rosset** and **Annette Olénina**, though the "O" could refer to one of the **Ushakóv** sisters (spelt *Ouchakoff* in French transliteration). *l. 4 N and W*: **Netty Vulf** (*Wulf* in the inherited German spelling of her name). In lines 2 and 4 the translator has replaced Pushkin's iambic dimeters with trimeters.

586   On his way from Moscow to St Petersburg in autumn 1829, Pushkin paused to visit friends in **Tver** province from mid-October to early November. This poem, apparently completed after he reached St Petersburg, was sent as an apology to one friend, **Yekaterína V. Velyásheva**, whom he had failed to visit. It was first published in 1830. Pushkin refers to the addressee by the formal pronoun *vy*. *l. 1 Izhóry*: The last post station before St Petersburg on the road from Moscow and Tver.

587   Written at Pávlovskoye, one of the Vulf family estates in **Tver** province, where Pushkin had stopped off on his journey from Moscow to St Petersburg. It was first published in 1830. Pushkin dates the poem as if it were a diary entry, but it is clear from his notes that some at least of the details (e.g. the two visiting sisters) are fantasy.

588   Dated 3rd November 1829, the day after the preceding poem; first published in 1830. Again the details are more imagined than autobiographical.

589   A fragment written in early November at Pávlovskoye, like the previous two poems, and unpublished in Pushkin's lifetime. The identity of Helen is unknown; she may be fictional.

590   A fragment written probably in the first half of November, unpublished in Pushkin's lifetime.

591   Written in November 1829 and first published in the following year. The epigram is aimed at **Nikolái Nadézhdin**. Years previously, Pushkin's uncle **Vasíly Pushkin** had written a short poem about a fifteen-year-old poet who had submitted to **Apollo** two odes full of poetic clichés, whereupon Apollo, bored and displeased, had ordered the youngster to be given a caning. Nadézhdin, in an unfavourable review of Pushkin's recent work, had referred to this derogatory poem as though it was addressed to Pushkin himself. In his own epigram Pushkin summarizes his uncle's fable

in the first four lines, then imagines the (ex-)seminarist Nadézhdin submitting his own tedious and time-serving writings to Apollo, provoking the god, bored and annoyed once more, to sentence him to an adult beating. *l. 7 Horace*: The Roman poet **Horace** opens one of his odes with praise for the Emperor **Augustus** (IV, 15). By, tongue in cheek, having Apollo upbraid him for writing hackneyed, unimaginative and uninspired material, Pushkin is implying that Nadézhdin's servile writings too are tedious and without merit.

592   An unfinished draft, from late 1829, of a poem recalling Pushkin's journey through the Caucasus in the summer of that year. Unpublished in Pushkin's lifetime.

593   Unpublished in Pushkin's lifetime. The dating and purpose of this unfinished poem and of 594 below are uncertain. They must postdate the Treaty of Adrianople, signed by Russia and Turkey in **Adrianople** on 2nd September 1829. Scholars have surmised that the two fragments may have been intended for incorporation into a single work. The Treaty confirmed Russia's victory in the Russo-Turkish War of 1828–29, and granted Russia gains of territory at the mouth of the Danube and along the eastern coast of the Black Sea.

594   Unpublished in Pushkin's lifetime. See under No. 593 above. The Treaty of Adrianople also confirmed the long-contested independence of Greece from direct Turkish control.

595   Unpublished in Pushkin's lifetime. The poem is unfinished, and the text of the last three stanzas is hard to decipher from Pushkin's notes. Though it was begun in June 1828, the present draft was dated 14th December 1829 (the fourth anniversary of the Decembrist uprising). Pushkin is here consciously revisiting his earlier 'Recollections in **Tsárskoye Seló**' (No. 25 in Vol. 1), which he wrote in 1814 while still a schoolboy at the Imperial Lycée there. He uses the same metre and elevated style as in the previous poem, and includes similar references to Russia's victories over the Turks in the war of 1768–74, commemorated by many monuments in the park, and to her recent triumph over **Napoleon**. *ll. 5–8 Thus too the wastrel son… wept*: Jesus's story of the prodigal son, recorded in Luke 15:11–24. *ll. 31–32 bronze memorials / to Catherine's eagle champions*: Literally "bronze commemorations of Catherine's eagles (Russian: *orlóv*)". Pushkin is referring to the three **Orlóv** brothers, **Catherine the Great**'s favourites during the early part of her reign, each of whom was commemorated by a monument in the park; **Grigóry Orlóv** was honoured by the Orlóv Arch for his handling of a plague outbreak in Moscow in 1771; **Alexéi Orlóv** commanded the Russian fleet during their victory over the Turks at Chesme in 1770, memorialized by the Chesme Column, surmounted by a bronze eagle; and **Fyodor Orlóv**'s defeat of a Turkish flotilla off the Peloponnese later

in 1770 was recognized by the Morea Column. *l. 35 the Thunderer*: Pushkin wrote **Perún**, Slavic god of thunder and war; he is referring to Count **Pyótr A. Rumyántsev**, the Russian general who, also in 1770, inflicted a crushing defeat on the Turks by the river **Kagúl**. Rumyántsev's victory was commemorated in the park by the Kagúl Obelisk. *ll. 37–38 the norther fleet's… all*: These lines refer to the burning of the Turkish fleet at Chesme. *l. 39 his loyal brother too, hero of that armada*: Pushkin wrote "hero of the archipelago", referring to the Russian naval expedition to the Aegean archipelago, aimed at supporting a Greek uprising against the Turks and drawing Turkish forces away from concurrent military engagements to the west and north of the Black Sea. The "loyal brother" is Fyódor Orlóv, who took part in the Archipelago Expedition and defeated a Turkish flotilla at Hydra. *l. 40 Navarino's Gannibál*: Pushkin is referring to a great-uncle, Brigadier **Iván A. Gannibál**, who played a leading part in the Russian capture of the Turkish fort of **Navarino** on the Greek coast in 1770. *ll. 43–64 meanwhile the tide of strife… Borodinó… Kulm… Lithuania's forests… Montmartre's banlieu*: Pushkin is referring to the Napoleonic Wars, the last phase of which was taking place while he was a young teenager studying at the Imperial Lycée. The pupils were forbidden to enlist in the Russian army, as many of them would like to have done.

596   Written on 23rd December 1829; its apparently unfinished ending is deliberate: it was first published in this form the following year. The poem reflects a low point in Pushkin's courtship of **Natálya Goncharóva** – see *Introduction: Rehabilitation 1826–31* on p. XXII.

597   Written on 26th December 1829 and first published the following year.

598   The poem is a close translation from late December 1829 of the first thirty-two lines of a poem by the English poet **Robert Southey** entitled 'Hymn to the **Penates**' (1796). Pushkin had recently acquired a collection of Southey's poetry published earlier in 1829 (which also contained Southey's *Madoc* – see No. 599 below). Pushkin's translation (which is five lines longer than the English original) was unfinished, and remained unpublished during his lifetime. He undertook this work, it seems, partly to further his English studies, but also because the Hymn's references to exile and to a solitary life devoted to poetry resonated with his own feelings. Pushkin's lines, like Southey's, are unrhymed. I have translated Pushkin's text back into English without prior reference to Southey's original in an attempt to reproduce the same effect on the modern reader as Pushkin's version would have had on his own Russian contemporaries. *l. 8 you dwell far off, in deepest heaven*: As Southey himself comments in a note, some ancient writers suggest (wrongly) that

the name "Penates" is derived from the Latin word *penitus*, mean-
ing 'deep within'. *l. 12 his venerable spouse*: Southey, following
Homer, describes **Zeus**'s spouse, the goddess Hera (Juno), as
"white-arm'd", but Pushkin, whether deliberately or by error, has
altered the epithet to "white-headed".

599   Written at the end of 1829 and unpublished in Pushkin's lifetime.
Like No. 598 above, this is a translation of lines by **Robert Southey**,
this time the first twenty-five lines of Part One (subtitled "Madoc
in Wales") of his epic *Madoc* (1805). Once again Pushkin's lines,
outnumbering Southey's by one, are unrhymed; and once again
Pushkin's motivation may have been partly his wish to improve
his knowledge of English and English poetry and partly the appeal
of the subject matter – the feelings of one returning home, like
Pushkin three years earlier, after a long absence. As with No. 598,
and for the same reasons, I have translated Pushkin's text back into
English without prior reference to Southey's original. Southey's
narrative poem recounts the legend (now regarded as fictional,
but which Southey believed to be based on fact) of the Welsh
prince Madoc. According to this, Madoc, one of the children of
the deceased king of North Wales, wishing to escape bloodshed
among the king's heirs in the late twelfth century, fled with a band
of followers across the Atlantic and settled in the Mississippi
basin, an area previously occupied by the Aztecs before they moved
southwards into Mexico. Years later Madoc returned to Wales to
recruit another band of settlers, and Southey's poem opens with
an account of this homecoming. *l. 3 at her prow*: Pushkin writes
"before her stern (*kormá*)", but surely means "prow". Southey
had written "[she]... round her prow / scatters the ocean spray".

600   Written around the turn of 1829–30 and published three months
later. The epigram lampoons several contemporary writers for
whom Pushkin had a low regard. In the published text, each name
is concealed behind asterisks corresponding to the number of its
syllables. The epigram provoked a swarm of conjectures, and there
is still some uncertainty about the identity of the last two targets.
Epigraph: Two lines from **Iván Krylóv**'s fable 'The Curiosity Seeker'
(*Lyubopýtny*), about a man who spent three hours in **Peter the
Great**'s Kunstkámera Museum in St Petersburg, amazed by the
variety of animal life on display; however, so engrossed was he
by the insects, "some smaller than a pin's head", that he failed to
notice the elephant.

601   First published at the beginning of March 1830 and apparently
written the previous winter. The poem's addressee is uncertain: it
is usually thought to be the unconventional **Agraféna Zakrévskaya**,
but the unprincipled **Karolina Sobańska**, still youthful-looking
despite her greater age, is another candidate.

602   Dated 1st January 1830 and written for an imperial fancy-dress ball at the Aníchkov Palace in St Petersburg to be held on 4th January; it was published later in the year. Pushkin wrote the verse for Countess **Yekaterína F. Tizengáuzen**, who attended the ball dressed as a one-eyed cyclops. The verses that each fancy-dress wearer brought were to be addressed to the Empress, hence Pushkin's use of the formal pronoun *vy*.

603   Dated by Pushkin 1829, but inscribed by him in the album of **Karolina Sobańska** on 5th January 1830; published later that year.

604   A reply, composed in St Petersburg at the beginning of 1830, to a playfully unsigned letter (now lost) from Pushkin's young Moscow friend, **Yekaterína Ushakóva**; it was first published early the same year. Pushkin addresses her with the formal pronoun *vy*, perhaps to indicate a platonic friendship. *l. 16 your home*: Pushkin writes *Présnya*, the name of the Moscow suburb where Yekaterína and her younger sister Yelizavéta lived with their parents and where Pushkin often liked to call when he was in Moscow.

605   At the turn of 1829–30 Pushkin published his deeply pessimistic and sceptical poem of 1828 'Gift of chance, O gift so senseless…' (No. 516 – see Volume 3). Within a week or two the Metropolitan of Moscow Filarét (1782–1857), an eloquent and respected churchman of progressive outlook, had written a response in the same poetic form, putting words of repentance and Christian commitment in Pushkin's mouth (No. 605a). Filarét's poem remained unpublished, but Pushkin was shown a copy, and No. 605b is his answer. It was written in St Petersburg on 19th January 1830 and published a month later. *605a ll. 11–12 You will create… pure*: words drawn from Psalm 51:10: "Create in me a pure heart, O God…"

606   Written in the opening months of 1830 and first published the same year. This is Pushkin's adaptation (perhaps via a French version by Sainte-Beuve) of **Wordsworth**'s sonnet about sonnets. Wordsworth mentions (in this order) **Shakespeare, Petrarch, Tasso, Camões, Dante,** Spenser and **Milton**; Pushkin has omitted Tasso, Spenser and Milton, but has added **Mickiewicz** and Delvig. *Epigraph*: Words quoted by Pushkin in English from the first line of Wordsworth's sonnet (1827), which opens as follows:

> Scorn not the sonnet; critic, you have frowned,
> mindless of its just honours…

607   Written in March–April 1830, and unpublished by Pushkin in his lifetime. **Bulgárin**, stung by an adverse notice about a novel of his, had published an article accusing Pushkin of attacking him as a

foreigner. This epigram is Pushkin's response. Bulgárin dodged the bullet by publishing the epigram himself, replacing the last two words of the Russian (*Vidók Figlyárin*) with his real name (*Faddéy Bulgárin*) and claiming that this was the authentic version. Pushkin's friend **Delvig** later tried to publish Pushkin's original text, but the censor disallowed it. *l. 2 great Mickiewicz – he was one*: Pushkin wrote "**Kościuszko** is a Pole, **Mickiewicz** is a Pole". *l. 6* **Vidocq Figlyárin**: Pushkin's satirical nickname for Faddéy Bulgárin.

608   A fragment written in March–April 1830, and unpublished in Pushkin's lifetime. The lines seem to be based on a passage from Canto I of **Walter Scott's** poem *The Lady of the Lake* (1810) describing a Scottish deer hunt.

609   This verse letter to Prince **Nikolái Yusúpov** was written in Moscow and dated 23rd April 1830; it was first published in May that year. *l. 14 crowned and sceptred dame*: Empress **Catherine the Great**. *l. 15 Ferney*: **Voltaire's** home in later life. *l. 23 a young enchantress on the throne*: Queen **Marie-Antoinette** of France. *l. 27 Trianon's loud revelry*: Le Petit Trianon was Queen Marie-Antoinette's personal château in the grounds of Versailles. *ll. 32–33 perching... ecstasy*: In ancient Greece the oracles at Delphi were delivered by a priestess in a trance seated on a tripod. *l. 38 twofold council*: The British parliament: House of Lords and House of Commons. *ll. 42 ff. Beaumarchais*: Yusúpov met **Beaumarchais** in London. *ll. 63 ff. the tempest*: The French Revolution, which began in 1789. *l. 83 women they admire*: Pushkin refers to *Temíra*, a standard girl's name in poetry. *l. 95 sublime Alyábyeva, enchanting Goncharóva*: Alexándra Alyábyeva (1812–91) and **Natálya Goncharóva** were both well-known Moscow beauties; Goncharóva subsequently became Pushkin's wife.

610   Written in Moscow around the end of April 1830, and first published at the end of the year. The verse is apparently addressed to Pushkin's Moscow friend **Pavel V. Nashchókin**, known for the miniature house he was making as he moved from apartment to apartment in the early 1830s.

611   Fragment of uncertain date and purpose, probably from 1830.

612   Written in Moscow in early July 1830 and first published the following year. *l. 14 shake your tripod's feet*: Pushkin is likening the poet to the priestess at **Apollo's** shrine at Delphi, who delivered her sacred oracles seated on a tripod. The translation uses iambic pentameters in place of Pushkin's hexameters.

613   Written in Moscow on 8th July 1830 and first published the following year. The poem is addressed to **Natálya Goncharóva**, Pushkin's future wife, to whom he was by now engaged. Subsequently, on 30th July, he wrote to Natálya from St Petersburg:

Les belles dames me demandent à voir votre portrait, et ne me pardonnent pas de ne pas l'avoir. Je me console en passant des heures entières devant une madone blonde qui vous ressemble comme deux gouttes d'eau, et que j'aurais achetée, si elle ne coûtait pas 40000 roubles.

"The ladies keep asking me if they can see your portrait and don't forgive me for not having it. For consolation I spend hours on end gazing at a blonde Madonna, which is as like you as one drop of water's like another, and which I'd have bought if it didn't cost 40,000 roubles" (French).

614   Written after mid-July 1830 and unpublished in Pushkin's lifetime. *l. 2 Firs*: Nickname for Pushkin's friend Prince **Sergéi Golítsyn**. Pushkin's jesting verse was based on an incident at the gambling tables: Golítsyn had been asked what funds he was playing for – "For these or for those [i.e. for ready funds or for borrowed funds]?" Golítsyn had replied: "It's all the same: both for these and for those, and for those, those, those." *l.5 Rosseti*: I.e. **Alexándra O. Rosset**; *Rosseti* was a semi-Italianized form of Rosset sometimes used by the family.

615   A fragment, written after mid-July 1830 and unpublished in Pushkin's lifetime.

616   Written after mid-July 1830 and unpublished in Pushkin's lifetime. Another unfinished poem, recalling Pushkin's visit to the Caucasus in 1829.

617   Commenced in the autumn of 1829 and completed at Bóldino on 7th September 1830; first published at the end of 1831.

618   Written at Bóldino and first published in 1834. Pushkin dated his manuscript 8th September 1830, the fourth anniversary of his return to Moscow from exile.

619   A poem drawing on Pushkin's memories of his Transcaucasian journey of 1829. Completed at Bóldino on 20th September 1830 and first published in 1831.

620   Another poem reflecting Pushkin's Transcaucasian journey of 1829, when he passed within sight of Mount **Kazbék** along the Georgian Military Highway. Completed at Bóldino on 20th September 1830 and first published at the beginning of 1831.

621   Written at Bóldino on 26th September 1830 and first published in 1831. In the summer Pushkin had been touched to receive an anonymous poem congratulating him on his engagement to **Natálya Goncharóva** in May and assuring him that marriage would bring him fresh poetic inspiration, at a time when others had been forecasting that domestic happiness would be damaging to his talent. This is Pushkin's reply to the author, who turned out to be Iván Alexándrovich Gulyánov (1789–1841), an eminent diplomat

and Egyptologist. Pushkin's lines are rhyming couplets; the final line, however, lacks its pair, and Pushkin's publication of it in this form suggests that he left the poem incomplete on purpose.

622 Written in Bóldino at the end of September 1830, and first published in 1832. Pushkin is referring to completion of work, after seven years, on his verse novel *Eugene Onégin*. Pushkin's original, like the translation, is in unrhymed dactylic couplets. *l. 6 the gods where I've dwelt*: Pushkin refers to "sacred **Penates**".

623 Written in Bóldino in October 1830 and unpublished during Pushkin's lifetime. *l. 5 Dreaded Fate*: Pushkin refers to *Parka* – i.e. Parca, a Roman goddess of fate. In classical mythology the Fates (usually a threesome) were sometimes imagined as malevolent old women spinning the threads of human lives.

624 Written in Bóldino in October 1830. Either Pushkin left the work unfinished or the end is lost; it was unpublished during Pushkin's lifetime. The poem's incompleteness and lack of proper names make it hard to interpret. Some elements call to mind the Imperial Lycée and adjacent park with its classical statuary at **Tsárskoye Seló**, and suggest a loosely autobiographical account of Pushkin's passage from boyhood to adolescence. Alternatively, the *terza rima* metre, used most famously in **Dante's** *Divine Comedy*, may point to a connection with the Italian poet, and Pushkin may be portraying in allegory the transition in European culture from medieval Christianity to the Renaissance with its more classical and pagan inspiration. *l. 4 A woman very meek*: The woman's identity is obscure: there were no female teachers at the Lycée, and she may be a personification of traditional Christian instruction, as given either to Pushkin in his childhood or more generally in premodern European society. *l. 37 The Delphic idol*: The Greek god **Apollo**, one of whose main shrines was at Delphi in central Greece. *ll. 40–42 The other... rich in beauty*: **Aphroditē**, the Greek goddess of beauty and love.

625 Written in Bóldino and unpublished during Pushkin's lifetime. These are two parts of an unfinished poem, the first written on 1st October and the second on 10th October 1830. A middle section seems to be missing. Pushkin had increasingly been criticized in the literary reviews by **Bulgárin** and others for using lofty poetic forms to describe down-to-earth matters in down-to-earth detail and in down-to-earth language. As he himself wrote at about this time,

> With new days come new aspirations;
> the soaring imagination of my springtime
> has now come down to earth
> and into the wineglass of my verse
> I've mixed a goodly dash of water.
>
> *Onégin's Journey* XVII, ll. 10–14

Though Pushkin's precise target in these fragments is uncertain, they are clearly intended as a satirical response to these criticisms. Pushkin's lines are rhyming couplets throughout. *ll. 24–27 quarantine… Caucasus' grim gateway*: When returning home from Turkey in summer 1829, Pushkin had been held in quarantine for three days at Gyumrí in Armenia because of an outbreak of cholera; by October 1830 cholera was rife in Russia, and travel was subject to quarantine.

626   Two epigrams about Pushkin's friend **Nikolái Gnedich**, who worked on a translation of **Homer**'s *Iliad* into Russian verse from 1809 until it was finally published in 1829. In January 1830 Pushkin had published an enthusiastic review of the translation.

626a   An epigram dating from between December 1819 and April 1820 only known from a friend's reminiscence long after Pushkin's death. Pushkin is said to have composed it impromptu during a meeting of the Green Lamp club at which Gnedich was reading extracts from his ongoing translation of the *Iliad* and some present commented on the roughness of certain passages.

626b   An epigram in the style and metre of a mock epitaph from the classical Greek Anthology. Pushkin wrote it at Bóldino on 1st October 1830, but then firmly deleted it in his notebook, no doubt because, as a friend of Gnedich and admirer of his work, he did not want to upset Gnedich by a verse that might have seemed disparaging or offensive. In the second line Pushkin seems to be referring to the fact that Homer wrote two major epics, the *Iliad* and the *Odyssey*, while one-eyed Gnedich had translated only one of them.

627   Written at Bóldino on 1st October 1830 and first published in 1832. The poem is in unrhymed elegiac couplets – i.e. alternating dactylic hexameters and pentameters – in the style of much of the Greek Anthology and of Roman lyric poets such as **Ovid**. It refers to a fountain in the park at **Tsárskoye Seló** created in 1816 by the sculptor Pavel Petróvich Sokolóv (1764–1835): a statue of a girl sits mournfully over a broken pitcher from which a stream of water pours unendingly.

628   Written at Bóldino on 2nd October 1830 or shortly thereafter and unpublished in Pushkin's lifetime. Pushkin included it as an "ancient epigram" in an article he never finished, to illustrate the incomprehension between writers, critics and reading public. He seems to have reworked the verse from an epigram ('Les trois sourds') by the French writer Paul Pellisson-Fontanier (1624–93). The translator has replaced Pushkin's hexameters with pentameters.

629   Written at Bóldino on 5th October 1830 and first published in a musical setting a year or so later. Addressed in thought to **Elise Vorontsóva**, whom Pushkin had loved in Odessa six years earlier.

630   Written at Bóldino on 7th October 1830; unpublished in Pushkin's
       lifetime. The epigraph and the mention of "my countess from the
       south of Spain" in the penultimate line make it clear that Pushkin
       had in mind Chérubin / Cherubino, the amorous young page
       in **Beaumarchais**'s play *Le Mariage de Figaro* and in Mozart's
       Le nozze di Figaro, both set in Seville. Mozart and Beaumarchais
       were both in Pushkin's thoughts at this time, as he was writing
       Mozart and Salieri (in which Beaumarchais is mentioned), one
       of his *Little Tragedies*, this same October. Pushkin also seems to
       have been influenced by certain songs from the *Contes d'Espagne
       et d'Italie* (1829) by the French poet Alfred de Musset (1810–57),
       a copy of which he possessed.

631   Written at Bóldino on 9th October 1830; first published in 1834
       as the lyrics to a song by Glinka. Pushkin possibly intended it as a
       Spanish song for *The Stone Guest*, another of his *Little Tragedies*,
       which he was composing at Bóldino and which he completed there
       at the beginning of November; in the end, though, *The Stone Guest*
       was set in Madrid, not Seville.

632   Written in autumn 1830 at Bóldino, but never completed or pub-
       lished. The translator has varied Pushkin's metre by substituting
       trimeters for tetrameters in even-numbered lines.

633   Written at Bóldino on 10th October 1830; first published in
       1832. No doubt to match the subject matter drawn from classi-
       cal mythology, Pushkin uses classical unrhymed elegiac couplets.
       Thus, ironically, Pushkin's poem commemorating rhyme is itself
       composed without rhymes.

634   Written at Bóldino on 10th October 1830; first published in
       1832. Pushkin again uses classical unrhymed elegiac couplets.
       The poem refers to the career of the great Russian polymath
       Mikhaíl V. Lomonósov. *ll. 2–4 Lad, leave the fisher behind…
       fisher of minds*: This disembodied command recalls the words of
       Christ to the fishermen Andrew and Peter and to James and John
       (themselves a fisherman's sons) to leave their nets and become
       "fishers of men" (Mark 1:16–20).

635   Pushkin began work on this defence of his ancestry at Bóldino
       on 16th October 1830 and continued with it in early December. It
       was unpublished during his lifetime, though widely circulated in
       manuscript. In August Pushkin's literary enemy **Faddéy Bulgárin**
       had published an article ridiculing a comment by a friend of
       Pushkin's that Pushkin and his fellow writers belonged to a kind of
       literary aristocracy. This verse is Pushkin's bitterly ironic response,
       reflecting his recurring complaint that Russia's ancient boyar aris-
       tocracy (from which the Pushkins were descended) had declined
       in power and status over the centuries and had been displaced by
       a new upstart aristocracy created by **Peter I** and his successors.

ll. 17–22: The references here are to members of the "new aristocracy" elevated by Peter I and his successors: Prince Alexándr Ménshikov (1673–1729), a close associate of Peter I, was said to have started life as a pie salesman; Count Grigóry Chernyshóv (1672–1745) had begun as an orderly to Peter I; and Count Iván Kutáysov (1759–1834) had begun as a valet and barber to the future Paul I; Count Alexéi Razumóvsky (1709–71), a favourite of the Empress Elizabeth, had been brought to St Petersburg as a boy to sing in the palace choir; Prince Alexándr Bezboródko (1747–99), son of a minor Cossack official in the Ukraine, had risen to power and noble rank under **Catherine II** and Paul I; and the father of the current Russian minister of foreign affairs, Count Karl Nesselróde (1780–1862), had begun his career as a soldier in the Austrian army, before moving on to the Dutch, Prussian and Russian services. *l. 25 Racha*: A thirteenth-century Prussian adventurer who moved north to fight with **Alexander Nevsky**. *ll. 27–28 though an offspring… Iván IV*: It is unclear what incident Pushkin is referring to here. *ll. 29–38 The Pushkins… thanks bestow*: In the early 1600, Russia endured a period of anarchy during which Polish forces occupied Moscow. In 1611–12 **Kuzmá Minin**, a merchant from Nizhny Nóvgorod (*"Nízhgorod"*) raised an army which succeeded in driving the Poles out and creating conditions for the election in 1613 (supported by several Pushkins) of the sixteen-year-old Mikhaíl Fyódorovich Románov (1595–1645) as the first tsar of a new dynasty. *l. 38 the new tsar*: I.e. Mikhaíl Románov. Pushkin wrote *stradáltsa syn* ("the martyr's son"): Mikhaíl's father Fyódor Nikítich Románov (1553–1633) had been forced years before to take monastic vows to disqualify him from the throne; from 1611 to 1619 he was held prisoner in Poland. *ll. 43–44 my ancestor… hanged for that*: Fyódor Matvéyevich Pushkin was executed in 1697 for his part in a conspiracy against Peter I . *ll. 49–54 My grandsire… made prisoner*: In 1762 Peter III was deposed and murdered by supporters (notably the three **Orlóv** brothers: Grigóry, Alexéi and Fyódor) of his wife Catherine, who succeeded him as Catherine II; however, Pushkin seems to have been mistaken in thinking that these events led to the imprisonment of his grandfather Lev Alexándrovich Pushkin (1723–90), who, whatever his sympathies, was not involved in the coup. *l. 62 as Pushkin (not Musín) I'm known*: Wachtel comments: "The Pushkins and the Musín-Pushkins were descended from the same ancestor, but the latter had remained wealthy, titled aristocracy, while the former had lost their wealth and stature". *l. 66 my black great-granddad Gannibál*: **Abrám Petróvich Gannibál** – see *Introduction: Family, Birth and Childhood* on p. XIII. *l. 69 the great ship-master*: I.e. Tsar Peter I, who had studied shipbuilding in his youth and always

taken an interest in nautical matters. *l. 77–80 another Gannibál…
Navarino fell*: Iván Abrámovich Gannibál. *l. 82 a commoner midst
lords*: In Russian: *vo dvoryánstve meshchanín*, which is the Russian
title for Molière's comedy *Le Bourgeois gentilhomme*, about a
commoner who makes a fool of himself by aping nobility. *l. 84
a courtier midst bawds*: In Russian *v Meshchánskoy dvoryanín*
("a courtier on Meshchánskaya street"): Bulgárin's wife had been
brought up in Meshchánskaya, a street notorious for its brothels.

636   Dated 16th October 1830, and first published at the turn of the
year. *l. 1 [Avdéy] Flyugárin*: Another of Pushkin's nicknames for
Faddéy Bulgárin. *Flyugárka* means a weathervane. *l. 2 your foreign
forebears*: Pushkin's alludes to Bulgárin's Polish origins. *l. 3 another's
work as yours you're scoring*: Pushkin wrote: "you're a gypsy on
Parnassus", referring to the fact that Bulgárin plagiarized passages
from Pushkin's *Borís Godunóv* for his novel *Dimítry Samozvánets*,
published in 1829 and set in the same period. *l. 4 Vidocq the sleuth*:
Pushkin writes "**Vidocq Figlyárin**". *l. 5 your novel's boring*: I.e.
Bulgárin's novel *Dimítry Samozvánets* – see above.

637   Written at Bóldino on 17th October 1830; unpublished in Pushkin's
lifetime. The poem is almost certainly addressed to the memory
of **Amalia Riznić** – see Index of Names. Leila is the name of the
heroine of Byron's *The Giaour*, who, having been put to death for
infidelity, appears to her lover from beyond the grave. *l. 19 Why
they killed the friend I miss*: There were rumours that Amalia
had been murdered at the behest of her husband, who resented
her unfaithfulness and wished to remarry more advantageously;
the rumours were probably false – she almost certainly died of
consumption – but Pushkin was tempted to believe them.

638   A rough draft, dating from mid-October 1830, unpublished in
Pushkin's lifetime. The third stanza is unfinished; and there are
indications that Pushkin intended to drop the second stanza.

639   Unfinished draft, from mid-October 1830, unpublished in
Pushkin's lifetime. Pushkin's lines are rhymed to an irregular
pattern. There is no consensus among commentators over the
meaning or purpose of the piece or over the identity of the
"mournful island" described in the second half of the fragment.
ll. 9–17 that land where heavens… still re-echo: The phraseology
of these lines evoking Italy follows closely that of ll. 1–9 of the
also unfinished and unpublished No. 510.

640   This soliloquy forms Scene 2 of Pushkin's one-act play *The Mean-
Spirited Knight*, one of his four *Little Tragedies*, which were com-
pleted at Bóldino between late October and early November 1830.
The Mean-Spirited Knight is dated 23rd October and was first
published in 1836. The Baron, the leading character in the play, is
a study in all-consuming avarice, and in Scene 2 he is visiting his

vaults to gloat over his treasures. Pushkin's original, like the translation, is in unrhymed iambic pentameters. *ll. 10–16 I'm sure that I've read somewhere... at sea beyond:* The story originates from an episode related by the Greek historian Herodotus (*c*.485–*c*.425 BC) in describing the Persian king Darius's invasion of Scythia near the beginning of the 5th century BC. As Darius was marching north to the Danube through what is now Bulgaria, "he indicated a certain spot where every man in the army was ordered to deposit a stone as he passed by. This was done, with the result that when Darius moved on he left great hills of stones behind him." (*Histories* IV, 92) The story was later elaborated and adapted to other epochs and locations. *l. 42 a Spanish gold coin:* In Russian, *dublón*, from the Spanish *doblón* (English: "doubloon").

641   This soliloquy opens another of Pushkin's *Little Tragedies*, his one-act play *Mozart and Salieri*, which was completed at Bóldino in autumn 1830 and dated 26th October; it was first published in 1831. The play is a study in overpowering jealousy: it portrays the Italian composer **Salieri** as an industrious mediocrity, who craved success and recognition for himself, while gripped by a murderous resentment of the apparently effortless genius of his younger contemporary **Mozart**. This attitude of Salieri's to Mozart reflects the professional jealousy that Pushkin experienced from some of his less gifted contemporaries. Pushkin's original, like the translation, is in unrhymed iambic pentameters. *l. 32 Gluck:* Christoph von Gluck (1714–87) was renowned across Europe as an innovative composer of operas. Born in Germany, he spent most of his career in Vienna, with visits to Paris and elsewhere. *l. 50 Niccolò Piccinni:* An opera composer (1728–1800) from Naples, who moved in 1776 to Paris, where an intense rivalry developed between his supporters and those of Gluck. In 1778 the directorate of the Paris Opéra arranged for each to compose an opera (with different libretti) based on the story of the mythical Greek princess Iphigenia (*Iphigénie en Tauride*). Gluck's opera (produced in 1779) gained the greater success.

642   An unfinished verse letter (in places conjectural), drafted by Pushkin at Bóldino in September–October 1830 and unpublished in his lifetime. In recalling their close friendship since schooldays, Pushkin is aligning himself with **Delvig** in their increasingly bitter literary dispute with **Faddéy Bulgárin** and his allies.

643   The poem was written at Bóldino in late October 1830; Pushkin had it published the following year, but insisted that he be not named as author. Pushkin's lines are rhymed throughout to an irregular pattern. *Epigraph:* Pontius Pilate's words at the trial of Jesus (John 18:38). *l. 2 tongue of flame:* The words recall the description of the Holy Spirit coming to rest on the heads of the apostles at Pentecost (Acts 2:3). *ll. 14–17: Just one... dark at dawn:* The references here

and in the rest of the poem are to **Napoleon Bonaparte**. *ll. 20–21 from the Alps... sacred Italy*: Napoleon led his armies into Italy via the Great St Bernard pass in 1800. *l. 22 when he grasps the battle standard*: At the Battle of Arcole in northern Italy in 1796 Napoleon is said to have rallied his troops by personally raising the French flag aloft in open battle. *l. 23 dictator's sceptre*: Napoleon seized dictatorial powers as First Consul of the French Republic in 1799. *ll. 28–29 troops acclaim... towering pyramids*: During the early stages of his Egyptian campaign in 1798, Napoleon defeated an Egyptian force near the Pyramids of Giza. *ll. 30–31 in desolation... keeps silence*: Napoleon occupied a deserted and burning Moscow in 1812. *l. 34 Caesar's son-in-law*: In 1810 Napoleon, now emperor, married the archduchess Marie-Louise (1791–1847), daughter of Francis I, Austrian ruler and erstwhile Holy Roman Emperor ("Caesar"). *ll. 35–39 sitting there... in idleness*: Napoleon, deposed after Waterloo, was exiled to the island of St Helena from 1815 until his death in 1821. *ll. 41–49 rows of beds... engenders courage*: During the French campaign in Egypt and Palestine in 1798–99, Napoleon is said to have visited a hospital at Jaffa housing soldiers stricken by the plague and to have touched them to show sympathy and raise morale. Other contemporary accounts dismissed this as Napoleonic propaganda, claiming further that on evacuating Jaffa Napoleon ordered dozens of his most seriously infected men to be poisoned to stem the spread of the disease and to prevent their capture and torture by the enemy. Pushkin was certainly aware of both versions, but in foregrounding the former he was reminding his readers of **Tsar Nicholas I**'s recent courageous visit to Moscow to raise the morale of citizens there during the cholera epidemic that had struck the city that autumn. *ll. 55–57 Poets' dreams... pronounced*: As Pushkin confirms in a note, he is referring to the *Mémoires de M. de Bourrienne sur Napoléon*, which challenged the truth of the Jaffa hospital episode.

The poem is dated "29th September 1830, Moscow" – not the date and place of composition, but the date of Tsar Nicholas I's entry into Moscow in response to the cholera outbreak.

644   Another Caucasian reminiscence, completed on 29th–30th October 1830 and published at the turn of the year. The poem describes an avalanche like one that had temporarily blocked the **Terek** gorge in 1827, two years before Pushkin's journey.

645   A piece of mock-vernacular verse included by Pushkin in his satirical *History of the Village of Goryúkhino*, a work commenced at Bóldino between mid-October and early November 1830, but unfinished and unpublished in his lifetime.

646   Written in early November 1830, but unpublished in Pushkin's lifetime.

NOTES

647 Pushkin completed *A Feast during the Plague*, one of his *Little Tragedies*, on 8th November 1830, while living in quarantine at Bóldino as a deadly epidemic of cholera raged through Russia; it was first published in 1832. The work is Pushkin's translation of a scene from *The City of the Plague* (1816), a play by the Scottish writer **John Wilson** set in the plague-ridden London of 1665. A group of revellers is holding a party in the street in defiance of the plague. One of them, Mary, a Scottish girl living in London, sings the group this song about a plague-stricken Scottish village. The song, unlike the translated drama, is Pushkin's own composition. Pushkin rhymed odd as well as even lines.

648 For *A Feast during the Plague* see the preceding note. This contrasting song, also Pushkin's own composition, is sung by Walsingham, Wilson's "Master of Revels". In Pushkin's stanzas, the third and fifth lines are rhymed, as well as the others.

649 Written at Bóldino; first published in 1831. The poem draws on Pushkin's experience of Moldavian Gypsy life during his posting to Bessarabia in the early 1820s. The subtitle "from the English" refers to a sixteen-line poem, 'The Gypsy's Tent', a more saccharine description of Gypsy life in rural England, by the Revd. **William Bowles**. Pushkin's poem is not, however, a translation, but an original poem, the only point of contact with the English work being the two lines in Bowles's final stanza:

Lo! Houseless o'er the world they [Gypsies] stray,
But I at home will dwell...

Pushkin sometimes presented his own works as translations if he wanted to veil their autographical reference.

650 Probably written at Bóldino in the autumn of 1830; first published in 1831. The poem, though presented as a translation of a lyric by **Barry Cornwall**, is in fact a free adaptation of it, shortening it from four to three stanzas, tightening the rhythm and rhyme scheme, and replacing much of Cornwall's sense with material of Pushkin's own. *Epigraph*: Pushkin quotes, in English, the first line of Cornwall's poem.

651 Dated 8th November 1830 and first published at the beginning of 1832. The epigram commemorated the publication of **N.I. Gnedich**'s translation of **Homer**'s *Iliad*.

652 Written at Bóldino on 27th November 1830; unpublished in Pushkin's lifetime. The poem is addressed to the memory of **Amalia Riznić**. *l. 2 Your dear homeland*: Though born in Vienna, Amalia had regarded the Italian port of Trieste, her husband's city, as her home since her marriage and returned there when she left Odessa. *l. 11 This land where you've been banished*: At the time (1824) Pushkin was living in exile in Odessa.

383

653   Unpublished in Pushkin's lifetime. Written in Moscow, apparently just before the poet's wedding to **Natálya Goncharóva** on 18th February 1831. Pushkin had asked Princess **Vera Vyázemskaya** to be his matron of honour at the ceremony, but she was taken ill, and he had at the last minute to find an alternative. He hurried off – it seems, after dark – to invite Countess Yelizavéta Potyómkina (1796–1870), whose Moscow residence stood on Prechístenka Street, vowing that if he found her at home, he would be content to be regarded by posterity as a writer no better than his despised rival **Bulgárin**. In the event Pushkin located the countess, and she played her part at the wedding. The wit of Pushkin's verse rests mainly on an untranslatable triple pun: *Potyómkinu* (the countess), *potyómkakh* ("darkness"), and *potómkakh* ("posterity"). The translator has substituted an amphibrachic metre for Pushkin's iambic tetrameters.

654   Three fragments from an unfinished composition, unpublished in Pushkin's lifetime, probably reflecting the polemics between Pushkin and his critics from 1830 onwards. *l. 8 cribbed from the Marquis de Bièvre*: The Marquis de Bièvre (1747–89) was a French writer and compiler of puns; a collection of his puns, the *Biévriana*, was published in Paris in 1799 by Albéric Deville (1774–1832).

655   Unfinished, and unpublished in Pushkin's lifetime. The addressee (for whom Pushkin uses the formal pronoun *vy*) is uncertain. The composition dates from between September 1826 and Pushkin's death.

656   The opening fragments of a discontinued poem about the doge of Venice Marino Faliero (1274–1355), who, to avenge a Venetian patrician's insult to his wife, staged an unsuccessful coup against the ruling oligarchy and was executed. The text of lines 2 and 4 of the second stanza is uncertain. Pushkin's original is fully rhymed. The translators have changed his metre of trochaic tetrameters. *l. 7 Bucintoro*: The doge's ceremonial barge.

657   Unfinished, and unpublished in Pushkin's lifetime.

658   A sketch for an imitation of a folk song, unpublished in Pushkin's lifetime.

MARRIED LIFE AND FINAL YEARS (1831–37)

659   Lines from the end of Scene 14 of Pushkin's historical drama *Borís Godunóv*, written at **Mikháylovskoye** in 1825, but only published in 1831. The scene portrays a ball at a Polish castle. Most of the play is written in unrhymed iambic pentameters, but in this little exchange between two elderly Polish noblemen Pushkin has rhymed all the lines to form a fourteen-line sonnet, with a fifteenth

line repeating the rhyme of the fourteenth. *ll. 10–11 dig us out...
herbage*: Good wine was buried in the earth to allow it slowly to
mature at a stable temperature.

660   Written in mid-June 1831 in **Tsárskoye Seló** and first published
(the first three stanzas only) in 1836. The poem reflects Pushkin's
frustration, at the time of composition, with the failures of Russian
forces to quell the Polish uprising of 1830–31. The tomb referred
to is that of the revered Russian general Field-Marshal Prince
Kutúzov in St Petersburg's Kazán Cathedral.

661   Written on 2nd August 1831 in **Tsárskoye Seló** and published
a month later, along with No. 663. The poem is addressed to
politicians and commentators in France who criticized Russia's
attempts to crush the current Polish uprising and called for armed
intervention in support of the Poles. The background is centuries
of hostility and warfare between Russians and Poles. *l. 3 Poland*:
Pushkin writes "Lithuania": for over two centuries before their
annexation by neighbouring powers in 1795, Poland and Lithuania
had formed a united commonwealth, and Pushkin uses the two
names interchangeably. *l. 19 Kremlin*: Pushkin is thinking both of
the Polish occupation of Moscow between 1610 and 1612 and of
the capture of Moscow in 1812 by **Napoleon**, whose international
army included Polish contingents. *l. 20 Praga*: Praga is a suburb of
Warsaw on the eastern bank of the Vistula. It was the scene of a
notorious massacre of Polish civilians by Russian troops in 1794
prior to the Russian occupation of Warsaw and extinction of Polish
independence; fierce fighting between the Russian army and Polish
insurgents also took place there during 1831. *ll. 23–30: Is it that we
alone... liberty and peace*: The reference is to Russian defiance of
Napoleon's invasion despite the capture and burning of Moscow in
1812 and to Russia's victories over Napoleon during the next two
years, which resulted in the liberation of Europe from French control.
l. 32 Izmaíl's great men: Izmaíl was an allegedly invincible Turkish
fortress on the northern shore of the Danube. It was captured
after a famous assault by Russian forces under **Suvórov** in 1790. *ll.
37–38: Perm... Tauris... Colchis*: Perm, a city at the eastern edge of
European Russia; Tauris, an ancient name for the **Crimea**; Colchis,
a region of modern Georgia on the eastern shore of the Black Sea.

662   The opening of a light-hearted letter from **Tsárskoye Seló** dated
14th August 1830, unpublished in Pushkin's lifetime. The letter,
otherwise in prose, was addressed to Pushkin's friend Prince
Pyótr Vyázemsky, congratulating him on the award by the Tsar
on 5th August of the title of chamberlain. *ll. 1–4 My greetings...
Faithfulness*: The first line (apart from the name) and the second
half of l. 2 in the Russian are quoted from a verse of 1812 by
Pushkin's recently deceased uncle **Vasíly Pushkin** congratulating

a friend on being appointed chamberlain. *l. 4 wear the key*: A symbolic key of gold was worn at the back of a chamberlain's uniform *l. 5 the sun*: An oblique reference to the Tsar. *l. 8 the faithful Princess Vera*: Vyázemsky's wife. In Russian *vera* means faith (cf. l. 4).

663   Written in **Tsárskoye Seló**, dated 5th September 1831, and first published a week later along with No. 661. The poem celebrates the seizure by Russian forces of the Warsaw suburb of Praga on 26th August, the nineteenth anniversary of the momentous battle of **Borodinó** between Russian armies and European invaders under Napoleon. The fall of Praga presaged Russia's recapture of Warsaw and suppression of the year-long Polish uprising. *ll. 3–5 nations in array... Europe*: **Napoleon**'s invading army was drawn not only from France, but from many European nations, including Poland, which was then under French dominion. *l. 12 they forget*: I.e. contemporary French politicians, journalists and public. *l. 26–27 Warsaw... break through*: Before the recapture of Warsaw in 1831 Russian armies had taken control of the city during the turmoil of 1794, and again after the fall of Napoleon. *ll. 33–36 point a righteous finger... to the ground*: In 1611 the Polish forces occupying the Moscow Kremlin had set fire to the city. *stanzas 5, 6 and 7*: Addressed primarily to French critics of Russia. *l. 42 Chambers' volatile discussion*: The reference is to anti-Russian tirades in the French parliament, which at that time consisted of two Chambers. *ll. 51–52 remove our bastions... to the sea*: Pushkin is ironically contemplating successive Russian withdrawals eastwards from Warsaw to previous Polish frontiers – to the River Bug, in eastern Poland; to the River Vorskla, a tributary of the Dnieper, much farther east; and to the Limán, on the north-western edge of the Black Sea. *l. 53 Volhynia*: A former region of Poland (now in north-western Ukraine), most of which largely passed to Russia in 1795. *l. 54 Bohdán's old legacy*: Bohdán Khmelnítsky (*c.*1595–1657) was a Ukrainian Cossack leader who in the 1640s led a rising against the Polish-Lithuanian Commonwealth. He succeeded in establishing an independent Cossack state in central Ukraine, but later accepted the suzerainty of the Russian tsar. Central Ukraine and Kiev, capital of ancient Russia, passed thereafter under Russian control. *l. 56 Lithuania*: Lithuania had been annexed by Russia in 1793. *l. 75 he now convalesces*: The Russian General **Iván Paskévich** was wounded in the left arm in the assault on Warsaw. *l. 78 Taurus*: Name of a mountain range in southern and central Turkey, loosely applied by Pushkin to the eastern Turkish mountains where Paskévich had campaigned. *ll. 79–80 triple victory... Suvórov's laurels*: Paskévich's three victories over Persians, Turks and Poles recalled the legendary General **Suvórov's**

three victories at the end of the previous century over Turks, Poles and the revolutionary French. *l. 86 your suffering, your peaceful rest*: Here "your" means Russia's. *l. 89 young grandson*: General Suvórov's grandson, Alexándr Arkádyevich Suvórov (1804–82), who had been serving as an officer under Paskévich in Poland, had just brought news of Warsaw's fall back to St Petersburg.

664   Unpublished in Pushkin's lifetime. This note in French, with uncompleted Russian verse, was inscribed on a copy of a booklet containing poems Nos. 661 and 663, which came off the press on 10th September 1831. It was addressed to Pushkin's friend **Alexándra Rosset** in **Tsárskoye Seló** in mid-September. Pushkin had learnt the news of the fall of Warsaw when it reached the imperial palace from Poland, hearing it first from his neighbour, the Countess Ulyána Mikháylovna Lambert (1772–1843) and then from Rosset herself. The missing second line of the verse was either lost or never written.

665   Written in **Tsárskoye Seló** in early September 1831 and first published the following year. In Greek mythology Echo was a nymph condemned for ever to repeat the last sound she heard. The poem imitates in metre, and distantly in subject matter, an eight-stanza poem by the English poet **Barry Cornwall**, 'A Seashore Echo'.

666   Written probably in **Tsárskoye Seló** in the autumn of 1831, and unpublished in Pushkin's lifetime. The fable was prompted by Pushkin's friend, the poet **Zhukóvsky**, having trained a pet starling to repeat the Easter greeting "Christ is risen!".

667   An unfinished piece written probably in autumn 1831 and unpublished in Pushkin's lifetime. The verse is a free adaptation of a short passage in the novel *La Confession* (1830) by the French writer Jules Janin (1804–74), in which the eligible bachelor Anatole is targeted by a variety of single girls – but "*Anatole ne comprenait pas*", and referred the choice of bride to his mother.

668   Written for the annual reunion of Pushkin's contemporaries at the Imperial Lycée on 19th October 1831, the twentieth anniversary of the school's opening. Unpublished in Pushkin's lifetime. *ll. 17–18 Six places... sighting*: As well as **Antón Delvig** (see next stanza), those of Pushkin's classmates who had already died included **Nikolái Kórsakov** and **Semyón Yesakóv**.

669   Unpublished in Pushkin's lifetime. Written in the aftermath of Russia's suppression of the Polish uprising of 1830–31 and addressed to an acquaintance (identity unknown) who disapproved of Russian actions. The text has been reconstructed from an incomplete transcription of a lost autograph. *l. 10 that blabberer of drivel*: **Joachim Lelewel**.

670   Written around the second half of 1831 and unpublished in Pushkin's lifetime. These are two short cantos in imitation of

Dante's *Inferno*, in which the author is conducted by the poet **Virgil** into hell to witness the punishment after death of various malefactors, in this case moneylenders and (apparently) procuresses. *l.* 27 *Ararat*: A high mountain in eastern Turkey. Pushkin saw it during his transcaucasian journey of 1829.

671   Unpublished in Pushkin's lifetime. Probably written early in 1832 and addressed to Pushkin's wife **Natálya Púshkina**.

672   Written in St Petersburg and unpublished in Pushkin's lifetime. Pushkin dated the poem, a loose translation of **Catullus**'s lyric 27, 18th February 1832, the first anniversary of his wedding. *Epigraph*: The first three words of the first line of Catullus's poem (*Minister vetuli puer [Falerni]*: "Boy who serves the aged [Falernus wine]"). *l.* 2 *Falernus*: A district of southern Italy north of Naples, famous for its wine. Pushkin's original, like the translation, is not strictly rhymed.

673   Pushkin wrote this poem in the person of his friend **Alexándra Smirnóva** (née Rosset) and inscribed it on 18th March 1832 as an epigraph in a new album that he presented to her for her birthday and in which he hoped she would write her memoirs. It was unpublished in Pushkin's lifetime.

674   Written in St Petersburg on 9th April 1832; unpublished in Pushkin's lifetime. A verse for the album of Princess Anna Davýdovna Abamelék (1814–89), whom Pushkin must have seen at **Tsárskoye Seló**, where her father was serving, while Pushkin was a pupil at the Imperial Lycée. By 1832 she was already an acclaimed beauty, and was soon to be appointed a maid of honour to the Empress. She became famous as a poet and translator, translating works by Pushkin and others into French. Pushkin uses the formal pronoun *vy* in addressing her here.

675   An album verse, written in St Petersburg on 16th May 1832 for Countess Yeléna Mikháylovna Zavadóvskaya (1807–74). First published, without identification of the recipient, in 1834.

676   Probably written in Moscow between late September and early October 1832, and addressed to Countess Nadézhda Lvovna Sollogúb (1815–1903). Unpublished in Pushkin's lifetime. The translator has replaced Pushkin's hexameters with tetrameters.

677   Written on 27th October 1832 in St Petersburg, where Pushkin had returned after leaving Moscow ten days earlier; unpublished in Pushkin's lifetime. The addressee, for whom Pushkin uses the formal pronoun *vy*, is unknown.

678   Two fragments of an unfinished poem, believed to have been written in 1832, and unpublished in Pushkin's lifetime. In them Pushkin seems to be recalling his journey across the Caucasus to Georgia and eastern Turkey in 1829 to visit his brother and other officer friends who were fighting in the Russian army there.

679   Written probably in 1832; unpublished in Pushkin's lifetime. The addressee is not known, nor does the text reveal their gender.

680   Nos. 680, 681 and 682 are songs from Pushkin's uncompleted drama *Rusálka*, unpublished in his lifetime, on which he worked intermittently from 1829 to 1832. In Slavic folklore *rusálkas* were the spirits of jilted brides whom disappointment had driven to suicide, but who lived on in the depths of rivers and lakes; at night they emerged naked onto the banks to amuse themselves, comb their hair and lure young men to a watery death. In Pushkin's drama a prince is engaged to a miller's daughter, but the prince throws her over to marry a princess. At the prince's wedding a choir of local girls employed to sing to the guests sing a nonsense song, then end with a cheeky ditty demanding more money from the matchmaker. The translator has changed Pushkin's Russian folk-song metre.

681   See the note to No. 680. At the wedding the choir girls' ditty is followed by a mysterious solo voice singing an ill-omened song about a jilted girl who commits suicide on a riverbank. The translator has substituted an English folk-song metre and style for Pushkin's original.

682   See the note to No. 680. These two songs are from a later scene in the play, set on the banks of the Dnieper at night. They are sung by a group of *rusálkas* who have emerged from the river for their nightly outing.

683   Dated 1st January 1833 and first published in 1834. The first of several Greek epigrams Pushkin drew from the compilation of **Athenaeus** and translated with the help of earlier French or Russian versions. A sepulchral verse by the poet Hēdylus (fl. *c.*280 BC) forms the basis of this poem, though the French prose translation contains many errors and misunderstandings. Pushkin's version shortens the text, but restores the Greek poet's metre of unrhymed dactylic couplets. *ll. 2–3 inspired… Theon*: The French translator (misunderstanding the original) took the Greek name Theōn, related to the Greek word for 'god', as referring to the divine quality of Theon's flute playing. *l. 6 hello*: Pushkin is translating the French *bonjour*; but the word used in the Greek original (*khaire*) could equally, and perhaps more aptly, have been rendered "goodbye".

684   Dated 2nd January 1833 and unpublished in Pushkin's lifetime. Seemingly this is Pushkin's own composition in the style of a classical Greek epigram, though it reflects sentiments expressed in a passage of **Athenaeus** immediately following that on which he drew for No. 685 below.

685   Pushkin's free rendering of phrases describing wine by the Greek poet Iōn of Chios (*c.*490–422 BC), which Pushkin found in his edition of **Athenaeus**. Written in early January 1833 and unpublished in Pushkin's lifetime.

686   Pushkin's translation of the opening lines of the Roman poet
       Horace's first poem (*Maecenas, atavis edite regibus...*) in his
       first book of *Odes*. After a brief address to his patron **Maecenas**,
       Horace goes on for thirty-six lines to speak of the various activi-
       ties by which men seek fame and fulfilment, and ends by declaring
       his own ambition to win fame as a poet. Pushkin left the transla-
       tion unfinished; it was unpublished in his lifetime. Pushkin has
       replaced Horace's unrhymed metre with rhyming iambic tetra-
       meters. *l. 11 citizenry*: Pushkin uses the Russian form (*kviríty*) of
       Horace's Latin word *quirites*, meaning the whole body of Roman
       citizens, responsible for electing magistrates.

687   Completed on 12th January 1833 and first published in 1834.
       Pushkin has drawn on his French edition of **Athenaeus** for this
       description of an ideal banquet by the Greek philosopher and
       poet Xenophanēs of Kolophōn (6th century BC). Xenophanes's
       Greek original consisted of twenty-four lines of dactylic couplets
       (alternating hexameters and pentameters); Pushkin has fairly
       accurately compressed the sense of Xenophanes's first twenty
       lines into thirteen lines of dactylic hexameters.

688   Probably written in January 1833; unpublished in Pushkin's life-
       time. The poem is Pushkin's reworking of the first part of a poem
       by the Greek poet Eubulus (4th century BC), which Pushkin again
       sourced from **Athenaeus**. The translator has replaced Pushkin's
       (unrhymed) trochaic metre with an iambic one.

689   An unfinished piece, probably the opening lines of a fairy story,
       unpublished in Pushkin's lifetime.

690   Written between late 1832 and 1834; unpublished in Pushkin's
       lifetime. The poem was begun as a reply to a letter from **Gnedich**
       in 1832, subsequently published, commenting on Pushkin's *Tale
       of Tsar Saltán* (1831). Although Gnedich died in February 1833,
       Pushkin completed the poem later as a manifesto on the breadth
       of a true poet's taste and activity. *ll. 1–12 Alone with Homer... into
       fragments*: The poem's first half is constructed around an extended
       comparison between Gnedich and Moses, the Old Testament law-
       giver and prophet: Gnedich had absented himself from Russian
       society for long periods to complete his translation of **Homer**'s
       Iliad, eventually to return, radiant with success, to (Pushkin sug-
       gests) a debased cultural world. Moses, for his part, had left the
       Israelites in their desert encampment for too long while conversing
       with God on Mount Sinai; with shining face he brought back with
       him to the camp the stone tablets inscribed with God's law, only to
       find the Israelites in profane revelry around the image of a golden
       calf; unlike the more tolerant Gnedich, however, Moses in anger and
       disgust smashed the inscribed tablets and had many of the errant
       Israelites executed (Exodus 31:18–32:28).

691   Dated 18th April 1833 and first published the following year. The ballad is based on a Ukrainian folk tale. A hussar was a soldier in a light-cavalry regiment. *ll. 49–50 my lover softly leaping / down off the stove*: In traditional Russian houses one slept on top of a large tiled stove in winter to keep warm. *l. 89 I spat*: In folklore, spitting was a way of warding off evil spirits.

692   An unfinished satire on contemporary literature, dedicated to the French seventeenth-century writer and critic **Boileau-Despréaux**. Unpublished in Pushkin's lifetime. Pushkin's lines are rhyming couplets. *l. 29 Zhukov*: Vasíly Grigóryevich Zhukov (1795–1882) was a wealthy Russian tobacco manufacturer. *ll. 35–36 seeking... trash*: A barbed reference to **Nikolái Polevóy**.

693   A rough draft of a poem in folklore style, unpublished in Pushkin's lifetime.

694   The uncompleted draft, probably dating from August or September 1833, of the start of a verse letter to his friend and publisher **Pyótr Pletnyóv**. It was unpublished in Pushkin's lifetime. Pushkin clearly designed it as an "Onégin stanza", a stanza in the same metre Pushkin used for his verse novel *Eugene Onégin*. The eight chapters of the novel, previously issued separately, had been published together in March 1833, and evidently Pletnyóv thought it would be to the advantage of both men if Pushkin were to compose a sequel.

695   The beginning of a folk tale about the legendary warrior **Ilyá of Murom**, written in mid-September 1833, when Pushkin was on his way through Murom country to the Urals. Unpublished in Pushkin's lifetime.

696   An unfinished poem, written probably during October–November 1833, unpublished in Pushkin's lifetime.

697   Written at Bóldino in October or early November 1833. Though at the end of 1836 Pushkin had plans to publish it, he did not live to do so. His subtitle "A Fragment" suggests that the poem's apparent uncompletedness and open-endedness are deliberate. *Epigraph*: A line from **Derzhávin's** 1807 poem 'For Yevgény: Life at Zvanka' (Zvanka was Derzhávin's summer residence in the country).

698   A draft written at Bóldino in late October or early November 1833 and unpublished in Pushkin's lifetime. It seems to refer to an incident that took place in September somewhere on Pushkin's journey to or from the Urals, but the place and person to which the lines refer are unknown.

699   Two poetic fragments of uncertain reference, perhaps connected with No. 698. They were unpublished in Pushkin's lifetime.

700   Written probably in October at Bóldino and unpublished during Pushkin's lifetime. Pushkin wrote it on request as a song for an opera (never finished) entitled *Gypsies*.

701   An unfinished fragment, unpublished in Pushkin's lifetime, apparently intended to celebrate the launching of a new battleship on the Nevá. Pushkin's lines are rhymed alternately.

702   Written at Bóldino and dated 28th October 1833. First published in 1834. The poem is a free translation of a ballad by the Polish poet **Adam Mickiewicz**.

703   Written at Bóldino and dated 28th October 1833. First published in 1834. Like No. 702, the poem is a translation of a ballad by the Polish poet **Adam Mickiewicz**.

704   Pushkin's narrative poem *The Bronze Horseman* was written at Bóldino between 6th and 31st October 1833, but never published in full during his lifetime. This Introduction was printed separately in 1834, but without ll. 39–42, which were excised by the censor. Tsar **Peter I** founded St Petersburg in 1703 on the delta of the River Nevá at the head of the Gulf of Finland on land won from Sweden in the Great Northern War of 1700–21. Peter transferred the Russian capital there from Moscow in 1713. The site was exposed to storm surges from the Gulf of Finland; one serious flood took place in 1824, and is described in the remainder of Pushkin's poem. *l. 16 window on the West*: Pushkin quotes a saying of the Venetian traveller and writer Francesco Algarotti (1712–64), who had visited Russia in 1739: "*Pétersbourg est la fenêtre par laquelle la Russie regarde en Europe.*" *l. 68 Field of Mars*: An open space in St Petersburg used for military drills and parades. It was named after the *Campus Martius* ("Field of Mars") in ancient Rome, used there too for army musters and drills. *ll. 73–74 hats of brass… in the fray*: The bronze helmets of senior officers of the Pávlovsky regiment were made with holes pierced through, in imitation of the marks left by enemy fire.

705   Written between 1830 and 1836; unpublished in Pushkin's lifetime.

706   A fragment that Pushkin hastily jotted in an old notebook. Written in St Petersburg and dated 9th December 1833, it was unpublished in Pushkin's lifetime.

707   A verse, dating from 1833–36 and unpublished in Pushkin's lifetime, which the poet had jotted down on a slip of paper that he was apparently using as a bookmark.

708   The opening of an unfinished poem, unpublished in Pushkin's lifetime.

709   The sixteen ballads in this cycle, composed between October 1833 and December 1834, are for the most part Pushkin's translations of material published anonymously in 1827 by the French writer **Prosper Mérimée**. This material came from a collection, entitled *Guzla*, of thirty-two pieces that the ostensible author presented as his translations (into French prose) of folk songs from present-day Croatia, Bosnia, Serbia and Montenegro; in fact, however,

they were Mérimée's own concoction with some ingredients from Balkan sources. Pushkin, with his interest in Slavic folklore, was at first taken in by Mérimée's hoax and began translating some of the pieces into Russian verse in folk-song style. However, having heard unconfirmed reports of the deception, he asked his friend **Sergéi Sobolévsky**, who knew Mérimée well, to write to him for clarification, which Sobolévsky did late in 1834. In the mean time, Pushkin continued to prepare his own work for publication, and it appeared at the beginning of March 1835. At around that time Pushkin saw Mérimée's reply to Sobolévsky, dated 18th January 1835 from Paris, in which Mérimée acknowledged the true origin of the ballads and sent apologies to Pushkin for the hoax. Accordingly, when the cycle was republished in September 1835, Pushkin prefaced it with a lengthy note, incorporating the text of Mérimée's letter.

Of the sixteen ballads, eleven are Pushkin's translations into verse of Mérimée's material, two (X and XIV) are translations of genuine Serbian folk ballads from the collection of **Vuk Karadžić**, and three (XI, XII and XV) are apparently Pushkin's own compositions. In rendering Pushkin's cycle into English for this volume the translators have attempted to reproduce Pushkin's verse forms: Nos. I–VI, VIII, XI, XII, XIV and XV preserve the folkloric metre of Pushkin's originals, in which the lines, each with three stressed syllables, are unrhymed; for the others see notes below.

709 I   Pushkin appended the following note, derived from Mérimée:

> In 1460 Tomaš I [King of Bosnia] was secretly murdered by his two sons Stefan and Radivoj. Stefan succeeded him. Radivoj, angry with his brother for seizing power, divulged the ugly secret and took refuge with Mehmed II in Turkey. Stefan, encouraged by the papal legate, resolved to go to war with the Turks. He was defeated and fled to Ključ [a fortress in western Bosnia], where he was besieged by Mehmed. Taken prisoner, he refused to adopt the Muslim faith and was skinned alive.

However, this is largely unhistorical. Radivoj was actually Tomaš's brother, not his son, and the rumours that he and Stefan had conspired to kill Tomaš were probably false. After Tomaš's death in 1461, Radivoj and the new king Stefan worked together to resist the Turkish invaders, but both were captured in Ključ and executed by Sultan Mehmed II in 1463.

l. 33 Bogomil: The Bogomils were a heretical sect in the Balkans, rejected by both Catholic and Orthodox Christians. *l. 53 Now that Bosnia… ruler*: As Pushkin's and Mérimée's notes acknowledge, Radivoj never became governor of Bosnia: he and other members of the Bosnian royal family were put to death by the Turks. *l. 58 Radivoj's to be given a kaftan*: According to Mérimée it was customary for newly appointed Turkish governors to be presented with a kaftan of rich material. *l. 81 boomed an explosion*: Both Mérimée and Pushkin refer to a "bomb". Both acknowledge the anachronism in their notes.

709 II   *l. 1 Bey*: "Bey" is a Turkish title or term of respect.

709 III   *Title*: Zenica is a city in central Bosnia, between Banja Luka and Sarajevo. The battle is legendary: the setting is soon after the final Turkish conquest of Bosnia in the early sixteenth century, but neither Mérimée nor Pushkin were aware of the battle's basis in history. *l. 1 Radivoj*: Not to be identified with the Radivoj of the first ballad. *l. 12 hanging the Jews... boughs*: Pushkin comments: "In Turkish areas Jews are constant victims of persecution and hatred. In times of war they have suffered abuse from both Muslims and Christians..." *l. 13 Pasha*: A Turkish title given to senior officials. Mérimée and Pushkin use the term Beylerbey, meaning a senior provincial governor in the Ottoman Empire. *Bosniak*: A term mostly used of Bosnians who acquiesced in the Turkish occupation and converted to Islam. *l. 14 Banja Luka*: A city of western Bosnia that fell to the Turks in 1527 and became the provincial seat of government in early Ottoman times. *l. 29 the Pasha's commander*: Mérimée (followed by Pushkin) uses the word *selichtar*, which he explains as a Turkish word for "sword-bearer", used for a senior member of the Pasha's court.

709 IV   Pushkin has drastically shortened the beginning of Mérimée's folk tale (hence the lacuna), which tells that the beautiful Jelena's husband Todor had left home for Venice for a year; while he was away, the elderly Italian Piero Stamati had tried unsuccessfully to seduce her. The setting is most probably Dalmatia during Venetian rule, between the fifteenth and eighteenth centuries. *l. 14 find a toad*: Pushkin comments that toads have everywhere been popularly regarded as poisonous.

709 V   The setting is during the domination of Dalmatia by Venice between the fifteenth and eighteenth centuries. Many Dalmatians travelled to Venice to seek their fortunes, but the Slav speakers found they took second place there to the Italian-speaking Venetians and others who had adopted Italian language and culture. *Title*: Mérimée entitled his piece 'Le Morlaque à Venise', which Pushkin translated into Russian as *Vlakh v Venétsii*. Both ethnic terms, Morlach and Vlakh, referred to the Slavic-speaking population of the Dalmatian hinterland. *l. 9 dolman*: A long, open-fronted robe in the Turkish style. *l. 11 gusli*: A multi-stringed musical instrument of the zither family.

709 VI   During the Turkish invasions between the fourteenth and sixteenth
          centuries many Serbs and other Balkan nationals were displaced
          from their homelands. Some fought with the armies of Austria,
          Hungary or Poland as irregular soldiers; others took refuge in the
          mountains, where they lived on for a couple of centuries as bands
          of brigands and freedom-fighters, plundering rich travellers and
          resisting Turkish oppression. These were the *hajduks*.

709 VII   A brother's funeral song for a *hajduk* killed during a brush with
          armed irregulars working for the Turks. It purports to have been
          improvised by Jakint Maglanović at the funeral. Maglanović was,
          according to Mérimée's fabrication, a minstrel-poet of the Western
          Slavs who performed traditional folk songs and composed new
          ones. Mérimée included with his compilation a biographical note
          about Maglanović, who was alleged to have been born, probably in
          Bosnia, in the late 1750s and to have been still living in the Kotari
          district of central Dalmatia in 1817; Maglanović is presented as
          the source of all the published folk songs. *l. 1 God be with you*:
          In Russian *c Bogom* (literally "with God"), an expression used
          normally to wish someone Godspeed at the start of a journey.
          In Serbian-Croatian, the language of the Western Slavs, it is run
          together as *zbogom*, the regular word for "farewell". *l. 19 yataghan*:
          A short sabre originating in Turkey and also used in the Balkans.
          ll. 21–23 Lizgorje... Tvark: Fictional names invented by Pushkin,
          not in Mérimée's original. The translation preserves Pushkin's
          metre of rhymed trochaic tetrameters.

709 VIII A vampire story. Mérimée comments that belief in vampires was
          widespread in eastern Europe. *ll. 63–64 The monk... smeared him*:
          According to Mérimée, earth from a vampire's grave, mixed with
          its blood and smeared on the victim's skin, was thought to be a
          cure for its poisonous bite.

709 IX   This light-hearted piece does not seem to reflect any histori-
          cal event. Although **Napoleon** annexed the Dalmatian coast-
          line for a few years after his conquest of Venice and defeat of
          Austria, he never campaigned personally in that region or invaded
          Montenegro. Mérimée himself, in a note to this folk song, writes:

          There is no nation, however small, that does not imagine itself to
          be the focus of attention for the universe. Even so, I do not believe
          that Napoleon ever bothered himself over the Montenegrins.

          The translation preserves Pushkin's metre of rhymed trochaic
          tetrameters. *ll. 11–12 Mamelukes... cuirassiers*: Mamelukes
          were an Egyptian military class, from whom Napoleon recruited
          troops for his army during the Napoleonic wars. Cuirassiers
          were armoured cavalry; Pushkin calls them *kosmátye* ("shaggy",

"long-haired"), because their helmets were often topped with a tuft or mane of hair. *Lacuna between l. 20 and l. 21*: The dots mark a missing stanza in Mérimée's text.

709 X   Pushkin did not take this piece from Mérimée, but from a collection of genuine Serbian folk songs published in Germany in 1824 by the Serbian scholar **Vuk Karadžić**, where it is entitled 'Three Overwhelming Troubles'. The translation retains Pushkin's unrhymed trochaic tetrameters. *l. 8 I was married off too early*: Pushkin has misread this line, which in the Serbian means: "Mother's found no wife for me yet".

709 XI   An original composition of Pushkin's about an alleged incident in the life of the Serbian rebel leader Đorđe Petrović ("**Karađorđe**") around 1800, during the Serbs' struggle for independence from Turkey. His father Petar favoured surrender to the Turks to prevent further bloodshed and destruction, while Đorđe and his fellow rebels wanted to continue fighting for independence. The quarrel ended with Đorđe killing his own father. *l. 50 called Karađorđe*: *Kara* is Turkish for "black".

709 XII Another original composition of Pushkin's, based on recent history, about a rival Serbian rebel leader, **Miloš Obrenović**. *l. 2 Sultan's guardsmen*: Pushkin refers to "janizaries" (see note to No. 570).

709 XIII A piece drawn from Mérimée's compilation. *ll. 15–16 I must take... prayer*: Earth from a vampire's grave was supposed to give protection from the vampire (cf. No. 709, VIII). The translation preserves Pushkin's metre of rhymed trochaic tetrameters.

709 XIV Pushkin translated this poem almost word for word from **Vuk Karadžić**'s collection of Serbian folk songs (see note to No. 709 X), where it is entitled 'God Stays in Debt to No One'.

709 XV   Pushkin's note on this piece reads: "The original of the ballad about Prince Yanysh is very long and divided into several parts. I have translated only the first part, and not all of that." However, no "original" has been discovered, so this may be Pushkin's own composition. The story is perhaps most likely to be based in Czech folklore; but, as the geographical setting and language of the original are uncertain, the personal names have been transliterated directly from Pushkin's Russian. *l. 19 river Morava*: There are two rivers of this name in the Slav lands: one flows south through Czechia and Slovakia and joins the Danube at Bratislava, and the other flows north through Serbia and joins the Danube east of Belgrade. *l. 46 or are you... a demon*: Pushkin wrote: "or [are you] a *vila* cursed by God?" In Slavic folklore, *vilas* were female spirits, often water spirits akin to *rusálkas* (see note to No. 680), who might lure men to their deaths in a river or lake.

709 XVI Another piece that Pushkin translated from Mérimée's compilation. The setting is the same as that of the first ballad in the cycle,

the steed being that of King Stefan of Bosnia. Pushkin's trochaic tetrameters are rhymed throughout.

710   Probably written in St Petersburg in June 1834, when Pushkin was trying unsuccessfully to get leave to go away into the country. It was unpublished in Pushkin's lifetime and seems from his notes to be unfinished. It is apparently addressed to **Natálya Púshkina**.

711   An unfinished poem, unpublished in Pushkin's lifetime; it was written in St Petersburg and dated 10th August 1834. The lines refer to the Polish poet **Adam Mickiewicz**. Pushkin's original is unrhymed.

712   Unpublished in Pushkin's lifetime. Written soon after Pushkin had seen the painting *The Last Day of Pompeii* (1833) by Karl Pávlovich Bryullóv (1799–1852), which was first exhibited in the Hermitage in St Petersburg in August 1834.

713   Unfinished and unpublished in Pushkin's lifetime. Written probably during a visit to Bóldino in the second half of September 1834.

714   Written probably in December 1834 in unrhymed folkloric metre for inclusion among the *Ballads of the Western Slavs* (No. 709), shortly to be published. However, it remained unfinished and unpublished, perhaps because at the time **Miloš Obrenović** was still in office as Prince of Serbia, and mention of his murder of **Karađorđe** might have fallen foul of the imperial censorship. *l. 1 Menko Vujić*: Not, it seems, an historical character.

715   *Scenes from the Age of Chivalry* is an unfinished dramatic work dating from 1834–35, unpublished in Pushkin's lifetime.

716   See note to No. 715 above. The song is said to be Pushkin's translation of a Scottish folk song.

717   Written on 6th January 1835, apparently for incorporation in his unfinished short story known as 'A Tale from Roman Life'; it was unpublished in Pushkin's lifetime. The Greek verse here translated by Pushkin was ascribed to **Anacreon** (a poet popular in the ancient world) as his Ode LV; it is, however, by a later imitator, since the Parthians here mentioned (a race originally from north-eastern Iran) only impinged on the Greek world a couple of centuries after Anacreon's time. Pushkin describes the piece as a "fragment", but it seems to be a complete poem. Pushkin did not know Greek, but worked mostly from an earlier, unrhymed translation of Anacreon's poems by the Russian scholar and translator Iván Ivánovich Martýnov (1771–1833).

718   A free translation of **Anacreon**'s Ode LVI, written on the same day and for the same purpose as No. 717; unpublished during Pushkin's lifetime.

719   A free translation of **Anacreon**'s Ode LVII, written on the same day as No. 717; unpublished during Pushkin's lifetime.

720   Written in 1834 or early 1835; unpublished in Pushkin's lifetime.

721   Translation in unrhymed folkloric metre of part of a genuine Serbian folk song, perhaps dating from early 1835 and intended by Pushkin for inclusion among the *Ballads of the Western Slavs* (No. 709), but uncompleted and remaining unpublished during his lifetime. Mérimée placed a prose version of the ballad among the collection on which Pushkin drew for No. 709, but in this case Pushkin also used other sources, including perhaps the Serbian original. The setting of the ballad is apparently Bosnia, then under Turkish control. *l. 6 aga*: the title of a senior official in the Turkish Empire. *l. 14 the lady*: Pushkin writes *Kaduna*, a Turkish word for "wife".

722   A free translation of an ode (*Odes* II, 7) by the Roman poet **Horace**; unpublished in Pushkin's lifetime. Written probably in St Petersburg in January 1835 and destined (like Nos. 717 and 718) for inclusion in the unfinished story 'A Tale from Roman Life'. Horace's ode is addressed to his friend Pompeius Varus, with whom he had served in Brutus's republican army at the Battle of Philippi. After Brutus's defeat and Horace's desertion from the army, Pompeius, unlike Horace, had continued to support the republican cause. As a result he was exiled from Rome by the victorious Octavian (**Augustus**), and it was thirteen years before he was pardoned by the Emperor and allowed to return and rejoin his old friend, the event celebrated in this ode. A subtext of Pushkin's poem is his recollection of the failed Decembrist uprising of 1825, involvement in which he had been lucky to avoid, and his vain hope that the Emperor would use the occasion of the tenth anniversary of his accession (1835) or coronation (1836) to pardon those (notably Pushkin's "first friend" **Iván Pushchin**) who, for taking part, had been exiled to Siberia. *l. 11 no soldier*: Pushkin writes "trembling *kvirít*", *quirites* being the Latin word for Roman civilians, as distinct from soldiers. *ll. 15–16 in a sudden cloud… Hermes*: Horace is here referring ironically to passages in **Homer**'s *Iliad* where gods save warriors from peril by enveloping them in clouds and spiriting them from the battlefield (e.g. **Aphroditē**'s rescue of Paris in *Iliad* III, 380 ff.).

723   Written in St Petersburg and dated 7th April 1835, Easter Sunday; first published in 1836. The "general" of the title is Prince **Mikhaíl Barclay de Tolly**, one of Russia's leading commanders in the Napoleonic Wars. *l. 1 a splendid chamber*: Pushkin is referring to the Military Gallery in the Winter Palace, where are displayed over three hundred portraits of the senior officers who served in the campaign of 1812. Tsar **Alexander I** commissioned the portraits in 1819 from the British painter **George Dawe**, who spent several years in Russia fulfilling the assignment. The Gallery was opened in 1826. *l. 43 he*: Alexander I. *l. 54 your successor*: **Kutúzov**, who

succeeded Barclay de Tolly as commander-in-chief, adopted the same strategy of scorched earth and retreat. *ll. 51–56*: These lines were modified and shortened in the published version in case they caused offence to the family and admirers of General Kutúzov.

724 Written in St Petersburg on 13th April 1835 and first published the following month.

725 Written probably in mid-April 1835; unpublished in Pushkin's lifetime. The target of the epigram, Prince Mikhaíl Alexándrovich Dondukóv-Kórsakov (1794–1869), was a civil servant of (reputedly) little talent who was said in his youth to have had a homosexual relationship with Count **Sergéi Uvárov**. Certainly Dondukóv-Kórsakov later benefited from the protection of Uvárov, who in March 1835 appointed him a vice-president of the St Petersburg Academy of Sciences. *l. 1 Dundúk*: Pushkin's nickname for Dondukóv-Kórsakov; *dundúk* is a Russian word for "fool". The translator has substituted his own metre for Pushkin's trochaic tetrameters.

726 This fragment, dating apparently from 1835 and unpublished in Pushkin's lifetime, is a monologue apparently intended for a dramatization of legendary events in the life of King Roderick (Rodrigo), last Visigothic ruler of Spain. Pushkin seems to have taken his material from the long narrative poem *Roderick, Last of the Goths* (1814) by the English poet **Robert Southey**, on which he also drew for No. 727. Historically, Roderick was defeated and probably killed by Moorish invaders from north Africa at the Battle of Guadalete in 711. According to legend, however, Roderick brought this disaster on himself by raping the daughter of one of his nobles, Count Julian; Julian thereupon sought revenge by defecting to the Moors and abetting their invasion. In Southey's version, Roderick does not die on the battlefield, but wanders off incognito, exhausted and despairing, and becomes a hermit and later a priest; Julian meanwhile falls out with the Moors, is mortally wounded and returns to his Christian allegiance; in a final encounter with Roderick, the two men forgive each other and are reconciled before Julian dies. Pushkin's monologue is best understood as being spoken by Julian just before his final encounter with Roderick in Chapter 24 of Southey's epic. In the original only the first seven lines are rhymed.

727 Unpublished in Pushkin's lifetime. For the historical and literary background see note to No. 726. Pushkin's lines give a much-abridged version of the first two of the twenty-five chapters of Southey's *Roderick, Last of the Goths*. Pushkin's original, like the translation, is unrhymed.

728 A loose translation into verse of the first few pages of *Pilgrim's Progress* (1678), the prose parable of the Christian life by John

Bunyan (1628–88). Written in St Petersburg and dated 26th June or July 1835; it was unpublished in Pushkin's lifetime, though he was preparing it for publication when he died. The translator has substituted iambic pentameters for Pushkin's iambic hexameters, except at the end of each section or paragraph. *l. 72 pass the narrow gate*: A reference to "the narrow gate… that leads to life…" in Matthew 7:13–14.

729   Three unfinished and unpublished drafts, dating from mid-August to mid-September 1835, of replies to **Pyótr Pletnyóv** and other friends who had urged Pushkin to add further chapters to his novel in verse *Eugene Onégin*.

730   Written on 10th or 11th September 1835 at **Mikháylovskoye**. Unpublished in Pushkin's lifetime. Pushkin's version of an anecdote about the celebrated Italian castrato singer Farinelli (stage name of Carlo Broschi, 1705–82).

731   A first, incomplete draft of a translation of the first section of **Samuel Taylor Coleridge**'s poem 'The Good, Great Man' (1802). Pushkin probably wrote it at Mikháylovskoye in September or October 1835. Because of the fragmentary and obscure quality of Pushkin's lines 3–6, and because the remaining lines indicate his aim of producing a literal translation, it has seemed more sensible to print Coleridge's original lines than to attempt a retranslation into English. The second (ten-line) section of Coleridge's poem, subtitled "Reply to the Above", protested at the "canting" tone of the first five lines, arguing that virtue was its own reward – "Greatness and goodness are not *means* but *ends*!" We do not know if Pushkin meant to translate this second section.

732   Written at **Mikháylovskoye** on 26th September 1835 and unpublished in Pushkin's lifetime. In the poem Pushkin recalls the two years that he spent in exile at Mikháylovskoye between 1824 and 1826. The original, like the translation, is unrhymed. *l. 18 other shores and other waters*: Pushkin is thinking of his sojourns by the Black Sea in Crimea (1820) and Odessa (1823–24). *l. 28 Grandfather*: Pushkin's maternal grandfather, Osip Abrámovich Gannibál (1744–1806), had inherited the Mikháylovskoye estate from his father Abrám Petróvich, after whose death it had passed to Pushkin's mother.

733   Written at **Mikháylovskoye** in spring or autumn 1835, the reworking of a draft from four years earlier; unpublished in Pushkin's lifetime. It is not known to whom Pushkin was referring in this poem.

734   Probably written at **Mikháylovskoye** in autumn 1835; unpublished in Pushkin's lifetime. The lines originate from *The Falcon*, one of the *Dramatic Scenes* by the English poet **Barry Cornwall**; Pushkin's text is an approximate translation of the first ten and a half lines

of the opening monologue, spoken by Frederigo, a young Italian nobleman who has fallen on hard times. The passage no doubt caught Pushkin's eye because at the time he was himself in particularly straitened financial circumstances. Cornwall's original and Pushkin's translation are both unrhymed.

735   Uncompleted and unpublished in Pushkin's lifetime. Written probably at **Mikháylovskoye** or elsewhere in the Pskov region, where Pushkin stayed in September and October 1835. The manor house Pushkin describes is probably Gólubovo, home of Yevpráxiya Vrévskaya (née **Vulf**) and her husband, whom Pushkin visited at that time.

736   Written in St Petersburg in November 1835 and published soon afterwards. Though subtitled "after the Latin" to mystify the censorship, the work is in reality a satire by Pushkin addressed to the wealthy Count Dmitry Sheremétev, but aimed at Count **Sergéi Uvárov**. *Title*: Lucius Licinius Lucullus (*c*.117–56 BC) was a Roman administrator and general who fought with success in wars in Asia, accumulating such huge quantities of booty that, after his recall to Rome in 66 BC, he became a byword for opulence and extravagance.

737   Written in St Petersburg on 9th November 1835 but unpublished in Pushkin's lifetime. This narrative fragment is based on Chapters 4 and 5 of the Book of Judith in the Eastern Orthodox Church's Old Testament (assigned by Protestants to the Old Testament *Apocrypha*). It tells of the opening stage of a legendary Assyrian invasion of Judah by the governor (satrap) and general Holophernes; his overwhelming forces besieged the Israelite city of Bethulia (Russian: *Vetilúya*), which was saved by a God-given Israelite victory facilitated by the piety and courage of a Bethulian citizen, Judith. Pushkin's lines are fully rhymed to an irregular pattern.

738   Prepared by Pushkin during 1835 for inclusion in his short story 'Egyptian Nights'. It remained unpublished during his lifetime. Pushkin's original is fully rhymed, to an irregular pattern.

739   Written during 1835 and first published the following year. Pushkin hoped (in vain) that this celebration of **Peter the Great** and the example of his clemency towards opponents might encourage **Nicholas I** on the tenth anniversary of his accession to pardon the surviving Decembrist insurgents who had now served ten years in custody, many of them in Siberian exile. In his autograph Pushkin had noted down a quotation from 'A Eulogy of Peter the Great' (1755) by **Mikhaíl Lomonósov**: "After pardoning many notable offenders, Peter invited them to his table, and in their company celebrated their reconciliation with a salvo of guns." For the highlights of Peter's reign mentioned in stanzas 2–4 see Index of Proper

Names. *l. 17 Brandt's frail boat*: This boat was originally a present from England to Peter's father Tsar Alexéi. The young Peter had it renovated by a Dutch shipbuilder, Carsten Brandt (*c.*1650–93), who gave Peter his first lessons in handling ships. Peter later had his "little boat" brought from Moscow to St Petersburg for the celebration in 1722 of Russia's victory in the Great Northern War, and displayed there on subsequent ceremonial occasions as "grandfather of the Russian fleet". *ll. 29–32 Catherine's name day... raven-browed*: The reference is to Peter's second wife, who bore him eight children (and succeeded him as Empress Catherine I – r. 1725–27). It became the practice to fire a salvo of guns from the Peter and Paul Fortress to celebrate the birth of a new heir to the imperial throne.

740   Written around 1835; unpublished in Pushkin's lifetime. Despite Pushkin's title, no Arabic original or model has been identified, though the core metaphor in the last couplet has a precedent in the *Gulistan* of the thirteenth-century Persian poet **Saadi**. It is likely that, as in some other cases, Pushkin presented his own work as a translation or adaptation of a foreign text to forestall an adverse reaction from the censorship or public opinion.

741   Written probably in 1835; unpublished in Pushkin's lifetime.

742   Pushkin's unfinished free translation of a Serbian folk song from the collection of **Vuk Karadžić**. The folk song was entitled 'The Horse That Was Angry with His Master', and concerned a man who had seduced two girls, leaving one with a son and the other in tears.

743   A fragment from 1835 or 1836, unpublished in Pushkin's lifetime.

744   A fragment dating probably from 1835 or 1836, unpublished in Pushkin's lifetime. The identity of the "bald old man" is uncertain. Pushkin could be recalling his youthful infatuation with the writings and thought of **Voltaire**.

745   Pushkin's free translation and adaptation (unpublished in his lifetime) of the opening of a novel by the Polish writer Jan Potocki (1761–1815), who spent his last years in Russia. The novel (*Manuscrit trouvé à Saragosse, ou Dix journées de la vie d'Alphonse Van-Worden*) was written originally in French and purported to be a translation of a (fictitious) Spanish original; it recounts the adventures of Alphonse Van-Worden, a nobleman from the Spanish Netherlands recruited as captain of the Walloon guards in the service of King Philip V of Spain, who came to the throne in 1700. Pushkin's original is fully rhymed to an irregular pattern.

746   Written probably in late 1835 or 1836, and unpublished in Pushkin's lifetime. *l. 2 cage bird*: In Russian *chizhik*: a siskin, a kind of finch.

747   Written in late 1835 or 1836, and unpublished in Pushkin's lifetime. The poem is a translation of an Arabic poem that Pushkin found in French translation in a book of oriental and French literature published in Paris in 1835. *ll. 8–14 Hair as dark as musk... for*

the dead: Musk is a reddish-brown substance used in perfumes. Camphor is greyish-white and was sometimes used for embalming corpses.

748   Written in St Petersburg and dated 18th January 1836; unpublished in Pushkin's lifetime. During one of Denís Davýdov's rare visits to the capital at the beginning of 1836, Pushkin wanted to present him with a copy of his *History of the Pugachóv Rebellion*, which had been published at the end of 1834. (Pugachóv, a Cossack from the Don, had led a widespread peasant uprising in the Volga and Urál regions between 1773 and 1775, described not only in Pushkin's *History* but in his historical novel *The Captain's Daughter*.) Pushkin wrote this verse to accompany the gift.

749   Written in St Petersburg and dated 25th March 1836; unpublished in Pushkin's lifetime. The artist to whom the poem is addressed, and whose workshop Pushkin had recently visited, is the sculptor Borís Ivánovich Orlóvsky (*c*.1792–1837). Born a serf, he was later given his freedom and sent to Rome to develop his talents as a sculptor under the Danish master Thorvaldsen. In 1829, after six years' absence, he returned to St Petersburg; among the works he created between then and his death were the statues of Generals **Barclay de Tolly** and **Kutúzov** that stand outside the Kazán Cathedral and the angel that surmounts the Alexander Column in Palace Square. Pushkin's original is unrhymed.

750   This is the first of several poems written while Pushkin was staying for the summer of 1836 in a dacha on Kámenny Ostrov ("Stone Island") in the Nevá delta on the edge of St Petersburg. The poem, dated 22nd June and unpublished in Pushkin's lifetime, is a free adaptation of a sonnet by the Italian poet Francesco Gianni (1750–1822) via a French translation by Antony Deschamps (1800–69), who had also produced a French translation of **Dante**'s *Divine Comedy*. *l. 1 choking... drooped*: Judas Iscariot's suicide by hanging is recorded in Matthew 27:5. *l. 10 lips... had placed a kiss*: See Matthew 26:48.

751   A brief poem or uncompleted fragment written on Kámenny Ostrov between the end of June and 5th July 1836; unpublished in Pushkin's lifetime.

752   Written at Kámenny Ostrov and dated 5th July 1836; unpublished in Pushkin's lifetime. *l. 3 frail... pallid*: In his manuscript Pushkin had crossed out these two words (бледные and слабые in the Russian), but had not replaced them. *ll. 3–6 stood two women... all fathoming*: Images of Jesus's crucifixion are commonly portrayed with women standing nearby; the presence of Mary Magdalene ("the Mary who had sinned" – see Luke 8:2) and of Mary, Jesus's mother, is recorded in John 19:25. Pushkin's lines are rhyming couplets throughout.

753 Written at Kámenny Ostrov and dated 5th July 1836; unpublished in Pushkin's lifetime. The subtitle refers to the Italian poet Ippolito Pindemonte (1753–1828), but was evidently chosen by Pushkin to confuse the imperial censorship, as the poem is not a translation but Pushkin's original composition. *ll. 7–8 if a zealous... journal*: Pushkin was at this period struggling with the imperial censorship over publication of his new periodical *Sovreménnik*. *l. 9 words, words, words*: Pushkin is here quoting from *Hamlet* (Act II. Sc. 2), where the title character gives this reply to Polonius's question "What do you read, my lord?" Pushkin's lines are rhyming couplets throughout.

754 Written at Kámenny Ostrov and dated 22nd July 1836; unpublished in Pushkin's lifetime. The last seven lines of the poem give Pushkin's rendering in contemporary Russian of a prayer customarily recited in Russian churches during Lent and attributed to St Ephrem the Syrian (*c.*306–73), preacher, poet and one of the fathers of the Eastern Orthodox Church. Pushkin's lines are rhyming couplets.

755 Written at Kámenny Ostrov and dated 14th August 1836; unpublished in Pushkin's lifetime. *l. 17 want to spit*: In folklore, spitting was a way of warding off evil spirits. The translator has substituted iambic pentameters for Pushkin's hexameters.

756 Probably written at Kámenny Ostrov in August 1836; unpublished in Pushkin's lifetime. These are unfinished free translations from the Latin of two passages (ll. 1–5 and ll. 188–91) from **Juvenal**'s Satire X on the vanity of human wishes. Pushkin undertook translation of this work at the request of his friend Prince P.B. Kozlóvsky, but found Juvenal's work uncongenial, as he began to explain to Kozlóvsky in No. 757. Pushkin's lines were to be rhyming couplets.

757 The incomplete draft of a verse letter to Prince Pyótr Borísovich Kozlóvsky (1783–1840), probably written in late August or September 1836; unpublished in Pushkin's lifetime. Kozlóvsky was a Russian diplomat who served in several western European capitals till his retirement in 1820, then stayed on abroad, returning home only in 1835. A classical scholar and *littérateur*, with an interest too in science, he became a friend of Pushkin and contributed to his new periodical *Sovreménnik*. He had pressed Pushkin to translate into Russian **Juvenal**'s Satire X (see No. 756), a work he particularly admired. *l. 2 you friend to English bards*: While in western Europe Kozlóvsky had made the acquaintance of Lord **Byron**, among others. Pushkin's lines are rhyming couplets.

758, 759 Two verses in unrhymed dactylic couplets composed by Pushkin after he had visited an exhibition at the St Petersburg Academy of Arts in late September 1836. The poems (first published in December 1836) describe statues he saw there of young men engaged in two traditional Russian games – *svayka* and *babki*. Wachtel explains that the point of the first game "was to throw the *svayka* (an iron object the shape of an oversized nail with a very large head) deep into the ground inside a metal ring", while *babki* "was akin to skittles, except that it was played with the bones of domestic animals". The *svayka* statue was by Alexándr Vasílyevich Loganóvsky (1812–55) and that of the *babki* player by Nikolái Stepánovich Pímenov (1812–64), both of whom had studied at the Academy. *No. 758 l. 3 Discobolus*: Pushkin is referring to the famous statue of the discus thrower by the Greek sculptor Myron (5th century BC), a copy of which the Academy possessed.

760   An unfinished poem that Pushkin wrote for his classmates' reunion on the twenty-fifth anniversary (19th October 1836) of the inauguration of the Imperial Lycée at **Tsárskoye Seló**; unpublished in Pushkin's lifetime. *ll. 27–32 those great events… renown*: The Lycée was opened in 1811; Pushkin was part of the first intake and remained there till 1817; by "great events" Pushkin is referring to the final phase of the Napoleonic Wars, which began in 1812 with **Napoleon**'s invasion of Russia and ended in 1815 with his final defeat and exile. *l. 34 given by the Tsar palatial quarters*: Tsar **Alexander I** gave the new Lycée accommodation in a wing of the Catherine Palace at Tsárskoye Seló. *ll. 35–36 On our first day… speech*: Alexándr Petróvich Kunítsyn (1783–1840) was a teacher, admired by Pushkin, of moral and political science at the Lycée; on the day of the inauguration he made a rousing speech before the Emperor, his guests and the whole school. *ll. 41–44 lines of soldiers… marched past*: In 1812 soldiers marching to the front from St Petersburg would pass along the road through Tsárskoye Seló close to the Lycée. *l. 50 Our High Lord*: I.e. Alexander I, who commanded the allied armies that drove Napoleon back across Europe and in 1814 captured Paris. Pushkin refers to him here as "Agamemnon", the legendary king who commanded the Greek forces in the Trojan War, which ended with the capture of Troy. *l. 54 this whole place*: I.e. the palace complex at Tsárskoye Seló. *l. 61 a new emperor*: **Nicholas I**. *ll. 62–64 took a firm stand… hurricane*: Probably a reference to Nicholas's ruthless crushing of the Polish revolt of 1830–31, which had threatened once again to curtail Russia's empire in eastern Europe and expose it to pressure and interference from the West.

761   Written at Kámenny Ostrov and dated 21st August 1836, but placed last in this collection as Pushkin's own assessment of his poetic career made within five months of his death; the poem was unpublished in Pushkin's lifetime. Though the poem is very largely Pushkin's own, it is modelled both on an ode (III, 30) by the Roman poet **Horace**, which gives Horace's summary of his

own poetic achievements (and from which Pushkin's epigraph is taken), and on **Derzhávin**'s adaptation of Horace in his ode 'Monument' (*Pámyatnik*) of 1795. There is a similar passage at the end of **Ovid**'s *Metamorphoses* (xv, ll. 871–79), which would also have been known to Pushkin. *Epigraph: Exegi monumentum [aere perennius…]*: The opening words of Horace's ode: "I have set up a monument [more durable than bronze]". *ll. 3–4 granite pillar… deeds*: Pushkin is referring to the Alexander Column in Palace Square in St Petersburg, set up to commemorate Tsar **Alexander I** and his victory in the Napoleonic Wars and unveiled in 1834; it was the highest structure in the city. *ll. 11–12 Finns, Kalmyks… untamed*: At this time Finland was part of the Russian Empire, which also stretched eastwards across the steppes to Asia and the Pacific Ocean, taking in peoples such as the nomadic Kalmyks (see note to No. 564) and the Tungús of eastern Siberia. *l. 16 mercy, too, for those who've erred*: Pushkin is thinking particularly of the exiled Decembrists, among them several of his friends, whose pardon he had unsuccessfully urged in some of his verses.

Extra Material

on

Alexander Pushkin's

Lyrics and Shorter Poems

Volume 4

Editor's Note

This volume contains all 218 of Pushkin's lyrics and shorter poems likely to have been composed in the period between his departure for the Caucasus in 1829 and his death in early 1837. Brief fragments, collaborative poems and poems of doubtful authenticity are not included.

The Russian texts are based on those established by modern Russian scholarship. But the process of establishing these texts has not always been simple, and indeed is still the subject of scholarly debate. Many of Pushkin's poems were never published during his lifetime; they may have been written just for circulation among friends; he may have feared they would offend those he did not wish to offend; or the censorship considered them – or seemed to Pushkin likely to consider them – morally or politically unacceptable for publication; or Pushkin may simply never have got round to finalizing them. In some cases Pushkin's autographs are lost and we have to rely on copies or memories preserved by friends (which may differ). When we have autographs, these are sometimes in the form of untidy jottings, where the arrangement of material and even the handwriting may be hard to make out. We may have several autographs or published texts of a single poem, one later than another and incorporating Pushkin's corrections or second thoughts. Where multiple versions attested by Pushkin exist, the policy of this edition, as for some of the most modern Russian editions, has normally been to prefer the latest text he approved, even when it dates from some years later than the initial composition. As a result, the Russian texts printed here sometimes differ from those underlying earlier editions, including the Milner edition – one reason why some of the Milner translations have had to be changed.

Russian Text and Ordering of Poems

Pushkin sometimes dated his autographs; or dates may be deduced from the subject matter, or from the study of Pushkin's notes (including the analysis of their ordering and of the paper, ink and pens that Pushkin was using), or from other records. In some cases, however, dates remain conjectural or quite uncertain. Recent scholarship has led to the traditional dating of poems to be revised. Again, this edition, which attempts, like most Russian editions, to arrange the poems in approximate chronological order, generally reflects the most recent Russian thinking.

Understandably, in view of the uncertainties, there are still issues of text and timing that are debated among Pushkin scholars. It is beyond the scope of this edition to undertake fresh research in order to reach an independent judgement on disputed questions, so I have chosen, with few exceptions, to base the text and order of poems on the relevant volumes (still incomplete) of the new twenty-volume Nauka edition of Pushkin's works and on the Klassika complete edition of Pushkin's works of 1999 (see bibliography). For the dating of poems I have relied, where possible, on the still incomplete Encyclopedia of Pushkin's Works published in successive volumes by Pushkin House in St Petersburg since 2009.

Timing and numbering of poems

Identifying Pushkin's poems in a consistent manner presents problems. Often poems were left untitled by Pushkin, or were given vague or generic titles such as 'To Her' or 'Elegy'. Where Pushkin supplied titles I have used them; where the subject of a poem is unmistakeable or a matter of fact (e.g. the addressee of a verse letter or epigram) I have supplied a title; but in other cases, rather than invent fanciful or subjective titles, I have followed Pushkin in leaving poems untitled. In the absence of standard titling, poems have hitherto had to be identified either by titles, when Pushkin gave them, or by first lines, a cumbersome practice, particularly in translation, where different translations of the same poem will produce different titles and different first lines. To assist readers, scholars and reviewers I have therefore numbered the poems in series. Volume 3 ended with poem no. 562. So the 199 items in this volume (including, in a few cases, groups of linked poems) are numbered from 563 to 761. A complete numbered list of these poems, with titles or first lines, is provided at the beginning, and an alphabetical index of Russian (or French) titles and first lines is given on pp. 417–25..

The Milner edition translations of the lyrics and shorter poems *Translators* were sourced from over twenty different translators. A few were taken (with permission) from the published work of established translators, alive or dead; but most were prepared specially for Milner. However, the limited resources and time available for the Milner edition resulted in too many typographical errors and in the lack of any adequate commentary. The present edition attempts to correct these deficiencies. All the translations have been thoroughly checked and, as necessary, amended or replaced with new versions. Explanatory material has been added. In the English text, the translators are identified by initials at the end of each poem: a key, showing full names and the translations contributed by each translator, comes at the end of this note.

My intention, whether as editor or translator, has been to present Pushkin's poems in clear and natural modern English, unobscured by archaic or obsolete "poetic" language (unless called for by the context). This, I felt, would be truest to Pushkin's own normally direct and informal style, as well as being most accessible to today's English reader.

Pushkin most often uses an iambic rhythm ($\cup$ –), the com- *Metre* monest metre being the iambic tetrameter, i.e. four iambs (strong ending), or four iambs followed by an extra weak syllable (weak ending):

$$\cup \; – \; \cup \; – \; \cup \; – \; \cup \; – \; (\cup)$$

But he also frequently writes lines of five iambs (pentameters) or six (hexameters), always with the option of an extra weak syllable at the end; and occasionally he uses lines of three iambs (trimeter) or even two (dimeter). With iambic hexameters he normally places a caesura (word break) after the sixth syllable. Sometimes he mixes lines of different lengths.

In a minority of cases (usually for humorous, invective or folkloric verse) Pushkin adopts a trochaic rhythm (– $\cup$), again usually in groups of four trochees, with the final weak syllable optional:

$$– \; \cup \; – \; \cup \; – \; \cup \; – \; (\cup)$$

Several times in this volume Pushkin uses the standard metres of classical Greco-Roman verse based on the dactyl rhythm (– $\cup\cup$): dactylic hexameters once (No. 687) or, in thirteen cases, alternating dactylic hexameters and pentameters – "elegiac couplets" – (Nos. 622, 626b, 627, 633, 634, 651, 683–685, 720, 749, 758 and 759). In two other verses he uses shorter dactylic lines (Nos. 616 and 707). In nineteen cases, usually when imitating the poetry of Slavic folklore or other cultures, Pushkin introduces different metres: anapaests (◡◡ –) (Nos. 650 and 703) or amphibrachs (◡ – ◡) (Nos. 619, 631 and 646), and, particularly for Slavic folk songs and poetry, a looser, traditional metre with three stressed syllables (Nos. 681, 714, 721 and eleven pieces in the 709 cycle).

The translations in this volume normally aim to replicate Pushkin's metres. Exceptions are mentioned in the Notes.

Rhyme   Pushkin normally rhymes all his lines, according to various patterns; in narrative poems and other longer pieces Pushkin's rhyme schemes tend to be less regular and less predictable. This volume, however, also contains a number of pieces unrhymed by Pushkin: notably those taken from a quasi-epic or dramatic context (Nos. 598, 599, 640, 641, 711, 726, 727, 732 and 734), those modelled on Greco-Roman verse (see under Metres above, plus No. 688) and those to a traditional Slavic folkloric rhythm (see above).

Fully rhymed English translations are problematical. Because of the uninflected nature of the English language (nouns and verbs mostly lacking regular endings) and the rigidities of English word order, it is much harder to find natural rhymes in English than in Russian. Despite this, the present translators have striven to produce faithful and fluent versions that in most cases still replicate Pushkin's rhyme schemes. Witty epigrams lose their pointedness without rhyme, and unrhymed translations of song-like poems written in regular stanzaic form will not do justice to the formal elegance of Pushkin's originals. Once or twice we have compromised by rhyming every other line (as frequently in English poetry) where Pushkin has rhymed each line; and in a dozen and a half cases (usually narrative, epistolary or more discursive poems, where meaning should trump form) Pushkin's rhymed lines are presented as unrhymed English verse.

Dates   Unless otherwise stated, dates refer to the Julian ("Old Style") calendar, which was in force in Russia during the nineteenth century.

– Roger Clarke, 2022

Translators, and the Translations
Contributed by Each

Initials	Translator's name	Poems translated
RC	Roger Clarke	563, 564, 568–571, 576b, 577, 578, 581, 583, 586*, 587*, 588, 590*, 592, 594–596, 598, 599, 601–605, 608, 610, 611, 612*, 613–615, 616*, 621–623, 625–627, 629, 631, 633*, 635*, 636*, 637–643, 645, 647–650, 652, 654, 655, 656*, 658, 659, 662, 664, 665, 667, 668*, 669, 670*, 671, 674, 675, 677, 679, 685, 686, 689*, 690, 692–695, 700, 701, 703*, 706, 707, 709 I*, 709 II, 709 IV*, 709 V, 709 VI*, 709 VII, 709 VIII*, 709 IX–XII, 709 XIV*, 709 XV*, 709 XVI, 710–712, 714, 717, 718, 721, 723, 726, 727, 729, 732–735, 737, 738, 741–745, 749, 750, 752–754, 756, 757, 760, 761
WA	Walter Arndt	580, 587*, 635*, 698
MB	Maurice Baring	724
CC	Carleton Copeland	566, 609*, 617, 618*, 619, 620, 624, 627, 634, 644, 660, 661, 663, 673, 683, 684, 687, 691, 697, 704, 705, 720, 722, 736, 739, 747, 758, 759
JC	John Coutts	565, 572–575, 582, 584, 590*, 591, 593, 600, 607, 628, 632, 633*, 636*, 653, 656*, 666, 680–682, 696, 702, 725, 728
BD	Babette Deutsch	751
JD	John Dewey	730, 748
JF	James Falen	567, 576a, 597, 606, 630, 646, 657, 672, 676, 678, 688, 699, 708, 713, 719, 740
IH	Irina Henderson	586*

Initials	Translator's name	Poems translated
JH	Jill Higgs	589, 616*, 689*, 703*, 746
MH	Mary Hobson	715, 716
WM	Walter Morison	612*
RM	R.H. Morrison	579, 651
AR	Adrian Room	585, 668*, 670*, 709 I*, 709 III, 709 IV*, 709 VI*, 709 VIII*, 709 XIII, 709 XIV*, 709 XV*
ER	Eugene Raitch	609*
AS	Avril Sokolov	755
IZ	Irina Zheleznova	618*

* indicates a part or joint translation.

Select Bibliography

Books about Pushkin and His Work:

Arinshtein, Leonid Matveyevich, *Pushkin: Neprichosannaya Biografiya* (Moscow: Rossiysky Fond Kultury, 2007)

Binyon, T.J., *Pushkin: a Biography* (London: HarperCollins, 2002)

Lotman, Yury Mikhaylovich, *Pushkin* (St Petersburg: Iskusstvo-SPB, 1995)

Tomashevsky, Boris Viktorovich, *Pushkin* (Moscow-Leningrad: Izdatelstvo Akademii Nauk USSR, 1956)

Russian Texts, Commentaries and Reference Works:

Texts are available in numerous collections of Pushkin's works, published in the Soviet Union and in Russia during the last half-century and more, notably:

Sobraniye Sochineniy Pushkina, Vols. I–III (Moscow: Gosudarst-vennoye Izdatelstvo Khudozhestvennoy Literatury, 1959–62). This ten-volume collection is also available online through the *Russkaya Virtualnaya Biblioteka* at www.rvb.ru/push-kin/toc.htm

Polnoye Sobraniye Sochineniy Pushkina v Dvukh Tomakh (Moscow: Izdatelsky Tsentr Klassika, 1999)

Polnoye Sobraniye Sochineniy Pushkina v Dvadtsati Tomakh, Vols. I, II (Books 1 and 2) and III (Book 1), containing lyrics from 1813 to 1826 with extensive commentary (St Petersburg: Nauka, 1999, 2004, 2016 and 2019)

Letopis Zhizni i Tvorchestva Alexandra Pushskina v chetyryokh tomakh, Vols III and IV, covering the years 1829–1837 (Moscow: Slovo, 1999)

Slovar Yazyka Pushkina v chetyryokh tomakh (Moscow: Rossi-yskaya Akademiya Nauk, Institut Russkogo Yazyka im. V.V. Vinogradova, 2000)

Pushkinskaya Entsiklopediya: proizvedeniya, Vols. I–IV (St Petersburg: Rossiyskaya Akademiya Nauk, Institut Russkoy Literatury, 2009, 2012, 2017, 2020)

Pushkin's Lyrics: Discussion and Commentaries in English:

Kahn, Andrew, *Pushkin's Lyric Intelligence* (Oxford: Oxford University Press, 2008)

Michael Wachtel: *A Commentary to Pushkin's Lyric Poetry, 1826–36* (Madison: The University of Wisconsin Press, 2011)

Index of Titles and First Lines
in Russian (and English)

Alexander PUSHKIN COLLECTION

EVERGREENS SERIES

Beautifully produced classics, affordably priced

Alma Classics is committed to making available a wide range of literature from around the globe. Most of the titles are enriched by an extensive critical apparatus, notes and extra reading material, as well as a selection of photographs. The texts are based on the most authoritative editions and edited using a fresh, accessible editorial approach. With an emphasis on production, editorial and typographical values, Alma Classics aspires to revitalize the whole experience of reading classics.

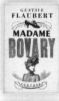

For our complete list and latest offers

visit

almabooks.com/evergreens

101-PAGE CLASSICS

Great Rediscovered Classics

This series has been created with the aim to redefine and enrich the classics canon by promoting unjustly neglected works of enduring significance. These works, beautifully produced and mostly in translation, will intrigue and inspire the literary connoisseur and the general reader alike.

THE PERFECT COLLECTION OF LESSER-KNOWN WORKS BY MAJOR AUTHORS

almabooks.com/101-pages

GREAT POETS SERIES

Each volume is based on the most authoritative text, and reflects Alma's commitment to provide affordable editions with valuable insight into the great poets' works.

Selected Poems
Blake, William
ISBN: 9781847498212
£7.99 • PB • 288 pp

The Rime of the Ancient Mariner
Coleridge, Samuel Taylor
ISBN: 9781847497529
£7.99 • PB • 256 pp

Complete Poems
Keats, John
ISBN: 9781847497567
£9.99 • PB • 520 pp

Paradise Lost
Milton, John
ISBN: 9781847498038
£7.99 • PB • 320 pp

Sonnets
Shakespeare, William
ISBN: 9781847496089
£4.99 • PB • 256 pp

Leaves of Grass
Whitman, Walt
ISBN: 9781847497550
£8.99 • PB • 288 pp

MORE POETRY TITLES

Dante Alighieri: *Inferno, Purgatory, Paradise, Rime, Vita Nuova, Love Poems*;
Alexander Pushkin: *Lyrics Vol. 1 and 2, Love Poems, Ruslan and Lyudmila*;
François Villon: *The Testament and Other Poems*; Cecco Angiolieri: *Sonnets*;
Guido Cavalcanti: *Complete Poems*; Emily Brontë: *Poems from the Moor*;
Anonymous: *Beowulf*; Ugo Foscolo: *Sepulchres*; W.B. Yeats: *Selected Poems*;
Charles Baudelaire: *The Flowers of Evil*; Sándor Márai: *The Withering World*;
Antonia Pozzi: *Poems*; Giuseppe Gioacchino Belli: *Sonnets*; Dickens: *Poems*

WWW.ALMABOOKS.COM/POETRY

ALMA CLASSICS

ALMA CLASSICS aims to publish mainstream and lesser-known European classics in an innovative and striking way, while employing the highest editorial and production standards. By way of a unique approach the range offers much more, both visually and textually, than readers have come to expect from contemporary classics publishing.

LATEST TITLES PUBLISHED BY ALMA CLASSICS